Chasing History

Chasing History

Quixotic Quests for Artifacts, Art, and Heritage

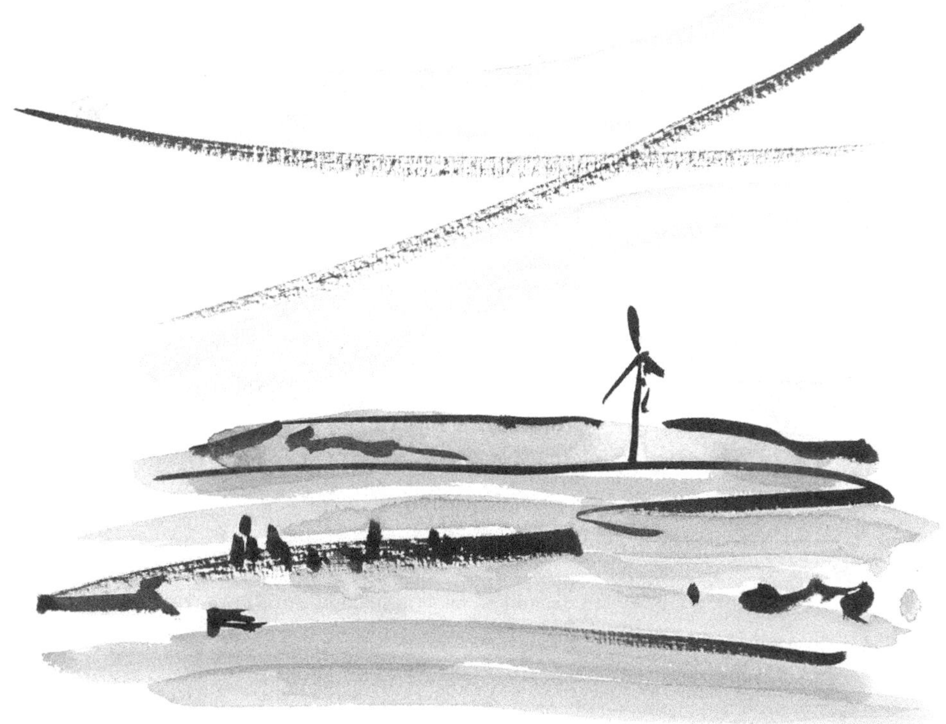

Thomas E. Chávez

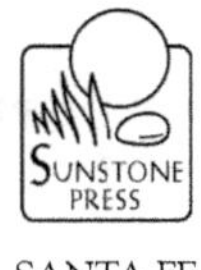

SANTA FE

Sunstone books may be purchased for educational, business, or sales promotional use.
For information please write: Special Markets Department, Sunstone Press,
P.O. Box 2321, Santa Fe, New Mexico 87504-2321.

Cover and Text Illustrations by Andrew John Cecil
Book and Cover design › Vicki Ahl
Body typeface › Goudy Old Style
Printed on acid-free paper
♾

Library of Congress Cataloging-in-Publication Data

Chavez, Thomas E.
Chasing history : quixotic quests for artifacts, art, and heritage / by Thomas E. Chávez.
p. cm.
Includes bibliographical references.
ISBN 978-0-86534-898-1 (softcover : alk. paper)
1. Museums--Acquisitions--New Mexico. 2. Cultural property--Protection--New Mexico.
3. New Mexico--Intellectual life. 4. Creative ability--New Mexico. 5. Chavez, Thomas E.
6. Cervantes Saavedra, Miguel de, 1547-1616. Don Quixote--Influence. I. Title.
F793.C45 2013
978.9--dc23

2013003745

WWW.SUNSTONEPRESS.COM
SUNSTONE PRESS / POST OFFICE BOX 2321 / SANTA FE, NM 87504-2321 /USA
(505) 988-4418 / ORDERS ONLY (800) 243-5644 / FAX (505) 988-1025

Dedicated to my three sisters,
Carolyn, Maria, and Roberta,
who have
sallied forth on their own quests.

Contents

Part III: The Value of Sancho's Hindsight / 133

Part IV: Every Windmill is in the Eye of the Beholder / 185

Preface

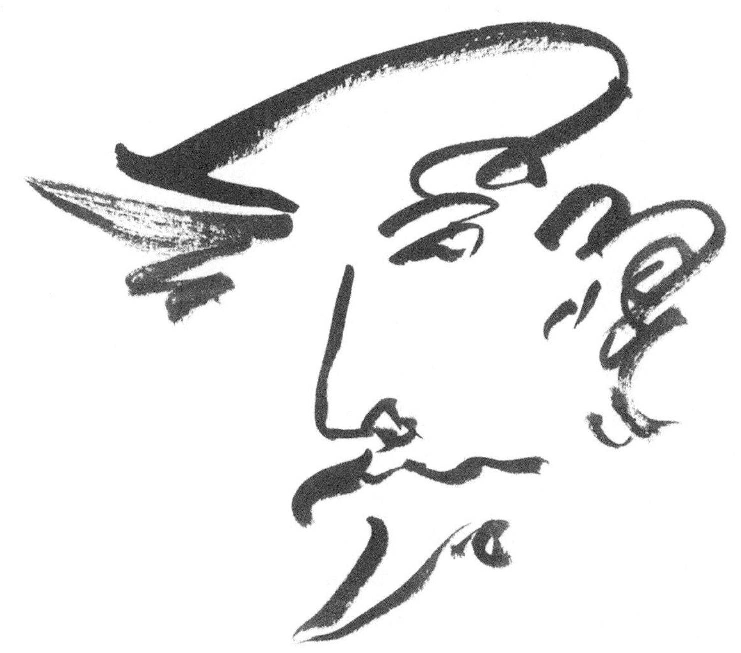

Four centuries ago Miguel de Cervantes, a wounded veteran, impoverished, and released from debtors prison, wrote two books that became one. His own attempt to create and leave something for the benefit of society must have, at times, felt like he and not his novel's main character was chasing fictional giants who turned out to be windmills. That feeling, along with his book, has prevailed through the centuries. Cervantes's classic satirical novel *Don Quixote* became one of the most popular novels of all time. Even today it continues to teach and entertain. Many "sensitive minds;" writers, artists, teachers, creators, philosophers, etc., who are cultural crusaders, have wondered "why" they do what they do. Nonetheless they continue to struggle with a single purpose of mind that what they are about is important now and in the future.

Almost a hundred years ago Frank Springer, a prominent attorney, amateur scientist, and community activist spoke at the dedication of the new Museum of Fine Arts in Santa Fe, New Mexico. In the museum's Saint Francis auditorium he said, "It is when the doers and the dreamers work hand in hand; or better still, when the dreamer is himself a doer, that epoch-making events are achieved."[1] Without naming himself, he referred to himself as well as others, especially Edgar Lee Hewitt, the Museum of New Mexico's first director. In his adopted New Mexico, Springer's words resonated for people like Adolph Bandelier, Ralph Emerson Twitchell, Charles Lummis, Alice Fletcher, Jesse Nusbaum, John McFie, Kenneth Chapman, L. Bradford Prince and many others who had a hand in the creation of the Museum of New Mexico, its antecedents the School of American Research and Historical Society of New Mexico, and the many subsequent organizations and institutions that would grow out of their efforts. These same people were instrumental in preserving the 1610 Palace of the Governors that housed the School of American Research and the Historical Society of New Mexico. Because of that effort the Museum of New Mexico was established and soon thereafter the Museum of Fine Arts across the street from it was erected. Generically, Springer's words applied to every person who has had the fortitude and persistence to accomplish the seemingly impossible. Those people, he continued, had "the duty...to keep the lights of human intelligence and creativity burning brightly."

In New Mexico the doers and the dreamers have continued to sally forth in pursuit of dreams. New museums, an internationally renowned opera, botanic gardens, a first-class zoo, orchestras, music and art festivals, schools, etc. have blossomed across the landscape. Natural as well as historic preservation are a priority. More recently, the National Hispanic Cultural Center and New Mexico's new state history museum have opened. The sons and daughters of *Don Quixote* are still challenging and defeating real giants and not just windmills.

For the majority of my life I have had the pleasure to work in the ranks of these creative and productive people. Trained as a historian, my career has been in cultural institutions. I worked with intelligent, creative, and sensitive people. My colleagues were dreamers and doers. We could have been neither but we came to our life's work intentionally with the realization that there was something inherently important in what we were doing. We succeeded in some quests and failed in others; but we always tried. The dreams easily came and the doing was hard.

Toward the end of my active career as an administrator of cultural institutions I thought about my many colleagues, their achievements, and some of the effects of their deeds. I quickly realized that these people unselfishly worked and, for the most part, did so without recognition. Their record has become obscured. Yet their deeds where invaluable in keeping "the lights of human intelligence and creativity burning brightly."

I decided to give expression to my thoughts in a three hour public lecture. I knew that people were fascinated with the story of the Segesser Paintings, or how the money was raised to purchase and renovate an old city library, or my version of the F.B.I.'s attempt to claim some of the Peruvian artifacts from the museum. Now, as I focused on a larger picture and reminisced about the many people "who made it all possible," I realized that all the previously told stories were connected and, moreover, there were many other accounts that should be shared before they were lost to memory.

I started the lecture by casually stating that many times people in my line of work feel like Don Quixote. I quickly rejoined that "our windmills are real." There is meaning in our "quests." When we begin to think about some of the successes or, even, failures, we begin to realize the lasting effect that progresses through time and beyond place. There is enlightenment, a richness, however unquantifiable, that positively bespeaks of a civilized people. Quality of life is improved in ways that cannot be imagined.

That lecture became the basis for this book. The analogy to Cervantes and *Don Quixote* persisted and grew. As the concept developed, I, as the stories' chief witness, became the book's major protagonist. That was not intended but it proved to be the best *entre* for what needed to be conveyed.

This book is about life in the world of cultural institutions; the arts and humanities. This book is about all the people who without fanfare dedicate their time and resources to the cause. This book is about people who believe and are passionate in what they do. Of necessity, this book focuses on New Mexico but is about everywhere and all time. This book tells of the confluence of the dreamers and doers, the thinkers and creators. This book relates the many-times humorous happenstance of their quests. Most importantly, this book conveys the priceless value of those people who work and volunteer in cultural as well as educational institutions; those solitary figures who excavate sites, investigate in archives, consult a student or colleague, or encourage someone to do something so apparently meaningless as to string words together to create beauty and music. For the most part, they are unheralded modern-day Don Quixotes and Sancho Panzas whose exploits will enrich society for generations to come.

Loosely modeled on the organizational structure of Cervante's novel, this book is divided into five parts containing short chapters, some of which are connected and others that are diversions. As a whole, the book has a chronological order, for it begins with the inception of my career and ends late in the same career. However, the reader should not be mislead into thinking that this is a chronological story, for like life itself, events overlap, themes run simultaneously, and multi-tasking is normal.

Each part has a loose theme and is given a playful *Cervantesque* title. The first part, "Don Quixote and the Cultural Crusade," sets the context and begins the story. Here is given a definition of history as a discipline, the value of learning from others, and some youthful dreams and early successes. An early master plan included the purchase and renovation of a city library, a new history museum, a support group, an endowment, and aggressive acquisitions policy—all with no money and less approval. Those plans, along with winning over community support resulted in some early successes including the new library building, property acquisition, and the Segesser Paintings.

Part II, titled "Dulcinea Does Not Exist," plays on Don Quixote's "fair maiden" who, in reality, does not exist. The cultural warrior encounters many things that may or may not exist. To make a point, the story of finding and acquiring the Martínez de Montoya documents illustrates how even recently discovered documentary evidence will not change the minds of many. This part continues to relate stories of missing artifacts and art, a search for a lost eighteenth century campsite, and a golden scorpion thought to exist. Here, too, is the story of Peruvian gold brought to the Palace of the Governors in Santa Fe, New Mexico, the F.B.I.'s false claim, and the loss of major gift that almost was. Part II ends by giving account of the lost or misplaced remains of a few of New Mexico's more noted personages.

Part III is about history and the value of books. Appropriately titled, "The Value of Sancho's Hindsight," this section imparts a theme of learning as you go. That, plus a little luck, can be very beneficial. This part opens with the wonderful success of a museum program in the world of book arts and fine printings. Then follows the trials and tribulations of doing research and getting published. Stories of learning and benefitting from others, sometimes in a surprising manner, continues a theme from Part I. The last chapters relate how the museum and its staff made a little history itself, which, in the case of the bull, hindsight clearly illustrates, was not smart.

"Every Windmill is in the Eye of the Beholder," the title to part IV, refers to things that are real but seen differently, perceived differently, or are intentionally deceptive. The value of artifacts, even the mundane, varies from creator to curator. The viewing public will interpret the same work of art from varying points-of-view. How staff has some fun to improve morale or make a point demonstrates the use of perception. The value of photographs to make points, historical as well as societal, became an invaluable educational tool. Finally, how the public came to see our cultural institutions and myself became an important aspect to the success or failure of a life's work. Stories of old photographs, an internment camp, runaway sheep, phantom staff, and a special map all make a point about perception.

While the book focuses on the cultural world and its warriors, there is the contextual reality in which they exist. Part V is titled "The Joust is For Real" and is a play on the made up joust that resulted in Don Quixote returning home and retiring from his quests. But, he was knocked off his horse and, for him, the joust was for real. Financial, political, and societal parameters are the reality in which the dreamers must work. Stories of political firings and patronage abound. The consternation caused by an exhibited image of Guadalupe or the interesting story of raising money for the construction of a performing arts center demonstrate the nexus of culture, politics, and fundraising. Accounts of politicians and well-meaning but misguided public pressure trying to dismount cultural crusaders off of their figurative Rocinantes (horses) abound. A governor's insatiable appetite for political patronage or a community's personal desire for how history should be conveyed, are just a couple of challenges to be overcome. Part V winds down as the quest continues with an attempt to pass on to future generations a legacy brought forward by the current generation. The end of Part V and a short Epilogue bring the tome to an end on a positive note for the future.

While this book, by its very nature, is subjective, every effort has been made to be objective. The narrative is footnoted wherever possible. Many of the people depicted in its pages have read the manuscript. Much of the information can be found in cited archival collections. Nonetheless, some of the story remained as a matter of the author's memory.

This book is intended to be a history as well as record of a time and place. Like all history, this one has lessons. Cervantes's wrote in the prologue of his book: "I would like this book, the child of my understanding, to be the most beautiful, the most brilliant, and the most discreet that anyone could imagine...."[2]

Whether this current effort will approach Cervantes's lofty goal is for you, dear reader, to determine. If, in some small way, this book encourages a current or future cultural crusader to keep those "lights of human intelligence and creativity burning brightly," then I will feel that my personal quest has been well worth the effort.

Read on.

Part I

Don Quixote and the Cultural Crusade

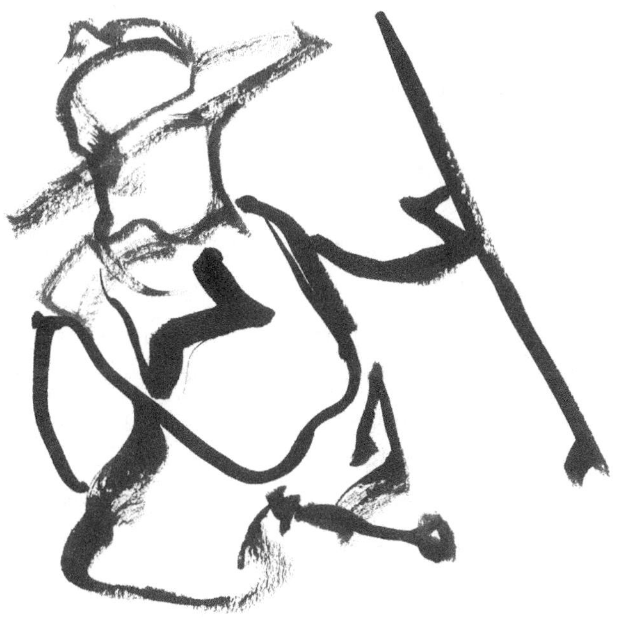

1
In which history is defined and the chase begins

During the beginning of the seventeenth century, Miguel Cervantes, one of the greatest writers of all time, penned his famous novel *The Adventures of Don Quixote*, which was a story of an elderly man who set off on romantic adventures as a "knight errant." Over the centuries the book has become so popular as to inspire plays, musicals, many movies, and even add words to the English language, "quixotic," that came from the character's very name, being one of them. The word is defined as "Extravagantly chivalrous or romantically idealistic," even "impractical." Not content to leave all definitions to subsequent historians, Miguel Cervantes, as the narrator of his story, inserted himself into his own book to define history and historians. "History," he wrote is, "the mother of the path of truth," the "rival of time, repository of great deeds, witness of the past, example and adviser to the present, forewarning to the future." "Historians must and ought to be exact, truthful, and absolutely free of passions, for neither interest, fear, nor affection should make them deviate from the path of truth."[3]

Without having noted Cervantes' definitions I became a historian who before even studying the subject saw history as meaningful. I learned to appreciate history as the story of people and their foibles as well as their successes. I could visualize that if people really studied history and did not make false assumptions then fools would not intentionally fly airplanes into buildings or attempt to change centuries' old cultural systems, or even try to create official languages.

My studies led me to a career of working in museums and cultural institutions, society's showcases. I worked in places where a term like "humane" or "humanity" is not lost from the current dialogue. These are institutions that, at their very base, are educational institutions. They are places where vestiges of the past as well as the present are collected, preserved, and studied for their knowledge that is then disseminated. They provide information through exhibitions, demonstrations, lectures, publications, etc. They serve as archives of material culture as well as libraries for books, images, and documents.

I learned as Harry Truman said, "There is nothing new in the world except the history you do not know."[4]

As a historian, my life's work opened up a whole worldview for me. Sometimes history is learned with a statement of the obvious not unlike a child who learns that fire is hot by sticking his or her hand in the flame. It suffices that we all learn and benefit from someone else's experience or, more aptly, we learn from history.

I also learned that history cannot, nor should it be, convenient much less politically correct. History happened—good, bad, or indifferent. For example, how can the historian be politically correct when describing the Buffalo soldiers who were late nineteenth century Black cavalrymen who fought against the Apaches in the American Southwest? Their very name came from their pigmentation and kinky hair that their enemies likened to buffalo hair and thus gave them their name. Indeed, many of these men and one disguised woman, Cathay Williams, achieved fame. Some of them received Medals of Honor from the government, for their exploits in fighting and killing Native Americans. That may not be politically correct by today's standards but that is what happened. Indeed, how can the reality of war be accurately described in politically correct terms when the very act of war is human beings committing mayhem on each other. In other words, war is very politically incorrect in, and of, itself.

In the City of Santa Fe, the four hundred year old capital of the state of New Mexico, the "culture police," in the form of one individual, acted when the word "savage" was chiseled out of the obelisk in the town's main plaza. The word was used to describe the enemy Apache Indians while commemorating soldiers who died fighting them. The monument was erected in 1866. Yet when asked, some Pueblo Indians agreed that the Apaches were savage.

Historians can clarify what happened, why it happened, and what resulted. History is cause and effect, as well as the narration of infinite story lines that travel through time. We need only to look at our own personal histories to see this. For example, we went to school on such and such a date at such and such place because it was convenient, affordable, we had a scholarship, our parents went there, etc. While at school we received an education that directed us on a career path. We also met lifelong friends, maybe even our spouse, hopefully a lifelong partner. Each of these events in our lives resulted in respective storylines and as we have gone through life other events have created new storylines. For example, your job dictated where you live. Every veteran will agree that those years in the military service, assuming they were not a career path, resulted in more than a few storylines in their lives. I know, personally, that the battle death in Vietnam of a best friend, who celebrated his birthday the day after me, influenced my life's direction. If this example of individual history seems complicated, imagine applying that very concept to societies, cultures, nations, and over millennia!

So, some focus is needed and why not concentrate, as I did, on New Mexico. I have written elsewhere that I came to believe that New Mexico's history has a message that just might be the basis for humankind's very survival. I theorized that New Mexico's long history of inclusivity and its handling of the various technological and scientific revolutions while maintaining its sense of place provided an example for all of humankind for a more positive future.[5]

So before completing graduate school I started working in museums, first as an intern, then on a grant as an educator, then as a curator, and, finally, after threatening legal action, I became director of the Palace of the Governors where for the next twenty-one years I worked with a staff of first class individuals and professionals.

2
On the value of mentorship and traveling exhibitions

A story must begin somewhere. Don Quixote began in his home where he read profusely. His books influenced him to sally forth as an adventurous knight. The experience of most cultural crusaders has begun the same way. They read and study and, then, embark on their respective careers. Cervantes wrote that Quixote's reading "deadened his mind." Thankfully, though, Cervantes continued with his story of Quixote, for society is richer as a result. So, too, is the case for those souls who struggle in the arts and humanities, for in the long run the pen does indeed triumph over the sword.

Michael Weber was my mentor. While at the University of New Mexico I took a graduate course on museums and history that he taught. Then, in 1979, I was selected for a summer internship under his tutelage that was held at New Mexico's state history museum, the Palace of the Governors in Santa Fe. The following year, he and Michael Warner, both historians, decided to hire me under a National Endowment for the Arts grant that they had just received. The two of them had just created a Palace of the Governors education program that quickly morphed into the Museum of New Mexico Education Program. The Museum of New Mexico was a state bureaucratic entity that included four museums and the state monuments. Simply put, my job was to survey all the museums in the state, which, over the next ten months, I attempted to do. I could not have had a better introduction to New Mexico's museums.

Michael Warner, who was to be my supervisor, took another job and Elizabeth "Liz" Dear became my first museum "boss." When the chief curatorial position opened at the Palace of the Governors, Mike Weber offered me the job. For obvious reasons, the most pressing of which was that the job was a permanent position and my current job was temporary, I jumped at the opportunity. So, now, I could be on a career track in my chosen field.

Liz Dear, who was passionate about creating a first-class museum education program at a time when museum education was a new concept, became upset with my decision to leave. She felt that I had not completed my work and insisted that I stay. Mike Weber, who outranked her in the museum bureaucracy, did not want to wait. So, I became the focal point of a short bureaucratic tug of war. Of course, Weber won out. Apparently frustrated over the delays in my transfer to the new position, he finally telephoned Dear and told her that I was to move over to my new job immediately.[6]

Liz Dear, of course, did not appreciate being ordered and this was exacerbated by the fact that she was left with no alternative but to acquiesce. So, she hung up the telephone, marched into my work area where I shared space with two other people and told me "to get my shit and get out of here." Without replying, I was out of the office within five minutes. Nevertheless, I did fulfill Dear's request to compile a report of the work that I had done up to that moment.

Thus began a career at the Palace of the Governors. Mike Weber took me into his confidence and gave me the freedom to improvise, while, also, maintaining his own vision for the Palace. He had brought the Palace of the Governors from almost step-child status to a full fledged museum. He had converted the building from a deteriorating almost four-century old structure into a restored and stabilized landmark in Santa Fe. Under his leadership new exhibitions had been installed throughout the building. He set the table for everything that would be accomplished after he left. As it turned out, Mike Weber would be my immediate predecessor as the Director of the Palace of the Governors.

I believe that I may have inherited Weber's concept to create a vibrant museum while expanding New Mexico's history to beyond the geographical confines of Santa Fe and New Mexico. He borrowed exhibitions and artifacts from other institutions like, for example, a collection of oil on copper "Mestizaje" cast paintings from the Museo de América in Madrid. The paintings depicted different racial mixing as it occurred in colonial Mexico.

He was also instrumental in discovering, organizing, and securing a loan of an exhibition of northwest coastal Indian artifacts collected at the end of the eighteenth century during a Spanish scientific expedition led by Alejandro Malaspina. The artifacts had been lost until discovered in their original packing crates by Dr. Donald Cutter of the University of New Mexico and the staff at the Museo Naval (Navy Museum) in Madrid, Spain.[7] Dr. Cutter was the dissertation director for both Weber and I.

Then Weber went to his field of expertise to put together a stunning exhibition about Spanish Cartography of the Spanish Borderlands, which is northern Mexico and the southwestern United States. *Tierra Incognita: Spanish Mapmaking of the Spanish Borderlands*, which was designed in-house by Alfonso Ulibarrí, remains one of my favorite exhibitions to this day.

Weber's last exhibition at the Palace of the Governors was *New Mexico in the Gilded Age*, which examined the influence of the dominant Victorian culture in the United States on distant New Mexico. Because I participated in the creation of that exhibition from its inception, that experience influenced me for the rest of my career.

Weber initiated two other exhibitions that would have a profound influence. These were *Spanish Colonial Ironwork* and *The Center Space: Pueblo Indian Architecture.* The first exhibition had an accompanying book written by historians and furriers (blacksmiths) Marc Simmons and Frank Turley that still is the primary tome on the topic.[8] The ironwork exhibition featured the collections of the Palace. Once again, Al Ulibarrí accepted the challenge to design the exhibition. He was given the task of designing and constructing an exhibition that looked good in the Palace but, also, would have reusable cases that could travel. Ulibarrí created a masterful, beautiful exhibition. He made the old ironwork look like diamonds. His natural wood-finished cases with self-contained lighting would travel and be used for many subsequent exhibitions, which allowed us to do those exhibitions at a much reduced expense.

Mike Weber left the museum on educational leave to write his doctoral dissertation. He never returned, for he was offered and accepted a job in Tucson, Arizona to direct the primary museum of the Arizona Historical Society. In his place I was named the Acting Director of the Palace of the Governors. I was thirty-three years old and quickly became known as "young Chávez" by my colleagues.[9] I would work as the Acting Director for the next two years before I received the permanent appointment.

With the *Ironwork* exhibition open, we wanted to utilize the traveling cases and send the whole exhibition to the Museo de Arte e Historia in Ciudad Juárez, Mexico. The director there, José Lizárraga, was a new friend and colleague who I met at a New Mexico Association of Museums conference. Lizárraga was a robust, bald man with an always positive outlook. Educationally and professionally he was an architect who taught the subject at the university in Juárez. Every year he drove an old Volkswagen beetle throughout New Mexico to attend the annual NMAM conferences. He also drove the same car up to Santa Fe to attend the opera, which he loved. When I became the president of NMAM my friends, Charles Bennett and Jim Hamilton, and I decided that we needed to save Lizárraga a trip and hold the annual conference in Juárez. With José as our host, we had a wonderful meeting and it was over lunch at one of our planning sessions in Juárez that he introduced us to *crema de membrillo*, a delightful after-dinner liquor. "Membrillo" means "quince" in Spanish and the liquor is made from that fruit. Quince candy is a gelatin affair that used to be made in New Mexico. However, the liquor cannot be found in the United States.

Juárez, which faces El Paso, Texas from across the Rio Grande, is historically connected to New Mexico. The staff and I felt that the *Ironwork* exhibition had as much to do with the history of that area as it did with northern New Mexico. So, I proposed traveling the exhibition to Lizárraga's museum. Our newly hired director of the Museum of New Mexico, Jean Weber, questioned the reasonableness of sending our collections to Mexico. She granted us the historical ties but worried about the act, which had never been done in the history of the Museum of New Mexico.

I expressed my confidence in Lizárraga, a colleague well-known to us all in New Mexico and, after all, I quipped, "We have more in common with Mexico than Minnesota."

Jean Weber acquiesced and curator Diana Ortega and I headed south with the exhibition packed in a U-Haul truck. True to expectations, Lizárraga had arranged everything at the border crossing and in his museum.

Al Ulibarrí met us there and helped install the exhibition. We opened the show with a formal reception that included local television and the newspapers. Lizárraga was very happy and subsequently reported that the exhibition was a big success.

After the exhibition closed, Diana Ortega and I returned to Juárez to truck the exhibition home. After a careful inspection by the United States Border agents, who allowed their dogs to crawl all over our cases, we brought everything back completely intact. Eventually, we installed the *Ironwork* exhibition at the State Fair where we felt we would receive good exposure for the museum. The whole affair taught us that we could actually enact some of our "crazy" ideas. We could travel exhibitions, even to other countries.

Before he left Mike Weber collected over $400,000 to fund *The Center Space* exhibition. With planning as well as implementation funds from both the National Endowment for the Humanities and the National Endowment for the Arts, this was going to be the largest, most extensive exhibition done at the Palace. With Weber gone, the exhibition fell into my lap to do.

Jeremy Iowa had the idea for the exhibition. He was a blondish, articulate man of about my age. Trained as an architect, Iowa had parlayed his interest in Pueblo Indians with his profession to come up with the idea that would be *The Center Space* exhibition. He approached Mike Weber who quickly accepted the idea of doing the exhibition. The two of them wrote the successful funding grants and Weber named Iowa the "guest curator" for the show.

After taking over for Weber, I quickly moved to hire Charles Bennett in my now vacated chief curator position. Charles and I met in graduate school. After receiving his Masters of Arts degree in history he left school to take a job directing a small museum in Kansas. He left Kansas to work in the newly created Education department at the Museum of New Mexico. Six months later I was hired in the same department. We worked in the same office and discovered that we shared a love for our work, history, the outdoors, music, travel, and slight hedonistic tendencies. Charles stands six feet three inches tall and, for most of the time we worked together, sported a long pony-tail. Always non confrontational but quietly determined and willing to take a risk, he combined a good intellect with excellent writing skills to be a perfect fit for the Palace of the Governors. He would have been an asset to any institution. An argument easily could be made that his was the best of my hires at the Palace.

The staff and I had worked with Jeremy Iowa for two years when I became the permanent director. Charles and I knew that Iowa's exhibition would be another experiment in that the approach was new, mostly in Iowa's creative mind, and that we would need to convert the whole Palace of the Governors for its installation. The addition of Bennett to the staff was a welcome addition at this critical moment.

As the exhibition evolved we began to see, if not quite understand, the genius of Jeremy Iowa. The show would contain art, artifacts, recreated architectural features such as a "T" doorway copied from Pueblo Bonito in Chaco Canyon, technical facets demonstrating the Puebloan use of passive solar heating, a multi-media slide show, and lots of text. Besides creating a visual wonder Iowa wanted to create an intellectual exercise that made visitors "feel" the sense of the Puebloan constructed world.

Iowa postulated that Pueblo Indian architecture took advantage of natural elements like rocks, mud, and the sun to create living environments that reflected their worldview. So, for example, Pueblo Indians believe that they came into this world from the underworld through a hole called a *sipapu*. That concept is played out in a series of concentric circles that begins with a symbolic *sipapu* in a larger subterranean *kiva*, or place of worship, that is located in the villages' centrally located plaza or common grounds where dances and other ceremonials take place. Iowa used plans of ancient as well as current pueblo village to demonstrate the point. Even such things as rock art, pottery, pottery designs, and jewelry came into play.

So with an amalgamation of funding sources, hired experts, a guest curator, the inexperienced museum leadership of Bennett and me, we embarked on one of the more daunting exhibitions that we would ever do—and, in the end, we succeeded!

The Center Space exhibition was another learning process. We learned that diplomacy and empathy are important aspects of museum administrative work. Trial and error can play a role but we have to be willing to accept a challenge, wherein comes the trial. In this case, the error came from the exhibition's size. The Palace of the Governors, with its many small rooms did not lend itself to such a magnanimous exhibition. We learned that we needed true galleries, with large spaces and high ceilings; and this was the germ of the idea to build a new museum or annex immediately behind the Palace of the Governors. Never again would we attempt to install such an extensive exhibition in the old building.

The Center Space attracted attention. With Jeremy Iowa helping to promote the show we received a lot of publicity. About halfway through the show's duration we received an inquiry for the Los Angeles County Museum of Natural History. They wanted to know if we would consider travelling *The Center Space* to Los Angeles. Sure, why not? So we started on another adventure. We took down the exhibition, packed it, and carried it out through the museum's front doors piece by piece where it was loaded into two eighteen wheel trucks. Jeremy Iowa directed the installation in Los Angeles where, in a proper gallery, the exhibition looked even more impressive. The opening was a glamorous, almost spectacular affair that did the exhibition justice.

If the creation and subsequent histories of the *Spanish Colonial Ironwork* and *Center Space* exhibitions were any indication, then the inspiration of Mike Weber had undergone a smooth and permanent transformation at the Palace of the Governors.

3
Relating to a master plan that would become our fate

As a beginning curator, I immediately discovered a treasure trove in the Palace's collections. There was D. H. Lawrence's satchel with pills, check stubs, and a prescription. I also found a rusty plowshare that, in century's past, had been beaten into a sword blade. Even the frivolous-like contraption whose maker claimed it to be "the greatest mousetrap in the world," held a fascination and stimulated curiosity. At one point, I found three flags still folded in the boxes in which they had been sent to the museum. My curiosity about them, as will be seen, resulted in what I consider my most important book.

But these treasures were not there to be used as a kind of grown up toy box. They were and are the intellectual foundation of the very institution that keeps them. The staff and I were in a position to use the collections, to study the artifacts as if they were documents. Besides artifacts, the Palace had a history library with books dating to the sixteenth century, documents dating to the seventeenth century, and over 400,000 photographic images.

We realized that we needed to protect the collections. We understood the importance of the collections and that the most significant item in the collection was the Palace of the Governors itself. So we began to meet on a regular, if informal basis. After I became acting director, we had what I called seminars that were held in my office on Friday afternoons. Over chips and salsa, wine, beer, and soda pop we traded ideas as well as goals and even dreams. Out of these discussions we concluded that we wanted to be something more than mere state employees. We decided that our expertise, the Palace of the Governors, and a little fate had presented us with an opportunity to do something that would effect generations to come. As a result, in 1983, we drew up a master plan for the Palace of the Governors.

The master plan was fairly straightforward. The Palace and its collections had to be preserved, which meant that we needed to find a way to let the Palace be shown as the Palace, build proper storage, and move changing non-Palace related exhibitions into new galleries. The books and documents also needed proper storage. We decided to be proactive in the acquisition of collections, for, in the past, the collections had shrunk as items were transferred to other museums. We also decided that our exhibition policy should not be predicated on the number of exhibitions rather than the quality of exhibitions. With these premises we concluded that a new history museum needed to be built adjacent to the Palace and that the Santa Fe Public Library also adjacent to the Palace needed to be purchased and renovated to house the library, archives and photographic images. To help pay for future operations, we argued that the Palace needed an endowment.

Doc Weaver, a retired airforce officer, artist, community activist and good friend, helped us create a slide presentation of our master plan that had color graphics of the lots in question and how they would be used. I took the presentation to a Museum of New Mexico administrative staff retreat and, upon making the presentation, I was met with a combination of silence and, then, ridicule from Helmuth Naumer, who had become the State's Cultural Affairs Officer. "How much do you think this will cost? Where do you think you are going to get the money? What about staff?" That actually was in the master plan but he did not want to see or hear that, for expanding staff meant going to the legislature, which, when trying to add staff, was painful. In so many words he derided me as being immature and audacious. I was more determined than ever.

At the time, the Museum of New Mexico Foundation operated as the Museum of New Mexico's not-for-profit support organization. The Foundation was charged with supporting the Palace, the Fine Arts Museum, the Museum of International Folk Art, the Laboratory of Anthropology, the State Monuments, the MNM Press, museum Education and Exhibitions Departments, as well as the MNM Administration; all of which made up the Museum of New Mexico. The Palace of the Governors received an annual Foundation allotment of $14,000 to supplement its state budget. This, we knew, was hardly enough.

A key component of the Master Plan was to form a Friends of the Palace group, which would consist of twenty to twenty-five people who wanted to support the Palace. We knew who some of these people would be and a first meeting was held at the house of Mary Jane Cook, a historian and prominent Santa Fean. The attendees all agreed to proceed and a second meeting was held at the house of Anita Gonzales Thomas, former New Mexico Secretary of State and long-time supporter of art and culture. Everett Ellin, a relative newcomer to town who was trying to start up a high tech company, was selected as the first chairman.

Ellin and some others met with Helmuth Naumer, the President of the Foundation, and presented him with a friendly ultimatum to accept them as a support group within the Foundation. He was not pleased with the idea of a museum in the Museum of New Mexico system having its own support group. Nevertheless, he was reminded about the precedent of the International Folk Art Foundation that mainly supported the Museum of International Folk Art and, in fact, had never given money to any other museum in the system.[10] The Folk Art Foundation had an endowment from which it dispersed funds for the Folk Art Museum. Still not convinced, Naumer was told that, as members of the public, the group could incorporate itself as a not-for-profit in support of the Palace of the Governors and thus become a competitor of the Foundation. Thus pressed, Naumer accepted the group, which named itself the Friends of the Palace or Los Compadres del Palacio.

Over the years the Friends where so successful on behalf of the Palace that every other museum as well as the state monuments formed Friends groups that worked within the Foundation. As a result the Foundation started raising more money much faster, for they learned that people wanted to donate and support the individual museums rather than a general entity. The Friends met every month and became my sounding board as well as an immediate morale boost for the staff.

While the Friends formed I challenged the staff to think about raising an endowment. I presented them with a plan wherein if they could raise $2,000 annually, I would match it in some way. The idea was for the staff and me to come up with fundraising programs. On paper we charted a modest beginning to show how the annual addition of $4,000 plus accrued annual interest that would grow the endowment to over $80,000 in ten years. Of course, we knew and felt that if we made this sacrifice, others, like the Friends and people we did not know, would join in. Indeed, that is what happened, for we surpassed the $80,000 mid way through our second year.

Initially, the Foundation resisted the Palace endowment idea, for it had its own endowment out of which we were receiving the support mentioned before. With the exception of the Museum of International Folk Art, none of the museums in the system had a separate endowment. The Foundation was leery of the additional record keeping a separate endowment would require. Nonetheless, the Foundation did not want a confrontation over the matter so it offered the solution that if we could raise $20,000 then we could have a separate endowment account. We accepted and fulfilled the requirement within months.

Our effort to raise endowment monies was not a small matter. I did the "Annual Chávez Lecture Series" every January and February, which raised around $120,000 over the next two decades. The staff and Friends put on "The Palace Rendezvous and Buffalo

Roast," organized downtown walking tours, created our own press that published out-of-print historical novels, initiated educational foreign tours to Mexico, Spain, Portugal, Argentina, Guatemala, and Peru. The Friends helped in all of this through actual work as well as monetary support.

A fact overlooked today was a source of income that came from the Foundation. While we tried to fulfill our master plan, the Foundation enjoyed unprecedented growth. As a result of the Friends' influence and a changed attitude in the Foundation, more support came to the Palace. The Foundation gave money to supplement an almost nonexistent state budget for programs and exhibitions. This support was very much appreciated. However, the Palace staff decided to dedicate $11,000 of the Foundation's annual support for endowment. In other words, the staff decided to tighten its program budget to build an endowment. They wanted to sacrifice their present gratification in order to save for future generations of Palace staffs.

Then, one day, I was invited to lunch by Michael O'Shaughnessy. He and his wife, Marianne, operated a local book publishing business called Red Crane Press. Moreover, they had become very generous and vocal supporters of various non-profits. Michael, as I would come to call him, asked me for a progress report and, after an abbreviated answer, he progressed to, "what would you like to leave as your legacy?" I thought for a second or two and replied "an endowment so that future staffs would not have to beg to get something done."

Michael listened to an extended explanation and said that "Marianne and I have approached my family's foundation, the I. A. O'Shaughnessy Foundation, and we are prepared to contribute $250,000 to your endowment." He went on to explain that the payments would be made in increments of $50,000 for each of the next five years and that they would need to be matched.

During this same time I was speaking for and consulting with the Union County Historical Society in Clayton, New Mexico where they ran the Herzstein Memorial Museum. Morris Herzstein, of Sephardic ancestary, was a "Pioneer Jew" who settled in Clayton at the end of the nineteenth century. There he operated the town's most notable mercantile store that became the basis of family wealth and eventually, The Albert and Ethel Herzstein Charitable Foundation. Albert was Morris' son, worked in the store, and became a successful businessman.

He and Ethel frequented Santa Fe and were members of the MNM Foundation. Mr. Herzstein ingratiated himself with the Palace of the Governors staff, for he liked history. Upon discovering that I was helping out with the people at the Herzstein Musuem in Clayton he asked L. Michael Hajtman, the President of the Herzstein Foundation to get in touch with me. The Foundation had been supporting the Clayton museum with annual grants and Albert wanted a third party opinion of how things were going. Mr. Hajtman met with me in Clayton to convey the message. I wrote a positive report that suggested that the Foundation leverage support from the City of Clayton as well as continue to support the museum.

Soon thereafter Hajtman telephoned me to express his gratitude and ask a few follow up questions. Then he announced that the Herzstein Foundation wanted to grant $250,000 to the Palace's endowment. I replied that no, that money should be used for the Herzstein Museum. Hajtman replied, "Tom, don't worry. We have enough resources to support both institutions."

The success of our endowment campaign resulted in another surprise, for the MNM Foundation decided that our model should be applied to each of the Museum of New Mexico's museums and the state monuments division. In an unprecedented act of generosity the Foundation board voted to give each entity, including the Palace, $250,000 for their specific endowments.

The endowment continued to be benefited in unexpected ways. For example, retired historian Robert Frazer, whose books I used in my own research, moved to Santa Fe late in his life. He came into the history library two or three times a week and got to know the staff. In the course of a casual conversation, for everything was casual with him, he matter-of-factly announced that he would set aside $60,000 in his Last Will and Testament for the history library. Years later, Dr. Frazer passed away in California and the Foundation received notice "out of nowhere" that the Palace endowment had been bequested over $300,000 for the history library from the estate of Robert W. Frazer!

Subsequently, members of the Friends also contributed or will leave bequests. Eddie and Phyllis Gladden always threatened to leave "a significant amount" when they sold their "mountain ranch." The ranch sold and their gift amounted to $100,000, which has grown to $150,000. Ambassador Frank Ortiz, left works of art, artifacts, and $60,000 for the endowment that he helped start.[431] There are others yet to come. Today the Palace's endowment is over two million dollars and on its way to three million dollars. Many times I heard various members of staff saying that they would never reap the direct benefits of the endowment that they started; and so it came to pass.

4
Concerning the purchase of a library and land

Money was needed for more than endowment because the master plan called for a new library as well as a new museum that we called an annex at the time. The city's old public library building had been vacated as the city library moved into newly renovated and larger facilities. The old library building sat in back of the Palace of the Governors and next to its administration building. The staff and Friends believed that, if fixed up, the old library building would be the perfect fit for our needs. The old building sat on land contributed by the Woman's Board of Trade and Library Association in 1892 under a covenant that the land be used forever for a library.[12]

The City of Santa Fe wanted to sell the property to the highest bidder, which at the time appeared to be someone who wanted to turn the building into an art gallery. AA Investments owned the vacant lot immediately behind the building. AA Investments was run by Arnold Horwitch whose wife Elaine, already ran a very successful downtown art gallery. A rumor circulated that Arnold and Elaine Horwitch wanted to purchase and demolish the library. Then they could build a new gallery over both lots.

The city wanted to sell or trade the property. As we would learn, they were working out a deal that did not include the museum. To help facilitate their plans the City had a friendly state legislator quietly introduce legislation that would change the covenant on the library property that mandated it to be used as a library. Arnold Horwitch hired an architectural firm headed by Art Trujillo, who was a former mayor of Santa Fe. Horwitch also hired an attorney to legally fend off any opposition. The Palace needed to act quickly.

Architects designed the new gallery and Mr. Horwitch's attorney represented him before city committees to secure approval for the plans. Meanwhile the Friends and I decided to approach the problem on two fronts. First, we needed to convince the city, especially Mayor Sam Pick, to let the museum have the library. Even though the building was not specially designated or on any historical registrar, it was eligible for such historical recognition. It was over eighty years old, had Public Works Programs (WPA) murals painted by Olive Rush in its entrance, and had been renovated by renowned architect John Gaw Meem. That information alone would halt any plans for demolition. Then the deed, if not changed in the legislature, left the city no option but to let the museum use the building as a library.

The Friends assigned one of their members to meet with Mayor Sam Pick about the museum's desires. Frank Ortiz, one of the early members of the Friends had recently retired from a career in the State Department where he had served in many diplomatic missions throughout the world. Among other posts he had been United States Ambassador to Peru, Guatemala, and Argentina. He had returned to his native city with an enthusiasm for community work and almost immediately took up the Palace's cause. Ambassador Ortiz went to visit the Mayor to talk of the Palace's plans and see how we could arrange with the city to get the old library building. Mayor Pick, normally a jovial person, knew both Ortiz and I on a first name basis. Yet this meeting proved to be hostile, for Mayor Pick exhibited a temper. At one point he asked Ortiz, "Who the hell do you think you are?" The city, he informed us, had already struck a land swap deal with a real estate partnership that owned thousands of acres south of town. They would convert the building into a commercial gallery and the city would receive land next to the National Guard's building. The Guard was moving into new facilities and the mayor hoped to acquire that property as well.[13]

Apparently, Ortiz's persistence during that meeting did not please the mayor. Ambassador Ortiz's suggestion that we have a referendum and his suggestion that we go public with what we wanted and what the mayor intended, struck a raw nerve. Nevertheless, the mayor saw the value of what we were trying to do and despite what would have been a better deal for the city, Mayor Pick agreed to sell the old library to the State for the Palace's use. In the end, the city came out well, for it received fair market value for the library as well as acquiring the National Guard properties that it desired.

We were disappointed that the mayor wanted money for the property but under the circumstances we understood. So we went to the legislature and talked with Governor Gary Caruthers to secure an appropriation of $1,250,000 to buy the building. In return, we promised the politicians that we would raise all the money needed for renovation.

We could not wait to enjoy our first major accomplishment. One beautiful Saturday Everett Ellin, along with Jerry Richardson and Doc Weaver, both of whom would succeed Ellin as the Chairman of the Friends, many other of the Friends, and all the Palace staff showed up for a clean up party in our future library building. The city left the building in a horrible state of disrepair. Trash was strewn throughout the building. Rather than wait for the state bureaucracy to allocate money and then arrange for state maintenance workers we decided to "do it ourselves." Our enthusiasm paid off, for we were able to salvage the building enough to use it for minor functions like meetings and loose storage before we began restoration.

Besides, we needed time to raise the necessary funds for the building's restoration and that would be the Friends first real fundraising effort. R. C. "Doc" Weaver, who I met while serving on the City Arts Board, accepted the challenge and came up with the idea of constructing a commemorative tile wall. The wall would include tiles that people could sponsor for $100, $1,000, and $2,500. People sponsored the small tiles by selecting a name or event from New Mexico's history. The sponsor's name appeared in smaller print under the selected person or event. To avoid popularity contests, we decided to deny repetitive nominations. The selected name or event would appear once on the wall but a sponsor could purchase as many tiles as he or she wanted.

Thirty-four tiles that went for one thousand dollars each were placed on a line across the top of the wall. We called these "family tiles" and started with the idea that old New Mexican families would want to have a tile with their name, family shield, and the date when their first ancestor came to New Mexico. We soon learned that not all families had shields nor were they all Hispanic or centuries' old New Mexican families. So we came up with the idea of producing photographic images on the tiles.

The most expensive category came about because of Doc Weaver's appreciation of the art of José Cisneros. Cisneros was a well-known artist out of El Paso who painted historical figures after researching old costumes and occupations. He was colorblind and had to depend on his wife, the former Vicenta Madero, to advise him with his colors. He specialized in pen and ink drawings, some in black and white and others in color.[14] Authors of southwestern books competed to have him illustrate their books.

Weaver knew that he was a long-time family friend and asked whether I would approach him about the possibility of us using his illustrations on our tile wall. We wanted to use twenty-two illustrations for corporate level tiles that would be sponsored for $2,500 each. Cisneros agreed without hesitation. He was honored that his work would grace a tile wall that would stand in the main reading room of the new History Library of the Palace of the Governors.

Weaver had a great idea and the wall's design that he worked up with the local Arius Tile Company was really attractive. We thought that we had a winner and selling the sponsorships would be a snap. We were wrong, for we soon learned that even great ideas take time and require work. At first, we asked the Friends and staff to sell an allotment of sponsorships, then the Friends split into two teams that they called the "Tacos" and the "Tamales" in a friendly competition to sell sponsorships. Then there was the logistics of keeping the money, information, orders, and final product organized before the tiles were put up on the wall. Doc Weaver spent many hours promoting that wall. When done, the wall became an immediate attraction. More importantly at the time, was that it raised over $300,000 and generated so much interest that we were able to raise another $225,000 through room naming opportunities and grants.

While all the donors are commemorated on the wall and on plaques in the various rooms, two of these gifts deserve special mention. The Palace received $100,000 from the Henry Luce Foundation strictly through the efforts of Riley and Betty Parker. Riley Parker, who eventually chaired the Friends, had roomed with one of the board members of the Luce Foundation while in college. Riley and Betty ran an antiquarian bookshop specializing in Southwestern literature and history two blocks from the Palace. They loved history and music. Both became good friends as well as strong supporters. Among the Friends, the Parkers were distinct for their melodic Texas drawls when they spoke. And there was no one quicker to smile and laugh than Riley. He felt so strongly about the library that he volunteered to use his friendship to convince the Luce Foundation that it should support us. I believe that this was the only time that he ever asked the Luce Foundation or his friend for anything.

The second of these gifts came from the good graces of Robert Olson's wife Joan. Robert Olson took an interest in the Palace after a tour through the facilities. He was a retired publishing executive, finishing his career at *Readers Digest*. He was a quiet, unassuming man who seemed to have an endless curiosity about the museum and, so, he joined the Friends. Unfortunately, he contracted cancer and passed away. Robert's wife, Joan, a beautiful woman with her own deep appreciation for the museum came to the office one day to announce that she had decided to donate $60,000 towards the library's renovation in the name of her late husband. Joan Olson Dayton still supports the museum and the map room is named for Robert.

Eventually, with legislative help after all, the Friends succeeded in raising all the necessary funds for the building's renovation. As a result I suggested that they had earned the opportunity to name the building. I was never criticized for this but probably should been, for we could have generated a fairly large chunk of change with that naming opportunity. Nevertheless, we rationalized that the library should be named after someone or something associated with research and history. The Friends initially considered Gaspar de Villagrá. He was a captain under New Mexico's first governor Juan de Oñate who wrote an epic poem titled *La Historia de la Nueva Mexico*, or *The History of New Mexico*, and published it in 1610. We had recently located and paid around $8,000 for a very rare original edition of that book.[15]

After some discussion, the Friends decided to name the library after Fray Angélico Chávez who was alive and my father's oldest brother, or my uncle. Fray Angélico, as he was called, was well known as New Mexico's foremost man of letters. He was a Franciscan priest then living at Santa Fe's Cathedral who had published twenty-two books of history, poetry, short stories, Spanish translations, and a novel. He wrote regularly in *New Mexico Magazine* and had published numerous articles in various professional history journals. He was also an artist who illustrated some of his own books and was most known for the murals of the Stations of the Cross that he did while ministering at the Our Lady of Guadalupe Parish Church in Peña Blanca. Fray Angélico spent many hours in the History

Library and knew its collections well. He was a good choice. The Friends had done well.

There was one problem. Fray Angélico was alive and lived two blocks from the new history library. We needed his permission to name the building after him. The Friends asked me to seek his blessing. I kind of knew that this would be problematic, for Fray Angélico, as a normal human being, liked recognition, but, as a Franciscan who took certain vows of humility, he normally refused such formal praise. I also knew him. He had become somewhat cantankerous in his later years and could be pretty abrupt. So with some trepidation I went to him and told him what the Friends had decided to do.

The answer to my inquiry came back without hesitation, with an emphatic "no." "Tell them to find someone else." And something to the effect that "You should know better than to bother me with this type of nonsense."

Impertinent nephew that I was, I, for some reason, followed up with, "What about after you die?"

"After I am dead, who gives a shit?" This was all that I needed. I reported back to the Friends. The naming could wait while we raised money and renovated the building. With the patience of historians we would wait until the building could receive the name that we chose.

Now that we had the library in hand we needed to pursue the privately owned property behind the library. The master plan called for the State to have possession of four lots behind the Palace of the Governors, which sits on the north side of Santa Fe's plaza. In total that would mean that we had land stretching across the block so that we could parallel the Palace itself. When we started, we owned the Palace and the two lots immediately in back of it. One lot contained Santa Fe's old armory building that housed our library, Palace administration offices, education offices, and, in the basement, collections storage. The other lot contained Santa Fe's old Elks building that housed the Museum of New Mexico's administration offices and, in the basement, more of the Palace's collections. Staff parking between the two buildings was actually a convenience likely never to be repeated. With the acquisition of the old public library building we had only one vacant lot to acquire to have the land necessary to proceed. We planned to tear down the old armory and Elks buildings, restore the library building and build the new museum annex around the library and connect it to the Palace.

While raising money for the library's renovation we opened negotiations for the vacant lot. At the time, we were confident for the lot had a large "for sale" sign on it. The price seemed reasonable so we approached the real estate agent who passed our interest on to Mr. Horwitch, the lot's owner who, as mentioned, initially wanted to build a gallery on it. We proffered the idea of a reduced price and partial donation in support of the new annex. The answer came back "no." We then agreed to pay the asking price with the caveat that we would have to go to the legislature to garner the funds. New Mexico's legislature meets annually in alternating sixty day and thirty day sessions beginning in the middle of every January. Money appropriated in any session usually did not become available until after the beginning of the state's fiscal year the following July. So we asked Horwitch to wait on the political process. He had no interest in delays and moreover had no guarantee that we would be successful with the legislature. To do what we wanted would cost us more money.

In an attempt to appease Horwitch we asked whether he would be interested in a land swap. Charles Bennett and I had gone to the State's Property Control Division to identify some state lands that could be used for the exchange. Horwitch expressed an interest in the idea and agreed to look at the properties. A couple of the Friends drove him to the various sites but returned with the news that he was not interested.

Then we heard that Horwitch still planned to use the lot to build an art gallery for his wife. He soon verified the rumor as true. Before long he was scheduled to present the plans for his new gallery before the city's Historical Design Review Board. This was a daunting proposition for anyone, for the Board was made up of community members appointed by the mayor and was a "heavy hitter." The Board was charged with preserving Santa Fe's historical styles in downtown. It worked under the guidence of a series of city codes and laws and had a lot of discretion. In addition, the Palace of the Governors traditionally had a staff member on the board. I recently had completed a three-year term.

We decided to take a stand before the Historical Styles Review Board by arguing against the gallery. Fortunately the plans gave us a lot of ammunition for our position. The plans seemed hurried with a two story, indiscreet edifice built to the property lines with windows that would eventually face a blank museum wall just three feet away. Horwitch must have anticipated us for he had his attorney Earl Potter represent him. Potter is a soft-spoken, very good attorney who is a student of New Mexico's history.

The presentation and arguments took about forty-five minutes. I represented the museum, which was the proposed gallery's closest neighbor. We also had a number of Friends in the audience and Charles Bennett, as always, was there to offer support. I criticized the intended structure in every way that I knew would strike a cord with the members of the Board. Potter presented a very lucid, reasoned argument. At one point we were both standing at a table before the Board when he pointed out something in the plans lying on the table. I walked up next to him, threw my arm around his shoulders and asked to point that out again because I missed it. A little levity always helped at those meetings. The Board voted to table the request for further consideration. This was victory for the Palace, for in my arguments I let everyone including members of the press, who always attended these meetings, know that the museum wanted the property for its future plans. Now word was out and Horwitch was quick to let us know that he was displeased as we left the hearings.

Still, Horwitch would not agree to sell the property to us. One afternoon we had a meeting in the Museum of New Mexico's director's conference room. James Snead, a tall, thoughtful, politically connected, influential attorney and Tom Catron another respected long-time Santa Fe attorney respectfully represented the Museum of New Mexico Board of Directors and Foundation. Snead, at the time, was the chairman of the MNM board and Catron was the long-time president of the Foundation board. Catron had just left the post while accepting a well-deserved lifetime emeritus board position. Jerry Richardson and Frank Ortiz represented the Friends. Richardson was personal friend of mine, an original member of the Friends, and also an attorney who worked for the state. There were others present that are lost in time.

The whole discussion was about the Palace's pursuit of the Horwitch property. I initially thought that we would be ordered to stop because we were embarrassing the museum and would lose some public support. The meeting started with a summary of what had happened to date. Then someone said that we are "out of our league in dealing with Horwitch." He was a man who played hardball. In his world he is "a mean son-of-a-bitch and did not take the museum seriously."

"Well, why don't we condemn his property? Use eminent domain." I replied. "Then he will take us seriously."

There was a short silence and then someone said, "You cannot condemn property for a museum and, even if you could, condemnation is not something a museum should do. Such an action would give the museum a bad image and as a result the foundation would lose support."

I continued with, "We would not be condemning the property of some poor person, nor would we be moving someone out of their home. We would condemn the property of a very wealthy man who spends most of his time in New York and who wants to build another downtown gallery. The public would love us."

A chorus of voices commenced talking but Jim Snead's commanded attention. "Eminent Domain is used for the public good. This is not a bad idea." Jerry Richardson agreed.

I quickly added my biased point-of-view that "what could be more for the public good than a museum?"

Snead recommended a good lawyer who was expert in eminent domain. The attorney had recently retired from a career of condemning property for the State Highway Department. But before we could proceed we needed the approval of the State's Attorney General's office because the condemnation action would be brought in the name of the

State of New Mexico. Without that approval we could not condemn the property.

Attorney General Hal Stratton, we knew, did not like using eminent domain but if his deputy who was assigned to the Museum of New Mexico approved of the action, most likely he would go along. Stratton denied our first request to condemn.

Jerry Richardson volunteered to meet with a designated assistant Attorney General to make our case. Richardson began preparations. He researched the state laws dealing with eminent domain and wrote a summary memorandum for the assistant A. G.'s review. Then he made an appointment to meet with the man. Along with the memo Richardson verbally stressed the language of the condemnation, which authorized the condemnation of the property for "a public purpose" and argued that building a state museum was clearly a public purpose. The assistant A. G. agreed and with his recommendation, Stratton granted approval for us to proceed.

The expert attorney was hired through the Attorney General's office and the legal complaint to condemn the property was drawn up and presented to Horwitch. Somehow the *Santa Fe New Mexican* learned of the museum's action and ran an editorial criticizing the museum. "This," it stated, was not the "Santa Fe way." The museum's own regents split on the issue. One of the regents publicly expressed her opposition to our action. Horwitch called our proposed litigation "un-American."

Frank Ortiz fought back and wrote a sharply worded letter to the editor and then he proposed to picket the existing Horwitch gallery with some prominent community members including, he claimed, some New Mexico Supreme Court justices.[16]

Ortiz and Horwitch had mutual friends who lived in New York and maintained a house in Santa Fe. Chuck Diker and his wife knew and appreciated the importance of what we were trying to do. Chuck Diker had joined the Foundation Board. On Ortiz's suggestion, Diker telephoned Horwitch from New York to convince him to let the museum have the land. Apparently, that call, along with all the publicity, convinced Horwitch to agree to sell the land at a mutually agreed upon price.

Now the way had been cleared to purchase the land but, as with what happened with the library, we did not have any money. The State legislature was the obvious source of funds but we felt that convincing the politicians would be a lot easier if we could secure other funds to use as a match. The Foundation apparently convinced that our grandiose dreams could become reality, quickly agreed to contribute $150,000. Then we did something unprecedented for a State institution in New Mexico. We went back to Mayor Pick and asked him for support from the City of Santa Fe. By now he was very aware of our plans to build a new museum as well as our positive efforts to cooperate with the city when it came to construction. We knew that the city's plaza lacked public restrooms and that this had become a source of irritation with the downtown businesses that had to accommodate the town's many tourists. We suggested that in return for some city funding, we would provide the public restrooms in the new building. The idea, as we discussed it, was that we would build the restrooms and pay for their utilities if the city could maintain them. Mayor Pick proceeded to secure the approval of $60,000 from the city council. So with this historical accomplishment we now had $210,000 out of the required $650,000. Once again, the state legislature and the governor appropriated the required money to make the purchase. Now, all the property was in place for the future history museum.

Meanwhile, the Friends and staff worked hard to raise the necessary funds for the library's renovation but that quest seemed an endless task, for the more time taken to raise money, the expense increased as well. For example, to fulfill the requirements of the Federal American Disabilities Act (ADA), we decided to add an elevator to give access to the two floors. This was an unforeseen expense. Even with a subsequent legislative appropriation the funds came up short. The Friends then decided to take a one time, unprecedented act and draw funds from the beginning endowment. With that transfer, along with the tile wall money and other raised money, we had enough to renovate the library, which was completed in 1996. The building looked wonderful and with the help of many volunteers we installed shelves and transferred collections. Frank Ortiz's daughter, Christina, single-handedly put together all the steel shelving in the basement that temporarily would house the newspapers and uncatalogued collections. She showed up daily for more than two months to get the job done.

The original building had a hand turned, floor to ceiling wood grill that separated the main reading room from what we planned to be the rare book room. Our architect, Bernabé Romero, wanted to replace it with a wrought iron grill. Charles Bennett and I agreed that the original should stay. To avoid problems, we dismantled and stored the old grill during construction. When most of the work was complete and before Bernabé Romero could order materials for a new grill, Charles and I laid out the old wood grill and had the museum maintenance staff install it. Then we invited Romero to see what we had done. To his credit, he accepted the deed as done and proceeded to work with us to use the grill as the basis of the interior color schemes, which turned out to be light blue, beige, and maroon. Today, as people walk into the main reading room, the grill, tile wall, book cases, and tables carry out a very pleasant environment for research that was based on the grill inherited with the building.

As mentioned, the grill separates the main reading room from the rare book room, which also doubles as the head librarian's office. Both the cases and the furniture were hand made by local artisan Walter Miera. He chose to leave his work in its natural wooden hues, for he correctly knew that it would complement nicely with the color scheme of the grill and main reading room.

In a nice touch, Miera carved the Spanish words, *"Libros y Libería"* into the top of one of the cases. His good intent resulted in a debate, for while *Libería* is commonly used to mean "library" in New Mexico, it really means "bookstore" and is used as such in the rest of the Spanish-speaking world. Julio Dávila, a native of Mexico and retired head of the cardiovascular section at Johns Hopkins Hospital, insisted that the word be changed to the more popular "biblioteca." Walter Miera was incensed at the idea of changing the word. The decision fell on me. I felt that if left as was, the word would bring criticism, even some ridicule on future staff at the library and museum so I decided in favor of changing the word. But how? I knew that Miera would refuse. Fortunately, Dr. Dávila, himself an excellent woodworker, volunteered to do the task. Today, Walter Miera's beautiful cases with one minor change still grace the library's rare book room.

We opened the building with a grand celebration. Invitations went out, the street in front of the library was closed, a tent was pitched, dignitaries came, and we had music, food, and organized tours. It was great.

Just before the ribbon cutting, I noticed that state representative Luciano "Lucky" Varela was out in the crowd. He apparently happened to walk by and had stopped to see what was going on. I immediately reintroduced myself to him, for he had been a key supporter of all the Palace's initiatives in the legislature. I asked if he would like to get some public exposure and he looked at me a little puzzled. So, I explained that he helped with the library's purchase and should be up front with the dignitaries.

"What do I do?" he asked.

"Nothing. Just stand up there with the rest of us and I will acknowledge you. Follow me."

Now with Representative Varela in tow, I secured a dignitary's sash from Sheridan Phillips, a Friend of the Palace who would become a chairwoman of the group and who had organized the festivities as well as designed and created the sashes. Thus Representative Varela joined the other dignitaries to receive his proper and well-earned credit.

Notwithstanding our best efforts not everything went smoothly at the opening. In anticipation to the construction of the new museum that would connect the library and the Palace of the Governors, we built a temporary entrance into the library where, as mentioned, we installed a temporary elevator. It was a glass elevator. To me, it looked really neat moving between the two floors in the temporary entranceway. So, with great élan, I entered the elevator and pushed the "up" button. The door closed and the elevator did not move. It malfunctioned and there I was trapped inside the glass cage with everyone including my wife, Celia, watching and, then, laughing. We soon got the elevator running but the whole episode, while embarrassing, brought some levity to the ceremonies.

Fray Angélico Chávez passed away earlier the same year that the library opened.

Everyone knew that the building would be named for him. Now, upon his death, friends and family wanted to place a statue of him in front of the library named for him. One of his brothers, Fabián, approached Judge Harry Bigbee, a long-time fan and supporter of Fray Angélico, who agreed to fund the whole project. This was not a surprise, for Judge Harry Bigbee and his wife, Helene, had paid for the publication of a couple of Fray Angélico's books. They also funded a part of my own research in Spain.

Donna Quasthoff, a local sculptor, was selected to create the statue and Judge Bigbee donated a total cost of $25,000. Quasthoff was also a friend of Fray Angélico. He had chosen her to create the bronze reliefs on the Cathedral doors. So, in a way, there was a sense of poetic justice being served. With photographs in hand Quasthoff began work while keeping the family appraised of her progress. She created a simple statue of Angélico standing upright in his Franciscan robe, holding a book. My father, Antonio, recommended to me that a rose be used as a bookmark in a book in Angélico's hands. He added that a stanza from Fray Angélico's poem, A *Single Rose*, be quoted on the plaque at the statue's base. The poem used the rose as an analogy to God.

Donna Quasthoff liked the idea and included the rose and book. After months of work, the statue was cast. A huge truck with a crane on back, blocked traffic as it lowered a granite base and, then, placed the statue on top. Three days later with Judge Bigbee, now in a wheel chair, most of Fray Angélico's family, and many friends present, Father Crispin Butz, O.F.M., who was a long-time friend, officiated at the statue's unveiling. The likeness was stunning and along with the necessary information the plaque gave credit to Judge Bigbee and concluded with Fray Angélico's words.

"THE LOVE I love in one, but one,
The only Rose!"

5
In which the pursuit for collections is described

Part of the master plan included the idea to be progressive, even aggressive when pursuing additions to the collections. We appreciated what we had, grieved over what had been lost before we came to the museum, and anticipated what we could get. Specifically, the master plan named the Segesser Hide Paintings as a goal for adding to the collections. Such an addition would make our point with an exclamation.

Rather than wait for something to come to us, we would pursue items as well as collections that we knew might be available. As a result, within the next fifteen years, the Palace of the Governors collections grew to over eight hundred thousand photographic images, fifteen thousand artifacts, six thousand books, and some three hundred linear feet of documents. We befriended former curators like Bruce Ellis and received his invaluable collection through his estate. The Bruce Ellis collection included Fort Marcy's quartermaster desk (c. 1850), Brigadier General Stephen Watts Kearny's field desk (c 1846) that traveled with the General down the Santa Fe Trail and out to California during the Mexican War, and *corbels* and *vigas* that came from buildings dating, at least, to the eighteenth century. The collection was extensive with many very rare and important artifacts. We were elated to truck the collection to the museum.

We were not above going after single and, seemingly, innocuous artifacts. Charles Bennett heard about a *vara* stick that was in private hands in southern New Mexico. He wanted to meet the owner and make an attempt to convince her to donate it to the museum. A *vara* was a Spanish colonial measurement of slightly less than a yard. A *vara* stick is a rough equivalent to the modern yard stick. The Palace already had a couple of *vara* sticks in its collections but Charles noted that this one had a provenance as the official measuring stick for the village of Mesilla and the surrounding area. This was very important historically. Besides, we had learned that *vara* sticks could differentiate in size by up to an inch, so having one that was the legal basis for determining property size, etc., was crucial to us.

While driving south to Ciudad Juárez in Mexico for the afore mentioned conference of the New Mexico Association of Museums, we stopped off in Mesilla to visit the owner of the *vara* stick. After introductions Charles launched into his effort to convince the owner to donate the stick. He talked about its historical value, the beauty of placing it in the care of a museum, the logic of it being in the state history museum, and so on. The lady politely paid attention and asked occasional questions. She wanted to know a little about us. Charles answered her every inquiry with even more explanations—and he was good at it.

Finally, it seemed to me that we were heading to an impasse, so I interrupted Charles with the statement, "Charles, just tell her that we want the sucker." That broke the ice and the *vara* stick with the date *"1776"* carved into it became a part of the Palace's collections.

We now had an invaluable artifact in our car as we headed for Mexico and we needed to do something. We did not want to take it across the border and risk losing it. Charles suggested that we stash it at his cousin's house in El Paso. It was a simple solution that worked to perfection.

As will be shown we aggressively pursued, won out over Sotheby's and the Smithsonian Institution and then we convinced the state legislature and Governor Garrey Carruthers to purchase the Segesser Hide Paintings, which we located in Switzerland. We located and purchased from a London firm the Martínez de Montoya documents that established who the founder of Santa Fe was and that he did it before the commonly accepted date of 1610.[17]

We also tried to expand the context of New Mexico's history. We learned that over time the state's politically created borders did not bind the cause and effect as well as ebb and flow of events. History is incomprehensible without context.

So, we did some exhibitions and put on some programs that raised eyebrows. We installed the *Art of Ancient America* exhibition that, as will be seen, even attracted the attention of the Federal Bureau of Investigation. We researched and created an exhibition on the pioneer Jews of New Mexico, the story of which began in Europe and moved through the eastern seaboard before it settled upon New Mexico. The Mountain Man Buffalo Roast and Rendezvous, now the Mountain Man Trade Fair, should have made obvious sense but it did not to some people. The re-creation of the traditional New Mexican Christmas play called *Las Posadas* was staged over state bureaucratic protests.

Retrieving art, artifacts, and documents that had been taken from New Mexico, in some cases, centuries ago became a goal. Two interesting cases in point are the Segesser Paintings and the Martínez de Montoya documents.

As mentioned earlier we knew about the Segesser Paintings when we formulated the master plan. One afternoon in 1983 I received a telephone call from Marsha Gallagher, a curator at the Joslyn Museum of Art in Omaha, Nebraska. She wanted to know if I was interested in exhibiting the Segesser Paintings at the Palace of the Governors. The Joslyn, she explained, had secured a loan from their owner on the condition that they are exhibited in the Southwest as well. She was telephoning me on the advice of Dr. James Gunnerson, the director of the University of Nebraska State History Museum. My answer was akin to something like, "Um, yes." At the time, I remembered reading something about the paintings in graduate school but could not remember anything more.

That night I rummaged through my library at home and found the book that I wanted. Gottfried Hotz, a Swiss ethno-historian, wrote a book about two paintings that he discovered in the attic of the Segesser family home in Lucerne, Switzerland in 1945. His book had the misleading title of *Indian Skin Paintings from the American Southwest: Two Representations of Border Conflicts Between Mexico and the Missouri in the Early Eighteenth Century.*[18] After refreshing my memory, I knew that the paintings belonged in New Mexico. We were talking about the remnants of two paintings done in New Mexico sometime before 1758 and maybe as early as 1720. For convenience sake, they had been labeled

Segesser I and Segesser II. They originally measured nineteen feet long and four and a half feet high. The canvases of each painting consisted of three panels of buffalo hide sewn together with sinew. The pigments appeared to be naturally based. We realized that the murals recorded events uniquely pertinent to New Mexico, for they depicted events from New Mexico's history. Moreover, Segesser II, depicted individuals whose descendants still populated New Mexico.

The paintings were in Switzerland because Phillip von Segesser von Brunegg, a Jesuit priest who was stationed in Pimería Alta, today's Sonora, Mexico shipped them to his brother in Switzerland in 1758. Father Segesser sent three paintings, two of which survived in the Segesser family. Now, a descendant, Andre von Segesser was willing to loan them to the Joslyn Museum and us!

I could hardly wait to talk to Gallagher. The Segesser Paintings were incredible as well as unique pieces of New Mexico's patrimony. Exhibiting them would be a real eye-opener. But, Gallagher's next telephone conversation brought bad news. Herr Segesser had withdrawn the loan offer and now wanted to sell the paintings for $2.2 million! Gallagher announced that the exhibition of the paintings was canceled because, she explained, the price is "too rich for our blood."

But wait. What does it cost to correspond with Herr Segesser to express the Palace's interest in exhibiting or even acquiring the paintings? The answer is "nothing." Gallagher gave me the name and address of the attorney who was representing Segesser. Until that moment I did not realize that the Joslyn Museum had not corresponded or talked directly to Segesser. They dealt with a Swiss attorney by the name of Eric Ferraris.

I wrote a letter that Howard and Meriom Kastner, who had spent careers working in Austria and Switzerland, translated into German and sent it to Segesser in the care of Ferraris. Upon receiving the letter, Ferraris telephoned and, then, wrote to me from Europe. He spoke good English and explained to me that he represented Herr Segesser and his client did not want to be bothered by inquiries such as mine. He added that Segesser was elderly and a recluse.

Not wanting to ruin any chance at the paintings I repeated the information that was in the letter. That was fine with Ferraris but before we continued he wanted a finder's fee of 7% because only through him could we reach a deal with Segesser.[19] To this I replied that as Segesser's representative it seemed to me that he should convey the information and, in fact, forward the letter to its rightful recipient. And no, there would be no finders' fee paid on my behalf. With that, the conversation ended and I hung up the telephone with little confidence that anything would come of it. But, to make sure, I wrote to Segesser and asked him how I should proceed.[20]

To my surprise, Segesser did receive my letters and wrote an amicable reply. He said that I should negotiate directly with him and he always felt that the paintings should go to the Palace of the Governors. Thanks to Gottfried Hotz whose book was originally published in German, Segesser knew that New Mexican troops from the very presidio that was now the Palace of the Governors had participated in the battle illustrated in Segesser II. So, yes, he was willing to consider the possibility of selling them to the State of New Mexico so they could be placed in the Palace of the Governors.[21] With this good news I immediately dashed off a letter informing Ferraris that his offer to be the intermediary was rejected and that, at Segesser's direction, I would be working directly with Segesser.[22]

Further reading and research, including a trip to the National Archives of Mexico in Mexico City shed more light on the paintings as well as Hotz's good research skills. Segesser II depicted the ambush in 1720 of the Pedro de Villasur expedition that had been sent out of Santa Fe on the Viceroy's orders to search for a rumored French force. Spain and France had gone to war and the Viceroy in Mexico City feared a French attack out of the "Ilinois Country." The troops left Santa Fe in June and traveled through the present states of New Mexico, Colorado, Kansas, and into Nebraska. They picked up Pueblo Indian auxiliaries, mostly form Taos and Picurís Pueblos as well as some Padouca Apaches at Cuartelejo, which was a series of Pueblo Indian villages out on the plains near the present-day border of Colorado and Kansas. While breaking camp on the morning of 13 August 1720 Pawnee and Oto Indians attacked them. Whether or not any Frenchmen were present is debatable but the attackers definitely had French firearms.

Segesser II was the more popular of the two paintings. Its image had appeared over a two-page spread in a book in the Time Life Books series of *The Old West*. That photograph clearly showed some detached pieces on the far right of the paintings,[23] which had disappeared since. By using the 1976 publication date of the book we realized that the missing pieces might have existed at least until then. We later learned that the photograph dated to as early as 1960, for Hotz used it in black and white in his book.[24] Still, we had a mystery. What happened to the detached end pieces?

Segesser I presented even more mysteries than Segesser II. This painting is an image of what look like Indians on horseback attacking an Apache village. On further inspection the attacking Indians wear Spanish clothing and have European weapons. Their very attack formation was standard European attack array. Women and children, some smiling, watch the attack from behind palisades or on a mesa top. These women and children appear to be Pueblo Indians rather than Apache Indians. Segesser I could refer to any number of expeditions that set out from New Mexico between 1693 and 1720.

Segesser I has more missing pieces then Segesser II. Hotz learned that the painting had hung in the Huenenberg castle, a Segesser family home in Ebikon outside of Lucerne and in the late nineteenth century the painting was cut to fit around a doorway. The piece cut out was apparently a self-contained image, for it was given to a family friend. Another piece that measured thirty inches wide by four and one half fee high was cut out of the middle of the painting and given away as well. This last piece depicted the Apache village with tepees, some of which have open doors facing the viewer. Pots and pottery with clearly defined designs can be seen through the openings. Hotz published a photograph of the missing tepee piece, as it came to be called, while it was still attached to Segesser I.[25] The two pieces disappeared although the latter piece may have existed as late as 1960.

6
Relating to a trip to Switzerland to inspect the Segesser Paintings

The Museum of New Mexico Foundation provided funding for Herr Segesser to make arrangements to have a conservation report done at the offices of Sotheby's in Zurich. He created a team of experts that included a chemist from the Hoechst Company in Frankfort, Germany, the director and curator from the Deutches Ledermuseum or Leather Museum in Offenbaugh, Germany, himself, and some of Sotheby's staff. The chemist would analyze the pigments while the curator could determine if the paintings were actually animal skins.[26] The paintings had been placed in Sotheby's of Zurich for safe keeping so the team could meet there. Segesser inquired whether I would like to join him and his team. Of course! The Foundation had included my travel to Switzerland in its support. Charles Bennett, who had become as enthused with the Segesser Paintings as I, agreed with me that we could not purchase the paintings site unseen. They needed to be authenticated. So, in February of 1985, with Foundation support, Charles and I split his travel costs and flew to Zurich on an adventurous trip that included our 747 jet blowing out an engine over the North Atlantic Ocean and being diverted first to London and then passed on to Paris instead of our initial destination in Frankfurt. Nevertheless, we made it to Zurich on the night before the appointed meeting. Zurich was white with snow and very, very cold. It was February after all.

We were a little overwhelmed with the idea of seeing the paintings and meeting with what seemed to be so many impressive people at Sotheby's. I came up with the idea of purchasing some hand lenses. My inspiration was Dr. Richard Rudisill, the Palace's Photographic Historian who was, in my mind, a genius in his field. He always impressed me with the way he used his hand lens in front of inquiring researchers. So, why not? Charles and I might impress the team of experts if we came ready with hand lenses.

We barely slept that night, for we knew that we would be the first Americans to see the paintings since they left the continent in the middle of the eighteenth century. They had not been seen by someone from the Americas for over two centuries! Also, this would be our first face to face meeting with Herr Segesser. We bundled up, left our room early, and took the short walk to Sotheby's. We had been warned that the Swiss are very punctual. They start on time; neither early nor late. Even though we actually walked over to Sotheby's the night before to make sure we knew where to go, here we were facing Sotheby's downtown high-rise a full forty minutes early. This was not good.

Fortunately, we spotted a coffee shop facing Sotheby's immediately across the street. Perfect! We trundled into the shop and ordered some good and very strong coffee. We talked of our anxiety while seated at little round tables but soon stopped for fear of being overheard. Who knew whether the people enjoying coffee at the neighboring tables were staff at Sotheby's or worse, Segesser and his team? Charles and I changed subjects and, then, laughed at ourselves. The time had come.

We walked back across the street, entered the building, ascended a stairway, and entered into a foyer, the opposite end of which had a reception desk. The receptionist immediately recognized us for who we were, for before we could say anything, she said, "You must be the gentlemen from the United States." It must have been the cowboy boots that we both wore.

Even though she had made an observation and not a question, we answered, "Yes."

She directed us through a door to her right. Upon passing through we were greeted by a group of people standing around a table strewn with enlarged colored photographs of different sections of the Segesser Paintings. Our reception was almost jovial. With the exception of myself, all the others were tall. The one woman in the group, the curator from Offenbaugh, was the closest to my height.

No sooner did we finish shaking hands all around when the room's double doors were thrown open and a man very formally announced. "Lady and gentlemen, the paintings are ready for viewing." We followed him through the doors, turned left and immediately entered the foyer that Charles and I had just passed through on our original entry. There laid across the floor were the two Segesser Paintings. Segesser II, the longer of the two because it was more intact actually stretched across the floor and up the first stair of the stairway. Two things crossed our minds at the moment. As I wrote later, we were "fascinated by the subject matter and stunned by the sheer size of the paintings. Here was the earliest visual testimony of these dramatic events, perhaps the first true historical paintings ever made in our part of the New World." Secondly, I know that I, and am fairly certain that Charles, was aghast at the paintings being unrolled on the floor, the result of which ended our anxiety about meeting these people.

Then, as if on cue, the experts immediately pulled out hand lenses and dropped to their knees to study the works. Charles and I apparently overwhelmed with seeing the paintings could not be bothered by an immediate microscopic analysis. Charles quickly did a mental comparison of the hides before us to the existing hide paintings housed in the Museum of New Mexico collections back home. He noted to me that they look authentic. Nevertheless, it did not take us long to follow suit and pull out our own new hand lenses to study the paintings. Charles, kneeling next to me asked, "What do you see?"

"I see the paintings up close." This is to say, I have no idea.

Then we heard the tick, tick, tick faintly getting louder as someone descended the stairs in high heels. Sure enough a woman appeared and proceeded to walk across both paintings on her way out. Then the chemist pulled out a small pair of scissors and snipped off a piece of the painting! I could not believe what I was seeing. Then he pulled out a cigarette lighter and lit the piece! As the smoke wafted upward he used his hand to move the smoke into his face and he sniffed. Apparently convinced by his experiment he began waving his arms and saying in German to anyone who would listen,

"*Es ist felz! Es ist felz!*" It is felt! It is felt!

When we understood what he was saying, Charles said that the paintings "look and feel like the hide paintings in New Mexico."

But the chemist would not budge. He repeated, "It is felt! It is felt!" And, to this day, I believe that I heard him call Charles *dumkalf,*" or "stupid."

Charles tried one more time to tell him that he thought the paintings were hide but received the same reply.

Irrespective of the chemist's proclamations as well as the treatment that the paintings were receiving at Sotheby's, Charles and I left the meeting convinced that the paintings were authentic. We were justified sometime later when the chemist and curator mailed their reports concluding that the paintings were indeed done on hide and that the pigments appeared to be natural. The chemist even went so far as to apologize for his behavior.[27]

At Herr Segesser's invitation Charles and I accompanied him to his hometown of Lucerne were we met his wife and visited the large downtown family home. Still furnished, the large mansion was unoccupied. Herr Segesser explained to us that the local authorities had strict preservation laws and he needed money to restore the house and this is why he wanted to sell the paintings. He toured us through the house where the paintings had been discovered in the attic. We asked about the missing pieces, especially the end pieces. Could they be in the attic still?

"No, there is nothing in the attic."

"Could we go up and look around."

"No, that would be a waste of time."

Among the many works of art hanging on the walls we encountered a portrait of Father Phillip von Segesser, the man who had sent the paintings to Switzerland. Then we were shown an oil painting of the Segesser family tree. Charles, who is an excellent photographer, took images of both paintings for further use or reference.

We left Switzerland determined to pursue the purchase of the Segesser Paintings. Their value to New Mexico could not be calculated in dollars. So we returned home with many slides and photographs and even more enthusiasm. Showing the slides and talking to our colleagues soon curbed our initial flush of optimism, for the reaction was somewhat akin to showing home movies.

7
On how the Segesser Paintings returned home

The only alternative was to borrow the paintings for exhibition at the Palace of the Governors. Then people would see their value and fundraising could begin in earnest. The Friends supported this effort but the Museum of New Mexico administration felt differently. Jean Weber, then the director, formed a pan Museum of New Mexico committee to study the matter. I learned from Dr. Donna Pierce, who had become a good friend and colleague and was the assistant director at the Museum of International Folk Art, that Weber wanted the committee to subvert our attempts at getting the paintings. Weber's intent in itself was subverted, for Pierce not only did not criticize the paintings but enthusiastically extolled their uniqueness and value. She dominated the committee, which concluded with an opinion opposite of Weber's desire.

Then I was asked to draw up a budget of how much it would cost to borrow or purchase the paintings, have them conserved enough for exhibition, and installed. In short, I needed to put together the justification for a definitive exhibition budget. At the time, everyone knew that such a budget was impossible. Any budget would be tenuous.

I was irritated because the written request was unreasonable. It concluded with a statement that until a complete budget, "is determined" and the Foundation has appropriated "all" the required funds, the Museum of New Mexico would not make a commitment nor provide interim funding.[28] This statement ran counter to the process that I was following and had received permission to pursue. We were moving one step at a time because the results of each step determined the route and expense of subsequent steps. For example, we needed to know if the paintings were in condition to travel and, if so, how? If they could not travel, could they be conserved enough to travel? And, if they could not travel under any circumstance then there was no need to budget for travel or an exhibition. Aside from Charles and me, no one from New Mexico or the United States had seen the paintings in person. Obviously, all of these questions needed to be answered before any subsequent expense. Estimating a price was premature at a time when negotiations for the price had not begun in earnest.

The budget request along with the secret committee put me on alert. The museum administration was working against me. I wrote a caustic reply to the budget request in which I gave a figure for each step of the procedure "to satisfy the bureaucratic appetite strewn in this museum...." I wrote in a memorandum headed with, "Segesser Paintings and other assorted attempts at memo warfare." For the cost of conservation, I wrote, "A wild guess: $1,500.23" and to make myself clear I concluded the missive with an expression of my irritation "of this matter" and that I would "not quietly sit back and let people mess this up.... If administration chokes now, I will not take the blame, nor will I make excuses for the failures of others." One of Weber's deputy directors and a close advisor received the memorandum and used a purple magic marker to print boldly across the document, "Do you believe this crap?" [29]

"Everything in life is politics," as the saying goes. So rather than deal with my immediate supervisor and her recalcitrant deputies, I started approaching the Board of Directors of the MNM. Finally, in late 1985, we received a unanimous vote of the Board to proceed.

We immediately proffered an offer to Herr Segesser. Would he lend the paintings to us for eighteen months, to allow us to arrange for appraisal, conservation and exhibition? By doing so, we argued, we could garner public backing, which would be important for receiving legislative support for their purchase. Along with the proposal sent through the mail, we were fortunate enough to appeal to Segesser personally, for Howard and Meriom Kastner, traveled to Switzerland on vacation. As mentioned Howard translated all our letters to Segesser into German. He also translated all the German correspondence from Switzerland into English. Kastner had been an interpreter for General Patton during World War II and parlayed that into a career of business and government work in Europe. He and Meriom had been long-time museum volunteers and, in fact, seemed to volunteer for every organization in town. They loved to travel and ski. Both had a great capacity for history. They attended every lecture I gave and I used to joke that Howard Kastner was my first PhD student. Naturally, he also was a member of the Friends of the Palace. The Kastners and Segessers had a great time together and sent me a jovial postcard that they wrote on the balcony of the Segesser's flat in Lucerne.[30]

Dr. Segesser agreed with our proposal. On Segesser's orders, Sotheby's shipped the paintings to New Mexico. Unfortunately their transfer to New Mexico did not go smoothly. Sotheby's had an interest in the paintings and had become, in fact, a competitor to the museum. The paintings were shipped through the Sotheby's office in New York, where they were held up. We were told that Segesser only authorized their transfer to New York, which in a telephone conversation he vehemently denied. Still, the New York people would not move them so we had Segesser contact them directly. Reluctantly, it seemed, the paintings were sent on their way to New Mexico. Then the airline on which they had been sent went on strike and all the planes were required to land at the nearest appropriate airport. The paintings made it as far as St. Louis where they were put into an airport warehouse. Once again I made some telephone calls to locate the paintings and find a way to get them moving again. The airline officials apologetically explained their situation and, in the process, shared the information that they were down to one flight per day from St. Louis to Albuquerque. This was an opening, for I painted a scenario to them of invaluable paintings, weltering in warehouse, which, if ruined would cost someone a lot of money. All of a sudden I could hear a series of connections being made to the point that a decision came back to put the paintings on the next day's flight. Finally, after two-and-a-half years of negotiations and a prolonged trip, the paintings arrived at the Palace of the Governors.

Even before we could get them on exhibition, they attracted attention. Historians from all over the country traveled to Santa Fe to see the paintings. For everyone's convenience, we had them unrolled over some large makeshift tables in one of our collections rooms. As we listened to these people react to the paintings we understood that each of them had a different perspective and some information to share, so with the help of a grant from the New Mexico Endowment for the Humanities (NMEH) that Charles Bennett and contract worker, Diane Block, wrote, we put together a three-day symposium for which we later won a national award for "Excellence in the Humanities," and invited over twenty-five scholars to come together view, discuss, and share ideas about the paintings.

The invited experts enjoyed two-and-a-half days of intellectual exchange. We started with a general meeting of introductions and orientation. Tom Livesay, the new director of the Museum of New Mexico who replaced Jean Weber, welcomed everyone. Then we viewed the paintings after which the scholars were split into three groups; historians, anthropologists and archaeologists, and art historians. The groups met the rest of the first day and most of the second day. At the end of the second day the whole contingent met in a general session to hear what each of the groups had concluded. That meeting was probably the most interesting time of the whole symposium.

The whole group met momentarily at the start of the third day and, then, broke into the respective groups to further ponder their conclusions in light of what they had heard in the general sessions. Finally, each group named two representatives who made presentations on their behalf in a public forum.

The NMEH produced a poster featuring Segesser II to commemorate the occasion, for one requirement of the grant was a public forum where the scholars could share their conclusions and answer questions.

One obvious conclusion was that Gottfried Hotz was correct. The paintings originally came from New Mexico but there was no real documentary proof outside of the paintings themselves. The art historians were adamant that the paintings were from New Mexico. Some historical questions were raised while others were answered. Fray Angélico Chávez identified the artists as a father and son with the surname of Jijon de Tiron. Father Charles Polzer, a Jesuit priest and historian from Arizona theorized on how the paintings went from New Mexico to Pimería Alta, which is Sonora, Mexico today, and in the possession of the Jesuit Phillip von Segesser. The Anza's, who were good friends of Father Segesser, and had early connections to New Mexico and Pimería Alta probably conveyed them to Pimería Alta and gave them to Segesser. He pointed out that the timing as well as placement of individuals pointed to this possibility.

That symposium concluded with a public forum held on 8 August 1986 that attracted some two hundred people on a Friday afternoon. Both the symposium and forum did exactly what we wanted. The value and uniqueness of the paintings spread through the academic world and the local public had become engaged in our effort to keep them in New Mexico.[31]

8
In which is related the irony of a scholar's unfair criticism of Gottfried Hotz

While we were gathering information as well as support for the paintings, Dr. Donna Pierce informed me of a collection of papers at the Folk Art Museum that had belonged to E. Boyd. Long after her death E. Boyd remains a legendary scholar and curator in New Mexico. She was a fierce champion of New Mexican Hispanic arts. Boyd, the curator of Spanish Colonial Art at the Museum of International Folk Art, was the expert on New Mexican hide paintings.[32] Among her papers we discovered that, in the course of his research sometime around 1959 or before, Hotz wrote to Dr. Bertha Dutton, curator of ethnology at the Museum of New Mexico. Dutton forwarded Hotz's inquiry to Boyd. Hotz, of course, was seeking information relative to his research on the Segesser Paintings.[33] In what only can be concluded as insane intellectual jealousy, Boyd refused to help Hotz. After he wrote his book and submitted it to be included in the University of Oklahoma Press's *The Civilization of the American Indian Series*, Boyd wrote to Dr. Savoie Lottinville in an unfortunate attempt to prevent the publication.[34] Dr. Lottinville was the editor of the press and creator of the series. Boyd's letter, as well as correspondence to friends, about Hotz and his work, was mean spirited, even bilious. She even claimed that Hotz had never been to the southwest.[35] This proved untrue for he traveled and researched throughout the southwest and northern Mexico. He dedicated his book "to Martha" who helped him "visit dozens of tribes in North America." Boyd later acknowledged that he had been to New Mexico but insisted that he did not go to Mexico. Fortunately, the editors at the University of Oklahoma disagreed with her appraisal of the book, for they concluded that Hotz's book was "the product of a remarkable feat of ethno historical detection."[36] The book came out as volume 94 of the series.

Undeterred, Boyd insisted on belittling Hotz. Turned back by the people in Oklahoma she turned to her friend Eleanor B. Adams, an accomplished historian who was the editor of the *New Mexico Historical Review*, which was published at the University of New Mexico. Adams accommodated Boyd[37] by allowing her to write an uncommonly long, five and one half pages, diatribe criticizing Hotz and the editors at the University of Oklahoma. Unwisely repeating many of the ugly words that she used in private correspondence, Boyd described Hotz's interpretations as "bombastic and preposterous" and his sources "even fictional." She accused him of "Teutonic 'think' patterns" and cited a conversation with Oliver LaFarge in which the southwestern novelist and Pulitzer Prize winner and who corresponded with Hotz, summed up "Hotz briefly as an autodidact."[38] She thought that was an understatement. She summed up Hotz's book as "this plethora of Teutonic mystique" not worth "the expenditure of $9.95." As for the paintings themselves, she concluded that they were done in Chihuahua or Sonora, and that Father Segesser may have "made one or both of them himself."[39]

On the other hand, LaFarge wrote to Hotz that "Miss Boyd and I are agreed that... these paintings may be of great historical importance" and that Hotz "made a real contribution in calling attention to these paintings.[40] Another of Boyd's colleagues wrote to her that news of the paintings had put her in a "tizzy and if you get them in your mitts...I'm drooling.[41]

Boyd did suggest that it would be beneficial to have the paintings loaned to a museum in the United States "where qualified scholars (her implication here is that Hotz was neither qualified nor a scholar) may study them."[42] Indeed, this may have been the source of her frustration with Hotz because neither the paintings or, in her opinion, good photographs were forthcoming. It seems that Hotz was doing what Boyd wanted to do—be the first to reveal the paintings in print.[43]

Long after Boyd's death the paintings did travel to the United States and qualified scholars have studied them. They are still being studied. Boyd unfairly misjudged Hotz.[44] She was wrong on almost every score. Subsequent research, including a letter written by Phillip von Segesser found in the Archives of the Indies verifies that the paintings are from New Mexico, "done in the style of that country."[45] In fact, Hotz's book was ingenious for its time.

Boyd's tirade gave me special pleasure in doing what she suggested and then vindicating Hotz. I met Boyd once as a graduate student doing research. I found her direct and condescending. I learned later that she was one of the people most responsible for the shrinkage of the Palace's collections in the seventies. Until the moment of gaining access to her letters I never suspected her of anything but a great curator and high intellect who had used her authority to move collections out of the Palace to the newly created Folk Art Museum. This uncomplimentary view of her as a professional and scholar was unexpected. Nevertheless, as revealed in her book review, people knew that Hotz's erroneous insistence in calling the paintings "Indian Skin Paintings" galled her and she was correct on that point.

9
Showing how the Segesser Paintings became educational tools

As we cleaned and conserved the paintings in anticipation to putting them on exhibition, interest in them continued to grow. We granted permission to the Nebraska History Museum to recreate Segesser II, for the Villasur battle took place in what is today Nebraska. The conservation report and Nebraska project brought forth even more information.

First, we learned that the paints used were not all made from natural pigments. The blue proved to be "Prussian blue," which was a dye developed in secrecy in Prussia around 1700.[46] Second, the people in Nebraska learned that they could not find buffalo hides large enough to replicate a three panel canvas nineteen feet long. They had to settle for four smaller panels to make up the complete size. In other words, buffalo were much larger in the early eighteenth century.

The paintings helped me make a historical point. In 1982 I served on the Diego de Vargas staff for the Santa Fe Fiesta council. Vargas and his "*cuadrilla*," as the staff was called, reenacted Governor Diego de Vargas and his "peaceful" retaking of Santa Fe in 1692 after the 1680 Pueblo Indian Revolt. The fact that Vargas really retook Santa Fe in 1693 and had to resort to violence is subject of a different text. Suffice it to say, in this historian's mind, Vargas is a man worthy of study and even remembrance as Santa Fe does at its Fiestas every September. The Fiesta's Vargas and his staff have activities scheduled every weekend from May through the actual Fiestas in September, so my vision of riding a horse during the Fiestas parade, although true, was overshadowed by the seriousness and duration of the task. For example, with the Fiesta Queen and her court as well as Mariachis in tow, we visited hospitals, schools, retirement homes, and workplaces to share a little Fiesta joy. At one place an elderly lady, who could neither stand nor walk, and could not have weighed more than sixty or seventy pounds wanted to dance. I could not understand her words, for she mumbled horribly, but her smile and gleam in her face told me all that needed to know. She wanted to dance, but how? A nurse explained; "pick her up." And that is what I did.

As the only historian in the *cuadrilla*, I volunteered to give some history lessons about Vargas, and his times. The staff accepted my offer with enthusiasm and this gave me a chance to talk about the historical accuracy of our uniforms. I was especially concerned about the color of the Franciscan robes or "habits" that we used. Two positions of the

Vargas staff reenacted Franciscan friars. Up until then, the Fiesta officials used brown habits, the color most associated with Franciscans today.

Earlier, in 1957, Fray Angélico Chávez opened an old colonial casket made of locally quarried stone and found in the cathedral's walls. The casket had two compartments inside that contained the remains of two seventeenth century Franciscans who were reburied in the 1750s in the old *parroquia*, or parish church that preceded the Santa Fe cathedral. During the remodeling of the Conquistadora chapel, which is the north transept of the cathedral, Fray Angélico decided to remove the double crypt from the nave wall, open it to see what was inside, and then have it placed in a specially made niche in the west wall of the Conquistadora chapel. He found writing under the lid as well as on the side of the joined crypts that described the contents. Along with bone fragments the crypts contained remnants of the priests' robes and the rope that they tied around their wastes. He cut out pieces of the habits from each compartment. He also cut a length of knotted cord from one of the crypts.[47] The pieces of cloth and rope eventually ended up in possession of Father Chávez's youngest brother José, who with his wife, Bernice, donated them into the Palace of the Governors where they are now part of the collections.

The color of the habits is blue, the shade of today's blue jeans or Levis. This, along with some scattered documentation, indicates that New Mexico's Franciscans wore blue and not brown. Upon reading more I learned that brown did not become the official color of the Franciscans until 1898. Before then they wore different colors including brown. For example, the Franciscans in California and Texas wore grey. I tried to convince the Caballeros de Vargas and the Santa Fe Fiesta Council to allow the Vargas staff to dress the Franciscans in blue, which would be true to New Mexico's history. With the acquiescence of Ed Berry, the staff liaison, we decided to have the robes made and unveiled during the Fiesta weekend. The staff was worried but they believed in my protestation that we should strive to be historically accurate. "But what if people start asking questions?" They wondered.

"That is exactly what we want." I replied. "We can explain to them that blue was the color worn by the early Franciscans who came to New Mexico. We will have a chance to educate someone, including members of our own sponsoring groups, the Caballeros de Vargas and Fiesta Council."

So we did it. Our two Franciscan re-enactors wore blue habits for the three days of Santa Fe's Fiestas in 1983. We thought that we had made a positive contribution to the event but we found out differently, for the robes were destroyed soon thereafter and the decision was made to go back to brown.

Nevertheless, people like Ed Berry continued to serve on the Fiesta Council and as staff liaison. Berry was an energetic, outspoken, and generous man, who ran a Christmas shop in downtown Santa Fe year around. He probably spent more time in community activities than he did at the shop. He also matched his volunteerism with generous financial support. Quite naturally he became a member of the Friends of the Palace and used the Palace's staff expertise with the collections to constantly improve the uniforms of the Vargas staff. Berry invited me to give the re-enactors and the Fiesta Queen and her court an annual history lecture. In addition, I was invited to give the Fiesta council's annual public history lecture and Donna Pierce invited me to write a history of Fiestas in a special edition of *El Palacio*, the magazine of the Museum of New Mexico that she was editing. The magazine would be published in conjunction with an exhibition on Santa Fe's Fiestas that she was organizing.[48]

I constantly mentioned the color blue, both in connection to the Franciscans and to New Mexico, for by then I noted that the color had connections with Mary, the Mother of God as well as New Mexico's story of the mystical Lady in Blue, María de Agreda, a Conceptionist Franciscan nun who the Franciscans claimed appeared to preach among the Indians. Fray Alonso de Benavides, who brought the statue of Mary, called La Conquistadora that is still a major part of the Fiesta celebrations, was the first to write of the Lady in Blue.[49]

Aware that "a picture is worth a thousand words," I used the Segesser II painting, now in the Palace of the Governors. It prominently depicts Father Juan Mínquez, a Franciscan who participated in the Villasur expedition and was killed in the ambush. Farther Mínguez's blue habit can not be missed. Thus I rather bombastically concluded in my article and repeated verbally, *ad infinitim* that the color blue "is special to New Mexico and so entwined with the Fiesta story that the hue cannot be denied but should be gloriously acknowledged."[50]

Thus with Ed Berry's influence the Franciscans of the Vargas staff started wearing blue habits and has kept them as part of their uniforms to this day.

10
Regarding how the Segesser Paintings were almost lost before they were bought

On 31 August 1986, after six months of study and conservation, the Segesser Paintings were put on exhibition at the Palace of the Governors. The Foundation flew

Herr Segesser to Santa Fe for the opening. He hit the ground on the run. As we learned, he was a very energetic man. The Kastners hosted him. Howard and Meriom liked to party and be with people. They held many wonderful receptions in their modest home. They were the perfect choice to host Segesser and, indeed, had become good friends with him. They encountered one small problem—Segesser wore them out and they had to hand him off to another couple. Naturally, Segesser was the star of the opening of the exhibition.

More importantly, he seemed really pleased at how we had handled his paintings. He liked Santa Fe and the museum's supporters. Combined with his original intent in having the paintings in the southwest everything had come together to create a good environment for further negotiations.

Segesser already expressed his desire that we purchase the paintings. He could not be more receptive so we agreed to sit down over lunch to talk about realistic figures and timelines. So far, we had raised around $100,000 but that had been spent to conserve, study, and install the exhibition. This included expenses for the opening, publicity, and Segesser's trip. Segesser agreed to wait while we raised the purchase money either through public donations and/or the state legislature. He conceded that his initial asking price was too high so he would consider something less but wanted to think about that. This information was all positive. I felt confident that something would be worked out. I had grown very fond of Herr Segesser and completely trusted him. In return, he had made some good friends in Santa Fe. This, along with his long-held belief and desire that the paintings should be in New Mexico, eased the discussion.

Segesser informed me that Sotheby's had told him that they could auction the paintings for $650,000 and that was an acceptable price to him. I replied that Sotheby's would take twenty percent of that amount for their fee. I continued that he should ask Sotheby's to draw up a contract that specified exactly what he would receive, their standard fee notwithstanding. In addition the contract should assure him that his family name will remain with the paintings for posterity, that Sotheby's will have them conserved, and that the paintings will be easily accessible to the public through exhibitions and for study. I said this knowing that Segesser and I both knew that Sotheby's would not agree to such a contract.

Segesser waited for me to continue. "With the exception of the price, we will do all those things and are willing to put them it writing." He became pensive and not at all nonplused. I continued, "We will need to get a legislative appropriation, the money from which will be available next June or July, so I am asking you to wait. I would like you to accept the price of $400,000 as a beginning. If we do not come up with that amount by June, then the price will go up in increments of $50,000 for each of the next three months until the amount reaches $650,000," which was Sotheby's projected auction price.

Herr Segesser asked me to repeat what I had said to make sure that he understood. After all, this conversation was taking place in what was probably his third language after German and French. He acknowledged that I had made a good argument for my plan and that he would give it his consideration. With positive and good feelings all around Herr Segesser returned to Switzerland.

Then, as luck would have it, I received a Fulbright Fellowship to do research in Spain for ten months, which will be explained further on in this book. Tom Livesay, my boss at the time, granted me leave to go and named Dr. David Phillips, an archaeologist, to replace me as the acting director for the Palace of the Governors. Charles Bennett, the assistant director, and I brought both men up-to-date with the Segesser Paintings. With Charles left behind and the fact that both Livesay and Phillips had participated in the Segesser Painting symposium, I felt confident in leaving.

While in Spain from January to the end of November in 1987, I received regular reports form Phillips and corresponded with Livesay. Livesay asked that I not contact Segesser from Spain while insisting that all was well on his front. I had no reason to doubt otherwise.

Meanwhile, I devoted a little time researching the Segesser Paintings in the General Archive of the Indies in Seville. I knew that Father Phillip von Segesser sent the paintings from Mexico in 1758. I also knew that they were sent to Spain. So could the ship's records or its manifest be preserved in the archives? Probably not, but why not check?

The Archive of the Indies is the repository where the majority of Spanish records dealing with its fifteenth through eighteenth century overseas empire are located. King Carlos III in the late eighteenth century ordered the archive to be formed. The early records of all its colonies in the Americas as well as the Philippines are stored in bundles called *legajos*. That the Spanish used to call the Americas the Indies explains the name of the archive.

Then one day I came across exactly what I was looking for. A *legajo* revealed the cargo list of the ship *Nuestra Señora del Rosario*, alias "*el Alcón*," or "Our Lady of the Rosary," alias "the Falcon." Captained by Domingo Apodaca, the ship sailed from Veracruz, Mexico, stopped at Havana, Cuba and arrived at the port of Cádiz in Spain on 29 September 1760. The ship's owner, Thomás Apodaca, who was related to Domingo Apodaca, received the paintings along with some other "*regalos*," gifts sent by the Jesuit priest Phillip von Segesser.[51] The ledger listed three paintings, (the third of which is still missing and is mentioned later in this book), some semiprecious stones that translated to petrified whale sperm, and a paper model of a church. All the gifts were in a trunk, which given the size of the paintings, must have been large.[52]

One of the great pleasures of finding something when researching is sharing the discovery with a colleague, friend, or loved one. It so happened that the well-known borderlands historian, Farther Charles Polzer, had arrived to research in the archive. So I hurried over to his table and invited him to see what I found. He followed me back to my seat, looked at the documents, and silently exclaimed, "Oh my!"

Soon thereafter I moved to Madrid to do research in the National Archive and the National Library. While there I received a telephone call from Charles Bennett almost simultaneously to the arrival of Donna Pierce, who had just resigned her position as Assistant Director of the Museum of International Folk Art. Both told me the news that the paintings where in jeopardy of being lost to the Smithsonian Institution.

Both received the news from Dr. Myra Ellen Jenkins, the long-time state historian who had learned that Helmuth Naumer, Lonn Taylor, and my boss Tom Livesay were working out a deal for the Smithsonian Institution to purchase the paintings, or, at the very least, the Museum of New Mexico Foundation, not the Museum, and the Smithsonian Institution would end up in a joint ownership arrangement.[53] Naumer, who was head of the Foundation when I left for Spain had accepted the job as Secretary of the Office of Cultural Affairs, a sub-cabinet position in state government. But he kept his position at the Foundation, which was the 501-(c)3 not-for-profit support group of the Museum of New Mexico, a state institution of which the Palace of the Governors was a part. Naumer thus became Livesay's immediate supervisor as well as equal. Taylor, who had left the Museum of New Mexico as one of Jean Weber's deputy directors, was now working at the Smithsonian Institution. All of them knew each other previously in Texas before they came to New Mexico.

Naumer and Taylor had reason to resent me. Naumer was the person who resisted the formation of the Friends of the Palace and Taylor left the museum after a physical confrontation with me. He took a position at the Smithsonian Institution's National Museum of American History in the Education Department. Naumer, I was told, expressed his lack of appreciation for the Segesser Paintings to my staff, saying, "I don't care about those paintings. I care about [Georgia] O'Keefe. Those paintings have no value to me." His priority at the time was the Fine Arts Museum.

Naumer, Livesay, and Taylor had drawn up an agreement wherein the Smithsonian Institution and the Museum of New Mexico Foundation would each raise half the cost for the paintings and if one institution could not fulfill its obligation then the other had the right of first refusal to raise the balance and become sole owner.[54] This, to me, was a blatant sellout; a convenient arrangement among friends to move the paintings from New Mexico to the Smithsonian Institution in Washington, DC.

I was incensed and took action. First, I asked Charles Bennett to telephone Ambassador Ortiz, who had returned to Washington, DC to finish out his career. Ortiz had given me his personal number and invited me to contact him if I needed anything. At the time, Charles had not met Ambassador Ortiz but dutifully called to fill him in on what was going on. Ortiz fully appreciated the value of the Segesser Paintings, so I felt that he might make a few telephone calls in Washington to discourage the Smithsonian Institution from interfering in our effort to get the paintings. Ortiz would see what he could do and, to this day, we do not know what he did or what influence he had on the outcome.

The second task proved very productive. I asked Donna Pierce to contact a mutual friend in the press. As a state employee, I was forbidden to approach the press as a matter of Office of Cultural Affairs policy. Pierce no longer worked for the state so she called Barbara Anderson a curator at the J. Paul Getty Museum. She, in turn had her husband, Frank Gifford, contact Richard McCord, the founder and chief editor of *The Santa Fe Reporter*, tell him the story and have him contact me in Madrid.[55]

Dick McCord is about as conscientious a journalist as I have ever met. He is soft-spoken with a speech pattern that gives me the impression he thoroughly considers each word as he says it. He talked to Livesay and Naumer before telephoning me. His interview was irritating, enlightening, and a relief. I became irritated at the information he had and that my own supervisors kept from me. He enlightened me as he "filled in the blanks" from the information that I had. I was relieved to give my answers and thoughts.

I felt that I had been betrayed. I expressed my concern that these people had no concern at all about keeping the paintings were they belonged–in New Mexico. Upon hearing that my bosses did not believe that the purchase money could be raised, I was quoted as saying from Spain that "I don't buy that. We never had a chance [to raise the money]." Couldn't they have waited just a little bit [for my return to New Mexico]? I don't know why they were so fearful. I felt that we could have raised the money.[56] I even raised some questions like how could Naumer and Livesay usurp the state in negotiations and limit the agreement solely to the Foundation and Smithsonian? Had they even informed Herr Segesser of their plans? It turns out the answer was "no." The interview lasted for around forty-five minutes and I knew the result would be scandalous. Apparently, none of the parties involved understood that all the work that we had done to that point had built a strong public backing for the project and their reaction would be somewhat akin to mine.

McCord had Keith Easthouse write the article that came out on 25 November 1987, the day after I flew back to New Mexico. McCord did his usual brilliant job.[57] While in Madrid, I received various telephone calls about the pending article. I heard that Naumer and Livesay were very upset. I returned home to an uncertain reception on 24 November 1987. Would I be fired? Maybe, but if the paintings were saved for the Palace, it was worth it.

A few days after my arrival and a couple days before I was expected back to work I walked into Livesay's office and said, "I'm back."

The reply was swift, "You son-of-a-bitch. You ought to be fired." Then he tossed his pencil across the room hitting the wall on the opposite side.

"Nice to see you, too."

At this point we both sat down and had a frank conversation about what I thought I was doing and what I thought they were doing. I also expressed that if Naumer or he wanted me fired—frankly I never believed that Livesay wanted to fire me—"that we should do that in a public forum and while we were at it we can inquire as to whom Helmuth works for; the state or the Foundation."

Still mad at me, Livesay commented, "If you are so damn smart why haven't *you* raised any money toward the purchase?" I replied to the effect that Herr Segesser never officially agreed to a price and that neither Livesay nor anyone else had granted me permission to seek the money. At any rate, how could I raise money for something that did not have a price?

He continued with the challenge to go ahead and try to raise the money, if I thought I could, but do not expect any help from him. "Fine," I thought; even, "great." I had a go!

Lest the reader get the wrong impression, I want to express at this point that Livesay and I had our differences but we also achieved much together. As will be seen throughout this quixotic story, Livesay turned out to be the best director that I had while at the Museum of New Mexico. We became friends and he even came to trust my judgment.

So now I was faced with the ultimate challenge. I had to get the paintings. Herr Segesser proved to be no obstacle. He agreed with my proposal of almost a year earlier. Now my staff, the Friends of the Palace, and I needed to accept Livesay's challenge and raise the money.

Once again, all the preparation paid off, for Jeff Hengesbaugh, a mountain man re-enactor, historian, friend, and fan of the Segesser Paintings who was one of the scholars at the Segesser symposium happened to be flying to New Mexico from a family visit in San Diego, California. Seated facing him on that flight was the state senator Les Houston. Senator Houston was the most powerful man in the New Mexico legislator at the time. He had forged a coalition of minority Republicans and majority Democrats and, with a moderate Republican governor, pretty much ran things as he saw fit. Houston is a big broad faced and shouldered man who does not waste a lot of time with small talk.

On the other hand, Hengesbaugh is a medium sized ebullient, outgoing man whose enthusiasm is easily shared. He also knows no fear when talking to people. Upon introducing himself and without realizing that the man he was addressing was an important politician, Jeff immediately embarked on one of his patented tirades about the paintings.

He engaged the senator's interest. At this point Houston revealed to Hengesbaugh that he was a state senator. After warning Jeff that the paintings had better be as exciting as he described them the senator said he would help. The senator knew of me, and told Jeff to have me telephone him. When I did, he instructed me to contact my uncle Fabián to draw up a bill that he, the senator, would sponsor.[58]

Fabián Chávez, by that time had had a long career in politics. He had been senate majority leader, unsuccessfully ran for governor as well as Congress, worked as the director of the state's Department of Development, and as an undersecretary in the Department of Interior in President Jimmy Carter's administration. At this time he worked as a lobbyist at the sate legislature. Senator Houston and he, although of opposite parties as well as the political spectrum, knew and respected each other.

The bill was drawn up and introduced. Fabián and/or Senator Houston arranged for Representative Max Coll, the Democratic chairman of the House finance committee, to sponsor a companion bill in the lower chamber. Within ten days of my acrimonious meeting with Livesay I was able to return to his office to share with him copies of the bills. To this day, I do not know whether Livesay was pleased, angry or both. Naumer's reaction was clearer for he tried to prevent the passage of the bill and, as will be seen, expected the governor, Garrey Carruthers to veto it when it got to his desk.

Once again we were going before the state legislature. Charles and I prepared informational packets for each legislator.[59] We prepared the Friends in anticipation of appearances before legislative committees. We arranged for some positive press and we spent time at the legislature as well as the *Bullring*, a local bar next to the state capital building where many of the politicians liked to hang out. Fabián Chávez also helped with introductions and letting the decision makers understand that we were related.

Curiously, our bill had not been scheduled for any committee hearings. Going before committee was a normal procedure. My brother Mark, at the time, was a meat salesman who ran a circuit out of Albuquerque to Northern New Mexico. He spent every Tuesday night with me. To my gratification he had developed an appreciation and interest in the paintings. Each week he asked what was happening with the legislation for the paintings. My constant reply was we are waiting to go before committee. Perhaps sensing my consternation as only brothers a year apart can do, he stated, "You know what you need to do?"

"No, what?" With Mark, who is about as quick-witted as anyone I know, you never knew whether he would come out with a serious statement or set you up for the butt end of a quip.

"You need a bumper sticker!"

"A bumper sticker?"

"Yah. You know a sticker with an image of that priest in the painting. The priest running with an arrow sticking out his ass." This, I knew was the Franciscan, Father Mínguez, but, before I could react, he continued, "And put below the priest the words 'Save our hides.'" Mark was a genius! He was absolutely right. The whole point of what we were doing was to bring New Mexico's patrimony home and reverse the trend of it leaving the state. In this case, the patrimony upon which we were taking a stand was the hide paintings. Mark's idea was brilliant; here was a message that covered all of our sentiments.

We had the stickers made up and passed out to every legislator. Word got out. The Segesser Paintings were no longer known to a few of the politicians who were pushing for their purchase. Now everyone knew about "those hides." The bills raced through both chambers and passed without ever going before committee. Put together into one bill, the legislation now waited for Governor Carruthers' signature but Naumer advised him to use his veto. Naumer, however, did not realize that Senator Houston had a slight edge for the Governor's favor.

I received a smug telephone call from Naumer that the governor wanted to meet with him and me in his office. The state capital building is round with both legislative chambers actually below ground level and the governor's offices on the fourth floor. The place is affectionately called "the roundhouse," sometimes with the adjective "merry" inserted before "roundhouse." The building has given rise to the now old joke that while in that building "you can never corner a politician."

I walked over to the roundhouse and rode up the elevator with Naumer whose smugness was obvious. I had with me a poster of Segesser II that the New Mexico Endowment for the Humanities had done in connection to the symposium. I planned to give it to the governor.

Naumer knew his way around the executive offices and was showing off for me. I guess he wanted me to know how important he was. As we walked into the governor's office, the governor stood up from behind his desk. He came around the side and shook hands with us.

Naumer started to say something but I felt that I could not lose the moment so I interrupted with, "Governor, before we start I want you to have this poster," as I pulled it out of the tube and unrolled it before him on his desk.

The Governor looked down at the image and exclaimed, "Oh, these are those hide paintings! We've got to have them!"

There was nothing else to say but "thank you, sir," to which he thanked me for the poster and thanked both of us for coming up to his office.

Needless to say, the elevator ride down with Naumer was very quiet. Now I was the smug one. I became further pleased when Governor Carruthers further recognized the importance of the paintings by sending me a letter of appreciation.[60]

Governor Carruthers signed the legislation and we bought the paintings for a total price of $400,000.[61] After an attempt to mail the payment check to Segesser failed, Segesser traveled back to New Mexico to receive his money.[62] Charles and I personally handed it to him and on 31 October 1988 the Segesser Paintings officially became the property of the State of New Mexico. Once again, Herr Segesser was the guest of the Kastners and we all had a great time celebrating a fulfillment of our mutual goals.

I learned afterwards that Senator Houston personally met with the governor to make sure that he would not veto the money for the paintings. Senator Houston confirmed that the governor had been specifically advised to veto it but upon the Senator's intervention the paintings became New Mexico's. I also knew that the governor's wife, Cathy, who served with me on the Board of the New Mexico Endowment for the Humanities, had an interest in the matter. She, like the other members of the board and staff of the NMEH, had recently received word of the organization's first-ever national award for one of its funded programs. On 14 November 1987, the Federation of State's Humanities Councils presented NMEH with the Helen and Martin Schwartz Prize for Public Humanities programs for the Segesser Symposium.[62] "Those hide paintings," indeed!

The Segesser Paintings had come home to stay but their story will continue. Publicity continued in journals, magazines, national news stories, and on television. Then we received the good news that First Lady Hillary Clinton was coming to the Palace of the Governors in connection with her new national treasures program. We had nominated both the Palace of the Governors and the Segesser Paintings for designation. Clinton wanted to designate and save national treasures in the United States and we learned that both of our nominations had been accepted! The building itself as well as the paintings had been accepted as official national treasures. Ms. Clinton received a personal tour and explanation of both the building and the paintings. As a result of that designation, the Palace of the Governors has been able to request and receive federal funding designated for National Treasures.

Another benefit from the symposium was a collection of article length manuscripts written by the participants. We wanted to publish an anthology with the latest information about the paintings. The anthology was put together but neither the Museum of New Mexico Press nor the University of New Mexico Press was interested. We turned to the Historical Society of New Mexico that had a publishing agreement with UNM Press. The Historical Society had been publishing its own series of books for years. Their goal was to publish history that might not be published otherwise. It seemed that the Segesser anthology was a perfect fit. After all, the Historical Society had presented Senator Houston,

Representative Coll, Charles, and I with their *Edgar Lee Hewitt Award for Service to the Public* for "efforts in the acquisition of the...Segesser Hide Paintings for the citizens of New Mexico.[64]

The manuscript was submitted to the Historical Society but after almost a year of waiting for an answer I started inquiring about the submission and found out that the Historical Society's publication committee had lost the manuscript. So the Segesser anthology languished for years before a private Albuquerque press approached me about publishing it.[65]

With some relish we did convince the Museum of New Mexico Press to reprint Gottfried Hotz's book. We replaced all the black and white images of the 1960 edition with the same ones in color and we designed a new, more exciting color cover. I wrote an introduction and we changed the books sub title to give a better description of the book's subject matter, which would have pleased E. Boyd, for the sub title reads, "Masterpieces Depicting Spanish Colonial New Mexico." The book came out in 1991 and, like the earlier editions, has gone out of print.[66]

Following the examples of the two earlier exhibitions that we traveled, we arranged to share the Segesser Paintings. The Arizona Historical Society's museum in Tucson paid a rental fee and was the first to open the exhibition outside of New Mexico. Director Michael Weber, my predecessor at the Palace of the Governors, who had attended the symposium and followed the progress of purchasing the paintings, could not wait to get them to his museum. He, too, showed the paintings with a successful symposium. The paintings also traveled to Los Angeles where they were exhibited in the Los Angeles County Museum of Natural History. Charles Bennett went to the opening and gave a lecture. While in Southern California he experienced or suffered through an earthquake. Then the paintings traveled to Washington, DC where the Museum of American History of the Smithsonian Institution paid a slightly higher rental fee. So, although they did not own all or part of the paintings, they were able to exhibit them. We suffered the disappointment that none of the museums in Nebraska could come up with the modest fee to exhibit them in the very place where the whole process began.

The legacy of the Segesser Paintings will continue. Today the museum is using advanced technology to study their composition. I'm pleased that the room in which the paintings will be permanently exhibited will be named for Howard and Meriom Kastner.[67] Nothing could be more proper.

Part II
Dulcinea Does Not Exist

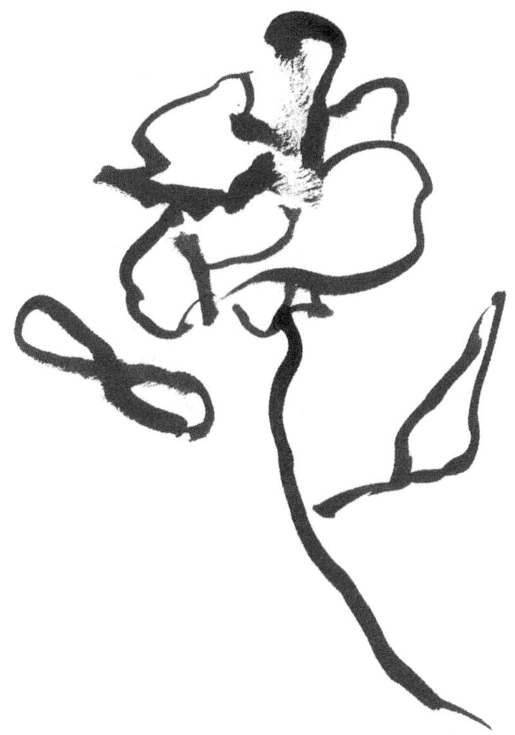

11
On how Sancho Panza's deception relates to history

As a matter of practice most of the staff members with whom I worked made themselves accessible to the public. If we were not otherwise occupied anyone could walk in the offices, sit down and visit with us. For my part, my office door was always open and I preferred to field my own telephone calls. Unannounced visitors commonly came in. This was more normal than not. The more affable Charles Bennett, who had an office facing mine, received even more people than me. This attitude permeated throughout the years.

So it happened one day that a man whom I had never met walked into my office with a small box in his hands. After introductions he told me that he had found some Spanish silver ingots in the hills south of Santa Fe. The ingots, he continued, dated to the reign of Carlos V in the sixteenth century. With that explanation he opened his box and unfolded a dark cloth that contained two roughly molded circular "ingots" measuring two inches in diameter. Their dark gray color did not hint of silver. The topside of the thick disk shaped ingots had markings while the reverse side was plain. The markings were a simple cross above a "V."

My visitor explained that the markings referred to Carlos V, who I knew was the Hapsburg Holy Roman Emperor from 1519 until 1556 and the King of Spain as Carlos I from 1516 to 1556. The ingots, he concluded, must have been left by one of the first Spanish expeditions to New Mexico.

This was all interesting and, if true, would be an important discovery. As he handed me the ingots, I expressed some doubt as to their authenticity. Such a reaction is common among museum people in such circumstances. The ingots did not look like silver and they were much heavier than they appeared. I also shared with my visitor that the historical record was silent on silver coming to New Mexico with any sixteenth century expedition.

He suggested that they might have been made locally in New Mexico. I replied that extracting silver was a complicated process that included the use of mercury, the vestiges of which researchers would have located. In addition, none of the expeditions that came to New Mexico reported finding enough silver to create silver ingots. Then, for some unknown inclination, I took one of the ingots and used it to write my name on a piece of paper.

"Look, they are lead. I can even write with them."

My visitor did not show any disappointment with this revelation. Instead, he told me to keep one of the ingots as a souvenir and with the other one in hand, thanked me for my time and left the office.

Historians as well as museum employees must deal with yesteryear's vestiges with some skepticism, for like don Quixote's imagined damsel, Dulcinea, people and history can present things that are not what they appear. At one point in don Quixote's story, the mad knight sent his squire Sancho Panza to fetch the beautiful Dulcinea. Sancho knew that she was a figment of Quixote's imagination so he decided to present Quixote with three peasant women who happened to be riding by. Sancho insisted that one of them was Dulcinea.

As Sancho Panza proclaimed that Dulcinea was approaching, don Quixote correctly surmised that he did not see anything "except three peasant girls on three donkeys." Sancho insisted that one of them was the maiden Dulcinea and convinced the knight errant that some evil had cast a spell on him thus making him see something that appeared other than it is. Convinced by the argument don Quixote exclaimed,

> Sancho, what do you think of how the enchanters despise me? Look at the extent of their malice and ill will, for they have chosen to deprive me of the happiness I might have had at seeing my lady in her rightful person.[68]

People charged with studying the past are presented with many such challenges. The episode of the silver ingot is a small and insignificant example. Nevertheless, history as mentioned earlier, is the mother of truth, so we come across many cases where different versions of the truth are claimed, sources need to be verified, a part of history is lost and retrieved, or a part of lost history has yet to be discovered. Sometimes the evidence is in existing knowledge that has been overlooked.

12
In which is revealed how Santa Fe is older than commonly thought and its founder is discovered

The Martínez de Montoya documents are a bound group of sixty-one pages dating from the beginning of the eighteenth century and extending into the third decade of the nineteenth century. They are the official record of a heraldry court in Spain that had them copied into its record. They include letters and testimony dating from 1605. Through the use of internal information within the documents themselves and taken in context of other known documents, the veracity of these documents make them very valuable. They divulge or clarify facts of New Mexico's early history, not the least of which is that Juan Martínez de Montoya, a captain under Juan de Oñate and, then, his son Cristóbal, established the village of Santa Fe sometime between late 1607 and August 1608.

Martínez de Montoya came to New Mexico as a leader of a group of recruited colonists who arrived in December of 1600. Gaspar Pérez de Villagrá, who later wrote *La Historia de la Nueva Mexico* that was published in Spain in 1610, was sent south to Mexico City to recruit more colonists. Upon hearing that he would not be in charge of the returning expedition, he deserted the enterprise. Martínez de Montoya continued with the expedition north with a disappointedly small contingent of eighty people. During the next five plus years Martínez de Montoya distinguished himself in various activities in New Mexico. In 1601 he participated in Oñate's expedition on to the plains where in present-day Kansas he gave good account of himself in a battle with the "Escajaque" Indians at the Quivera settlements. He also partook in a punitive expedition to Taos where other sources tell us that the pueblo was nearly completely destroyed. In 1603, he went to Acoma Pueblo, already reoccupied after the devastating battle in 1599. From there he went on to the Hopi pueblos. He participated on more than one campaign against the Apaches and in 1605, while Oñate rode to the Gulf of California, Martínez de Montoya was named *Alcalde Ordinario* (special or interim mayor) of the Spanish capital San Gabriel, where he was charged to maintain its defense.

Apparently in anticipation to leaving New Mexico Martínez de Montoya secured an audience with Juan de Oñate to certify his accomplishments and years of service. The captain wanted to make sure that, per the laws of the day, after five years of service in the new colony he would receive what was due to him. Specifically, he wanted the minor Spanish title of nobility; that he and his descendents would become *hidalgos*, a contraction of *hijo de algo*, which means "son of something" as well as be addressed as "Don" and "Doña," which is an acrynim for *de origen noble.* The governor dutifully bore witness to Martínez de Montoya's testimony. He also had it written down and signed and dated it on 6 October 1606.[69]

Martínez de Montoya did not immediately leave, probably because he was needed in New Mexico. He was called upon to lead two punitive expeditions against the Apaches and joined another expedition as an officer under Cristóbal de Oñate, Juan's son. He also served a second term as *alcalde ordinario* of San Gabriel.

Meanwhile, on 24 August 1607, Juan de Oñate sent a letter of resignation to the Viceroy in Mexico City. Oñate was bitterly disappointed and discouraged with the lack of support for his colony. Oñate stipulated that he would keep his soldiers and colonists in New Mexico until the following June. If no reply came by that time, he would order the abandonment of the colony.[70] No doubt Martínez de Montoya shared the same anxiety as everyone else while they waited for the viceroy's reply.

The viceroy penned his reply and sent it along with three Royal Orders, one of which originated from the King. The viceroy addressed the royal packet to Martínez de Montoya, not Oñate. So Martínez de Montoya was the first to learn that Oñate's resignation had been accepted and that the governor was ordered to remain in New Mexico until replaced or instructed otherwise. The biggest surprise was that the viceroy named Martínez de Montoya to replace Oñate as the interim governor of New Mexico.[71]

Historians have surmised that the cabildo or the colony's council, heavily influenced by Oñate, met and refused the viceroy's choice. They then named the governor's son, Cristóbal, the interim governor. The Martínez de Montoya documents hint at the acquiescence of Martínez de Montoya himself, for he remained on good terms with Oñate and desired to leave New Mexico.

Soon thereafter Cristóbal de Oñate, in his capacity as the new acting governor, witnessed and certified a second testimonial given by Martínez de Montoya. Signed on 8 August 1608, Oñate's son verified the almost two years of the captain's activities since his earlier testimony. Along with the aforementioned activities, Martínez de Montoya noted that he "populated" and "made a plaza in Santa Fe." Within a few months Cristóbal de Oñate granted Martínez de Montoya permission to leave New Mexico. He traveled as an officer in a small escort of Fray Lázaro Ximénez and Fray Isidro Ordóñez, who carried some letters for the viceroy. One of those letters mentioned that plans were underway to establish a new town and capital.[72] The unnamed town can only be a reference to the new plaza of Santa Fe established by Martínez de Montoya. No doubt the captain's presence in Mexico City was an additional source of information about New Mexico for the viceroy.

The viceroy quickly decided upon Pedro de Peralta to replace Oñate and in the fall of 1609 Peralta began the trip north. The new governor carried instructions to "found and populate" ... "la villa que se pretende,"[73] which refers to a town or place that already existed. Again, this could only refer to Santa Fe, for no other new towns had been established and that was indeed the town where Peralta made his capital. Maybe someday a historian will discover a report that Martínez de Montoya made for the viceroy. Then we will have a clearer understanding of the founding of Santa Fe.

Martínez de Montoya naturally wanted the establishment of Santa Fe on his résumé. Such an act was important and separated him from the vast majority of other settlers. Most likely he laid out a plaza and moved a few people to the place, which, apparently, was already occupied by some people.[74]

Martínez de Montoya did not stay long in Mexico City or even New Spain, for he returned to his native village of Navalagamella with his proof of service. He and subsequent generations of his descendents presented these documents as well as proof of their ancestry to the Heraldry Courts. The courts dutifully copied the documents as well as subsequent testimony into the record and it is this court record that has survived as the Juan Martínez de Montoya documents.

I learned that France Scholes, New Mexico's preeminent historian, discovered and copied the documents in the 1930s. He found them in a London rare book and antiquities shop. Scholes used the documents to publish an article in 1944 in the *New Mexico Historical Review*.[75] The article focused on Martínez de Montoya. His role in establishing the village of Santa Fe led Scholes to conclude that "it would appear ... that the beginnings of settlement there [Santa Fe] occurred as early as 1608 and that at such time the site was already known as Santa Fe."[76]

David Snow, an ethno historian who worked with me at the Palace of the Governors brought the article to my attention and suggested that this might be worthy of pursuing.[77] I read it with interest but what caught both of our attention was Scholes's footnote in which he cited the Martínez de Montoya documents. They were "owned by Maggs Bros. of London when I saw them." Scholes followed this with their long title.[78] No one but Scholes had seen these documents and he used them to refute the time-honored 1610 founding date of Santa Fe. He also used them to establish that Martínez de Montoya, not Pedro de Peralta, deserved credit for starting the town. We wondered whether the documents still existed and I took it upon myself to find out.

I picked up the telephone, figured out how to call information in London, and asked for a listing for Maggs Brothers. Sure enough the operator gave me a number. The company, if it was the same one, still existed. So I telephoned and asked the man who answered if this was the Maggs Brothers that sold rare books? "Why yes, we do. How can I help?"

I told him about the footnote and documents and wondered if anyone would know anything about them. The reply surprised me, for he said that he thought that they still had the documents.

Hardly able to control my excitement, I asked him if he could locate them because we would be interested in purchasing them. I then explained my position as a museum employee in New Mexico. Our conversation ended with his assurances that he would get back to me.

Then I asked Charles Bennett to draft and send a letter to the company reiterating the museum's interest in the papers. I waited over a month before I telephoned Maggs Bros. again. The same voice answered and he remembered our previous conversation. Unfortunately, he had not located the documents but he had not finished searching. Once again, he assured me that he would call.

Time passed again. The man at Maggs Bros. did not telephone. So, once again, I picked up the telephone and initiated the conversation. This time the same person gave a less favorable reply. "We sold the documents."

"When?"

"I do not have the record in front of me."

"Did you sell them recently?"

"Oh no, this was done some time ago."

I then asked him if he had records of the sale and who he sold them to. And, if so, would he mind contacting the person to ask permission to share with me his contact information. The documents, I explained again, were of significant historical importance to New Mexico and, if nothing else, I would like to get copies for their information.

I received a positive answer to what I considered a long shot. However, I was warned that the inquiry would take some time. With no other choice, I politely thanked the man for his willingness to help and hung up.

This time, three months passed before my patience ran out and I telephoned Maggs Bros. once again. Not surprising, the same man answered. This time the conversation was short. They could not locate the sale record for the Martínez de Montoya documents. We had reached a dead end. The chase was over.

Some time later, Homer Milford, a friend and historian who worked for the State in the Mining and Minerals Division telephoned me with the news that he was going to London to do some research. He is a friendly person who because of his job began researching the early mining history of New Mexico. His research eventually led him to New Mexico's first governor Juan de Oñate, a miner himself. Milford found and then published the 1625 reprinting of the 1584 laws and ordinances for mines that were written under the direction of Oñate.[79]

Milford wanted to know if there was anything he could do for me while in London. I asked him if he could go to Maggs Bros. and inquire about the Martínez de Montoya documents. In particular, I recalled hearing something about their miscellaneous closet. They thought that the documents might be there but found nothing. Maybe Milford could take a look himself. I gave him the address and he said that he would try.

"Try" was an understatement, for not only did Milford convince the people at Maggs Bros. to give him free reign in their miscellaneous closet but he found the documents! Almost a year to the day since my first contact with the people in London, Milford located the documents. In a telephone call from London he told me that they were bound in what looked like an eighteenth century cover that was tied shut with ribbons. The documents consisted of sixty-two pages.

With Milford's information, I again telephoned Maggs Bros. The same man answered. While feigning calm, he was embarrassed. Now we could talk turkey. I knew that he had the documents. I wanted to know if he was interested in selling them. Yes he was.

"Good! Well then, what do you want for them?"

"I cannot tell you. I need our Professor of Hispanic Antiquities to come in and give us an appraisal."

"When can he give you an appraisal?"

"Not soon, I am afraid. He is on holiday."

So we left it at that. When the appraisal was done I would be notified and we could come to an agreement. Obviously, I needed a price if the Palace was going to purchase them. My telephone conversant made clear that a donation of the documents was not a consideration. Once again, I was after something that would cost money while I had none in hand. Nonetheless, I never considered raising the funds a problem if the money was needed for a worthy reason. The documents were too important not to have in New Mexico.

Once again, time passed in silence. Finally, I telephoned only to find out that the Professor of Hispanic Antiquities was still "on holiday." A month had passed but by then I had come to realize that many Europeans take a month or more for vacation. So okay, but I did ask if anyone else was available to do the appraisal. "No."

More time passed with, at least, two more telephone calls with the same results. The Professor of Hispanic Antiquities was "on holiday." Once again, I was in a place where I could do nothing but wait. After almost a year and a half, we were waiting for a Professor who had an endless holiday. And, I could not overlook the fact that not once did the man at Maggs Bros. telephone me as promised. I initiated every call.

Then one day, Frank Ortiz came into my office. He was going to London.[80] As a Friend of the Palace he knew about our attempts at getting the Martínez de Montoya documents. Could he do something to help while he was in London? Yes he could. He could visit Maggs Bros. and impress upon them the importance of the documents. Maybe he could get them to get an appraisal.

As mentioned earlier, Frank Ortiz was a retired career diplomat who had been an ambassador at some important places. He could be intimidating. As an operative for the Palace of the Governors he was the perfect person for this job.

He went to Maggs Bros. and was met with the, by now, standard "our Professor of Hispanic Antiquities is on holiday." Well, the dapper Ambassador Ortiz, who no doubt introduced himself as "Ambassador," explained in no uncertain terms that he had traveled thousands of miles to be there and that it was time that the professor was called off of his holiday. I can imagine how that message was put. I know the result. The Professor was called in, gave an appraisal, and I received my first telephone call from Maggs Bros.

They wanted ten thousand dollars for the documents. I explained to him that the documents had been in their possession for over fifty years, they lost them, we found them, and we were the only people in the world who had an interest in them. Then I counter offered $2,500. After a slight pause, he agreed. The documents were shipped to New Mexico and arrived before Ambassador Ortiz returned. The Museum of New Mexico Foundation had no trouble contributing the purchase price.

With great fanfare we presented the documents to the public. Mayor Debbie Jaramillo participated in the ceremonies and historians came to the Palace specifically to see the documents. My wife Celia López-Chávez, who also is a historian, and I did a page-by-page English synopsis of the documents. The documents were clear. Sometime between the date of Martínez de Montoya's first testimony on 6 October 1606 and his second testimony given on 8 August 1608 he had established a town named Santa Fe. Along with other known information the documents were just as Dr. Scholes had concluded. Subsequent research by other historians, especially into birth records, also corroborates an earlier beginning date for Santa Fe.[81]

An interesting part of the documents is a genealogical tree that traces the descendents of Martínez de Montoya until the 1830s. Celia and I traveled to the old captain's birthplace and the town to which he returned from New Mexico. The town is called Navalagamella and is located about fifteen miles from San Lorenzo de Escorial outside of Madrid on a pleasant and beautiful drive. The town was nearly destroyed during the Spanish Civil War and has very little left from before then. While there, we asked to meet with the mayor and we were lucky enough to be invited into his office. We shared some copies of the documents including the family tree. The mayor's face lit up and before we knew it he was on his feet. He said in Spanish that there are many people in the village today with these surnames–including him. His secretary entered the office to remind him that people were waiting to see him but he would not be distracted.

He replied to her, with an excited, "Yo soy hidalgo! Yo soy hidalgo!" I am a hidalgo! I am a hidalgo! Then he charged out into the reception room repeating the same phrase. With this some of the city workers came out of their offices to see what the commotion was all about. The mayor explained about the documents and that one of their ancestors and a native of Navalagamella was the founder of the famous Santa Fe in the United States. Needless to say, the mayor and his staff treated Celia and me royally.

After we returned home we copied a complete set of the documents and sent them to Navalagamella. Hopefully, some day, the city leaders of Santa Fe, New Mexico in the United States will make an attempt to contact and even do something with the birthplace of their town's founder.

The acquisition of the documents received a fair amount of publicity but one of the more pleasing pieces came from Hazel Romero, the Palace's librarian. Hazel was a worker bee. She did all the cataloging in the library. The work is unglamorous, maybe monotonous but it is the basis of a good library and the History Library is what it is in good part because of her. As a result of a research inquiry about Navalagamella, she ended up writing a well done article in the local monthly historical/cultural journal called *La Herencia* in which she more succinctly recapped the tale above.

Years later, in 2006, the University of New Mexico Press used a photograph of the Martínez de Montoya documents opened to one of the two pages where he claimed to have established Santa Fe. The phrase, which reads, "y haber hecho plaza en Santa Fe," "and having made the plaza in Santa Fe," is on the cover of my seventh book.[82]

13
In which the examples of a missing painting, a lost Indian headpiece, a stolen gun, and a statue of the Virgin Mary illustrate the point of chapter eleven

In 1761 a new church on Santa Fe's plaza opened. Governor Francisco Marín del Valle commissioned Bernardo Miera y Pacheco, a cartographer, artist (he was *santero,* a person in New Mexico who paints and carves religious images), explorer, and minor politician, to carve the church's altar screen out of local white stone. Miera y Pacheco responded with a magnificent piece of work that can be seen today at Santa Fe's Cristo Rey Church.[83] The artist carved a three-tiered piece that was originally painted.[84] In keeping with the name of the original church, which was Our Lady of Light, the center section of the bottom row was reserved for an oil painting of that Virgin. Fray Francisco Atanasio Domínguez, who compiled a report of his inspection of all the churches in New Mexico in 1776, wrote about the painting; "In the center of the first [row of the altar screen], as if enthroned is an ordinary oil painting on canvas with a painted frame of Our Lady of Light."[85]

The altar screen and its painting stayed in the original church, which became known as La Castrense, until 1859 when Bishop Jean Baptiste Lamy sold the church.[86] He had the stone altar screen disassembled and stored in the *parroquia* where they remained until they were moved to the new Cristo Rey Church in the 1930s. The oil painting did not stay with the altar screen, for Lamy gave it as well as a stone plaque that had been a front piece in the Castrense altar to the newly arrived Sisters of Loretto.[87] The painting hung for years in the Sisters' reception room at Loretto Academy, a women's school. In 1968 the Sisters closed their school and left Santa Fe taking the painting with them.

Fray Angélico Chávez, remembered seeing the painting in the convent and wondered if the Sisters still had the painting with them in Denver where they moved. He also wondered whether this was the same painting that Father Domínguez described in the eighteenth century. So he received permission to inspect the painting and found it to be an image of Our Lady of Light. Even more telling was that the painting was too large for the niche where it supposedly was placed but that two vertical creases or evidence of fold marks perfectly fitted it to the altar screen.[88]

Much later this information interested the staff at the Palace of the Governors. Another telephone inquiry was in order and this one bore immediate fruit, for upon contacting the Sisters of Loretto's convent in Denver we learned that they still had the painting. In fact, it was their prized possession and had been cared for very well. With some reservation, the Sisters agreed to let the Palace of the Governors exhibit the painting. The Sisters worried that once the piece arrived in New Mexico, we or the Archbishop would lay claim to it. Staff assured her that if loaned to the museum, which is a state institution, it would be returned. Convinced that it would be returned, they agreed to a loan. From 14 October into November of 1994 the Palace of the Governors was able to exhibit a piece of history thought to be lost or, for the most part, not known.[89]

A curious aside to this story is that the stone used for the altar screen appears to be quarried from the same place as the stone casket now in Santa Fe's Cathedral that holds the remains of the two Franciscans mentioned previously. The priests were reburied at the request of Governor Marín del Valle, the same man who ordered the altar screen made for the Castrense. Is it possible that Miera y Pacheco also carved the stone casket? One telltale sign is the writing on the casket's outside as well as under the lid. It appears to be in his style as well as in his hand. So the crypt, altar screen, and oil painting are examples of history that have been rediscovered over time and for the latter, the museum was able to reintroduce it to the public.

Another example of known but overlooked history resides in a side chapel of the Franciscan Church of San Francisco in Mexico City. There a visitor will find a small statue of Mary known as "Nuestra Señora de la Macana." This statue, whose official name is Our Lady of the Tabernacle of Toledo (Nuestra Señora del Sagrario de Toledo), is an example of a known piece of New Mexican seventeenth century history that has not returned to New Mexico.

The statue came to New Mexico with the first colonists in 1598. Most likely, Pedro Robledo with his wife, four sons, two daughters and his son-in-law, Bartolomé Romero, the first of New Mexico's Romeros had the statue with them. The Robledos and Romero came from the area around Toledo and would have venerated Lady of the Sagrario.[90] In 1674 the statue passed into possession of Bartolomé's great-grand daughter María Romero, who at the time was ten years old and an invalid. One day, so the legend has it, the statue spoke to the bedridden María. The statue instructed the girl to rise up and go to the priest in the parish church. There she was to tell him to give a sermon warning all the people that if they did not start obeying God's clergy, destruction would come upon them in the form of an Indian rebellion.

Six years later, in 1680, the most successful Indian rebellion in North American history took place in New Mexico when the Pueblo Indians united and rose in revolt. Over three hundred settlers and twenty-one Franciscans were killed. Some of the survivors including the now teenaged María huddled in the fortified Royal Houses that roughly surrounded today's Santa Fe plaza. The Romeros lived in the southern part of Santa Fe, which was attacked first, so they were lucky to get into the fortification. In their haste they left their statue of Mary, which was broken as the attackers rampaged through the house.

Apparently, one of the Pueblo Indians was familiar enough with the people of Santa Fe to recognize that the statue belonged to the young lady so he wrapped it in a cloth and tossed it over the ramparts. María was reunited with her statue.

The story of María and her statue preceded the revolt, for Fray José de Trujillo, who was stationed at the Hopi Pueblos, wrote of the warning to his brethren in Mexico City. Now, he conjectured and hoped, he would achieve his highest ambition, which was to die for his Lord. Father Trujillo had spent his adult life seeking martyrdom, first in the Philippines and, then, in New Mexico. And, indeed his greatest wish came to pass during the Pueblo Revolt.[91]

On Governor Antonio Otermín's orders the colonists abandoned the fortification and fled south to the present area of El Paso. María took the statue with her on that difficult journey. In El Paso, the Franciscans, very much aware of the story of the miracle, convinced the young lady to give them her statue and by 1683 took it to the mission of Tlalnepantla, north of Mexico City, where the statue was repaired. Most notably a patch over a cut or dent in her head resulted in a permanent bump. Over time the Mexican Indians at Tlalnepantla began to call her Nuestra Señora de la Macana in reference to an Aztec war club, which they called a *macana*. The locals, thinking that her bump was the result of a blow from such a club during the rebellion in the far north, gave her the name.

An oversized oil painting illustrating the events of the Pueblo Revolt was commissioned and served as a backdrop to La Macana for years. The painting also had a narrative describing the miracle and revolt. Unfortunately, when the statue was moved to its final location in the Franciscan's mother house in Mexico City in 1754, the painting remained behind to be lost. To this day it has not been located.

Franciscan historian Agustín de Ventancurt, in his 1697 book, *Teatro Mexicano,* related the story of the miracle, Father Trujillo's martyrdom, and the Pueblo Revolt. Diego de Vargas, who successfully resettled New Mexico, knew of the story as well.[92] He actually described to the Viceroy that the rebellious Indians had beaten the statue "with a club, and the head of the divine Lady had been broken.[93]

Whether apocryphal or not, the story of Nuestra Señora de la Macana is a story that involved real people, real events, a statue of Mary that still exists, and a missing painting. There was some talk about requesting a return visit of La Macana to Santa Fe when it celebrated the 400th anniversary of its 1610 (sic) establishment. Sentiment for her temporary return continues. Maybe someday, when she does return, the painting will have been found as well.

While the challenge of locating items, discovering history, and musing over lost art that still may exist can take up a lot of pleasurable time, there occasionally is the incident in which history is lost. The largest disappointment of my career dealt with a rare artifact that the Palace of the Governors had in its collections before I started working there. It was an old converted Spanish *escopeta*, or rifle that had been remade into a percussion cap firearm. The sawed off barrel turned it into a one-of-a-kind handheld weapon. It was used at a bar in Embudo, today's Dixon, New Mexico in the 1830s and 40s. Even though it had not functioned for decades, it was a unique piece.

I was in the habit of taking artifacts to schools and public forums. Rather than talk about them I wanted to share them. I let children wear a real helmet from the sixteenth century, hold a breastplate, wear a hat from yesteryear, and imagine how miserable it must have been for women to use an old curling iron that was heated in a fire or over coals before wrapping their hair around it. I wanted the public to get a sense of history. Sharing actual pieces from the collections engaged people with the museum.

The gun from Embudo was one of my favorite "show and tells." On one such occasion, I met mountain man re-enactor Jeff Hengesbaugh at Bents Fort in La Junta, Colorado and, to this day, I believe that he was more taken with the sawed-off rifle than me. It was impressive. On another occasion I received an invitation from an organization holding it's meeting at the Santa Fe Women's Club. I gave a lecture and took the old weapon along to show. The lecture went well and everyone seemed impressed with the rifle. I went home to my one room apartment after the talk and made the mistake of leaving the artifact overnight in my car. The next morning as I prepared to drive to work I found that my car had been opened and ransacked. The weapon was missing. It was the only artifact stolen in my twenty-seven years of working at museums and it was completely my fault.

I am confident that the rifle will be found and returned. It is unique and photographs of it exist. There is no value in having it in private possession unless it is shared with others. Maybe some future or current curator will initiate a dogged pursuit that, like many of the stories in this book, will return a little bit of our patrimony.

One of the more intriguing stories of lost artifacts involves the defeat of the Comanche leader Cuerno Verde in 1779. Cuerno Verde had a hatred for New Mexican settlers, for his father had been killed fighting them. He sought revenge and became a larger than life scourge in northern New Mexico. People reported seeing him being carried on a litter and wearing a headpiece of buffalo skin and one horn, all of which was dyed green. So the settlers gave him the name Cuerno Verde, or "Green Horn."

New Mexico Governor Juan Bautista de Anza's main task in New Mexico was to end the constant raiding from Plains Indians. As the main culprits, the Comanches became his initial target and Cuerno Verde the primary objective. Anza led an expedition north out of New Mexico and then west through the Rocky Mountains that surprised and eventually defeated Cuerno Verde on the plains by present-day Pueblo, Colorado. The Comanche leader and his son both died in the conflict. Anza described Cuerno Verde in his diary of the expedition. We "...recognized from his insignia and devices the famous chief Cuerno Verde, who, his spirit proud and superior to all his followers left them and came ahead, his horse curveting spiritedly."[94]

The battle eventually brought peace to New Mexico with both the Comanche and Apache Indians. In truth Anza's successes in dealing with Plains Indians changed history. What interests us here is a subsequent letter that he sent to his superior Teodoro de Croix, the Commander General of the Interior Provinces of which New Mexico was one. In a letter that Anza sent with some gifts to Mexico City he described one item as,

> "The head-dress of the above named Chieftain, Cuerno Verde,
> because it was known and distinguished among his people, as
> well as, that of the second in command, Jumping Eagle, I give
> myself the satisfaction of sending to the hands of your lordship."[95]

The famous headpiece of Cuerno Verde, along with that of his assistant Jumping Eagle, was sent to Mexico City! What became of them? Were they forwarded to Spain? Are they an anonymous part of a private collection in Mexico? As of yet they have not been located if indeed they have survived. At one point, a rumor surfaced that the headpiece was in the Vatican Museum but this proved not to be the case—at least, not for now. One can only imagine the excitement if either of these invaluable pieces of history were found.

Unlike the unlucky don Quixote who never found his imaginary Dulcinea, historians are only limited by their persistence and imaginations in the search of lost history, for, on many occasions lost history becomes reality.

14
Relating to a story of a morrión and a breastplate

Gaspar Pérez de Villagrá joined Oñate as his legal advisor and as a captain in the original settlement of New Mexico. In the fifteen months that he served Oñate in New Mexico, he captured and executed some deserters, and participated in the siege and destruction of Acoma Pueblo before being sent back to Mexico to recruit reinforcements for the disintegrating colony. As mentioned in chapter twelve of this section, he deserted the New Mexican enterprise when the Viceroy replaced him as the commander of the returning expedition.

Villagrá, as he has become known in the United States, was born in Mexico, educated in Spain at the University of Salamanca, and spent some time at the Spanish Royal Court. After his short career in New Mexico he returned to Spain where he wrote a book length poem about the exploits of himself and his commander.[96]

In one part of his poem he told the story of what happened to him after he returned to New Mexico after capturing some deserters in Mexico. He wanted to report to Oñate who had left the settlement to explore west to the "South Sea," the Pacific Ocean. He decided set off alone following Oñate's route.[97]

Just after passing Acoma Pueblo, Villagrá entered a land of lava rock known today as Malpais, which translates to "badlands." He followed an Indian trail that survives today. With lava rock towering above him he had no choice but to follow the narrow trail. As a matter of convenience animals did the same thing so the Acoma Indians had set an animal trap. Unfortunately, Villagrá rode into the camouflaged hole. His horse was killed. "Pierced, without a sign of life," probably impaled on spikes set up in the bottom of the hole. Miraculously, Villagrá survived. Now on foot he continued his journey west but he had a sense of urgency because he believed that the Indians had set the trap for him. Now they would be looking for him.[98]

Then it began to snow and before long Villagrá was walking in a full blizzard. Villagrá wrote that he stopped to leave his armor in the rocks. Without the metal's weight he could travel much faster. His paranoia led him to place his boots on backwards,

> And, not to be caught by my tracks,
> I turned my boots around without delay,
> Putting my toes into the heels...[99]

Thus, he felt that the Indians would think that he was walking in the direction opposite from where he was headed,

> ...With which strategy the barbarians
> remained deceived for all the time
> that was duly needed by me...[100]

Apparently lost on the poet adventurer was that he was in a severe blizzard and his tracks were covered quickly by the falling snow anyhow. Then, later in his own narrative, we find out that he had a dog tagging along with him.[101] One wonders whether Villagrá, in his rush to avoid imagined pursuers and later to write down the account of his trip, ever realized that the logic of walking in backwards boots did not make sense with a dog accompanying him.

Pedro Rivera Ortega was a proud man. He taught Spanish and history at Santa Fe High School before he retired. He was a bibliophile who collected anything relative to New Mexico history and even had a New Mexico history and genealogical research center in the village of Truchas. To some people he was a gadfly around town, for while he was a very private man who never married, he loved to talk about history and culture to anyone who cared. He was appointed to many city committees, and was asked to be the town's representative historian on some of the sister city trips. Probably, he was proudest to be the longtime *majordomo,* or head of the confraternity of La Conquistadora. He was suited for the position because he adored the statue and, above all, he was an intensely devout man.

Rivera Ortega had come into possession of a breastplate and *morrión,* an iron helmet that Villagrá called a "*yelmo.*" Both pieces dated to the late sixteenth century and contained ornate engravings; an etched man in sixteenth century clothing kneeling before a cross graced one side of the helmet, while a depiction of the Nuestra Señora de los Remedios was on the opposite side. Our Lady of the Remedies was a very popular virgin among the Spanish at the time of Oñate. The breastplate did not match the helmet because it had an engraving of the Virgin of the Immaculate Conception.

Pedro Rivera Ortega simply told us that someone who had long since passed away had given him the pieces and that he had kept them under his bed for years. The man told him that he found them in a cave in the Malpais in western New Mexico.

Rivera Ortega wanted the pieces to go to the Palace of the Governors so he loaned them to us to study. We did not take long to realize that they were authentic and dated to the period of New Mexico's first Spanish settlement. The quality of the helmet especially and the engraved images told us that the pieces must have belonged to a person of some means or an officer at least.

We knew that our generous friend meant to donate the pieces to us but we also realized that he did not have much income. So, we made an offer to purchase the armor from him. The offer was a decent sum but well under the value of the artifacts. We made sure the Rivera Ortega knew how rare and valuable such pieces were and this convinced him all the more to place them in a museum. So we all agreed to the purchase and Pedro Rivera Ortega's legacy lives in the museum today.

Of course, such pieces will incite speculation. As will be seen in the subsequent chapters of this book, historians and the curious alike have any number of subjects to investigate that are subjects to speculation. We could not help but wonder whether Pedro Rivera Ortega had inherited the armor that belonged to Gaspar Pérez de Villagrá who left it in the Malpais to escape his imagined pursuers. The possibility exists but the definitive truth probably will never be resolved.

15
About the saga of Hernāndo Cortes's scorpion

Dr. Peter Keller, the director of the Bowers Museum of Culture in Anaheim, California and I like to talk about compiling a hypothetical book that would feature rare as well as spectacular artifacts. We used this excuse to play an intellectual game in which we would exchange our respective nominations. An original missing gospel, Pocahontas's dress that is in England, the flag on Magellan's ship that circumnavigated the world and is in Spain, and so on. Museum people tend to be easily distracted in such matters.

One such artifact came out of Mexico and disappeared supposedly to surface again but maybe not. Hernán Cortés, the conquistador who's audacity, diplomacy, legal knowledge, and a lot of luck helped him defeat the Mexicas or Aztecs in Mexico, almost lost his life more than once during his conquest. On one occasion, he survived a severe head wound that cracked his skull, knocked him unconscious, and resulted in severe migraine headaches for the rest of his life. He was fortunate to survive the blow.[102]

Another near death experience did not result from a battle but something quite natural in what would become Mexico. A poisonous scorpion stung him. As a result, Cortes developed a high fever that resulted into dangerously high temperatures and delirium. Those attending him could only see to his comfort and pray.

He and the others prayed to the Virgin of Guadalupe. This Guadalupe was not the virgin who would later become the patroness of Mexico but the one of Extremadura in Spain, the native region where Cortés and many of his men were born. Cortés and his attendants were praying for Guadalupe's intervention almost a decade before the famous miracle of Tepeyac. They prayed to the same Guadalupe after who Christopher Columbus named an island in the outer Lesser Antilles. She was the Guadalupe kept in her Extremaduran monastery where Columbus took the first Native Americans to be baptized in Europe.

Cortés recovered from the sting and gave thanks by ordering that a gold pendant be made in the form of a scorpion. The pendant is described as having forty-three emeralds and four pearls, two of which hang separately and the other two are set in the scorpion's claws or talons.[103] In 1528, while in Spain, Cortés traveled to Guadalupe to present some gifts in appreciation for the success of his exploits. Among the other pieces of jewelry, the pendant was singled out and noted for its connection to his survival from the scorpion sting.[104] Various letters in the Monastery of Guadalupe archive describe the pendant. One sixteenth century description contains a detailed drawing of the piece at the top of the page.[105]

However, some time in the past the gold pendant was lost, or, as the priests at the monastery would say; the pendant was stolen. While it was no longer in possession of the Monastery, closer research uncovered the knowledge that the unique pendant may have gravitated into private ownership and exists in Madrid in a private museum, the Instituto de Valencia de don Juan. One piece of jewelry in the Institute's holdings is reputed to be Cortés's gift to the Virgin of Guadalupe almost five centuries ago.[106] However, the Instituto's piece in photographs does not match the drawing or description of the pendant given to the Monastery of Guadalupe. This discrepancy was noted as early as 1942 by Federico Gómez de Orozco, the esteemed Mexican scholar and descendent of Martín Cortés the son of Hernán Cortés and his Indian translator Doña Marina, also known as Malinche. Gómez de Orozco published a short well-researched article in which he concluded that the piece in Madrid is not the scorpion that was in the Monastery. He left open the possibility that the Madrid piece could have been one of many of the other pieces of jewelry that Cortés donated.[107] Despite his article, the common perception that the piece in Madrid is the scorpion pendant that Cortés gave to the Monastery in Guadalupe has persisted. Here is an example where the scorpion pendant actually was thought to exist and can be seen, but like Quixote's illusive Dulcinea it does not quite fit expectations.

16
Concerning the introduction of art of ancient America

Then came the curious twist connected with the exhibition titled *Ancient Art of America.* Through the good offices of David Margolis and Jean Moss, personal friends and staunch supporters of the Palace of the Governors, I met John Bourne. David and Jean sell rare books, maps, photographs, and documents. Both of them have been long-time supporters of the Palace's photographic archives and history library. David continued as a member of the Friends of the Palace for years.

They met John Bourne through his interest in out-of-print books about Latin America. As they do with all their customers, they became friends with Bourne who, in turn, confided in them his idea and dream of giving his extensive collection of pre-Columbian art, Spanish colonial furniture and art, and a library of rare books to a cultural institution. Bourne wanted his collection to be shared with the public for posterity.

David and Jean suggested that he might be interested in the Palace of the Governors and explained our plans for building the new annex or museum, creating an endowment, and moving into the newly renovated library. They talked up existing collections, especially the library. They offered to introduce him to me and he agreed.

David paid me a visit and said, "Sit down and hold onto your hat." He then told me about John Bourne and that Jean and he wanted to take me to Bourne's house to meet him and see his collection. So a time was set for David and Jean to drive me to Bourne's house. I was impressed with Bourne from the beginning. He had a collection the importance of which I could only begin to understand. He shared his collection with me like an enthused child who had just received his first electric train set. But this was much more important. This was his life's work as well as hobby and it began with his mother who collected before him.[108]

John Bourne moved to Santa Fe from southern California. Heir to family wealth and his mother's interest in pre-Columbian Mesoamerican archaeology and art, he attended classes as well as educated himself to become familiar with the field. As a teenager he traveled to Mexico and went into the Yucatan Peninsula to live with and record Mayan people. He is credited as one of the discoverers of the very important site of Bonampak on the Yucatan Peninsula. At one time he was given a native wife and on another occasion his companion drowned in a boating accident while they were traveling through the Yucatan jungles.[109] Throughout his life, he studied, collected, and traveled into desperate places in the Americas. Reflecting both his curiosity and intelligence, when I met him he was working on the translation of Mayan hieroglyphics and had developed his own computer program to assist in the task. Above all he wanted to share his life's work with others.

Bourne and I seemed to understand each other perfectly. He liked what we were doing at the Palace of the Governors and I thought that the new expanded museum could accommodate his collection. He understood that the idea of having pre-Columbian art at the Palace of the Governors would raise some eyebrows. We concluded that the best thing to do was to open an exhibition featuring a part of his collection. This would give him an opportunity to work with the museum staff to see if they met his expectations. I had enough confidence in the staff to support the idea. He also agreed to pay for the exhibition.

I had to get busy and convince the staff, the Friends, and the Museum of New

Mexico's Board of Regents about this opportunity. Justification for doing such an exhibition came easily. First, as mentioned earlier, history does not occur in a vacuum. History's context is large. There existed connections and comparisons between pre-Columbian Mexico, Central America and South America. This was also true of the Southwest of the United States of which, for our purposes, New Mexico was the focal point. Corn, beans, and squash had migrated from central Mexico into the Southwest from 1500 B. C. to 800 B. C. From the pre-European contact sites of Mesa Verde straight south through Chaco Canyon, the Gila Cliff Dwellings, to Casas Grandes in northern Mexico trade and cultural influence was obvious. Casas Grandes was a major trade center involving many cultures and apparently was a conduit through which turquoise from New Mexico eventually made its way to central Mexico and parrot feathers from central Mexico came to New Mexico. So, I argued, we had historical context.

The second justification involved the concept that as a state history museum we had two overriding tasks to accomplish with our exhibitions. First, we needed to introduce and share our own history with the state's inhabitants and its many visitors. We needed to install exhibitions about ourselves. This was obvious. On the other hand, we also had an obligation to install exhibitions about elsewhere for the benefit of our local constituency. These would be exhibitions about society and history that New Mexicans might not have an opportunity to see unless they traveled out of state. My predecessor Dr. Michael Weber started with this concept when he installed exhibitions on the Saltillo Serape, eighteenth century cast paintings called *Mestizaje*, and the blockbuster exhibition showing some of the artifacts collected by the 1789 to 1794 Alejandro Malaspina expedition to the Pacific Northwest.[110] As discussed in Part I, Weber had created precedent.

We had some serious discussions, for while the state museum system had shown many exhibitions of pre-Columbian or pre-European contact,[111] it had never shown what I proposed. The Museum of Fine Arts had planned such an exhibition but turned it over to the Museum of Albuquerque that, not without some controversy, did the show. Nevertheless, the staff, Friends and the Board of Directors all agreed to proceed.

John Bourne and I were very pleased with the news. Yet, we needed to talk some more. Neither my staff nor I were expert in this field. We knew enough to realize the repatriation was a hot issue of the day. Theft, fueled by a high-priced market was common and new international laws were finally catching up to the rapidity of the loss of patrimony from various countries. Bourne agreed with us that any artifacts proven to be stolen or illegally smuggled out of their country of origin would be repatriated.

Bourne brought Dr. Peter T. Furst to Santa Fe to survey the collection. Dr. Furst was an expert and scholar from Philadelphia where he worked as a Research Associate in the American Section at the University of Pennsylvania Museum. He had spent a career researching indigenous cultures in South America and had over 150 published books and professional articles.[112] Over lunch Dr. Furst answered my direct question about whether he had found any artifacts that might be problematic. His answer was, "No, there are none." And, then he praised the collection while predicting an amazing exhibition.

Furst then agreed to write the essay in the gallery guide that Bourne was putting together for the exhibition. In the first paragraph he wrote:

> It is not often that residents of Santa Fe and visitors have the opportunity—as they have in this special exhibition at the Palace of the Governors—to step beyond the rich mosaic of the Southwestern past into the larger world of the great Pre-Columbian civilizations of Middle America and the Andes.[113]

He then went on to praise the pieces and explain the importance of such an exhibition concluding with his belief in the theories of Andean connections with Mexico as well as the common knowledge of maritime trade "between North and South America along the Pacific coast."[114]

That same gallery guide contained photographs of various artifacts in the exhibition. As will be seen, one of the photographed artifacts would become important. Listed as a gold pendant from the Moché Period in Northern Peru it was described as a "large bead finely modeled in the form of a monkey's head."[115]

As we planned for the exhibition and worked with staff, Bourne began to talk about his long-term plans. He appreciated what we were doing to raise an endowment, build a new museum, and, by then, open a new library. He agreed to help us. He joined the Friends where he quickly endeared himself with that group by bringing pieces of his collection to share in their monthly meetings. He helped us in every way he could from writing letters to politicians, sharing his house and showing his collection, and meeting key people on request. Governor Gary Johnson as well as the legislative leadership were given personal tours of his collection.

Bourne expressed his desire to give his collection, indeed, his estate to the Palace of the Governors. As if to leave no doubt about his intentions, he donated his magnificent library consisting of many rare books. He even paid for a special handmade custom bookcase to house it. Then he donated three pieces from his collection, including the monkey head. Next he helped design and then paid for the exhibition. Finally, he had the Palace written into his Last Will and Testament and invited me to be a witness, which I gracefully declined. I did not see the logic in bearing witness to something for which the institution that I directed would benefit. We, all of us, could not have been happier with the situation.

17
In which is explained the idea of dedicated galleries

As a member of the Friends and family of the museum, Bourne became involved with the planning for the new museum. We agreed to dedicate a gallery in the new museum to his collection. I suggested that it be named for him but Bourne, who is a shy and private man, declined. He wanted the gallery, which was to be on the top floor of the planned structure, to refer only to the title of the exhibition–Art of Ancient America.

The idea of a dedicated gallery was not unusual, for by that time we already had dedicated a gallery to the Segesser Paintings and another to the first exhibition ever installed in the Palace. In addition, the Palace of the Governors had three dedicated period rooms, each determined on historical research. Planning for the new building included dedicated galleries based on subject matter. In my mind the Segesser Paintings deserved their own gallery just like Picasso's famous painting *Guernica* had been exhibited in Madrid at the Prado Museum. We also decided to dedicate a gallery to Spanish Colonial Art because of a pending gift from the International Institute of Iberian Colonial Art (IIICA).

The IIICA collection originated with Charles W. Collier, a diplomat and world traveler. He formed the IIICA, which amounted to a board of people who would keep his collection intact after his death. Longtime Santa Fe resident, architect, and historian John Conron became the chairman of the board. Conron, who served over the last three decades of his life on the board of the Historical Society of New Mexico, had a keen appreciation for history and preservation. He had become involved with the Palace of the Governors long before I did. My predecessor Michael Weber and he were best of friends. Weber hired Conron, whose architectural firm specialized in the preservation of historic structures, to stabilize the Palace's west wall, reinstall the interior floors, as well as install various protective features to preserve the building. I inherited Weber's appreciation for Conron and hired him to oversee the replacement of the Palace's 110-year-old roof with an exact replica.

Part of the IIICA collection had been on loan at the Palace of the Governors for many years. The paintings of high colonial art made up one of the better private collections in the southwest. With paintings by some of the major Mexican and Peruvian artists of the seventeenth and eighteenth centuries, some on oversize canvasses, the staff planned for the IIICA collection to be the anchor for even more additions. In addition, Frank and Dolores Ortiz were talking about a bequest of a few of their paintings while staff members Charles Bennett and Diana DeSantis arranged for an estate gift of a major painting of *Nuestra Señora de los Gozos*, also known as *Los Siete Gozos de la Virgen*, the Seven Versus of Praise (Litanies) of the Virgin Mary, which is attributed to Bernardo Polo, a late seventeenth century Spanish artist. The painting dates to between 1680 and 1700, when Polo died. Bennett and DeSantis took advantage of the newly created New Mexico Art Acceptance Act to facilitate the donation. We unveiled the painting with a special reception during a legislative session and were able to attract some key legislative leadership.[116] Part of John Bourne's intended gift also included colonial paintings as well as furniture that would complement the IIICA collection as well as the gallery in which we intended to show it all. With all of these acquisitions and potential gifts we felt that a dedicated gallery made sense. And, we had two perfect rooms, both with high ceilings and at the west end of the Palace. As we envisioned it, the art on exhibition in those rooms would be worth a visit to the museum alone.

John Conron was a highly educated, intelligent, direct, curmudgeonly, and fair man. On one occasion I successfully opposed one of his projects before the city's historical styles committee by using an article he had written in a magazine he produced. While immediately disappointed, he later acknowledged the irony of my argument with his good sense of humor.

Charles Bennett and I pled with Conron and the board of IIICA to donate the collection to the Palace of the Governors. At the time the collection was divided and housed at the Palace of the Governors and at the University of New Mexico under long-term loans. We employed the tact of demonstrating to the IIICA that we should be their choice for the collection's permanent home by using the pieces in our care. At different times we installed exhibitions featuring the collection at the Palace and at the State Fair.

We did become over ambitious on one occasion. Charles and I had a mutual friend and museum supporter who enjoyed membership at the Albuquerque Country Club. She asked us if the museum would loan some of the paintings to be installed in the club's main hall. We quickly agreed, for, once again, here was an opportunity to get collections beyond the museum's walls and demonstrate to IIICA yet another innovative way that we could share their collection. So with great glee, Charles and I borrowed the museum van, loaded up the paintings, drove to Albuquerque, and installed them.

The very next morning I received a hurried call from our friend who wanted us to return to Albuquerque and take down the art. It seems that a rather large percentage of the club's membership was Jewish and the iconography of New Testament high art was not proper for the Club's secular environment. So, without question, we rushed back to Albuquerque and retrieved the art. This was one occasion where a well-intentioned attempt at goodwill did not work out.

The IIICA never made a decision to donate the collection to the Palace while Charles and I worked there. Even when, Roy Woods, John Conron's business partner and chosen heir to his architectural firm, won the bid to design the new museum and therefore be assured of the dedicated gallery, we could not convince Conron of our desire. We knew that the board favored giving us the collection but a minority wanted it to go to the University. Dr. Donna Pierce, who would eventually become a curator at the Palace of the Governors, was on the IIICA board of directors for a while. She wanted the collection to be given to the Palace but, as she put it, "eventually I was no longer invited to the meetings!"[117] A few years after Charles and I retired from the Palace, Frank Ortiz passed away. He bequeathed his paintings and, soon after that in 2006, the IIICA agreed to make the donation to the Palace of the Governors. Ironically, the Museum of New Mexico press release did not mention the many-years efforts of the Palace staff that made the gift possible. Instead the release gave credit to Dr. Gabrielle Palmer, who was one of the IICA board members who had opposed the collection going to the Palace in favor of the University of New Mexico.[118] As of this printing, John Bourne's Spanish colonial collection is still destined for the Palace.

So, in context of what we had done and were planning, the idea of a dedicated gallery for the Art of Ancient America made perfect sense.

18
Concerning the opening of a very successful exhibition

John Bourne worked with designer Nancy Allen to design a beautiful installation exhibiting choice pieces of his collection. Nancy, who had worked as a set designer as well as exhibition designer, became a good friend with Bourne. They talked the same language, as the saying goes. Their collaboration paid off with a spectacular exhibition. They chose to use high-tech fiber-optic subdued lighting in gray based, shadow cases, with non-glare glass to convert a long, rectangular room of the old Palace into a new, but connected to the past, environment. They left the *vigas,* old log ceiling crossbeams exposed but carpeted the wooden floor. Everything focused on the art and artifacts. Bourne did not want to use traditional exhibition labels. Instead he created a numbering system and a gallery guide for patrons. The final result was impressive.

We opened *The Art of Ancient America* exhibition with an elegant invitation only, private preview that was followed the next day with a public opening. Nothing like that kind of art and artifacts had ever been shown in northern New Mexico, much less Santa Fe. A huge crowd turned out. Bourne, attended but kept low profile, mostly hiding out across the Palace's courtyard. Peter Furst enjoyed himself and, it seemed, ran into many old friends there. He was in his glory. The museum's attendance increased after the opening and local colleges took advantage of the exhibition by sending students to study it.

The exhibition was described as,

> "...among the finest small collections of pre-Columbian art anywhere. In a gallery at the Palace of the Governors, dimly lit and hushed but for a viewer's occasional gasp, fourteen shelves, hold grinning Mayan deities, a 1,500-year-old ceramic incense burner..., a brawny stone man...dating to about A. D. 900... Museums often prattle on about a collector's 'singular vision' or 'exquisite taste'... In this case it is true... This collection dazzles."[119]

We had scored a coup. Everyone praised the exhibition. We heard no criticisms, not even about the intentional lack of interpretive signage: instead John Bourne requested an exhibition "checklist" in the form of a very tasteful exhibit guide. Nobody including the reviewer quoted above realized that we were exhibiting a portion of what was to come. John Bourne, Nancy Allen, and the staff even planned to recreate the same exhibition design, replete with *vigas*, in the new building. Only this time we would recreate two, maybe three rooms to exhibit the full breadth of Bourne's collection. The thought of it all more than "dazzled," it took our breadth away.

19
Regarding the sorry tale of Peruvian art and the Federal Bureau of Investigation

Some two years after the exhibition's opening two men came to my office and introduced themselves as special agents working for the F. B. I. The older man, who was perspiring and out-of-breath introduced himself as Robert Wittman and, then, introduced his lighter haired and younger partner as Brian Midkiff. Midkiff was stationed in Santa Fe while the former operated out of Philadelphia. After shaking hands all around I invited them to sit down and asked them what I could do for them. Wittman explained that he specialized in investigating stolen pre-Columbian art taken out of Peru and that he was in Santa Fe to check on the *Art of Ancient America* exhibition.

"Fine, no problem." I volunteered. "The exhibition is still up and open to the public. Please go ahead and take your time."

Wittman, however, had some questions mostly directed toward the provenance of the artifacts, which was explained in the gallery guide. He wanted to know who owned the collection. As an administrator of a state institution all of this was a matter of public record so I proceeded to answer his questions. There was nothing to hide. After all their questions were answered, the agents left my office to see the exhibition.

The two agents returned the next day to announce to me that they needed to take possession of three of the artifacts for further investigation. Wittman explained that the three artifacts in question might have been removed illegally from a site in Peru so he would need to place them in the Bureau's evidence vault in Albuquerque pending an investigation. No, he could not tell me how long he would need them.

To this I inquired, "Why can't they stay on exhibit? After all, they are secure, they will not go anywhere and have been available to public scrutiny for over two years."

I felt that the agents overlooked that neither John Bourne nor the Museum was hiding anything by the mere fact that we had put the artifacts on public exhibit. I learned soon thereafter that Bourne was even more transparent, for the two agents visited him unannounced at his house after seeing me the day before. Bourne invited them in without requiring a search warrant and gave them his standard tour. Obviously, neither of us had anything to hide. Like me, Bourne answered their questions.[120]

By this time the agents knew the position that Bourne and I had relative to stolen property. I made clear to them that if the artifacts were indeed taken illegally, they should be returned. I stated that a neutral expert should make the determination. The agents did not express any disagreement with that position

Unfortunately, I was told, that procedure required that the artifacts had to be taken. So, I called the State's Attorney General's office to apprise them of what had happened. They advised me not to turn the artifacts over until they sent a representative to witness the transfer. So we prepared a standard museum loan form for the transaction and, witnessed by a deputy attorney general from the AG's office, special agents Wittman and Midkiff signed the forms and took possession of the artifacts.

We then learned that an anonymous archaeologist had informed the F.B.I about the suspected artifacts. We were told that it was someone with whom we were familiar. As is standard, I suppose, the person's identity was never revealed nor did we care to press the matter.

We also learned that Wittman believed that the artifacts had been stolen from the site of Sipán in northern Peru. This site had made international news as one of the richest of all archaeological finds in Latin America. The National Geographic Society funded a great portion of the excavation and featured the work in its magazine.[121] Books had been written about the discovery. Finding an expert on Sipán would not be a problem.

The question of museum ethics also came up as the story broke in the local press. Hollis Walker, the journalist who penned all the articles about this subject, used an anonymous source with an obvious bias to condemn the museum.[122] I had been a nationally elected member of the board for the American Association of Museums and was placed on the AAM ethics committee. That committee formalized the ethics standards for the museum community in the United States. In this case the ethics question came down to the propriety of receiving stolen property. My answer was simple and, for clarity's sake, I used a simple analogy.

If a bank is being robbed and the thieves run out the front door and drop some of the stolen money in front of you, shouldn't you pick up the money and return it? Of course you should. Not only is that how I was brought up, but such an act was in keeping with national museum ethics standards. If, in my capacity as a museum professional, I have the opportunity to receive something that I know was stolen, I should receive it, report it, and return it. I was quoted as saying that by receiving and exhibiting such items museums could play a role on "getting the stuff back" if it was actually stolen.[123]

Nevertheless, the above principle did not apply in this case, for, I received assurances from the lender that everything was fine with the collection and moreover we could return anything found to be taken illegally. We had also gone to third parties like Dr. Peter Furst to make sure that the collection was "clean" and received MNM Board of Regents approval for receiving and exhibiting the material. I was quoted in the local newspaper stating as much. "I, as director of the Palace of the Governors, consider this action a proper thing to do and I am pleased to be a part of this process." So both personally to the agents and in the press I expressed these sentiments. But, special agents Wittman and Midkiff apparently did not care about my position, for they had their own agenda.

Wittman who specialized and was developing a reputation in these types of cases had a different process in mind. Rather than use a neutral referee, he wanted me to meet his "good friend" Walter Alva, who was in the process of opening the Brüning National Archaeological Museum, which is a public institution that specializes in artifacts excavated from Sipán. Alva is an archaeologist, who depending upon who you read or talked to, was a tireless leader in preserving Peru's patrimony or a shady character involved with killings and who was a major benefactor of the Sipán site that he helped excavate. He had published some well-received books in his field and has taken credit for the discovery of the Lords of Sipán and the site in which they were buried, a pyramid complex on the remote, dry plains of Lambayeque in northern Peru.[124]

At the time, I did some research on him and found that at one point he joined the press and the Peruvian federal police to ambush some people stealing from an archaeological site. After the ambush he entered a museum van then being used as a police van and sat next to one of the accused looters who had been shot in the back by Federal troops. The man bled to death before the police or anybody else could get him to a hospital. Alva commonly carried a pistol on his person and had participated in what the local people called a murder. Even though Alva commiserated over the death, he and I were not alike.[125]

At Wittman's suggestion, Alva telephoned me. The gist of the conversation was that he was told that we were alike and that he was happy that his artifacts had ended up in my possession, for he knew that I would do the right thing and return the questioned works of art. I replied that I knew nothing about the artifacts being his and that, nonetheless, an expert would make the determination on whether or not they had been removed under questionable circumstances from Sipán.

What I did not know but soon found out was that Wittman, Alva and company were confident that I would accept Alva as the neutral expert. They expected me to overlook the fact that Alva was the one man who would benefit the most from their return because they expected the artifacts to be given to Alva, not the Peruvian government, who would personally take them back to Peru. Contrary to what Wittman and his publicists claimed later, I was never informed that Alva represented the Peruvian government of President Alberto Fujimori. Nor did he provide any paperwork to anyone like, for example, the Attorney General's office. Ironically, not long after the corrupt Fujimori fled Peru to accept asylum in Japan. He was arrested in Chili in 2006 while trying to sneak back into Peru. Convicted in court he now resides in a Peruvian prison.

Initially, I did not understand what would become clear very soon. Wittman and Midkiff expected to use the aura of the F.B.I. to convince or pressure me into giving the three pieces to them and Alva. Any person with a reasonable knowledge of law and legal processes would immediately understand that the agents were embarking on a shady path. They banked on my ignorance of my personal rights as well as awe of the two of them. And they did it with the complacence of Hollis Walker of *The Santa Fe New Mexican*. The agents wanted me to violate law by ignoring the fact that I was a state employee and we were dealing with state property in one case and property for which the state was responsible in the other two cases. As mentioned, the monkey head had been donated to the museum. The other two items were on loan to the museum. Paperwork turning them over to the F.B.I. was on file in both the museum and the Attorney General's office.

If it were not for the fact that we hear stories like this involving our Federal officials more often than not, most people would not believe what happened next. Wittman arranged for Alva to travel from Peru to Santa Fe, New Mexico. I innocently agreed to meet with him and even suggested to Midkiff that we could meet for dinner on 24 October at Jack's Restaurant, which no longer exists

My wife Celia and I had earlier plans to meet with our friends John Reeder and Margo Chávez-Charles. Knowing that we would be meeting at Jack's they decided that they would have dinner there as well. Upon entering the dining room I sighted the table where Wittman, Midkiff, and several other people were seated. Reeder remembers one person looking especially untidy. That turned out to be the longhaired and bearded Alva. There was at least one other person seated there as well. I found the idea of my wife and me dining with all these people to be a little intimidating so I told them that we would eat with our other friends. We could meet after dinner at the more elegant and quieter Palace Restaurant and Bar across the street.

We finished eating about five minutes after the others. With some trepidation we paid our bill and walked out into the cold night's air. There across the narrow street, on a foggy night, which is unusual for Santa Fe, Celia and I met a contingent of four people. Huddled in buttoned up long overcoats with collars turned up, Wittman, Midkiff, Alva, and another person who was introduced as an interpreter waited for us on the sidewalk in front of the appointed bar. We looked in the bar but found that the place was full with no available tables so we met on the sidewalk.

After introductions, Alva began to talk to me in Spanish. The translator translated for Alva while my wife translated for me. Although I understood that he was repeating pretty much what he had said in his telephone call, Celia, a historian who I met in the Archives of the Indies in Seville, Spain while she was working on her doctorate at the University of Seville and is from Argentina, wanted to make sure that I had a good understanding of what was being said. She did not bargain for the setting and the message.

Alva, who kind of mumbled and spoke under his breath, began by stating how he and I share the same profession and that we colleagues understand each other. He then told me that he had seen the three pieces in Albuquerque and concluded that they were stolen from his site, meaning Sipán.

I replied by repeating my position that I was waiting to hear what an impartial expert would say and that, at any rate, if he was correct the expert would verify him and the artifacts would return to Peru.

"But," Alva responded, "that would not be necessary," for, according to him, no one was more qualified than him to render an opinion and I should turn the artifacts over to him.

To this I reminded him that I did not have the artifacts. The F.B.I. had them.

"Yes, yes. Of course, I know that," he replied.

At this point Wittman chimed in that based on Alva's testimony it would be okay to sign a release so Alva could return to Peru with the artifacts.

Now, I understood. The idea was to use me to grant them permission to take the artifacts from their own vault and give them to Alva. I was astounded that they thought I was either intimidated or stupid enough to agree to such a proposition. Here, on a cold foggy night, were three men, easily taller and larger than my wife and I, standing around us on a sidewalk, trying to get me to do something that I could not agree to do.

I immediately told them that I could not do what they wanted.

Wittman shot back with, "Why not? I thought that you were one of us."

On impulse I threw out my hands in exasperation and then smiled, for I would not be intimidated. I told Wittman, for he seemed to be the only one that mattered at that point, that he knew my position and that he should know that I do not have the authority to release the artifacts. I added that if he wanted the artifacts released he "should see my attorney."

"What attorney?" Wittman was clearly exasperated.

"The State's Attorney General. I am a state employee. You know that. I am represented by the Attorney General's office. I have no authority under any circumstance to arbitrarily turn over state property."

To this Wittman, who, despite the winter's night, seemed to be sweating again, stared at me and stated that Alva had come a great distance to receive his pieces and that if this was not solved tonight they would walk straight to the offices of *The Santa Fe New Mexican*, which was four blocks from us, where they had a reporter waiting. "Tomorrow's headline," he continued, "would embarrass my museum and me." So now this agent of my own government was attempting black mail.

Three years later Alva is quoted as saying that he was "confident we could reach an agreement for the return of the pieces quietly, like gentlemen, without harming the image of the museum."[126]

Alva was wrong or misled, for I replied to Wittman, "You have my answer. Talk to the Attorney General."

Wittman, looked at me incredulously and mumbled something to the effect of "Okay, we are going to the press," and all of them except for my wife, who was visibly shaken, left in the direction of the *New Mexican*'s offices where Hollis Walker was waiting.

20
In which a threat is carried out and some repercussions result

Wittman already told *The Santa Fe New Mexican* that the F.B.I. had seized the three pieces under the National Stolen Property Act, which implied that a criminal act had been committed. This was a vaguely concealed attempt to shame me. So, Wittman already had played the press card to no avail before threatening me. What surprised me was his easy access to the press as well as Hollis Walker's willingness to publish a subjective and biased article the next day under the headline "Archaeologist: Museum Items Were Stolen." She then went on to quote Alva extensively but, contrary to accepted journalistic tenets, did not bother to contact me.[127] I was incensed but knew that I had done the correct thing. Alva returned home, where in a few years he would open a new museum featuring Sipán art and artifacts to mixed reviews. I never saw Special Agent Wittman again. As far as I was concerned the resolution to Wittman's case was left to the U. S. Attorney and the State Attorney General. I was completely out of it.

Wittman was quoted later as stating that Alva's insistence about talking to the press was a big mistake and that from that moment on his case was in trouble. I disagree. Wittman, through local agent Midkiff, already groomed Walker to be ready. Alva was from Peru. He did not have the means to make arrangements with a reporter to stand by late in the evening. In my opinion, Wittman set up the whole strategy and should place the blame for destroying his case on himself. Alva, who understandably would like to have all Peruvian art and artifacts returned to his museum, was used by Wittman and then later blamed for alienating me. Wittman is also quoted as saying, "It was a strange evening and very, very awkward."[128] To this, I cannot agree more and can add that Wittman was the reason.

Celia took a while to get over the meeting. Unlike later accounts given by Wittman who claimed that Celia came out of the bar, which was really a restaurant, to separate Alva and me, she never left my side. Nor were Alva and I on the verge of a fist fight. As stated, my wife was there interpreting for me. Wittman has a very faulty and convenient memory and one wonders why the journalists who quoted him were so quick to believe him.

Celia grew up under dictatorships in Argentina. She went to schools where teachers were watched and some "transferred." Books were outlawed and plains-clothes police drove around intimidating people in unmarked cars. She has friends whose loved ones were "disappeared" and others who sneaked out of the country before they were killed.

This encounter with the F.B.I. brought back all her old memories of living under a police state. I, who had brought her to this country, was embarrassed and tried to assure her that no authority could operate beyond the law, not even members of the reviled F.B.I. She should not worry, they could do nothing to me. I added that I would be proven correct. Others of my friends, including a retired Superior Court Judge, wondered whether special agent Wittman had other than pure motives for his actions.

Aside from the F.B.I.'s informant, Walker's earlier articles used an anonymous source who was someone who claimed to be a colleague of mine in the Museum of New Mexico. Clearly, this person did not work in the Palace of the Governors and, apparently, the newspaper was anxious to create controversy despite overwhelming evidence to the contrary.[129] Walker's article using the unnamed source was the second of consecutive articles that headlined the newspaper's front page.[130] Why Walker did not simply cite the anonymous source, is a question the answer to which remains a mystery. Her use of that information was biased.

Both the source and article claimed that my activities could affect the museum's accreditation and thus lose its ability to win grants. They were wrong on both points. Ed Able, the Executive Director of the American Association of Museums that accredits museums, quickly denied that I had, or would, jeopardize the museum's accreditation. In fact, over ten years later the Palace of the Governors still had the exhibition and the artifacts in question. Its accreditation remained intact while it has raised millions of dollars in grants and government support.

Nevertheless, both of the articles along with the anonymous source were personal attacks and I understood the motive. As Wittman had threatened, they were out to embarrass my museum and me. In all three instances, I was wronged and although the outcome of the case would not be influenced, I felt that I needed to offer a correction, so on the same day as the publication of Hollis Walker's first article I wrote a letter to the editor reiterating the position that I had told the F.B.I. from our first meeting and repeated to them and Alva.

The letter did not get published so I went to see Billie Blair, the Associate Editor and Publisher of the newspaper. Billie Blair is a very intelligent, pleasant woman who knew me from our mutual participation in various projects. I met her while serving on the board of directors of the Santa Fe Chamber of Commerce. She had invited me to write a monthly history article for the Sunday edition of *The Santa Fe New Mexican*. I knew her to be an honest, forthright person so I had no qualms about visiting with her and my expectations were more than fulfilled.

After explaining the situation to her, she asked her staff for a copy of my letter. What she received was a heavily cut and edited version of what I had submitted. Somewhat irritated I told her that the letter in front of us was not anywhere near what I had written. She asked me to provide her with an original, which I did within minutes. Blair appeared to be a little upset as she compared the two notes. She agreed with me that the edited version was unacceptable, and told me that they would publish my letter unedited. Except for a typo, the letter came out intact.

The Santa Fe New Mexican gave my letter prominent placement on the editorial page of Tuesday's edition. A photograph of me accompanied the text, which included a headline that read, "Stories about the museum were one-sided." A by-line quoted from the body of the letter was set apart and printed in oversize italics. I took direct aim at the anonymous source and, by implication, Walker's articles. It also succinctly summed up my position, which was a position, that Wittman, Alva, and, apparently, Walker, found unacceptable. The by-line read,

> "As long as I direct the Palace of the Governors, I will conduct myself professionally as I would personally in such matters. I and my staff will openly continue to work within the laws and, if justified, return stolen property to the proper owners. To do anything else is just plain wrong–and this does not need to be anonymously stated."

I also condemned Walker and her newspaper for their subjective and prejudicial reporting. "Unfortunately, Ms. Walker chose to give more ink to a single anonymous person without checking any outside sources such as the American Association of Museums before running the story. Let me be clear...this person would secretly criticize a co-worker without any basis of information about what has happened."[131]

The publication of my letter worked, at least locally. The community knew enough of my staff and me to understand and believe that we were acting in a completely transparent and honest manner. I continued to take every opportunity to tell the museum's side of the story during my numerous public talks. People still ask me to tell the story. Wittman wanted to create a false image, just as Don Quixote, the old wannabe knight, believed Sancho Panza's claim that a peasant lady was the beautiful Dulcinea, despite her stench.[132] Wittman with Alva continued to talk about stolen art thus taking their false tale beyond the local level. But, Sancho Panza had an answer:

> "Let Satan carry off all the Dulcinea's in the world, for the well-being of a single knight errant is worth more than all the enchantments and transformations on earth."[133]

21
In which is revealed the outcome of false claims

Given Wittman's actions, I was not surprised to learn that his case did not hold up. Christopher Donnan, a friend and colleague of Alva's who had actually secured National Geographic money to help excavate the Sipán site and co-authored with Alva a book on the excavation just five years before,[134] was chosen to be the neutral expert. By now, perhaps realizing that someone other than himself would be called in to identify the artifacts, Alva was laying claim to only one of the artifacts–the gold monkey head. Journalist Roger Atwood, who as we will see, continued to write about this story, noted that Donnan's "standing among U. S. law enforcement as an identifier of Moche loot was unrivaled."[135] Donnan, himself an archaeologist, worked for the Fowler Museum of Cultural History at the University of California at Los Angeles. The U. S. Attorney with the compliance of the State Attorney General chose him to be the case's neutral expert. I knew nothing about him and did not know him. After his appointment I received a telephone call from him, who, as a courtesy, introduced himself and informed me that he was involved with the case. Upon hearing that he would not be traveling to visit the museum I asked if he needed photographs of the items in question. He replied that my offer would be unnecessary because the F.B.I and U. S. Attorney's office in Albuquerque had provided him with everything that he needed. I never talked to him again.

This "unrivaled expert" completely disagreed with Wittman and Alva. Donnan concluded that none of the items had come from Sipán. Their case was lost. What is important here is that neither John Bourne nor I chose Dr. Donnan.

Thus, I received a telephone call from agent Midkiff and was told that I could go to Albuquerque to pick up the artifacts. I replied that his organization took them from the museum and they should return them to the museum. He agreed and within days arrived with the artifacts. With a representative from the state's Attorney General's office present, the artifacts were returned and placed back on exhibition. Charles Bennett, with his understated sense of humor, asked Midkiff if he would like to become a member of the museum's Foundation. The surprised Midkiff soon realized that it was a joke; although we would have accepted his membership.

With the return of the artifacts, one would think, the story ended. We continued to plan for the new gallery in the new building just as we continued to raise money to pay for the building. Then, the School of American Research convinced Bourne that the SAR would be a better fit for his collection. Doug Schwartz, the long-time School's director, was noted for his aggressive fundraising style and he appeared to have added to his reputation. But a misunderstanding between him and Bourne over the building that would house the collection quickly ended the matter.

Again, with the help of Jean Moss and David Margolis, Bourne knew that we held no animosity toward him and still wished to include him in our plans although he was impatient with the bureaucracy of the State of New Mexico. Nevertheless, through the efforts of Moss and Margolis, John Bourne agreed that his collection would go to the Palace so we were able to continue as before and plan for his collection.

22
On how a story has legs

In journalism, a story that continues to draw attention is said to "have legs." So, it seems, this became the case of the F.B.I.'s sordid attempt to claim part of the Bourne collection. While the public continued to enjoy the exhibition, others wanted to continue the work begun by Wittman. One day I fielded an innocuous telephone inquiry about my reaction to the F.B.I and Alva. The caller was a journalist named Roger Atwood, who seemed very friendly and somewhat sympathetic over the telephone. I never met him personally although he later described me as "a tweedy, earnest man with the nasal twang of a New Mexico native" who "was a historian, educated at the University of New Mexico, who had written several well-regarded books on Southwestern history."[136] A few years later, Frank Ortiz described me in his autobiography as "a puckish leader who proved over and over again what dedication with a sense of humor can accomplish."[137] I wonder which is better, "tweedy" or "puckish."

Atwood's good interview technique was being used to develop an article that he would publish. Atwood, while not a noted author, had developed a reputation writing for liberal causes in liberal magazines. He has a stylish and engaging writing style and eventually would take up the anti-war in Iraq cause in a few years. He also apparently befriended Wittman and Alva. Wittman, as noted, had developed his reputation in garnering stolen plunder. Atwood, who talked to agents Wittman and Midkiff before interviewing me, proceeded to write an article for *ARTnews* that favored their point-of-view. At the time,

I only heard about it but never bothered to get a copy.[138] I figured that this would be Wittman's last shot and to let it go without comment. To paraphrase Harry Truman; why argue with someone who can counter with ink by the barrel-full?

A few years later I received a book in the mail. Roger Atwood's name on the return address meant nothing to me, for I had long forgotten the name of the interviewer. By this time, I had moved from the Palace of the Governors to take a new job as Executive Director of the National Hispanic Cultural Center in Albuquerque. I was faced with new challenges and was really enjoying the opportunity. The book contained a brief hand written note inside the front cover that read,

> "Dear Dr. Chávez,
> Thanks for interviews and for your
> frankness.
> Very best wishes for the New Year.
> Roger Atwood"

The book has the incredibly enticing title, *Stealing History: Tomb Raiders, Smugglers, and the Looting of the Ancient World.* Upon reading the book I found both the note and title misleading. Atwood had grouped John Bourne and me with a cast of very bad characters of thieves and murderers whose only motivation was to enrich themselves. Bourne and I fit none of those descriptions. In every instant, when my version of things contradicted Wittman or Alva, Atwood took their side. He completely missed the point that I had no authority to turn over the seized items. He erroneously claimed that I avoided Alva's attempts to meet with me before the infamous evening encounter. He incorrectly claimed that Alva spent a week in Santa Fe unsuccessfully trying to talk with me.[139] Anyone who is familiar with me knows that I kept an open door policy and always was easily accessible. I answered my own telephone. Apparently lost on Atwood was his own easy and successful attempt at contacting me. Nor did he consider the two unannounced meetings that Wittman and Midkiff had with me in my office.

Then Atwood misrepresented the meeting that Alva, the agents, my wife and I had on the street. Among other things, he claimed that my wife and I were in the bar waiting for Alva and company. He continued with the aforesaid misinformation about my wife having to break up a near fight between Alva and I.[140] No such thing happened. Actually, the logic of such a scenario is ridiculous on its face, for why would Celia need to break up a fight when two F. B. I. agents were standing right there?

Probably the worse insult, if not misrepresentation, is that Atwood went to great lengths to disparage me through the Palace of the Governors' success in getting the

Segesser Paintings. Irrespective of some errors in the details, Atwood gave a fairly accurate generalization of how we acquired the paintings. He concluded that I should have understood "the emotional fright of Peru's pleas and return" their pieces.[141]

After all, he wrote, "the bison-hides case was a textbook example of the benefits of repatriation" that restored "to the people of New Mexico a piece of their cultural heritage" and no one scorned New Mexican claims as being "cultural nationalism." Our action, he correctly wrote had taken "an important work of art out of a private setting" and "put it in a public setting." How could I not understand Alva's position? [142] Of course, Atwood's question implied the answer that I should have known better and should be ashamed of myself.

However, Atwood's argument is facetious. His parallels between the Segesser story and that of the Moche artifacts are inaccurate, for he omitted any mention that we never accused Herr Segesser or anyone else of stealing New Mexican art. Indeed, we never ran to the press, called in the authorities or demanded that the paintings be returned to New Mexico. Segesser was never confronted in the way that Alva and the F.B.I. confronted me. Finally, we never asked Segesser to do anything illegally. We patiently and hopefully waited as the potential return of the paintings went through the patrimony courts in Switzerland, the opinion of which is on file in the Palace of the Governors' library.[143] Then, we negotiated and *purchased* the paintings! Indeed, a significant piece of Segesser II is still in Switzerland because the current owner of that piece does not want to sell.[144] Our efforts do not compare to the F. B. I.'s technique used on me.

We spent years working with Herr Segesser and the State of New Mexico to get the paintings. Our relationship and negotiations with Herr Segesser to acquire the Segesser Paintings when compared to Wittman's and Alva's demanding and threatening tactics are like night and day. Our work with Segesser may have been, as Atwood describes, "textbook." Perhaps, if the F.B.I. and Alva had studied that example they could have been more successful with us but I doubt that they were capable of a patient and legal approach.

We remained good friends with Herr Segesser until his death. To this day, we are on good terms with his son and daughter-in-law. They continue to visit Santa Fe.

Also of note is that Atwood wrote about thieves and crooks that are or were out to make money. Outside of the monetary value, Atwood's protagonists have no appreciation of the artifacts and art with which they deal. Of necessity, they work in the shadows requiring special agents like Wittman to rely on informants or to go undercover. These people are dangerous criminals.

John Bourne, the Museum of New Mexico, and I pale in comparison. We openly exhibited the items and, true to my word to Wittman, they remained safely ensconced on exhibition. None of us personally profited or intended to profit from the artifacts.

Atwood's insinuation that we somehow equate to the other thieves and murderers of his book should be seen as pure and obvious bunk. Alva's statement, as quoted by Atwood, that "what that museum did was launder stolen property,"[145] is unmitigated nonsense. The property remained on exhibit at the museum until May of 2008.[146] If he were really serious about getting the monkey head, which was his true goal, he should have lowered and controlled his rhetoric.

Somewhat exasperated by Atwood's book in which the author included Bourne and myself with stories like the sacking of the ruins of Isin in southern Iraq, I set the book aside. I never contacted Atwood. Eventually, I loaned the book to some friends and family to get their reaction. All of them responded that Atwood showed a bias but that he could not avoid the bottom line that I was correct and that the outcome, even as he described it, suggested as much. Still I felt maligned in a book that probably sold well. This feeling, in part, became the reason for writing this book.[147]

Alva later wrote a letter in which he did not place blame or make accusations. Atwood did note that Alva eventually agreed that none of the items were taken or stolen from Sipán.[148] This is the basis from which he should have started. Maybe the outcome would have been different.

The larger question, of course, is whether art and artifacts, taken legally or not, should be returned. Should, for example, the Segesser paintings be returned whether or not the owners agreed? Obviously, I wanted them returned but a part of them remains in Switzerland. In principle, the answer is yes but if the owners have them in good faith and without fault, then it behooves those who want them to work to find an amicable way by which to have them returned.

Then, again, a lot of New Mexico's patrimony is in out-of-state institutions, which is not, in and of itself, bad. New Mexico's patrimony like its history did not occur in a vacuum and that point is as important for New Mexicans to understand as it is for others to appreciate that New Mexico shares a larger heritage. So it is okay that the Smithsonian Institution has artifacts and art from the Southwest, including New Mexico, or that a convent in Mexico City has Nuestra Señora de la Macana, the statue of the virgin, or that the Museo Nacional del Virreinato in Tepotzatlán, Mexico has an original Bernardo Miera y Pacheco map of New Mexico. Even the British National Library has a Miera y Pacheco map that they loaned to the Palace of the Governors for an exhibition. We did not claim that it belonged to us. We do not know how the maps came into the possession of these institutions - nor have we asked.

In February of 2003, the same month that Atwood published his *ARTnews* article, *El Palacio* published an excerpt of John Bourne's account of his trip into the Lacambá jungles of Chiapas and the discovery of the ruins of Bonapak[149] along with a two page color sampling of *The Art of Ancient America* exhibition.[150]

The Art of Ancient America exhibition had a long run at the Palace of the Governors. However, John Bourne decided to give his pre-Columbian collection to the private College of Santa Fe where it was to be exhibited in a building specifically constructed to house his generous gift. In 2009, the financially troubled college had to close. Bourne's collection is now going out of state to the Walters Museum in Baltimore. His decision is New Mexico's loss.

Almost fifteen years since the exhition opened and thirteen years after the confrontation with the F. B. I., the Museum of New Mexico voluntarily returned the monkey head to the Peruvian embassy. The transaction took place in December of 2001 and the Museum was careful to note that the act in no way acknowledged that "the head was improperly obtained. John Bourne expressed pleasure on two scores. He was happy to see it going back to Peru and pleased to note that many people in New Mexico had the opportunity to see "these kinds of things" that they might never have a chance to do.[427]

23
On the challenge of a son's desire to vindicate his father

A grave is a site associated with a person and many times becomes a monument. Other sites like buildings or landmarks are easily identifiable. Some sites, like trails are located over vast expanses. Trying to find a campsite or route of a trail requires physical evidence or documentary descriptions that combine with the lay of the land. In other words, sometimes the researcher needs to use common sense to figure out where a person would walk, ride a horse, or take a wagon. Finally, current tradition and oral history can provide pertinent information.

I was not expecting the challenge that Dr. George Baldwin brought into my office. Dr. Baldwin is a very smart person. He is a nuclear physicist who retired from a career working for General Electric and at the Los Alamos National Laboratories, where he had a reputation for his intelligence among his own colleagues. He spent a good part of his life trying to create a Graser (Gamma Ray Laser) but, after retirement, concluded that it was not feasible to do.[152] When I met him, he was in his early seventies. He had a medium build, had a well-trimmed small moustache with engaging blue eyes set in a round face under well-trimmed white hair. He had a way of stating things in an understated method while looking off from you. He did this in such a way as to make you sense that what he had said was obviously correct and that disagreement was unnecessary, in fact, a waste of time. This mannerism was not disconcerting so much as engaging, for he added a wry sense of humor and a strong determination. He would use all his traits in our meeting because he came to me with a proposition that seemed incredulous at first hearing. He said as much from the beginning by asking me to hear him out.[153]

At the time, both he and I had been briefed for the meeting. Baldwin's wife, Winnie, a lovely woman who adored her husband, was a volunteer at the Palace of the Governors' museum shop. She asked me if her husband could visit with me about a historical question of importance to him. I gladly agreed to a meeting and instructed her to tell him to come in anytime. I added that I looked forward to meeting him.

George Baldwin, as he explained to me, was born late in his father's life. An older sister had recently passed away and he inherited from her a map, some typed letters, and a newspaper article. They told a story that Baldwin barely remembered from family talk.

His father was a topographer who worked for the U. S. National Geological Society in the 1880s. He was assigned to survey an area on the Navajo Reservation that included the Mormon Ridge south of Navajo Mountain near Kaibito in northern Arizona. While working in this very open, arid, and remote land he set up an evening's camp near a large sandstone outcrop and came across what he described as a Spanish inscription carved at the base. Although he could not read Spanish he noted the date 1776, which he would never forget. He later described the location of the campsite as at the base of the east facing wall of the outcrop, which if a person turned his or her back to it, White Mesa could be seen about a mile away. A natural cistern holding water had been formed about half way up the wall's face.

Many years later, in 1939 in Salt Lake City, he read an article in *The Saturday Evening Post* in which an account of a 1776 expedition of some Hispanic priests had become the subject of research and discovery.[154] He noted that their conjectured route traversed the very area that he surveyed and became excited over the date. The article talked about some historians who were trying to retrace the journey. Harry L. Baldwin, by now, an elderly man with health problems, contacted Jesse Nusbaum and Herbert Eugene Bolton, the "historians" mentioned in the article.

Nusbaum was a fairly well known archaeologist who was the first curator at the Palace of the Governors. He worked for the School of American Research and, at the time, for the National Park Service, especially at Mesa Verde in southwestern Colorado not far from the Mormon Ridge.

Bolton, a historian, was nearing the end of his career and was a legend in his day. He taught and researched at the University of California in Berkeley. His work started a field of study that became known as Spanish Borderlands Studies. His graduate students and, in turn, their students now down to four and five generations of scholars are known as Boltonians. Like their namesake they specialize in the archives of Spain, Mexico, and the United States to reconstruct the history of northern New Spain (Mexico) and what is today the southwestern United States.

Dr. Bolton had transcribed and translated the journal of the 1776 expedition that Fray Francisco Anatasio Domínguez and Fray Sylvestre Vélez de Escalante led out of New Mexico northwest through the four corners area into Utah where they almost got to present-day Idaho.[155] They were in search of a rumored inland river down which they could travel to California. California just had been settled in 1767 and the Domínquez and Escalante expedition hoped to open a route for trade and commerce to Spain's newest settlement with its capital at Monterey. The river, shown on some maps as the Rio Santa Buenaventura, did not exist. So failing to find the river, the disappointed members of the small expedition decided to turn back. With winter approaching they planned to head directly south to the Hopi Pueblos and from there take known routes to return safely to Santa Fe.

Their return route took them directly to the north rim of the Grand Canyon, which with the help of Indian guides they entered the Glen Canyon near today's Page, Arizona and came out on the Grand Canyon's south rim near Navajo Mountain. During their descent they had to carve foot holds out of rock to progress. These impressions were found and the place became known as "Padre's Crossing." The site is now under the water of Lake Powell.[156]

Continuing south, in November, the weather turned nasty and the group apparently became disoriented. As the friar's journal notes, at one point, they camped on a cold snowy night. They had no food and had to eat a porcupine that they killed. They ultimately regained their bearings, and following Indian trails, they continued south to the Hopi pueblos. They had received a letter written by Fray Francisco Garces who was stationed at San Xavier del Bac in southern Arizona. Father Garces had been there in the Hopi pueblos in July while returning on a trek that had taken him from his mission west to southern California and back to the Grand Canyon where he spent some time with the Natives living in the canyon. Then he left the canyon to travel east and, then, south to the Hopi pueblos. He thought about going on to Zuni in New Mexico but was convinced to continue south to his own mission. He penned a letter to the "Father Minister at Zuni although I did not know his name" to report on his visit to the Hopi's. He asked that his letter be shared with the governor of New Mexico and the Father Custodian. Little did he suspect that Father Vélez de Escalante, who was the priest assigned to Zuni, would embark from Santa Fe not quite three four weeks later on the aforementioned journey that would arrive at the Hopi Pueblos in November.[157]

The maps drawn from the Dominguez-Escalante expedition as well as their journal clearly delineated the whole trip except for that one area where they were lost and ate the porcupine. Nobody, not even the scholarly Nusbaum and Bolton had located their route for that part of their trip. Understandably, the news from a sick, old man in Denver should have caught their immediate interest. But it did not, for they showed a scholar's disdain that anyone but one of their equals could enlighten them.

But Baldwin, like his son many years later, was persistent. He described the place, the date, and when he was there in 1884. The two scholars must have checked their notes and maps, for at some point they realized that the old man was talking about the only part of the eighteenth century expedition's route that they had not identified. Eventually, they replied to Baldwin and he sent them a map of the area on which he circled the general area of his camp site near the Mormon Ridge.

In October of 1939, Nusbaum and Bolton organized an expedition to personally inspect the area and to retrace the Domínguez-Escalante route. Finding the lost camp site would be a nice bonus. Roads would get them to the general area. Once there, they would have to go on foot or ride horses. They sent Baldwin an invitation to join them with instructions to meet at a prescribed place. Baldwin would have been the perfect guide and, with him, Nusbaum and Bolton could have added another academic feather in their caps.[158] Unfortunately, with deep disappointment Baldwin could not join the trip. He was bedridden in a hospital. The scholars would have to find the site on their own.

They drove out to the area where they spent two days on foot unsuccessfully searching for Baldwin's site.[159] They quickly dismissed Baldwin's description and advice. Forget the Mormon Ridge. They illogically determined that the expedition would have traveled south on a route further east along the base of White Mesa where they concentrated their futile search. Baldwin urged them to undertake a second search and volunteered to lead them to the site. Partially because World War II was raging and because the old surveyor was terminally ill and died in 1943, the second search never occurred.[160]

This story with all the attendant correspondence plus a second map with Baldwin's circle faded into memory. Nusbaum and Bolton never brought it up again. Upon Baldwin's death, his daughter inherited the correspondence and map in a trunk that she never inspected. When she died many years later, her younger brother George Baldwin received the trunk. His inspection of the contents led him to the correspondence and map and like that knight in the old Spanish novel, he had a wrong to correct. Credit must be given to his sister as well, for she had the good sense to keep the trunk. Most people would get rid of it arbitrarily.

George Baldwin studied his father's letters and map. He checked some sources and read Bolton's publication of the Domínguez-Escalante Expedition. He realized that his father could not have imagined nor made up his claim.

By the time George Baldwin came to see me, Bolton's publication of the Domínguez-Escalante Expedition had become a classic in the field. Subsequent scholars had published new, updated versions of Bolton's work, and many maps by the expedition's cartographer, Bernardo Miera y Pacheco, surfaced in various archives. Thanks to Michael Weber, the Palace of the Governors had copies of most of them and had purchased an original map that is actually an oil painting by Bernardo Miera y Pacheco, who participated in the Domínguez-Escalante expedition.[161] Still, none of this new information shed any light on where the two friars and their men traveled during that lost period of their trip. The mystery of "the porcupine camp site" remained unsolved.

24
In which is related the first search for a lost site

George Baldwin was determined to vindicate his father and asked that the state history museum help. As a matter of historical curiosity, I thought; Why not? Charles Bennett joined us in that initial meeting and he agreed. Both Bennett and I were longtime backpacking partners and the idea of exploring the Mormon Ridge for a historical site was very appealing.

George and Winnie Baldwin hosted a series of planning meetings in their house. Some of their friends were invited to participate. Two of these were Dr. Johndale Solem and his wife, Ann. Johndale had a pilot's license and was a high-ranking staffer in the "T" division (nuclear theory) at the Los Alamos Laboratories. Dr. Ross Melgaard, a retired physician from Kansas City and a longtime friend of the Baldwin's also attended the meetings. Charles and I included Tom Caperton who was the director of the New Mexico State Monuments Division and a person who had spent a lifetime identifying archaeological and historical sites in the Southwest.

Early on Johndale Solem agreed to fly over the territory to get a look of the "lay of the land." So he and Bennett took off from the Los Alamos airport and flew west to inspect the Mormon Ridge from the air. They came back with photographs that they shared at a subsequent meeting.

During our discussions I suggested that the 1776 date could have been left by Fray Garces and not the people of the Domínguez-Escalante Expedition. Garces could have traversed the same territory while traveling from the Grand Canyon to the Hopi Pueblos in the same year. Baldwin dismissed the idea out of hand. I continued to bring it up on occasion but the majority of the group sided with Baldwin in the matter. The identity of who wrote the inscription that Baldwin's father saw was never resolved to my satisfaction. I personally believed that the chances of it being Garces´s doing was very remote but could not be dismissed.

Aside from considering any other possibility for the inscription, Baldwin wanted the search to be systematic and his scientific friends agreed. The problem was how to systematically look for the proverbial needle in the haystack. The eleven square miles that encompassed the circle that Baldwin's father drew on the map seemed to grow as we planned. We decided that the search would be a museum project and that we would use some of the Palace's Foundation funds to defray the costs. Baldwin sweetened the pot by contributing some of his own funds. Naturally with museum involvement and funding, I saw myself as the project leader. George Baldwin knew that the project was his. Deferring to me was a necessary evil.

With dates set, we decided where to begin the search. Baldwin and his friends who were all older than the more adventurous "museum" members made reservations at a motel in Page, Arizona. The rest of the members decided to camp outdoors. But before we did anything we needed permission from the local Navajo Chapter House, because the search area was on the Navajo (Diné) Reservation. Charles Bennett, who had some previous experience at this, used the mails and telephone to prepare the way. State permits where granted but we still needed permission from the tribe on whose land we were going to search.

We car caravanned out to Kaibito, where we had a date with the current tribal representative. As is the custom we were welcomed into his house where he began to regale us about his family, himself, and friends. After about forty minutes of this George Baldwin became impatient. His fidgeting and facial expressions became obvious. Fortunately, he never tried to interject and hurry up the business of our visit. That would be seen as rude and permission would be denied. The tribal representative ignored him and Bennett signaled to Baldwin to be patient.

We could not belittle the person who could grant us permission to proceed. If he sensed that we considered ourselves and mission more important than him, the project would end right there. Baldwin was not used to this technique but our host could care less about who anyone of us was. He was determining whether or not he should allow this group of strangers to camp and explore on his tribal lands.

After another forty minutes, we were granted permission to search for the site. Our host volunteered to take us to a camp site on the ridge. He had no idea where the inscription was. Nor did he have any idea for the site. We would need to look on our own.

He hopped into an old pickup truck and led our caravan through a maze of old dirt roads on the Mormon Ridge's south face. We gained elevation until we crested the Ridge. He left us to camp far west of where we wanted to be. Then we learned that our guide had taken us on an indirect convoluted route, for, from above, we could see dirt roads heading down the north face to the main state highway 98, stretching from Kaibito to Page. With the help of GPSs, at the time a new instrument that the scientists had with them, we could not get lost ~ or so it seemed.

The campers spent a very cold night on the ridge. We dragged ourselves out of our sleeping bags the next morning and began to cook breakfast. Getting something warm inside of us was all that we could think of. But, as the bacon sizzled and the potatoes cooked, the others led by Baldwin drove up. Baldwin was anxious to start. The moment had come to find his father's site. Upon seeing us still stretching and rubbing our eyes with food still cooking, he treated us to another display of his impatience. We, like the tribal representative the day before, ignored him.

After breakfast, we split up into groups of two and three. Each group was assigned an area. Caperton and Bennett headed for the ridge's highest points, which seemed to be the most unlikely place of a lost eighteenth century expedition to camp. Baldwin and his friends broke into two teams and jumped into their SUVs to head to their designated area further east. Pat Trujillo, a recently retired chemist from LANL, and I would cover the area between the camp site and the area that Baldwin and company would search. Trujillo is a soft spoken, friendly man who loves history. We also had some mutual friends and shared some local family history. We had an enjoyable time together as we futilely searched.

About an hour into the search we began to realize that we were not even close to a potential site. We were too far west and too high on the ridge. Besides we could not see White Mesa. Why, we asked ourselves, would an eighteenth century expedition travel over the top of a formative ridge when, a couple of miles west, it could pass by or through the ridge on relatively level ground? Except for those paths that led up to religious sites, all the old trails would follow the path of least resistance. In this case they passed between the Mormon Ridge and White Mesa. I became discouraged. I wanted to find the site. The idea of hiking in beautiful high country became secondary.

At one point, Trujillo and I saw a member of our group trudging along in the opposite direction that we were going. We could not make out who he was from the distance but, it appeared that he was returning to the camp site. He was at least a half a mile away so we could not yell at him. He seemed to be in a rhythmatic, almost aimless walk.

A couple of hours later we finished our search and found the Solems standing by their SUV at the prescribed meeting place. They immediately told us that one of the scientists was missing. Ross Melgaard was last seen walking up and around a rock ridge immediately above us.

"How long has he been gone?" I asked.

"About two hours."

"Did you go after him? Have you looked for him?"

"Yes, we went up on the ledge but we did not want to go too far in case he returned."

"Where are the others?"

"They decided to drive back toward the camp site in case Ross came out from the other side of the ledge."

By now both Pat Trujillo and I had a very sinking feeling. We had an elderly man with no or little outdoor experience lost in a desperate land.

"Okay," I continued, "how was he allowed to walk off by himself?" We had made a point of telling everyone to stay pared up. The reasons now became obvious.

"He just left. We turned around and saw him walking around the bend on the ledge."

I was worried, very concerned. Ross was very smart, somewhat detached and unobservant of his immediate surroundings. Trujillo and I made a quick decision to look for him by following his path as best we could. Johndale and Ann agreed to wait where they were while Trujillo and I headed up the rock ledge to where Ross was last seen.

He walked on a defined path made by animals and we found his tracks in a sandy area. As soon as we rounded the bend we entered an area of high cliffs, canyons, and great distances. We were up high looking off the cliffs as our path took us east on a south-facing outer ledge of Mormon Mesa. We began calling out his name and heard our echoes in reply. There was no Ross. We realized that there was a possibility that Ross could have fallen off the ledge. We looked over the sides of the cliffs, hoping that we would not see Ross. Fortunately, we did not find him.

Eventually, the severity of the ledge began to give out and we were dropping down to a plain that made up a saddle on top of the Mormon Ridge. Looking off the ridge to the south we could see an expanse of desert with distant mesas, maybe even the Hopi Pueblo mesas, and Humphreys Peak near Flagstaff, Arizona. Hogans, like tiny intrusions to the forbidding land, were scattered on the desert floor miles apart. These are the traditional type of Navajo dwellings. We also saw a pickup truck winding its way up the side of the ridge below us. The truck eventually took a dirt road heading west toward our camp site.

About a half hour later Trujillo and I walked off the ledge to the plain where we met some of our people who had driven back looking for us. They brought the good news that

Ross Melgaard was back at the campsite. He was a little shook up but otherwise okay.

"What happened?"

He, indeed, had been lost and disoriented. Trujillo and I were on his trail for two, maybe three hours. He had taken the same route as us, dropped to the plain, and then walked down the dirt road to the desert floor below. There he headed for the nearest hogan that he had seen from above. So he walked about a half mile from the mesa's base to get to the dwelling where he met some people who did not speak English very well. With the use of gestures he was able to explain that he was lost. No doubt the locals knew this, why else would an elderly non-Indian man on foot, without water, and food be at their door step?

They also figured that he was a part of the group camping up on top of the mesa. They gave him some water and put him in their truck and took him to the camp site. Melgaard was very lucky.

As Trujillo and I listened to the story, we began to realize that he was the person that we saw aimlessly walking across the plain earlier that day. We also realized that the truck that we saw was the one that took him back to the camp site.

It is hard to kick a dog when it is down but I was mad and tired. Trujillo and I had spent hours searching and being concerned, and the latter had worn on us more. Ross Melgaard and the others were at the camp when we arrived. Rather than cuss him out, which would have served no purpose, I made a couple of quick comments such as; "you are a very lucky man," "now maybe you guys will listen to us when we tell you to do things for your own safety," and, the one that hit home with George Baldwin at least, "maybe we should call this whole thing off before something serious happens."

Everyone was properly scolded and reacted in kind. George Baldwin desperately wanted to continue and agreed that more attention would be paid to our collective safety. He knew that he could have lost a friend that day.

Somewhat relieved, if not chagrined, we decided to concentrate the search in a different area the next day. We agreed to explore the ridge's base further east. After a good night's rest we broke camp, drove down the north face on the shorter road, met the others who stayed at Page, and headed east on the main highway for a couple of miles. We turned on a dirt road heading toward the eastern end of the Mormon Ridge and found a place to park and begin the search. Once again, we formed small groups and assigned general areas. This time everyone was careful about preventing anyone from wandering off alone.

We were reinvigorated with the promise of the area in which we decided to investigate. Searching the base of Mormon Ridge with White Mesa in view to the west made more sense. Trujillo and I were together again. We headed off to our assigned area and spent the day looking at the base of western facing walls in dead end canyons. We hiked all day and found nothing, nor did anyone else. We became very familiar with the area but failed to find the inscription and campsite.

We gathered together very disappointed but none more so than George Baldwin. As we compared observations while standing among our cars, we all agreed that we would not give up. We will return and continue the search. Most of us felt that generally we were in the correct area. We also agreed that Bolton and Nusbaum were wrong to arbitrarily decide to ignore the Mormon Ridge in favor of White Mesa.

With a renewed resolve to continue the quest we returned home. I drove with Pat Trujillo in his camper truck. Both of us are trout fishermen so we took advantage of the opportunity and drove over to the quality water section of the San Juan River where we spent the night to rise early the next morning and go fishing. Our luck did not improve there either.

25
Relating to the second search

After another planning meeting we agreed on the dates and the locations for the second search. Jerry Richardson and Charles Kirkpatrick joined our group for the second search. Kirkpatrick's family owned the Inn at Loretto in Santa Fe. He was an hotelier who had an interest in history. Pat Trujillo, who with his wife had a curio store at the Kirkpatricks's hotel, could not join us on this trip. Dr. Robert Filice, a Santa Fe dentist, joined us in this next search. Also, on the search was James Knipmeyer, a student of western rock inscriptions. Knipmeyer heard about our search from Stanley Jones of Page, Arizona. He had been with us for part of the first trip and thought that Melgaard was very lucky to have survived. With a slightly changed group, we all drove out the day before to spend the evening in Page, Arizona. Bennett and Richardson chose to camp at the Navajo National Monument campground. We met at a proscribed place on the main highway and, once again, caravanned to our designated base.

This time we would explore the western edge of the Mormon Ridge beginning with a review of the area where we had finished on the previous trip. The Mormon Ridge runs in a slight northwest to southeast direction that makes it easy to describe its directions as west and east. The eastern edge is where the Mormon Ridge is closest to White Mesa, which is about a mile away further east. The latter received its name for its distinct white cliff sides.

Our entire group and most every historian believed that the eighteenth century expeditions traveled south to the Hopi Pueblos somewhere between the Mormon Ridge and White Mesa. The Domínguez-Escalante expedition, at least, left some evidence in its journal as well as subsequent maps that it had passed south from Navajo Mountain and ended up at the Hopi Pueblos. Navajo Mountain is easily visible from the base of the Mormon Ridge and a casual study of the lay of the land virtually dictates that the route had to go somewhere through the area between the Mormon Ridge and White Mesa.

But, the Mormon Ridge did not end abruptly. It had a small mesa connected to it with a saddleback, a depression connecting the two higher ridges.. The saddleback was much lower than either the mesa or the ridge and the inclines up to it were mild. An old dirt road went right up its north incline and down the south incline. Could the road have been a continuation of an old trail? Probably. The road still is used by the locals with some frequency.

Ross Melgaard's misadventure was not lost on George Baldwin. Along with a couple of extra GPSs, he brought along referee whistles that he passed out to everyone. He explained that we should use them if we were lost or searching for someone who is lost. The whistle would lead us to each other in case of an emergency.

With whistles hanging around our respective necks we trudged off on our search. Toward the end of the day as we were walking back to the cars, I could hear the distant sound of someone incessantly blowing on a whistle. This seemed odd to me because we could not have been more than fifty yards from the parked cars. Within seconds I saw one of the retired doctors standing on a boulder next to the cars blowing his whistle as long and as hard as he could. Upon seeing us he stopped and ran up to us to explain that he thought that everyone was lost and, as the first person back to the cars, he started blowing his whistle as a homing device for everyone. But, as everyone soon realized, the whistle's sound did not carry beyond fifty yards. The sound was swallowed up in the vast expanses of the area. Nevertheless, everyone returned without any problems.

Forgoing any lectures about safety we began our customary exchange of observations and thoughts. One of the group mentioned that he had walked down the road to the north to inspect rock outcroppings out away from the ridge. He found one site that he thought was interesting and that we should see. He did not see any old Spanish inscription but there was a lot of modern graffiti. Besides, he added, the site was about a hundred yards off the dirt road on our way out of the area. Checking it out would not be an inconvenience.

All agreed to see his site and hopped in the cars to travel down the road to a spot that he had marked. The thirty to forty foot high rock outcropping was familiar to me because I had been searching the territory west of it and never thought to walk around to its east side. The east side base was an obvious gathering place, probably for youth. The area was strewn with graffiti, trash, and recent fire circles. However, outside of modern inscriptions and paint on the sandstone wall, we saw nothing that looked like a centuries' old inscription. Still this was a popular place in use in modern times.

We also observed that with our backs to the east facing wall we could clearly see White Mesa. Then we agreed that the site was close to a road that probably was an old trail going over the saddle to the south. Still, our discussion led us to an ununanimous conclusion that there was too much speculation and not enough substance to determine whether this was the actual site. Besides, there was no inscription.

George Baldwin believed that we had found the site. He became frustrated with the direction of the conversation. He could not disagree with us more. "Look," he postulated, "the site fits dad's description. Of course there is no inscription. The rock is soft and judging from the sand piled at the base, has been breaking off for decades."

He just knew that we had found his father's site. But there was no more to say, except to agree to return the next morning and perhaps get a better view of the wall in the western morning light. Up until then we had been looking at everything in an early evening shadow. Baldwin was at once, frustrated, happy, and anxious with the decision. He had to settle for a return visit.

As we walked away from the site toward our cars that were parked on the dirt road, Tom Caperton and I stopped to take a last look at the wall. We were fifty to seventy-five yards away and we simultaneously noticed what looked like a well defined horizontal fissure or crack about two thirds of the way up the wall's face. But it could be more than a crack, even a ledge or a natural water tank. "Hold on," I exclaimed to no one in particular. Caperton and I looked at each other and began a rapid, rejuvenated walk back toward the wall. We pointed out our discovery to anyone who would notice.

James Knipmeyer immediately began to climb up the outcrop. Charles Bennett, Jerry Richardson, and I followed. A couple of the others followed us. We found a well defined natural impression with a sandy bottom. It was a natural water cistern. Although the tank contained no water, it would easily fill up with a thunderstorm. Knipmeyer quickly found an arrowhead in the sand. This was a place that had been visited for many years, possibly, centuries. More importantly, it was a telltale presence, for Harry Baldwin described just such a tank in his reports. Now, with the exception of the inscription, the site perfectly matched the old surveyor's description.

Then someone pointed out what could have been a "7" carved in the rock at the base of the cliff. Now George Baldwin had no doubts. He was convinced that we had located the site and that the "7" was all that remained of the eighteenth century "1776" marking. Some of us, however, had trouble accepting the carving as part of the old inscription. Nevertheless, the site had us talking. We left for the evening with a renewed sense of urgency for the next morning.

The morning's light revealed a more defined "17" although the "museum" contingent of the group could not conclude that it was carved two centuries ago. Under George Baldwin's direction, Knipmeyer took photographs of the marking. Knipmeyer apparently believed that we had found a part of the authentic inscription, for he included it in his subsequent book on historic southwestern inscriptions of the Colorado Plateau.[162]

Jerry Richardson, Charles Bennett, and I along with a couple others still had doubts about the inscription. We felt good about the search and that we had exhausted all the possibilities at the Mormon Ridge. While George Baldwin and his friends stayed at the site the rest of us took a hike up the small mesa that is connected to the ridge. The view from the top was very telling, for now we could see the relationship of Navajo Mountain, the outcrop, a route over the saddle, and the distant Hopi Mesas. At that point I felt reasonably assured that we had found the place where Harry Baldwin had camped on 16 November 1884. The lay of the land, the natural cistern, all pointed to an old trail and good place to camp. I also had no reason to doubt his word about seeing an inscription and remembering the date. He had no motive whatsoever to fabricate such a story and then insist on it until his death. Whether the inscription survived or not was a moot point although it would be nice to have found it intact.

Did we find the lost Porcupine camp site of the Domínguez-Escalante exhibition? Although we may never know for sure, I believe that we did.

George Baldwin had no doubt. He wrote up a report of the search and, on my advice, submitted it to *El Palacio Magazine*, which is the official magazine of the Museum of New Mexico. I thought that the editors would enjoy an article about an interesting museum project but they shortsightedly refused to consider the article, perhaps because of its length. Baldwin would not be deterred and he found a publisher in the *Journal of the Southwest*, which is published in Arizona. This made perfect sense, for the Mormon Ridge and Porcupine camp site are in Arizona.[163]

Baldwin's article is the definitive account of the search for the lost site. In his view we definitely found the site and a remnant of the inscription. As he tells it, he pretty much orchestrated the whole project and the museum's participation was a necessary distraction. Nevertheless, George Baldwin and everyone else involved could agree on one salient point–his dad had been vindicated.

26
In which a context is set for the following chapters

Most research is negative, which means that a lot of time is spent not finding that which is being sought. The life of a research historian is a life of intrigue, solving mysteries of the past, and learning what really happened. But, the process is slow and, many times, futile. And, sometimes, like Don Quixote, the illusive Dulcinea is never found.

Burials of famous or infamous people long have been a major attraction to the general public. Witness, for example, New Mexico's Governor Bill Richardson, who became fixated on the remains of Billy the Kid. Whether the governor wanted the outlaw's remains disinterred for publicity or not, his interest generated a lot of press.

New Mexico is not unique. The world is rife with strange burials, tombs, and *post mortem* shenanigans. There are the examples of Stalin's tomb, the sordid story of the body of Argentina's Evita, or the remains of any number of "incorruptible" saints that are left out for viewing. Then there is the international controversy over who actually has Christopher Columbus's remains; Spain, the Dominican Republic, or Cuba. A recent forensic study of the remains in Columbus's tomb in Seville, Spain, concluded that he is there. Nor is the United States divest of this phenomena. Let us not forget the time-honored question of "who is buried in Grant's tomb." The burial sites of many, if not most of the Presidents of the United States are majestic in scope.

Let us focus on the remains of a couple of scholars. James Smithson died in 1829. He was a wealthy Englishman who never visited the United States. He was a mineralogist and chemist who had an intelligence and curiosity that led him to seek ways for the further investigation and dissemination of "knowledge among men." He came to believe that the young United States of America was the place to best plant the seeds of his legacy. Before he died and was buried in Genoa, Italy, he made arrangements, pending the offspring of his only nephew, to leave his considerable wealth to the government of the United States to establish an educational institution that would be based in Washington, DC.

Decades later, in 1904, the leaders of the Smithsonian Institution, which had become the national museum of the United States, decided to move his remains from Italy to his institution. Today, in a small chamber to the left of the main entry to the Smithsonian Institution's "castle," its original building and location of the director's office, the tourist is invited to view the crypt containing the benefactor's remains. The crypt is surrounded with an array of paraphernalia that belonged to him.[164]

Not connected but similar to the Smithsonian Institution's example, the School of American Research,[165] located in Santa Fe, New Mexico, decided to transfer the remains of Adolph Bandelier, the Swiss born "father" of southwestern archaeology. By then Bandelier had a National Park named for him in the nearby Jemez Mountains. He and his wife, Fanny, spent a few years studying ancestral Pueblo Indian cultures, including the ruins in and around what would become the park named for him.

He left New Mexico to research in Mexico and Peru and, finally, in the Archives of the Indies in Seville, Spain. There, in March of 1914, he became ill and died. He was buried in Seville's municipal cemetery of San Fernando. His much younger wife intended to raise enough money for his remains to be moved back to the United States but she never succeeded in her plan. In the summer of 1927, Dr. France Scholes, while doing research in Seville, arranged for Bandelier's remains to be transferred to a crypt and paid a ten year deposit. By the end of that period Spain was in a civil war and Edgar Lee Hewett of the School of American Research opposed a plan to have the remains brought back to New Mexico. Instead he arranged for a permanent crypt and marker although it is unclear whether the reburial took place.[166]

In 1974 the leadership of the School of American Research negotiated with Spanish authorities to have Bandelier's remains located and returned to the United States. They wanted to bury him in Bandelier National Park. Spanish bureaucracy and the fact that it took a while to locate his unmarked grave because the marker had been stolen resulted in almost three years delay. Nonetheless, his remains were located and returned in a sealed lead casket about the size of a coffee table or steamer trunk. U. S. immigration officials had to use blow torches to conduct a required inspection of the contents.

The remains and the casket arrived at the School of American Research in March 1977. Then came the next hurdle, for Federal Government policy did not allow burials in national parks. As a result, Bandelier's remains waited, now transferred to a simple wooden chest that was kept under a table in the School's boardroom.[167]

Eventually, the School of American Research negotiated a compromise with the National Park Service. Bandelier's remains could be deposited at a designated place distant from the park headquarters if they were cremated. The School agreed. At the time Santa Fe had no facilities for cremation. This meant that the School had to send a staff member take the remains to Albuquerque to have them cremated. The story is told that the staffer took the remains to the designated funeral parlor and entered the office where he was greeted in the usual understated and respectful manner. Upon hearing that a cremation needed to be done, the parlor's representative inquired as to where the body was located. He, no doubt, was thinking that it may be at a hospital or, possibly, another funeral home.

Imagine his surprise when the reply came back that the remains were in the trunk of the patron's car, which was parked outside!

After further explanations the deed was done and the ashes taken back to Santa Fe where arrangements had been made for Bandelier's final interment. With some pomp but no circumstance, Bandelier's ashes were spread in the park of his name along the north wall of Frijoles Canyon between the park's visitor center and the ruined pueblo of Tyúonyi.[168]

27
Concerning the curious tales of some mysterious burials

Unlike the examples shared in the previous chapter, the burial locations of two of New Mexico's most well-known governors have never been located. While many parts of the world venerate, even elevate the reputations of their history's distant heroes with elaborate monuments and mausoleums at their gravesites, two of New Mexico's most known governors have no such distinctions while a third is mis-identified. The first two are New Mexico's first governor Juan de Oñate (1598–1609) and Diego de Vargas, the hero of the Spanish resettlement of New Mexico in 1692–1696. Each had a profound influence on New Mexico's history. Both were controversial. Like the third governor, Juan Bautista de Anza, who served as New Mexico's governor long after them, both were active up to their respective deaths. The remains of Anza, as will be noted, have been located but not acknowledged.

Oñate died as an old man while inspecting a mine in Guadalcanal in southern Spain.[169] Vargas became ill from a "stomach ailment" while pursuing Apache Indians east of the Manzano Mountains in central New Mexico. He succumbed in bed a few days later in Bernalillo. Oñate asked that his remains be placed in a chapel in Madrid and Vargas willed that his remains be buried in a church in Santa Fe, New Mexico.[170] To date, historians have not found either of the burial sites for Oñate or Vargas.

28
An interlude or, more likely, a transition regarding Juan Bautista de Anza

An interlude is defined as something unrelated to what went on before and what continues after. This interlude occurs in the context of final resting places, particularly those that have been located or relocated and, yet to come, those that have yet to be located. The case of Juan Bautista de Anza's grave site is a story of the location being known, even advertised, only to realize that the site did not belong to Anza at all.

Maybe this interlude should be more accurately described as a transition. And why not? Miguel Cervantes whose book is a loose organizational model for this effort, did the same and even offered apologies in his own way—which are not offered here.

Anza has been introduced in these pages in reference to his defeat of Cuerno Verde (Part II, chapter 13). He grew up in the Sonoran frontier then called Pimería Alta, the northern or upper country of the Pima Indians. Both his father and grandfather were killed by Apaches. He spent a lifetime defying the odds of surviving in a hostile environment. In 1774 he fulfilled his father's goal of opening an overland route from Sonora that traversed present-day southern Arizona to California. A few years later he returned to California and helped establish the new presidio of San Francisco.

He then received the appointment to be the governor of New Mexico in which capacity he served from 1778–1787. Anza is considered one of New Mexico's most successful Spanish colonial governors. He is most known for his efforts in successfully confronting the Comanche and Apache Indians and bringing some stability to New Mexico. He also collected a "tax" in New Mexico to help Spain fight Great Britain in the war that resulted in the independence of the United States.[171]

After his term in New Mexico, he returned to his native Pimería Alta where he died 19 December 1788 in the town of Arizpe. He was buried in the town's church of Nuestra Señora de la Asunción.[172]

Anza's lifetime accomplishments were such that centuries later historians and archaeologists published his letters, wrote his biography, named a national trail, and organized an annual conference dedicated to him. His name is on buildings and schools in both the United States and Mexico.

For years the Palace of the Governors had an original oil painting that purported to be a portrait of Anza. The painting was on exhibit when I arrived at the Palace and remained so throughout my tenure there. Dr. Herbert Bolton first published the portrait in his 1921 book on the Spanish Borderlands. At the time the painting belonged to one of Anza's descendants, James Ainsa of San Francisco. It changed possession within the family several times until 1970, when it was donated to the Palace of the Governors. The donor insisted that the painting was authentic. However, J. Ignacio Rubio Mañe, a renowned scholar and researcher with the Archivo General de la Nación in Mexico City expressed doubts about the validity of the painting. He based his conclusions on the subject's beard and seventeenth century French clothing. Richard Alhborn, a scholar and curator at the Smithsonian Institution's National Museum of History countered that full beards were still in vogue in New Spain's northern frontier at the time and that the clothing was probably from wardrobes that painters commonly kept for their subjects. Michael Weber, a friend of Alhborn's, who originally put the painting on exhibit at the Palace still had some doubts about its authenticity and while in Arizona he contacted staff about the possibility of having it scientifically tested in Mexico.

Diana Ortega de Santis, the Palace's curator, received the assignment of working with Weber on the project. In 1994, Weber took the painting to Mexico to have it x-rayed and its pigments analyzed. After many delays the inconclusive results came back. Apparently, the painting, while relatively old, may have been executed many years after Anza's death and, therefore, could not be a contemporary or true depiction. Thus Anza's only known authentic rendering had been debunked and is still in doubt.[173]

Meanwhile in Mexico, Anza's grave site was located and excavated. The scholars found the skeletal remains lying in a classic position dressed in fancy clothes of the time. Then the excavators made the decision to leave the remains exposed under glass. They wrote a label explaining the importance of the grave. From a historians point-of-view the location and exposure of Anza's remains was impressive. Over time many people traveled to the remote village of Arizpe to see the remains of the famous personage.

Then the unthinkable happened. Further research revealed that the exposed remains were not Anza's at all. Scholars and town fathers had exposed and misidentified a different person. Anza, they learned, was buried in a different spot in the church. Nevertheless, the decision was made to leave the misidentified grave alone. Apparently they felt that no one would know the difference, but they were wrong.

Word of the mix-up quickly spread through the academic community. The Anza conference attendees, including the general public, talked about the controversy. The only question remained was how long the local leaders of Arizpe could suffer the criticism. At this point, Anza's purported final resting place, like his only known portrait, is doubtful to say the least.

29
Relating to the request of Juan de Oñate

Yet, there are scattered hints and possibilities, intriguing information, and theories that give rise to continuing courses of investigation. Juan de Oñate died in 1626 at the age of seventy-six, "more or less." Five years earlier, in 1621, after the death of his wife, he left Mexico and traveled to Spain to petition for the exoneration of the convictions that he had incurred for his activities while governor of New Mexico. He succeeded in getting some of the charges dismissed but not all of them. He also received an appointment to be a royal inspector of mines in Spain. Oñate took his new responsibility seriously.[174] He oversaw the revision of Spain's mining codes that were published in 1625.[175] It seems that Oñate died a successful man, at least, in his own mind.

He requested in his Last Will and Testament that he wanted a fifth of all his substantial wealth given to the Jesuits to help pay for the construction of their Colegio Imperial in Madrid. He further requested that another 10,000 *ducados* be donated to help with the construction of the Chapel of San Isidro Labrador being built adjacent to the Colegio Imperial. One of the conditions for this request was that his remains be buried in the chapel and that the Oñate coat-of-arms be displayed on the wall.[176] This is interesting on a couple of scores. Oñate wanted to support a Jesuit project even though he had spent most of his life among Franciscans, some of whom were his own relatives. San Isidro Labrador is the patron saint of Madrid, Spain and had become very popular in New Mexico. Also the patron saint of farmers, the actual saint actually worked for the ancestors of Diego de Vargas who owned land in what is today downtown Madrid. Diego de Vargas became New Mexico's governor eighty-two years after Oñate left the colony.[177]

In the early 1600s Madrid was a small indiscrete town that was undergoing a transformation. Some forty years earlier in 1561 King Felipe II, who also built the massive mausoleum of Spanish royalty as well as monastery and royal residence that he named San Lorenzo de Escorial, established nearby Madrid as Spain's capital city. The king wanted a centrally located seat of government.

Felipe II and his son, upon becoming King Felipe III in 1598, petitioned the Catholic Church to officially recognize Isidro's good life through beatification. In the church of Santa Maria Mayor in Rome, Pope Paulo V beatified Isidro on 13 June 1619. The Pope fixed the new saint's day of celebration as 15 May.[178] Thus with the King present in Madrid's Plaza Mayor, the city's new patron saint was celebrated for the first time on

15 May 1620,[179] the same year the Pilgrims landed at Plymouth Rock. The pride and enthusiasm generated with this event may have been reason enough for Oñate to support the construction of the new chapel and school that would bear the saint's name.

Upon reading this information, I wondered whether the chapel and church was ever finished and, if so, did it still exist? The answer to both questions is "yes." Further inquiry revealed that the church had the remains for San Isidro and his wife and was attached to a *colegio,* a high school that retained the name San Isidro.

Through Charles Penny, a friend who had moved to Madrid to teach English, I was able to establish contact with the *colegio.* Don Pedro Vela Vázquez, who taught in the Department of Geography and History had an interest in the school's history and had been doing research on the old chapel building.[180] Initially, I received word that he could not find any reference to Oñate. Then, through Charles Penny, Vela Vázquez sent copies of a printed pamphlet that gave a history of San Isidro and his connection to Madrid. The pamphlet was printed for the chapel's chapter house that consists of a group of lay people who support the church and school. Later on they would become *socios*, or the board of directors for the school. The pamphlet contained a list of the directors for 1752. The Conde de Oñate appeared as the "*teniente Hermano Mayor.*" At least, the family, whether direct descendents or not of New Mexico's governor, continued to be involved with the building into the eighteenth century.[181]

Another source revealed the unconfirmed story that the Oñate coat-of-arms is prominently displayed on the chapel. Historian Eric Beerman wrote in 1979 that Oñate's last will and testament stipulated that the school's main door display the Oñate coat-of-arms.[182] Nancy Brown, who worked in the Center for Southwest Research at the University of New Mexico, wrote to me that she heard about Oñate's shield on the building but was unsuccessful trying to get a confirmation through correspondence.[183]

In July of 2007 Celia and I went to see the chapel and school for the first time. By then, the school had sent a photograph of the interior of the chapel. I was left with the impression that the old chapel's nave is used for lectures, banquets, and receptions. The floor is a polished wood while the white with gold trimmed walls appeared to be fairly barren. However, when we arrived at the church I was surprised to find that the chapel was a large church and nothing like the photographs that I had. The *parroquia de San Isidro Labrador* or parish church had gone through quite a history, for the original chapel grew to become the cathedral of Madrid only to lose that designation to a newer larger edifice next to the Royal Palace. Nevertheless, many people today refer to it as the Cathedral of San Isidro Labrador.

Once inside the building we found many side chapels with different devotions. A statue of San Juan that is prominently placed to the left of the main altar grabbed my attention. Oñate's patron saint is San Juan. But Celia quickly diverted my attention to another chapel devoted to San Isidro.

Celia had an interest in the church because she was researching and writing a book about Gaspar Pérez de Villagrá and Alonso Ercilla, two conquistador poets in the Americas. Her research indicated that Villagrá and Oñate remained in contact after Villagrá's desertion from New Mexico. Villagrá, who apparently continued as Oñate's legal advisor, traveled to Spain to represent himself and Oñate before the crown. Both had been accused and found guilty of crimes committed while they were in New Mexico. In this context Villagrá's epic, book length poem, dedicated to King Felipe III, makes sense as a published document that was intended to show both men in a positive light. Neither of them were ever completely exonerated but they did receive royal favors, for Oñate, as mentioned, became a royal mine inspector while Villagrá received an appointment to be the mayor of a town in Guatemala. The old poet, who was around seventy years old, died and was buried at sea while traveling to his new position. Villagrá, like his friend Oñate, had become involved with the Jesuits in Madrid.

So far we searched through the large former cathedral and found nothing that hinted of Oñate. As I scurried over to Celia in the San Isidro Chapel, she told me that this was it and pointed to a mounted marble plaque on the left wall. It explained that a miracle occurred in the late sixteenth century and that for this reason the chapel was built. Mary as the Immaculate Conception appeared to a man named Luís Gonzaga and told him "to enter the company of my son." Thus, on that spot he and the Jesuit order built the chapel and, eventually, an attached building for the Imperial Institute of the Royal Austrians.[184]

At the time the Jesuits were a relatively new order of priests. They were founded by Ignatius Loyola in 1539 and established as soldiers of Christ to fight against the Reformation. The order quickly dedicated itself to education and became devoted to Mary the mother of God.

All this information was corroborated with a label next to the main church's front door that stated that the church was completed in 1622, the same year as the school. The institution existed before the building but the building gave it a higher and more visible prestige.

The Jesuits had established their institute in the new capital in 1566. The lives of both Oñate and his captain in New Mexico, Villagrá, spanned the same years as this history of Madrid, the Jesuits, and the school. Villagrá died in 1620 and, as mentioned, Oñate succumbed in 1626.[185] Thus the histories of the saint, the church, the Jesuits, and Madrid all converged with the New Mexican explorers and settlers.

After inspecting the church, Celia and I walked next door to the institute. At the time of the building's construction, the only opportunity for a good formal education in Madrid was a two day journey to Alcalá de Henares, where Villagrá published his book about New Mexico in 1610. The next closest place was the more distant University of Salamanca. Both schools had a monopoly on higher education so the Jesuits filled a void in Madrid but their effort had to be limited to a secondary school, which is to say, high school. The school did gain prestige, for it became the source of formal education for many Spanish royal personages, including future kings.

The gate keeper at the institute directed us to Justo Corbacho, who wrote a short history of the institute in 1995 and is considered its expert.[186] He knew about Oñate and Villagrá's connection to the school because he remembered receiving correspondence about them. A very gracious man, he gave us a copy of his history of the institute, confirmed that the chapel dedicated to the Immaculate Conception was the original and that the church and school was built up around it. The chapel, he continued, had changed over the years and only a few vestiges of the original structure remain. The chapel grew into the larger building that became the Cathedral of Madrid and it along with most of the left side of the building received severe bomb damage during Spain's civil war. Franco's "modernization" completed the changes. If Oñate's coat-of-arms existed on the building, it disappeared during the destruction or renovations. As of now there is no physical evidence of Oñate's association with the church.

But, what about under the floor? Has that ground been disturbed? As was customary, could there be burials? And, if there are burials, might one of them contain the remains of New Mexico's colonizer and first governor? All this was possible. After all, his bequest paid for the chapel's construction on the condition that they inter his remains along with those of his descendents.

Of course, the answers to these questions require more historical as well as archaeological research. Hopefully, some kind of high tech non-intrusive scan of the floor could answer the question about the existence of burials. The staff at the school was enthused about the possibility of further research. However, they very clearly stated that they cannot bear the cost and proffered the hope that an institution in the United States could be convinced to fund the project.[187]

The engaging Corbacho shared some ideas for further research. Celia, who had researched and written about Jesuits, asked about the Jesuit account books that would be associated with the chapel and school. Corbacho agreed that those documents are an untapped source and could be very revealing. At least, there is a possibility that we could find entries for both Oñate's and Villagrá's donations. Upon review of our sources we discovered that historian Eric Beerman found Oñate's records in those account books and shared his findings in a 1979 article.[188]

On the other hand, Corbacho was very clear that burial records for the chapel had disappeared and did not exist. Were they lost in the war's devastation? Who knows? Left unsaid is the possibility or low probability that the records were transferred to some archive only to be lost in bureaucratic record-keeping.

So far, we had established nothing except that Oñate had developed a relationship with the Jesuits, he requested to be buried in their church, Oñate family members remained connected with the church and school, and the coat-of-arms did not exist. Whether or not Oñate was buried there is still a matter of conjecture. Through Penny's efforts the school seemed interested in further research. The possibility that Oñate's remains are there and that they have been undisturbed is likely. Yet, even a very remote possibility is an intriguing enticement for further research. The possibility of locating the final resting place of Juan de Oñate, the "last conquistador" as he has been called, is too great a temptation to lie fallow for long.[189]

Nevertheless, if found, the idea of returning Oñate's remains to New Mexico for reburial and the inevitable construction of some kind of monument would be uncalled for despite the precedent set by the admirers of Smithson, Bandelier, and Hewitt. One of the sentences imposed by Oñate's king and not overturned was his perpetual banishment from New Mexico. Getting the current king of Spain to forgive Oñate at this late date would be an intriguing but inappropriate idea. Besides, such a move would be contrary to Oñate's own wishes that he be placed in the new chapel of the church of San Isidro in Madrid.

30
On whether the desire of Diego de Vargas was fulfilled post mortem

In 1704, Diego de Vargas died in Bernalillo, New Mexico in the house of Fernando Durán y Chaves. Vargas requested that his remains be taken to Santa Fe to be buried in "the military chapel" after the proper services and prayers. Historians have never established the exact location of the military chapel. They know that the royal houses, the larger antecedent of today's Palace of the Governors, had a military chapel but without accurate plans or descriptions plus a silent archaeological record, the location could be anywhere in the vicinity of the town's main plaza.[190]

Over the years, the final resting place of Diego de Vargas, the hero of the reconquest of New Mexico, as well as today's annual Santa Fe Fiestas, and the namesake of the Caballeros de Vargas, has become the subject of much speculation. The staff at the Palace of the Governors was constantly confronted with the question. Popular belief has his remains located in the Palace of the Governors. This belief fails to realize that the current building was a part of a much larger complex. Besides, the extensive excavations so far completed under and around the old building have revealed nothing pertinent to Vargas's burial or even the chapel.[191] Approximately eighty percent of the building has been excavated. The most recent excavation took place immediately behind the Palace, where, unexpectedly, a whole complex of rooms was uncovered.[192]

Then there is another possibility, which, if true, more accurately places Vargas's final burial in the cathedral. This line of reasoning follows Vargas's desire to have a church built that would contain the throne from which Nuestra Señora de la Conquistadora could look after New Mexico. She had become popular among New Mexico's settlers since her arrival in 1625. By Vargas's time the statue had a long history with the area. Within six years of her arrival in New Mexico she had acquired her nickname of La Conquistadora and had a confraternity dedicated to her. She, like the small statue that became Nuestra Señora de la Macana, survived the Pueblo Revolt. Unlike Nuestra Señora de la Macana, this statue remained among the exiled New Mexicans and returned to New Mexico with them in 1693. Vargas, himself, was the *majordomo,* or head of her confraternity. He dedicated the resettlement of New Mexico to her. He also pledged to build a church that would serve as her seat to reign over her people.[193]

Vargas died seven years before the new parish church was finished in 1711 on the current site of Santa Fe's cathedral. The line of reasoning continues that his friends and followers would have reburied him in the new church.[194] The large adobe structure with crenalated walls had a cruciform floor plan. The north transept, a third of which is the only remaining part of the original structure, was dedicated to La Conquistadora. Eventually, in the last half of the nineteenth century, the cathedral was built up around the old church leaving, as mentioned, about a third of the old church's north transept where a visitor will find La Conquistadora today.

Three years after the dedication of the new church some of Vargas's former friends and colleagues gathered at the house of Juan Paez Hurtado to draft a fiesta proclamation. With a backdrop of thunder and lightning outside, they wrote up a testimonial to their former governor and military leader and proclaimed that henceforth Santa Fe, the capital of New Mexico should have an annual fiesta in his memory. Over the years, this became the basis for today's fiestas that still feature Diego de Vargas.

In 1966 the cathedral underwent some extensive interior renovations. The workmen uncovered burials inside the church and, with Church permission, proceeded to remove them. At first some bones were moved to Rosario Cemetery. But as more bones were uncovered the Rector Father Godfry Blank had a cement crypt dug inside the cathedral. The cement lined pit is about ten feet long "four or five feet wide and ten feet under the sacristy." The crypt was capped with concrete and labeled with a copper plate. According to an anonymous transcript, the rector claimed that most of the bones were buried in the crypt.[195]

One shallow grave, uncovered by a backhoe, had the remains of a male individual buried in a fetal position before the main altar. From his clothes and placement, the remains appeared to be those of a wealthy man. This discovery required further study. Palace of the Governors curator Bruce Ellis was given two days to study the site and remains. Because Church officials were anxious to finish the renovations, Ellis decided to remove the clothing from the skeletal remains and called in E. Boyd, a Spanish colonial specialist from the Museum of International Folk Art, to take the three piece suit to the museum for further study. The man was buried in a suit with a matching cloth hat, pantaloons, and jacket that dated to around 1700.[196]

The Archdiocese of Santa Fe loaned the suit to the Museum of International Folk Art,[197] which had it cleaned and conserved in London. Eventually the museum did a small but very tatsteful exhibition of the suit. Before its conservation the suit had stains from body fluids, along with bone particles and hair stuck to it. Unfortunately, the process removed all of that. This was not good because the suit belonged to someone of importance who had died around 1700. Given the location of the grave, that person likely was one of the first burials in the new *parroquia*, as the church came to be called.[198]

Speculation began. Did the construction crew come across Diego de Vargas's final resting place? The argument against that possibility was his clear request to be buried in the military chapel. But proponents of the theory that he had been found, countered that he could have been reburied in the church he wanted built. Given the available information, no one more important than him died during that time. People argued, who besides him would be placed in the most honored of all locations?

Other details argued against the Vargas theory. Bruce Ellis described the remains of those of "a tall male."[199] Vargas's voluminous record never refers to him as a tall man. Research has indicated that he was around 5' 2" tall, rather average for his day.[200] Another detail noted in the MOIFA files as well as by historian John Kessell was that Vargas joined the Third Order of St. Francis while on his death bed. This indicated the high probability that he was buried in a blue Franciscan habit, as was customary for members of that lay Franciscan order.[201] An overlooked line of reasoning would be to investigate if the remains, when found, gave any evidence of a reburial. If Vargas's remains were relocated seven years after his death, they would have been mostly or completely decomposed. Maybe a review of the literature is necessary.

Aside from Boyd's conclusion that the suit belonged to don Rafael Sarrasino, a Chihuahua merchant who was forty years old when he died, much later, in 1797, the documentation is silent on the issue and the remains did not contain an identity.[202] Boyd also concluded that the price for conserving the suit would be prohibitive so the suit was put in storage for future research.

Not until 1985 when Donna Pierce, then the Spanish Colonial Curator at MOIFA, brought in David Richman from Connecticut and Edward Maeder, textile curator from the Los Angeles County Museum of Art to study the suit did they conclude that the suit dated from 1695 to 1700.[203] Nora Fisher, MOIFA's textile expert dated the suit to 1700-1750.[204] Around this time Nora Fisher brought Terri Schindel to the museum. Schindel, a graduate student in conservation at the University of London's Textile Centre at Hampton Court, was looking for a project and agreed to take on the study of the burial suit as a partial requirement for her degree. She could take one piece but funds would need to be found for the other two pieces. Dr. Pierce wrote three grants, one for each piece of the suit to raise the extra needed funds.[205]

The desire to conclude that the suit belonged to Vargas was tempting as research continued. Donna Pierce noted that Vargas's own inventory included many examples of clothes like the suit. In November 1987 Schindel took the suit to be x-rayed at the Los Alamos National Laboratory and the event was published in the newspaper.[206] Historians were consulted but nothing could be definitively established. The lack of any burial records from 1700 to 1726 proved to be a hurdle that could not be overcome.[207]

In London, Schindel worked on the suit until her graduation. After graduation, the suit was left for the staff conservators to finish the work. The task took a total of three years.

Of course, not all was pleasantry, for when Schindel began to moisturize the suit it began to smell "a skunk-like odor." This problem followed the suit back to New Mexico where the plan was to put it on exhibition. Charlene Cerny, the Director of MOIFA dashed off a memorandum to Claire Munzenrider, the Museum of New Mexico's chief conservator. That memo and Munzenrider's reply speak for themselves. Cerny wrote under the subject "Smell of death" and followed with,

> "The burial suit came back looking just peachy but the odor is [it] now has renders it a pariah to all staff and potential visitors. How can we even dream of exhibiting such a smelly thing?"[208]

Munzenrider replied with the subject heading,

"CRY! CRY! CRY! THE BURIAL SUIT SMELLS."

She followed with,

> "Today I read your memo about the smells of the burial suit. You are right it smells now and didn't smell (so much) before it went to England. WELL, according to Landis,[209] who has had some previous encounters with burial material, it is likely smelling because there is more moisture present which has activated bacteria and the "smell"...when it dries, the smell will go...."

Munzenrider recommended that several open boxes of baking soda be placed in the burial suit's storage trays. Robin Farwell Gavin, a curator of Spanish Colonial Collections, was given the task.[210] And it worked.

As planning for the exhibition progressed the staff had to suppress the urge to call it the "Vargas burial suit." Needless to say the exhibition stirred up public speculation about who belonged to the suit.[211] Fray Angélico Chávez, interviewed at a local restaurant and bar, vehemently and definitely denied that the burial was Vargas. Ethno-historian David Snow, who worked in the cathedral site, is quoted as saying that connecting the suit to Vargas "may be too far a leap."[212]

Scholars are left with the fact that someone of importance who lived around Vargas's time was buried before the recently completed church's main altar. But, another opportunity for research exists. This author was told that the suit included a cloth hat that was not conserved. It still has hair particles and very small bone fragments. Moreover, Schnidel removed hair and bone pieces from the suit and placed them in a container.[213] Descendents of the Vargas family live today in Madrid. There is a possibility that a DNA analysis can be done and thus, definitely determine whether or not Diego de Vargas´s grave had been found, only to have his bones summarily piled with the others to be deposited in a cement lined vault in Santa Fe's cathedral.[214]

In a final draft report about the burial suit Dr. Donna Pierce summed up the mystery as well as can be done. The "remarkable point" is, she wrote,

> "...not that learned men and women disagree about the mystery of don Diego's burial–but rather that almost three centuries after his death, they still are [concerned]. All in all, a more durable memorial than a tombstone or a shopping mall."[215]

Juan de Oñate and Diego de Vargas, arguably New Mexico's most famous governors, lived full, sometimes controversial lives. Each of them has a plethora of buildings and monuments in their respective names. Yet, to date, what became of their remains continues to intrigue students of history. The answer to these still mysterious and unanswered histories remains to be solved.

Part III

The Value of Sancho's Hindsight

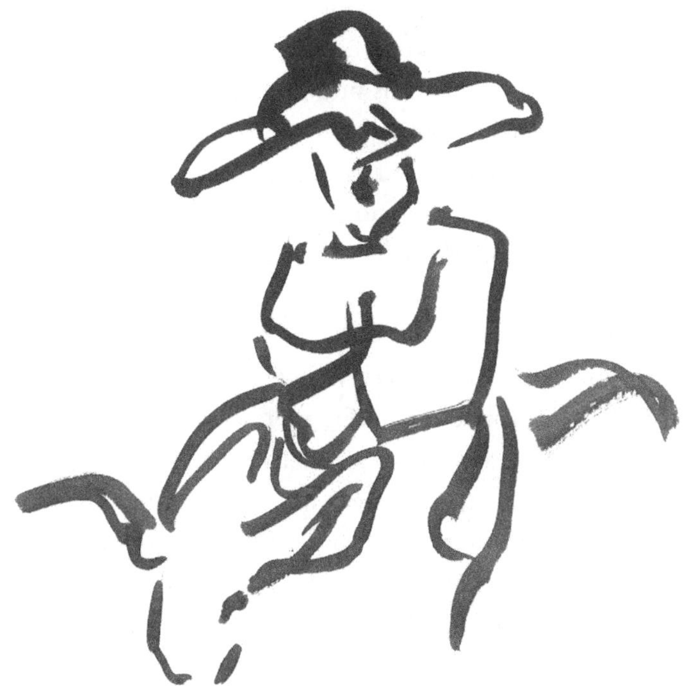

31
Relating to the genius and art of printing

Enamored by Don Quixote's unbounded enthusiasm for what the two of them were doing, Sancho Panza blithely stated,

> "I'll wager that before long there won't be a tavern, an inn, a Hostelry, or a barbershop where the history of our deeds isn't printed."[216]

Such, too, is the hope if not aspiration of any person, especially those who have become part of a cultural quest. For that matter, nearly everyone at some point in his or her life shares Sancho's thought. Unfortunately, more times than not Sancho would lose his bet.

One of the pleasures of working in cultural institutions like museums is that the task involves teamwork that usually is interdisciplinary. For example, the staffs at the Palace of the Governors and National Hispanic Cultural Center, where I worked, consisted of historians, poets, archaeologists, linguists, librarians, archivists, artists, and art historians. These varied professionals came together to create programs and share new information. All of these people strived to collect, preserve, and, especially, share knowledge. Based in the institutions' collections and their combined knowledge, they created projects that many times have had a lasting effect on society.

One specific outlet for sharing knowledge is books and this is where Pamela Smith, who ran the historic Print Shop at the Palace of the Governors, excelled. She dedicated her life to the art and technique of fine printing and bookmaking—and she succeeded. An intelligent boundless person, who is, above all, creative, Pam Smith was the perfect person for her job.

My predecessor Michael Weber deserves credit for hiring her and recognizing the potential of the Palace Print Shop program. Pam was a volunteer worker in a newly opened Print Shop exhibition at the Palace of the Governors. The idea for the exhibition germinated in 1960 and became reality in 1969 when the museum accepted a gift of all the printing equipment from the defunct *Estancia News Herald*, which had begun operations in the early 1900s and closed in the 1940s. The exhibition opened in 1970. That early gift along with existing collections and subsequent gifts led Weber to believe that the Print Shop needed an employee so he hired Pam Smith part-time. She soon became fulltime.

Pam was a writer and had worked in design. An appreciation of fine printing was a natural attraction.[217] The museum needed an educator who had the curiosity and intellectual capability to be able to work in a museum environment.

In Pam Smith, Weber hired someone who exceeded expectations. She took the original concept beyond anything anyone could imagine. She immediately recognized that the collections, the space, and the museum environment required something much more than an operating period print shop. She started a program that, at once, created a functional print shop and became a focus for the fine print and book arts world. She went to workshops and conferences to learn more of her new vocation. She first started printing postcards, exhibit labels, menus, and invitations. Then she reprinted replicas of old newspapers. Next she developed a series of limited edition works for which she oversaw the design, printing, and binding. In 1976 she issued the first of eleven of these finely printed works. Seven of them were recognized with a prestigious American Association of Museums design award.[218]

Pam brought in artists like Kirk Hughy and Sarah Laughlin and bookbinders like Priscilla Spitler and Carole Ronbinson. She trained volunteers and drew on the intellect of her colleagues as well as the public to produce a program unique in the country. Two of the Print Shop publications illustrate the above point about interdisciplinary museum work.

The museum had succeeded in purchasing a collection of old documents from a former teacher who lived in Peña Blanca. Mauro Montoya collected documents his whole life. Now, in the twilight of his life he wanted to sell his collection to the museum to supplement his retirement while being assured that his life's hobby would benefit future generations. He went to Orlando Romero Head Librarian of the Palace's history library who brought him to me. With the help of the Friends of the Palace, the state legislature appropriated $60,000 to purchase and care for the "Montoya Collection."[219]

The Palace's curator Diana Ortega DeSantis subsequently researched the collection in anticipation of an exhibition about eighteenth century New Mexico. She discovered a small, eight-page journal written from 1789 until 1818 by José Salaices, a New Mexico frontiersman. This attracted her interest for further research. She located Salaices's place-names and even found some of his descendents living in the Silver City area.

Diana shared her discovery and research with the staff. Pam thought that the journal would be a great candidate for one of the Print Shop's publications. She was right. Replete with Diana's annotations, including an essay, the limited edition publication went beyond information. The book's binding in handmade paper was a reproduction of an eighteenth century leather pouch, each of the journal's pages were reproduced, and the edition was enhanced with an illustration based on an original drawing of a Spanish colonial soldier. The latter was found on the cover of a eighteenth century prayer book that was also in the Palace's collections. Here was a one of a kind project that combined the artistic and technical talent of the print shop with the archival collections of the Palace and the expertise of a staff curator. The information was new and the publication was unique.[220]

The *New World Saints* project took five years to complete. The idea was to produce twenty-five hand colored prints of saints for each of 140 copies. Each illustration would have accompanying text giving that saint's history printed on letterpress. Galisteo Artist Catherine Ferguson[221] did the illustrations and Donna Pierce, who had become a curator at the Palace of the Governors and is an expert in the subject and iconography of Spanish colonial art, wrote the essays. Each saint was presented on a numbered paper triptych that was specially cut and embossed. Under the supervision of Bill Sneeberger, the "senior colorist,"[222] volunteers used a technique called *pochoir* to do the hand coloring.

The technique required a time consuming effort wherein a stencil was used to apply each color to each page by hand. The person charged with coloring sat at a table and used a thick, soft brush to tap the individual colors onto each page. The Palace staff and volunteers worked for two years coloring the illustrations.[223] In total, they hand-colored 3,900 triptychs.[224] I remember walking by the Print Shop on many occasions and hearing the tap, tap, tap, of staff and volunteers as they applied the colors to the pages. To say that Pam Smith had conveyed her dedication and enthusiasm to a loyal group of volunteers is an understatement.

Aside from creating limited edition, collector's works, Pam taught in the schools as well as in the museum. She and her staff taught printing, paper making, bookbinding, marbling, etc. From 1980 until 1984 the Print Shop hosted and put on the Annual Book Arts Festival. Pam recognized her good fortune:

> "From a privileged vantage point—proprietress of a working historic print shop at the state museum—I acquired a wealth of inspiration and information from a steady flow of museum visitors."[225]

While she learned from her "visitors," she inspired them as well. She encouraged Willard Clark to revive working with his woodcuts after a thirty some year hiatus.[226] She featured his work in the Annual Book Arts Festival, had him produce the festival poster, and then do the artwork for a1986 publication of a Lawrence Clark Powell lecture.[227] Powell delivered his keynote lecture at the Palace on 13 September 1984 for the Annual Book Arts Festival.[228] He was a legendary bibliophile, author, librarian, teacher, and champion of the literary arts. Putting Willard Clark and Lawrence Clark Powell together in the same limited edition publication was an act of genius.

As a member of the staff Pam helped plan for the new museum. Staff and architects concluded that a gallery would be dedicated to exhibitions about printing that would have a hands-on component. The new gallery would free up the print shop to become, as it was originally intended, a working period print shop. However, as time passed and because of a need for further fund raising and planning, Pam was hired out of retirement to curate her first planned exhibition for the new museum and have it installed in the Palace of the Governors. That exhibition along with a Museum of New Mexico Press book that she wrote to accompany the exhibition, was appropriately named *Passions in Print: Private Press Artistry in New Mexico, 1834-Present*. Because of her genius and leadership, the Palace Press led a revival of fine printing in New Mexico. Today the Palace Press, operated by Tom Leach, Pam's preferred successor, is New Mexico's longest continually operating fine printing establishment.[229]

32
In which is demonstrated another example of spending time with an elder

Charles Bennett and I had been exposed to book publishing from different sources. The Palace Print Shop taught us the value of a finely crafted book. Our friend Jim Mafchir, who directed the Museum of New Mexico Press, exposed us to the business of book publishing. Eventually, Jim published my first book. Charles and I served on the Board of Directors of the Historical Society of New Mexico (HSNM) that had made an agreement with the University of New Mexico Press to publish HSNM sanctioned books. The Historical Society wanted to publish its own series that focused on history and expose books that had little chance of being published otherwise. The UNM Press agreed to publish the books that the society selected if it could partially underwrite the cost of each book.

The HSNM series provided us with the opportunity to encourage former Palace of the Governors curator Bruce Ellis to finish a study that he had been working on for years but, in later life, he decided that no one would be interested in it. He was in his late seventies and into his early eighties when we met him. Although he had trouble breathing and used oxygen, his mental alertness, humor, and curiosity belittled his physical health and age. A tall, dignified, balding man, he was a gentleman in every sense. He took pleasure in subsequent generations of museum workers coming to him for information. He enjoyed teaching and sharing information as he sat his desk, a 1850s U. S. Army quartermaster's desk that came from Fort Marcy in Santa Fe.[230]

Charles Bennett, Diana DeSantis, and I visited him on a regular basis. We gleaned information from him about the Palace's collections, its institutional history, and history in general. On occasions we tape-recorded him. We constantly encouraged him to finish writing his manuscript on the history of the old church that preceded Santa Fe's cathedral and how the cathedral came to be constructed. Mr. Ellis was an archaeologist who had been a part of most of the excavations in and around the cathedral. As noted earlier, he was there when construction workers uncovered graves in the floor. He was there when the burial that may or may not be Diego de Vargas was found and he was there with Father Chávez when the stone crypts containing the colonial Franciscans were discovered. He had a wealth of information that needed to be shared.

Charles and I assured him that we could get his manuscript published but he had to finish it first. With our encouragement, and the support of his wife Florence Ellis, a renowned archaeologist in New Mexico, he pulled out his notes with a partially completed manuscript and started working. When he finished his manuscript, he handed it to Charles and me. After carefully reading it, we took it to the Historical Society and they quickly agreed to include it in their series. The University of New Mexico Press did a fine job and Bruce Ellis's book came out under the title of *Bishop Lamy's Santa Fe Cathedral with the Records of the Old Spanish Church (Parroquia) and Convent Formerly on the Site.* Mr. Ellis received advance copies of his book within weeks before his death. The book is an invaluable historical source and still is the definitive work on the church called the *parroquia* that preceded the cathedral.[231]

Not all goes according to plan, for I accepted the honor of writing a foreword in which I praised Ellis for taking "every opportunity to complete archaeological surveys before the bulldozer...." He did this, I wrote, "along with colleagues Stanly Stubbs and Walt Chapman,"[232] to which Ellis replied, "who is this Chapman? I never worked with him." Much to my chagrin, I had made a mistake and dampened the otherwise joyous occasion of presenting the advance copies of his book to him.

Of course, as mentioned earlier, Bruce Ellis left the Palace of the Governors a legacy through his collection of New Mexican artifacts. When, after his death, his wife and Andrea Dodge, his step-daughter, telephoned us to arrange to pick up the collection we already knew that we needed to rent a large truck for the task. Bruce Ellis lives on in his papers, his book, and his gift. He is, at once, part of our heritage and a reason for why we know more about that heritage. His quest was not for naught.

33
On how historical novels serve history

It seems that we will never be satisfied with how well we can share history with the general public. To be a historian who believes that the subject is a life's vocation, the challenge of attracting the general public to history is a lifelong pursuit. Combine that task with working at a history museum, then, trying to capture the public's imagination looms even larger.

Our experience with Pam Smith, the Historical Society's publication efforts, and the Museum of New Mexico Press, gave Charles and me an idea. Why not identify out-of-print historical novels, have the staff approve them for their relative accuracy and re-publish them? The idea probably came up in one of the Friday afternoon seminars and the reasoning went as follows. Historians are notorious sourpusses at the movies. They are the people who cry out that "they didn't wear zippers" or point out some other mundane Hollywood inaccuracy that nobody cares about. Yet, we have to admit that movies are one way to attract people to history. The concepts of entertainment and education are not contrary. They can complement each other. For example, a person watches a favorite program on television without taking notes yet can cite in detail the names, events, even story lines of that show. Their brain retained something from the entertainment. Naturally, we felt, if a history museum's education can be packaged through different forms of entertaining programs like exhibitions, demonstrations, and so on, then we will attract people to our mission.

Of course, making a movie was way beyond our capacity for all kinds of reasons. However, Charles and I reasoned why not historical novels? Based from our own experiences as avid readers, we felt that historical novels could be another way to "get the word out." We broached the idea to the Friends of the Palace. Technically, the project would be theirs. Through the foundation they would have to pay for the initial publication. If all worked well, the revenues from book's sales would pay for the expenses and any excess would go into the Palace's endowment.

The Friends agreed to the idea and designated Doc Weaver to work with the staff to get the program going. Either in anticipation or over confident, we already had our first book recommendation. We presented *The Royal City* by Les Savage, Jr. This was an easy reading novel about life in Santa Fe set in the decades before the 1680 Pueblo Revolt. The Friends approved our choice.

Doc Weaver, who had designed the tile wall for the library, had become a fan of José Cisneros's artwork. He wondered whether Cisneros would also agree to let us use his talents to adorn the cover of our first book. Cisneros was flattered and agreed to come up with a new piece for the cover. Doc got to work. He arranged for the printing, design, and all the proper Library of Congress information. The first historical novel came out under the publisher's name of the Friends of the Palace Press.[233] Then the problem of distribution came.

Another member of the Friends, Mary Noel, volunteered to handle the job. She was as an energetic woman as ever existed. With books in hand, she combed Santa Fe and convinced businesses of all kinds to sell the book. Of course, our biggest outlet was our own museum shop, which sold to an ever-expanding group of Palace of the Governors supporters. The three thousand edition run of *The Royal City* sold out within two years.

For our second publication, Charles recommended Walter O'Meara's 1954 novel

The Spanish Bride. Unlike the first book, this book's author was still alive. He lived out-of-state and Charles befriended him through correspondence. He was over ninety years old and expressed surprise as well as appreciation at our interest in re-publishing his book. He did not hesitate to agree to our proposal and was pleased to donate all royalties to the Palace of the Governors.

O'Meara's novel appealed to us because it was a story about the 1720 Pedro de Villasur expedition that ended in the ambush depicted in the recently arrived Segesser Paintings. In the process of writing his story O'Meara obviously did some serious research on the expedition and its ambush at the confluence of the Platte and Loup Rivers. He never saw the Segesser II painting that depicts the battle but he described its subject matter perfectly. His detail was very accurate.

Charles had come up with a gem for our second Friends of the Palace publication. Here was a connection to the history of an actual artifact and work of art that we had acquired for the state. This was another way to interest people in the Segesser Paintings.

O'Meara liked the project for a personal reason. His book featured a fictional woman he named Josefina María del Carmen Torres who sneaked herself on the Villasur expedition to Nebraska. She had fallen in love with the expedition's leader, the young dashing Pedro de Villasur, and decided to follow him onto the plains. O'Meara's last letter to us expressed his feeling that of all the fictitious characters that he had created in his many stories, Josefina stood out to him "most vividly—still a figure of absolute reality, an object of almost true-life affection...and so it is with a special kind of gratitude that I welcome Josefina's return, in this new edition of *The Spanish Bride*, to enchant a new generation of readers."[234] He continued that he thought it fitting that the Palace of the Governors was publishing the book, for that was "the very place in which Josefina played out her beautiful albeit tragic destiny." Mr. O'Meara died two weeks after writing that letter. He never saw the new issue of his book. Nevertheless, we had brought a bit of joy and satisfaction to a creative person in the last days of his life; and his legacy continues to benefit us all. We decided to publish his letter intact in the book where it appears under the heading of "Author's Note."[235] Truly, though, the pleasure was ours.

The third novel was *The Lady from Toledo* by Fray Angélico Chávez (now in a new edition from Sunstone Press) that told the story about the Virgin of the Macana. Like O'Meara, Fray Angélico was still alive and I was assigned the task of seeking his permission to publish the book and allow us to keep the royalties for the Palace of the Governors' endowment. As mentioned, he was my uncle and had a very big influence on me becoming a historian. To me he was a giant always watching the progress, or not, of my career. At this time, he was living at the rectory next to Santa Fe's cathedral and had retired as an active priest. He was a medium height, slender man who was brilliant, direct and, at many times, blunt. He was not prone to praising others. His approval came in nuances, with barely a passing word or gesture.

At that time, the Friends, staff and I had done much to win his pleasure. Upon our submission and backing, the Museum of New Mexico Press had re-published two of his other books in very handsome editions. The first of these was perhaps his most popular book *Origins of New Mexico Families.* This was a fourth edition of the original first published in 1954.[236] I was privileged to write a new introduction and we added a large addendum of additional genealogical material that Fray Angélico published in *El Palacio Magazine* after the first edition of his book.[237] Then, the following year, we convinced the Museum of New Mexico Press to publish *My Penitente Land: Reflections on Spanish New Mexico* (now in a new edition from Sunstone Press), which is a historical essay about New Mexico and, perhaps, was his most beautifully written book. Father Thomas Steel, a Jesuit priest and historian, wrote a nice foreword in which he described Fray Angélico as "this devil's advocate with the name of an angel."[238]

We showed him the first two novels that we had published and asked if he would agree to his novel becoming our third effort. We knew that his novel was based on real research from an article that he published in the *New Mexico Historical Review.* We shared with him our idea that we wanted to add his footnoted article as an addendum to his book. The idea really pleased him and he agreed to have the book re-published. Our publication of his novel and article illustrated exactly why we decided to publish historical novels. Fray Angélico, the poet and historian, clearly understood the value of a historical novel in getting history to a wider audience.

34
Relating to a personal history and writing

The idea for the book you are reading came out of a three hour lecture that I organized and gave.[239] I realized that the topic(s) could make for an interesting book as well as serve a number of purposes. Aside from getting things off my chest, events could be recalled that had been forgotten or otherwise miss-represented. Many people who sallied forth to make a positive impact had been overlooked. I also realized during the lecture that an underlying philosophy of what being a steward of culture is all about and that the seemingly but not really thankless tasks matter. Then, as in all human endeavors, there is humor.

Just as a lecture inspired this book, there are stories behind all other books published through the ages. Books always have stories behind the stories. Hints of this have surfaced in some of the stories already related but it is one thing to get someone else published and another thing to see your own name in print. As we worked with Pamela Smith, Bruce Ellis, Doc Weaver, and many others to publish books, I endeavored to write and publish my own history books. I also encouraged staff and colleagues to write and publish. The intelligence and information of the people with whom I had the pleasure to work is astounding and I always thought that they should share.

At least as much as my other life's experiences, the experience of my employment in cultural institutions has influenced my publications. In some cases the germ of an idea came from my colleagues as well as the experience of doing exhibitions.

The most obvious of these behind the scene stories is the process of actually doing the book from the initial idea and research, to the organization, writing, editing, publication, and, even, marketing. Every book is a journey and, like every journey, each book varies in its making. To be sure, the process is educational, can be aggravating even frustrating, scary and, when finished, can be very satisfying as well as embarrassing.

I say embarrassing rather than disappointed, for like every author, I tend to get impatient toward the end. The work is so long and tedious, that, as a result, the wait to see it in print is almost unbearable. After all the time and effort, the author does not want the manuscript checked one last time. By then the manuscript is too familiar to the author for him or her to be impartial. Besides, there is the assumption that the press has already done a thorough editing job.

Invariably, the book will come out with mistakes. The overall work is there. The intent is there. But, also there, are those errors. One of my publications repeated a long sentence in successive paragraphs.[240] In another book, I misread a Spanish word in a document that I had reproduced in the book. In the caption, I misread the Spanish word "*linda*," or "good looking," instead of correctly writing that the word was "*viuda*" or "widow."[241] The same book, published in hardback, misprinted the title on its spine. The book is a biography of Manuel Alvarez but the printer has it as "Manual," which, I suppose is a play on the old bi-lingual joke about the Hispanic worker with the name "Manual Labor." Fortunately, the dust cover has the correct spelling and most people have not noticed the error much less confronted me with the blame. In another book, some photographs were printed sideways. When it came to what I consider my most important book, the governor of New Mexico received a copy of an irate letter complaining that the captions of two of the photographs were incorrect. Actually, I reversed the catalogue numbers of the artifacts in the photographs, and the erroneous captions followed.[242]

But why copy a letter to the governor over a matter of such relative insignificance given the overall message of the book? Actually had Governor Bill Richardson, who ran for President of the United States in 2007, paid any attention and read the book he could have used it during a nationally televised presidential debate on Univisión. When all the presidential candidates were asked to name one important Hispanic contribution to the United States, Bill Richardson named a political colleague, Frederico Pena, the former mayor of Denver and cabinet secretary under Bill Clinton. Richardson missed the chance of startling a national Hispanic audience with "the birth of this nation."[243] He was given a copy of the book, some of his top aids had read it, and he had received the above mentioned complaint about it. Oh well, he had already demonstrated with his autobiography that research was not his strength.[244]

The book on Spain's role in U. S. independence had some footnotes out-of-order and I mistakenly miss-cited two documents from the Spanish Archives of New Mexico. I correctly cited the microfilm but failed to notice that the citation did not correspond to the actual documents. Fortunately, in these last two cases I was able to make the corrections in the subsequent editions of the book.

My more recent book was no exception. I kept a list of corrections and improvements in anticipation of a second edition. For example, I wrote about the Apaches who periodically traveled to Pecos Pueblo to trade. The walled pueblo conducted all trade with Plains People on a level piece of land outside of the fortified village. For some reason, I wrote that the location where business took place was on the "west" side of the pueblo. Actually, the trade fairs occurred east of the pueblo. This is a small matter that only a very few studious and knowing readers would catch, but this was an error that I found embarrassing. The error needed to be corrected in the subsequent edition. Otherwise, I could have gone down in posterity as the fool who did not know on which side of Pecos Pueblo the trade fairs took place. Worse, still, is that some reader, some student, will read that section and repeat the error as truth. Publishing history is, in its way, scary. There is, as Cervantes claimed, a responsibility for truth. There is a reason that many aspiring historians research and never publish. Conversely, does anyone really believe that the novelist Willa Cather let facts get in the way of her story about nineteenth century Santa Fe Bishop Jean B. Lamy?

My boss Tom Livesay once told me that a person could not make a career out of both administration and writing. He was not criticizing me rather than offering some constructive advice, for I was a young director and he wanted me to concentrate more on my administrative duties and, thus, I suppose, become less of a headache to him. I politely listened and noted the sentiment but there was no way that I would stop researching and writing.

I harkened to the words of Dr. Myra Ellen Jenkins (1916–1993), who was New Mexico's State Historian for many years. I had the pleasure of knowing and learning from her. She even became a member of the Friends of the Palace. Revered in her day, she was an archivist, an advocate, and an activist who sat on many boards and commissions. She appeared in court as an expert witness on many occasions. In short, she spent a lifetime chasing history. Yet, when asked what she was or when introduced with many accolades, she always stated that she was a historian and nothing more. That was not an embellished statement. She was a historian, period. I admired that single purpose of mind. As a historian, her many accomplishments proliferated and continue to do so today. I, too, am a historian. As such, Tom Livesay's well-intentioned advice fell on deaf ears.

Many years later when I unsuccessfully applied for the very job that Livesay held, I was told that one of the search committee members opinioned that I was a lousy administrator. Maybe, despite myself, Tom Livesay was correct.

35
About Manuel Alvarez and a new experience

Tom Livesay's advice was given to me after I had published my first two books, both based on my dissertation. The first book was published by the Museum of New Mexico Press. If the truth be known, I believe that my friend Jim Mafchir, who directed the press at the time, did me a favor. The book was not intended to be published first but rather was an off-shoot of my PhD dissertation. In researching the life of Manuel Alvarez, a nineteenth century native of Spain who moved to New Mexico and became a Santa Fe Trail merchant, mountain man, United States Consul, and political activist, I discovered a thirty-two page handwritten memorial about New Mexico and the Santa Fe Trail that he wrote in 1842 and sent to Daniel Webster, the Secretary of State of the United States of America.[245]

Alvarez complained about the mistreatment of U. S. citizens, including himself, under the Mexican administration in New Mexico. At the time, the governor's nephew nearly succeeded in killing Alvarez, who, as U. S. Consul, was a diplomat for the United States. After being slashed down his face by a knife, he was saved by the Mexican secretary of government. Nonetheless, the insistent Alvarez wanted to make sure that Webster, the Secretary of State, understood what was going on in New Mexico. Initially, Alvarez intended to confront Webster personally but his small party was caught in a major blizzard while crossing the Great Plains. Three of the nine men who were with him died. All of them suffered some form of frost bite. If not for Alvarez leaving his companions to get to the eastern settlements and secure help, all of them would have perished.

Thus, while recuperating in St. Louis, Alvarez penned his memorial and meticulously footnoted and attached copies of the cited letters to his document. He sent it on to Daniel Webster. Writing out of the bitterness of his experience and Washington's almost total lack of concern for the plight of U. S. citizens in northern Mexico, he related a detailed account of problems that U. S. citizens where having with the Mexican government. Such abuse would end, he wrote, only when the State Department interceded.

Alvarez soon followed the memorial to Washington, DC where he insisted and succeeded on having a meeting with the contemptuous and famous Daniel Webster. Alvarez's audacity and his memorial intrigued me so I decided to annotate it and have it published. Jim Mafchir took a great risk and agreed to produce the book. He hired another friend of ours who, at the time was an employee at the Palace Print Shop to do the cover illustration. Kurt Hughey was an accomplished artist and came up with a perfect drawing for the cover. The original hangs in my house today.

Thus my first book was published as a small edition of less than a thousand copies. The whole publication amounted to ninety pages and was given a convoluted title. Machir put it out in hardback and it looked great. Like any first-time author, the book looked like a best-seller to me.[246]

Alvarez's full biography did not get published so easily. The University of New Mexico Press had the manuscript. Luther Wilson, the director of that press, had asked for it and publication seemed eminent. However, because of the unfortunate combination of Wilson leaving the press and a separate manuscript that I submitted to the press, UNM never published Alvarez's story.

36

Alvarez continued, an illustrated history, and the problems of publishing

At that time, Luther Wilson was a medium sized, big-boned man with an understated sense of humor whose prowess as a director of university publishing houses might be surpassed only by his enthusiasm for fly-fishing. A proactive searcher for new manuscripts for his press, Wilson came to my office one day to ask if I would approach Dr. Richard Rudisill with the idea of doing a photographic history of New Mexico. Dr. Rudisill, as noted earlier, was the Palace of the Governors' photographic historian. He was a genius in his field and I still consider him the foremost historian of photography of the western United States. He was a natural choice for such a book. As usual, Luther Wilson had a great idea.

Dr. Rudisill, while appreciative of the request, had too much work with the photographic archives and an ongoing collaborative compilation of international photographers and collections to embark on a new book. Ever gracious, he suggested that I do the book and he would help with the selection of photographs. I became intrigued with this idea. Wilson thought that I was a good second option and he convinced me to proceed.

Very soon thereafter, Dr. Rudisill, who was always Dick or Richard to me, came to me with an idea that he had gleaned from another work. He thought that I should collect words as well as imagery of yesteryear, combine the two with brief introductions to historical periods and let that stand in the eye of the beholder as New Mexico's history. In other words, let the reader and/or viewer draw his or her own conclusions.

Simply put, he suggested that I put together a book in much the same way museum exhibitions were done. I should compile a book of images of people, artifacts, art, old maps, scenes, etc., with captions and some narrative. The new emphasis would be quotes taken from the people who lived at particular times in New Mexico's history. I saw it as analogous to baroque music, which I described in the book's introduction. In giving Rudisill credit I wrote that, "we created a book of melodic lines, each interesting in its own train of thought, that together create a harmony of the whole, permitting the reader/listener's mind to make its own connections." "[T]he quotes, if read alone, will tell a tale that, like a melodic line, will complement another melodic line created by the photographic images," that will complement a third line of narrative. "At times these lines may touch or cross, but they will always harmonize, for the score is about New Mexico."[247] Here was a book that would stimulate readers into making their own connections and discoveries.

Over time the manuscript was completed and submitted to the press. Meanwhile, Luther Wilson left the University of New Mexico to take a more lucrative job at Syracuse University Press. The editors at UNM made suggestions to improve the manuscript's selection of images, which I dutifully fulfilled. Then a letter arrived from one of the Press's assistant editors. The letter stated that UNM Press had decided to reevaluate "old agreements" and they were no longer interested in publishing the "Illustrated History." The message that stood out to me was the editor's sentiment that he and the governing board did not believe that readers could think for themselves. He noted that the press had "always been concerned about the connections between a brief text and a long section of photographs and the accompanying captions" and that "nothing less than a text of at least 150 pages" was needed. He conveniently overlooked the voluminous quotes that keyed the whole manuscript. Obviously, he did not like our baroque approach.[248] An incensed, hurt author that I can be, I asked not only for the illustrated history manuscript but also the Alvarez biography. I did not want a university press that could not imagine readers thinking for themselves to publish my books. So here I sat, a beginning, unheard of historian with two complete manuscripts and no publishers.

I shopped the Alvarez manuscript to different university presses thus beginning a rather thick and still growing collection of refusal letters. The University of Oklahoma, Texas A & M, and the University of Arizona presses, among others, turned down the manuscript. I did not know where to go with the illustrated history. Perhaps a local privately owned press would be best suited for it.

Luckily, Wilson, who was corresponding with me, had moved to a new challenge to restart and reinvigorate the University Press of Colorado. Ever in search for new manuscripts, he asked for both of mine. The biography of Alvarez came out in 1990 as my second book and the illustrated history was published in 1992 as a hardback that was quickly followed by a paperback edition. Ten years later, after Luther Wilson moved back to the University of New Mexico Press, *The Illustrated History* came "home" to be published once again. The book had gone full circle. It has gone through three editions and the last edition has had two printings. The book is still in print today.

37
Concerning a preposterous idea or when history can go awry

The consequences of writing history can take on many manifestations. As a graduate student I looked forward to being cited in a footnote by another historian. Then, I learned that publications meant more invitations to speak on the topics of the books. This resulted in immediate book sales that led to the best compliment of all; when I was asked to sign my books. Maybe this harkened back to my youth when I imagined myself a professional baseball player giving out autographs, for I always took such a request as a personal compliment that I had to repay with my signature and an inscription. In addition, as historian Marc Simmons once instructed me, I made sure to put the date and city/location of the signing. He even told me which page to sign; the title page with the author's name.

Other outcomes of publishing have been varied. The *Spain and the United States Independence* book went through two hardback and one paperback editions as well as a Spanish edition.[249] It also inspired my involvement with the publication of a pamphlet designed for high school and middle school students[250] and had something to do with inspiring a couple of subsequent books, an exhibition at the Smithsonian Institution, and a number of conferences. The book even gave rise to a gift to the Palace of the Governors of a rare portrait of one the of story's participants. The portrait, in turn, was used on the cover of a biography of that historical figure that was published in Spain.[251]

While, as mentioned, *The Illustrated History* is still in print, my first two books never had second printings after limited runs. Nevertheless, they did get attention, for they have fulfilled my graduate school ambition of being cited in numerous publications. They also became the basis for a whole chapter in a book about Manuel Alvarez's home town of Abelgas, in the region of Leon in Spain. Historian Román Álvarez, a distant relative of Manuel and who teaches at the University of Salamanca, became aware of my work through Elizabeth West, then a librarian in Santa Fe's Public Library. While on a trip to Spain, she went to Abelgas to see Manuel Alvarez's home village. In the process of her visit, she met Román and told him about my books. The rest, as is said, is history.

Román Álvarez did some additional research on this heretofore unknown son of Abelgas. As a historian, he has a passion for his field and appreciates the work of his colleagues. In the course of writing his book he used my work but he also had access to archives and records that I did not. Thus he found Manuel Alvarez's birth certificate in which the actual date of his birth was given. I had used secondary information that never gave a specific day or month to surmise that Alvarez was born in 1794. The new information had him born on March 29, 1796! I had missed the date by two years and even included the error in the biography's title![252] Nonetheless, this and other family information excited me as a historian.

Elizabeth West had put Román Álvarez in touch with me and we corresponded, always with the intent of getting together sometime but, to date, we have missed connections sometimes within an hour of each other. We shared a mutual pleasure with his discovery of Manuel Alvarez's baptism certificate and the publication of his book. He sent me two copies and, as fate would have it, I will have the opportunity to incorporate his new information in an upcoming publication of the Spanish translation of my biography of Alvarez in Valencia, Spain.

This is how history should work; historians learning and building on each other's work. If, as stated earlier in this book, the work of a historian has value, then the historian's efforts must be shared to benefit others.

But there are odd quirks. Whereas historians must be as accurate as humanly possible, they, too, must draw conclusions and propose questions and hypothesis. But these subjective stances still must be "absolutely free of passions" to repeat Cervantes.[253] This is the area where many fail, for historians, like journalists, fall into the abyss of trying to "scoop" one another. This kind of competitive one-up-man-ship is not good for history. The result is that historians start treating each other snidely. Criticism or the correcting previous as well as contemporary histories, becomes less constructive as well as condescending.

One such example came from a friend and former museum supporter in whose house the Friends of the Palace began. Mary Jane Cook, while not a trained historian, loves history and can be a determined researcher. She began by writing a very well- received book about Santa Fe's Loretto Chapel and, in the process, has become interested in the history of the Santa Fe Trail.[254] In a short article written for a Santa Fe Trail newsletter, she concluded that my account of Alvarez's burial was completely erroneous. She had very little substantive evidence to support her position. Instead, she posited an unsubstantiated theory in which Alvarez was secretly practicing Judaism, had family in Mexico and, therefore, when he died, his body was taken from the priest in Santa Fe who recorded his burial. His remains were pickled in whisky in a lead coffin, and transported on a very long overland trip from Santa Fe, New Mexico to Monterrey, Mexico. Upon its arrival, the body was dutifully taken out of its preservative and, under authority of a different priest, whipped before burial.[255]

Ms. Cook subsequently wrote and published a biography of one of Manuel Alvarez's nineteenth century contemporaries in which she brought up the same story with a slight nuance and different basis. The nuance is that she cited her earlier article as the source for the story while the undocumented claim of the whipping of Manuel Alvarez's body is presented as *fait accompli.* "Even more extraordinary are the facts surrounding the mysterious burial and lashing of Alvarez's body in Monterrey," she writes. Then, she follows with the caveat of, "The details of the covert burial and postmortem lashing presently remain unknown."[256] Her footnote for this assertion explains that she traveled to Monterrey and found a grave of a Manuel Alvarez. She was unable to attain definitive burial dates. This is the basis of her theory "despite Thomas Chávez's hypothesis in his biography."[257]

However, without any explanation, she changed the reason why this bizarre event took place. In the second account, the body was lashed because Alvarez may have been a "*hermano*, or member, of a flagellant brotherhood in Spain or New Mexico." She does this without any comment about her previous assertion that Alvarez's body was whipped because he was a secret Jew. This is quite a religious swing coming from a historian who has no evidence to back either position. Aside, from her rather unfortunate description of the very religious Hermanos Penitentes, she also offers no evidence that the Penitentes whip the bodies of their dead.[258]

The problem with this kind of "history" is that it sucks in the denigrated party and distracts attention from true, well-done history. When the dust is settled, nothing has changed except that the bereaved historian must reply or imply the truth of the undocumented theory by his or her silence. That person is forced to do what historians should avoid.

Miguel Cervantes reacted to an anonymous author who wrote a sequel to the first part of his *Don Quixote.* The false *Quixote* was published while Cervantes worked on his own sequel that became the second part of the novel. He confronted his nemisses with a "Prologue to the Reader" that he inserted before the second part. Appropriately enough, he ended that prologue with a statement that could apply to Manuel Alvarez.

> "Don Quixote who is, at the end, dead and buried, so that no one will dare tell more tales about him, for the ones told in the past are enough...."[259]

38
Concerning Spain's role in the independence of the United States and a new career path

As a beginning curator I had just received my PhD and the two Alvarez manuscripts mentioned in the previous chapter were well in process. Thus, I was an aspiring author at the start of a museum career.

I spent a good deal of time foraging through the Palace of the Governors' uncatalogued room. This was a room in the basement of the old Santa Fe armory building that contained all the artifacts that had not been catalogued. One day I came upon a box that contained three-hand painted silk banners with a typed letter from the Spanish embassy in Washington, DC. The letter stated in Spanish that the banners were copies of original regimental banners of Spanish contingents that had fought British soldiers in the United States' war of independence. The banners were given to the State of New Mexico by the government of Spain as gifts in commemoration of the bicentennial of the birth of the

United States. The Spanish government made gifts of the reproduced banners to all the states of the United States that had been a part of the Spanish empire.

As a recent graduate with a doctorate in history whose field of study was the Spanish Borderlands, which is to say, the study of northern Mexico and the Southwestern United States from the first Spanish explorations to the present, I was surprised. I had studied and been tested in United States history as well as Latin American history. Yet, I had not heard or read of Spain's involvement in the revolution that resulted in the independence of the United States. I was intrigued.

On a camping trip to the Rio Grande Gorge in northern New Mexico with Charles Bennett, I divulged to him that I wanted to pursue the subject and, possibly, write a book. His favorable response solidified my enthusiasm for the idea: he said that he would like to read a book on the subject. I knew that most of the research eventually would be done in Spain. Soon thereafter I was sent to the Smithsonian Institution's Museum of American History to work with Richard Ahlborn on an exhibition that he was organizing in conjunction with the division of Community Life at the Library of Congress. The exhibition was about cowboys in the Paradise Valley of northern Nevada, which is another story that will be described further in this book.

I spent the summer of 1982 in Washington, DC working with and under Ahlborn. The experience was a great learning opportunity for me. I used that opportunity to go to the National Archives to do some initial research, actually "checking," on the role of Spain in the birth of the United States.

I walked into an area where I explained to a receptionist what I was looking for and, after checking in my bag, I was sent to a second area. There an archivist asked about the subject of my research and shot back an answer that Spain was not involved in the "Revolutionary War." By then, a personal survey of some secondary sources had revealed some information for me to share with the archivist. This resulted in a plethora of information being brought to me by more than one interested archivist. We found a short letter book of Brigadier General Edward Hand in which he gave a partial account of Captain James Willing and his journey down the Mississippi River on his ship, the "Rattletrap," to receive covert supplies from the Spanish officials in New Orleans.[260] I followed my research at the National Archives with a visit to the Library of Congress where I was provided with secondary sources but nothing original.

I knew that I was on to something. Upon my return to New Mexico, my friend Roger Snodgrass became interested in my project. Roger is a pleasant round-faced man with a head of very curly hair. He was a filmmaker and became a member of the Friends of the Palace. Snodgrass and his film company, Sanjak Productions, had just finished a film on the signing of peace in Versailles and Paris in 1783. This was the treaty that ended the

Revolutionary War and granted the United States its independence. The film had actors, was shot in the Versailles Palace, used a narration, and was accurate to a point. The story was based on the classic and, at the time, considered definitive book by Richard Morris titled *The Peacemakers.* What was missing, of course, was the Spanish view, for while Morris and, then, Snodgrass had Spain's ambassador the Duke of Aranda present as one of the negotiators as well as a signatory to the treaty, he and his country did not get a full or balanced treatment.[261]

Snodgrass showed his film at a special gathering in the townhouse that Charles Bennett and I shared. We asked if he could do a preview at the Palace of the Governors and Snodgrass readily agreed. The film was shown to a full house in the Palace. I was, and still am, very impressed with Snodgrass.

He thought that my project would make an interesting film.[262] With my permission, for he was very careful not to tread on someone else's territory, he drafted a request for funds for the film. His written narrative and approach to the subject was beautiful. The film was never done for lack of funding but I used Snodgrass's prose as the basis for my narrative in a Fulbright Research Grant application.

Then, one day, I was surprised to receive a Western Union telegram. This preceded e-mail or even, as I recall, regular access to fax machines. The telegram came from the Fulbright people and, at once, announced and congratulated me for being selected as one of the Fulbright Research recipients for 1987.[263]

I read the missive twice and did not know how to react. Could this be true? I have friends who would arrange to have such a telegram sent to me just to see my reaction and to take advantage of the remote possibility that I might want to celebrate with them at my expense. I telephoned the local Western Union offices to verify the origins of the telegram. Only then did I begin to feel the pleasure, the ecstasy of having been awarded a Fulbright Fellowship. I was going to Spain to do research on Spain and "the American Revolution," as I called it then. Not only that, but the fellowship helped pay for family to travel as well. In this case, I would take my two young daughters Nicolasa and Christel. The experience would be life-changing experiences for us all.

39
Relating to a different definition of "American"

In January 1987, my two daughters and I boarded a plane and headed to Spain. *The Albuquerque Journal* noted that we were on a mission to "...spend most of 1987 in Spain doing research for a book on a forgotten part of American history."[264]

But there was more, for, in the next ten months I would meet my wife Celia in the Archives of the Indies and make lifelong friends and contacts that would change my life in diverse ways. I would spend quality time with my daughters and unknowingly plant the seeds of ideas that are still bearing fruit. And, all the while, I would do enough research to begin forming my most important book.

There is an old saying that "travel is an education." I would add that "travel is an opportunity" as well. In fact, education creates opportunity.

I planned to spend ten months in Spain. The first eight months would be in Seville where I already knew that the preponderance of material dealing with Spain's role in the American Revolution was housed in the Archives of the Indies. My parents, who had retired to the fishing village of Roquetas de Mar outside of Almería, met us in Seville. They had located and reserved an apartment in the Remedios neighborhood. I was left with finding a school for the girls, opening a bank account, and supplying the apartment with the necessaries.

Then I went to the Archive of the Indies, which was located in the old sixteenth century *Lonja*, that housed the Casa de Contratación, the institution through which passed all of Spain's commerce as well as passengers going to and from the Americas. The archive is located next to Seville's famous cathedral. In the eighteenth century Carlos III converted this institution into "el Archivo General de Indias," which is to say the place where all the documents pertinent to the Americas would be housed and preserved. Every scholar of southwestern, borderlands, and Latin American history knows of the Archive of the Indies. For people like me, researching there took on a dream-like requirement. At the very least, my arrival there was an awe inspiring moment.

Despite my Fulbright status I was not allowed access to the archive until I could present two letters of introduction to the archive's "*secretario*." In Spanish bureaucracy the *secretario* is not just a secretary but the equivalent to what we would call a deputy or assistant director. At the time that I went there the *secretario* at the Archives of the Indies was the penultimate bureaucrat. He was an elderly man who knew his job. Everything about him was gray. His desk, suit, tie, walls, typewriter, hair, even his skin and eyes appeared gray. He patiently and somewhat happily explained to me the two letter requirement.

"But," I replied in rather poor pigeon Spanish, "Yo soy un becario de Fulbright." I am a Fulbright recipient.

"No matter. The requirement is two letters."

"Bueno." Okay. "Can I write one for myself?"

"No, señor."

"Por qué no?" Why not? "I have written many letters for others to research here." The *secretario* was not amused with my logic probably because he correctly sensed a touch of sarcasm in my tone. The conversation was over.

I had no choice but to secure two letters of introduction. One came from the Fulbright office in Madrid and the other from the United States consulate office in Seville.

Thus I returned to the *secretario's* office where I patiently watched him meticulously study each letter. But, the rules were the rules. He approved my application to research, typed up my researcher's card and, then, arranged for me to have the required meeting with the director of the archive. Although no longer done, this last requirement, to me, was very impressive.

The *secretario* guided me to the director's office. After introductions, she asked me what I would be researching and I anxiously and proudly stated that I would be researching "Spain's role and help in the American Revolution." I thought that they would be impressed with such a brilliant idea but no. Instead, "my friend" the *secretario* snickered and looked at the director who smiled in return. He turned to me to smugly ask; "Which American Revolution?"

I immediately understood. Spain, the possessor of many American colonies had suffered through many American revolutions. I explained that this was the rebellion of the British colonies against Great Britain that resulted in the independence of the United States.

Since that moment I have never used the phrase American Revolution without a qualifier. In fact, I have found myself in situations in which I had to explain what I mean by American.

I did get my revenge on the *secretario*. The archive's administrative offices as well as the research rooms were on the second floor with large fourteen to fifteen foot windows opening up to an interior courtyard. When seated at certain seats, the researcher could peer through the window and across the courtyard and see the *secretario* dutifully working at his desk.

Very early in my research I became overwhelmed at the amount of documents in the Archive of the Indies that dealt with the U. S. War of Independence. I needed help and found some close by. My father; a twelfth generation Spanish-speaking New Mexican, who majored in history as an undergraduate and, then, went to law school, had recently retired as a Superior Court Judge. He and my mother had moved to Spain. He was extremely interested in my research and I reasoned why not use him as a research assistant. I could assign him a particular batch of documents that is called a *legajo,* to search for specific events or names. This would be of help to me.

As I had learned, I would need two letters of introduction to get him in the archive. No problem. One came from the U. S. consulate and I wrote the second letter, as an approved researcher in the Archive of the Indies I could make recommendations. I had the *secretario* snared in the web of in his own bureaucracy and I wanted to watch his reaction. He had to play by the rules.

The day came. My father and I walked to the archive where I directed him to the *secretario's* office and scurried to a select seat in the research room to watch from across the courtyard. My father introduced himself and explained that he wanted to do some research in the archives while presenting the required two letters. The *secretario* read the letters, rechecked the signatures, squirmed, hesitated, and reread the letters. He was not pleased. He was checkmated. He had to approve my father's access to the archives. My dad became my research assistant for the next few weeks. I eventually used some of his translations in the book while the *secretario* became a memory.

40
About the beginning of a beneficial international relationship

While in Seville, I received a letter from Dr. Jaime de Salas of the Fundación Xavier de Salas. He had been recommended to me by Dr. Donald Cutter, who was my doctorate advisor at the University of New Mexico. Jaime de Salas informed me in his letter that Cutter was a close personal friend of Jaime's father, Xavier, who had recently passed away. Xavier de Salas and his wife Carmen Ortueta de Salas, who I knew simply as Doña Carmen, formed the above mentioned foundation and, under its auspices, had started a "museum" housed in a four hundred year old convent in Trujillo. Jaime de Salas inherited his father's "dream" and wanted to make something of it.

Jaime de Salas was (and still is) a full professor who taught in the Philosophy Department at the Universidad Complutense de Madrid. He specialized in United States thought as well as in the Spanish philosopher José Ortega y Gasset. I would soon learn that Jaime had been educated in England and that his father had been a Spanish diplomat to Great Britain and Director of the Prado Museum in Madrid.

Dr. Cutter told Jaime that I might be of some use to him regarding the museum in Trujillo. I was a director of a museum housed in an old building that, like Jaime's institution, had a library. Jaime invited me to visit Trujillo to see the Museo de la Coria. In reply, I shared with him my willingness to travel to Trujillo for a weekend but that we would have to wait until after my daughters and I moved up to Madrid for the final two months of my grant.

I had been in Trujillo a few months earlier. After spending weekend in Madrid with my friends Alan Gates and Isabel Adame and we decided to return to Seville by taking the "back" route through Trujillo and Mérida. My father had told me that he had seen the Chávez family crest on a "castle" in the town so when we drove onto the old plaza mayor around midnight I was curious to see the place. Of course, during the summer in Spain midnight can be early and true to form all the restaurants lining the plaza were open. We parked on the plaza to eat a small meal at one of the nearby outdoor cafes.

I hopped out of the car, walked up a series of steps, past a church, and looked up over the main doorway of the first building I encountered. The building was over four stories high, centuries old, and abandoned. And, there it was! The Chávez family shield! I was flabbergasted. As a result of this brief introduction to Trujillo, I took Jaime de Salas's invitation as a foturnate opportunity to return to this curious town.

Trujillo is a small town of eight to twelve thousand people that sits on a hill. It has a rich history starting as a Roman outpost called Trugalium followed by the Visigoths, and then a subsequent long occupation by the Muslims who built the castle on the hill's crown along with the walled medieval section. King Fernando III, "the Saint" took the town from the Moors in 1232 and in the sixteenth century many *conquistadores*, explorers, and settlers, in total some 600 to 700 people, left Trujillo to test their luck in the Americas. Thus, outside the medieval wall further down the hill, a Renaissance plaza lined with buildings mostly built with wealth brought back from the Americas has become the town's center of activity.

In a quiet, understated way, Trujillo became a Spanish tribute to the *Mestizo* race, the mixture of Spanish and American Indian blood. Francisco Pizarro had a daughter by Inés Yupanqui, the daughter of the Inca emperor, Atahualpa, who he murdered. Francisco's mixed-blood daughter then married her uncle, Francisco's half-brother Hernándo, who returned to Trujillo with her. Together they built the Palace that towers over one side of Trujillo's plaza. All of Pizarro's direct descendents originate through her. The Pizarro Palace is dressed with imagery of Spain and Peru. Next to the *alcazar* or castle on top of the hill is a large boulder dedicated "*al mestizaje*...", "to the mixed-blooded people," that truly speaks to a history of people and place.

By the middle of the twentieth century Trujillo had become impoverished. Most of its once glorious buildings had been abandoned and were run-down. The place was ignored. Then interest picked up very slowly. Some wealthy Madrileños, the Salas family, and others, including a woman from the United States who married into Spanish nobility, began to restore a few of the old buildings into seasonal homes. Other Madrileños bought *fincas* or farms nearby. These new part-time inhabitants began to dabble in local history, even to the point of opening the tomb of Diego García de Paredes (1466-1534), a Spanish soldier and duelist known as "Sansón Extremeño," the Samson from Extremadura, for his legendary size and strength. To their disappointment the crypt in the church of Santa María Mayor was empty.[265]

The Salas family took a real interest in the community. Unlike many of the others, they were not dilettantes. Don Xavier and Doña Carmen, purchased and renovated a house that had been built into the old town wall. They then purchased the ruined convent next to the ancient "Coria" gate. Naturally, the convent and future museum was called "La Coria." They then raised and invested a lot of their own money to pay for local craftsmen to begin the reconstruction of the convent to fulfill their dream that it could be used as a museum, seminar center, and library.

I was able to leave my daughters with a friend in Madrid and take a bus south on, what I considered, a new adventure. When I arrived, the town looked depressed. The only taxi at the ugly bus station had a driver who never heard of the Museo de la Coria. He sought out others working at the station to see if they knew of the place. He made a telephone call to someone and, finally, received directions.

Upon being left off in a very narrow street that is best described as a passage way, I was confronted with a high wall and locked iron gate. The Coria was closed. In desperation I pulled on a chain connected to an old bell. The noise was overwhelming but did the trick, for a man, who I would come to know as Miguel for the next three plus decades, gave me directions to the Salas residence. Today, as I look back on the episode, I am amazed that I actually was able to find the home, for the route took me on a walk down the passage way, then right into a narrower pedestrian way that worked its way down hill. After coming out at the end of pedestrian way I turned right on another passage way, avoided a cross street, crossed a beautiful small plaza, continued straight on a small cobble-stoned and partially dirt road through a sharp "s" turn and an ancient gate in the old town wall. There, immediately to my left was the entrance to the Salas residence. I had to be fated to meet Jaime de Salas.

I was greeted by Jaime and his mother, given time to nap, called to pre-dinner drinks in a wonderful living room with a walk-in fireplace, sat to a multi-course dinner served by Miguel, and verbally introduced to the dream of Jaime's father. I spent the weekend touring the Coria, meeting the staff, and sharing the Salas's future plans for the place. I was intrigued and impressed. The Salas family had an obvious passion for Trujillo and their institution. To that point, the family had done a stellar and expensive job with the help of the European Community, the World Monument Fund, and the Kress Foundation in the United States, as well as help from other U. S. institutions. Still, there was much more to be done. The library had a good beginning collection and the museum had a panel exhibition. About half of the old complex had been restored.

I learned that the mission of the Museo de la Coria was to emphasize the role and influence of Extremadura on the Americas. Fully aware that Extremadura was considered the birthplace of *conquistadores* and that many New Mexican families, including my own, originated in the region, I became instantly interested in learning more.

After spending a wonderful weekend in Trujillo, Jaime offered to drive me back to Madrid where he has a permanent residence. With an opportunity to spend more time with him and, coincidentally save the return bus fare, I gladly accepted the invitation.

Then I learned that Jaime drove a vintage right-hand drive BMW. This meant that I would sit on the left-hand side while we drove on a two-lane highway in a country that, like our own, is right-hand drive. As we prepared to leave, Jaime put on a pair of fingerless driving gloves. And off we went.

Naturally, to pass slower traffic we passed on the left and to do this, Jaime had to depend on my judgment about oncoming traffic. There I sat concerned more about my immediate prospects for a longer life than any conversation. Jaime relied on me to say, "when." Needless to say the trip was a new, not always comfortable, experience for me. Nevertheless, by the time that Jaime dropped me off, the two of us knew that we had made a lifelong friendship. And, yes, I wrote a multi-page summary of my impressions of the Museo de la Coria.

A few years later, the BMW was replaced in favor of a newer, left-hand drive car.

41
On what Penitentes and cultural curiosity will get

My daughters and I made many friends when we lived in Seville. Alan Gates and Isabel Adame became very good friends. Alan taught school where Nicolasa and Christel attended. I became the godfather of their only son, Alan William. Their good friends José Suarez Labrador and his wife Reme Guillen became very close friends. While attending a birthday party all of us entered into a conversation in which José or Alan made an observation that was really a question.

"You really liked the *feria*," referring to a week long fair whose size and magnitude can match New Orleans's Mardi gras. I answered in the affirmative but mentioned that I preferred the activities of Semana Santa, Holy Week that preceded the *feria* by two weeks.

"The *fería*," I explained, "is a big week-long party. Don't get me wrong. I like parties but Semana Santa is unique." I then explained my fascination with the confraternities of *Hermanos Penitentes*, brotherhoods of Penance, their processions, the floats that were carried through the streets, the statues, imagery, and music.

"We have *penitentes* in New Mexico. We also carry our saints on floats through the streets. We don't call our floats *pasos* like here. What we have are *pasitos*, little floats that take only four people to carry. We have *cofradias*, confraternities made up of people who call themselves *hermanos penitentes.* Processions in Santa Fe annually carry a statue of the Virgin Mary through Santa Fe and she is the oldest statue of the Virgin Mary in the United States. Also, those sorrowful *saetas* that the gypsies[266] sing to the Madonna while in procession sound very similar to the *alabados* song by the *penitentes* in New Mexico."

At this point I had the complete attention of my friends, especially José, who was an active member of one of Seville's brotherhoods. I told them that my parents, daughters and I saw every *paso* during the recently completed Semana Santa. There were 111 of them. We became especially curious about the *costaleros,* the men who carried the heavy floats, some of which took over fifty men. The name comes from *costal*, the name of the headpiece the carriers wear to help relieve the burden of the float's weight across their shoulders. The headpiece is made up of a material akin to a gunny sack, which is really what *costal* means.

I did not know at the time that José had been a *costalero* for all of his adult life and took to heart my words. Soon after I returned to New Mexico, he arranged for his brotherhood to send a formal invitation to me to join them as a *costalero* the following

Semana Santa. I would have the privilege of carrying the float of [Our Lady of] Dulce Nombre. Dulce Nombre was also the short name of José's *cofradia.* The letter went on to state that "in the 400 years of our Brotherhood's existence no other person from the New Continent has been a member of the team of *costaleros.*[267]

Of course I accepted. The invitation was a rare honor and I already figured out how I would get back to Spain.

42
Relating to the convergence of three ideas that led to a fourth

By the end of 1987, or within five weeks after my return from Spain I had sent a multi-paged report/critique of the Museo de Coria to Jaime de Salas, received the invitation to become a *costalero,* and had begun planning for a museum fundraising tour to Spain that I, the museum's director, would lead. This plan to return to Spain worked brilliantly. We visited places that I knew. We started in Madrid from where we took day trips to Toledo, San Lorenzo del Escorial, etc. Then we traveled to Trujillo where with, great formality, we had a reception in the Coria. In front of television cameras and radio microphones, Jaime and I signed an agreement for the Museo de la Coria and the Palace of the Governors to become sister institutions. From there we visited Extremadura's famous Virgin of Guadalupe thus sharing another connection between the region and the Americas.

After visits to Cáceres and Mérida the tour traveled south to Seville where it received an insider's tour of the city. Celia López, who had become a good friend and colleague and would eventually become my wife, came out to our hotel and met us in the bar. Doc Weaver, who only heard about her, saw her coming and completely surprised her when he jumped up and blurted out, "Celia! How the hell are you?" and then gave her a hug. She had never seen him before, had never been greeted in such an extroverted manner, and, outside of her name, did not understand a word he said. Nevertheless, the smiles and laughter surrounding us clued her in. Doc has liked her more than me ever since.

Celia arranged to lead a tour through the Archives of the Indies. She even had the director welcome us. In very broken but practiced English, Celia gave us one of the better tours ever given of the place.

José Suárez and Reme Guillen, met the group and let them into the Church of San

Lorenzo to have a private view of the two floats that would leave there on Tuesday evening. They also arranged permission for anyone from the tour who wanted to walk in the procession behind the float that I would be carrying. Doc Weaver and Gene Law joined Celia and another friend Jesús Muñuzuri, the grandson of my landlord of my previous year's stay in Seville, to walk in the procession.

The convergence of the tour, Trujillo, and Semana Santa led to an opportunity that I could not overlook. The previous year's research on Spain's role in the independence of the United States was far from complete. I needed to finish research in the National Archives in Madrid. Now that I was in Spain, I took vacation time to spend an extra few weeks doing more research. It was during this time that Celia and I fell in love, only to decide that our lives were too diverse to make it work. In the great park of Madrid called Buen Retiro, we decided to remain "friends" instead of lovers.

Obviously, that agreement was not kept.

43
About the experience of doing penance

Being a *costalero* is serious. I trained in anticipation of the moment. I ran daily. Then I ran with weights on my shoulders. After that I ran up a hill that I named "*costalero* hill." All of this was done at Santa Fe's elevation of seven thousand feet. Even during the tour leading up to Semana Santa, I ran and took opportunities to carry on my shoulders the young daughter of Sheila Garcia, a friend from Albuquerque.

Upon arriving in Seville, José took me to the *paso* to explain to me what would happen and what I needed to do. While this gave me a good idea and curbed some of my anxiety, the information also gave me reason to worry.

First of all, I thought that there would be some kind of rehearsal. No. This explanation was all that I would get. Then, José explained how the *capataz*, the man outside the float who gave directions, would tell us when to lift the float, which weighs over 2,500 pounds. He took me underneath the float to explain that the frame's parallel 2x4 boards are what are used to lift the float. In six rows of five persons each, with the taller men front, making a total team of thirty men, we each would place the back of our heads firmly against a board so that it rested across the back of our necks and shoulders. The costaleros wait with straight backs, bent legs, and with hands pushed against the board in front on either side of the person's head in that row. Upon command the men straighten their legs in unison and lift to their extremity without leaving the ground to settle to their natural height with an obvious "whomph" as they exhale. This is done on command of the *capataz* who uses words to the effect of "are you ready?" If ready, the *costaleros* reply in Spanish with, "*al cielo!*" This technically means, "to heaven!" What it really means is that "we will lift her [the Virgin and/or float] to heaven!" Then with a door knocker attached to the front of the float he will tap it, in what became for me, an ominous three times. This followed a slight pause of a couple of seconds while the team underneath got in place and the *capataz* communicated with a *costalero* in the last row. Then came the one loud tap and the float is lifted. As José walked me through the process, he stressed that when lifting the float, I had to be in unison, "for if you go up when the *paso* is coming down, you can snap your neck."

A subdued, "great," in English was my reply.

On the next day, I arrived at the appointed gathering place with mixed feelings. All the *costaleros* for my particular *cofradia* gathered in an oversized room in the second story of a building behind the church. Mostly young men who were all dressed in T-shirts and blue jeans milled about. José introduced me to some of the people who would be working with me. They explained that we had plenty of time but before doing anything and that I needed to wear my shirt inside out and wear it backwards. This would prevent the shirt's label from rubbing the back of my neck raw. "Oh great," I thought again.

For the time being my new friends left me to myself, which gave me an opportunity to observe my surroundings. There were enough *costaleros* to carry the brotherhood's two floats. Other *cofradia* members milled around. Besides the float of the Virgin and St. John, the brotherhood had a larger float that depicted a scene out of the New Testament. The scene of life-sized figures froze the moment when Pontius Pilot slapped Jesus. This float gave rise to the brotherhood's second nickname after "Dulce Nombre" and that is "*La Bofetá*," the slap. The *Bofetá* float took over fifty men to carry and was over one-third again as large as the float I would be under. With *costaleros* enough to carry both floats plus some extra men to relieve the initial teams, there were around a hundred guys preparing for the upcoming ordeal about which I could only imagine.

Some elderly men walked around offering cigarettes out of large plastic bag while a couple of boys did the same with chewing gum. Some of the guys were busy folding and preparing their *costales*. Others were preparing their *fajas*, the long approximately eighteen inch wide strip of black cloth that, with the help of two others, was wound tightly around the body's mid section to support the lower back and protect against hernias. Still others talked, some joked. Many sought solitude to be with their own thoughts, or stretch, or pray.

"Wow!" I thought. "These guys are the descendents of the same people who left this very city to cross the sea to conquer and settle strange lands three and four centuries ago. Some of my own ancestors were among them." The scene in front of me conjured up the image of what it must have been just before embarking on such an expedition.

Romantic notions aside, my new friends helped me prepare my *costal* and wrap the *faja* on me. Then we were told to line up according to height. While in line the *capataces* measured us by a bone in the back of our necks. This is where the weight of the float would rest. Each row of five men had to be the exact size as measured from that bone. I was assigned to the second to last row under "Dulce Nombre." I also would start out and not be one of the backups. I would have the privilege of carrying the Virgin out of the church and into the streets.

As a confused believer best described as a "Jack Catholic," to borrow the term from Mormon terminology, I dutifully attended mass with the other *costaleros* the night before. I received the priest's blessing but did not go to confession or receive communion. Now, as I climbed through the thick skirt under the float, I dedicated my effort to the health of Don Pierce, the father of my friend and colleague Donna Pierce. Mr. Pierce, a very nice and enjoyable man, had a reoccurrence of cancer, and it was terminal.

Clap...clap...clap came the sharp noise of the float's clapper.

"?Costaleros, están listos?" "Costaleros, are you ready?"

"Si, señor! Al cielo!" "Yes, [We will lift her] to heaven!"

"Tos[268] por igual, valientes...a ésta es!" "Everyone equally, valiant ones...here it is!"

CLAP!

We lifted the float and started marching in place and then, upon orders, started forward with our feet never leaving the ground. The weight was almost, but not quite, unbearable. We marched in complete darkness, for the float above us contained a skirt that almost reached the ground.

Our first challenge was to get through the church door were the community and tourists waited. We had to lower the float by walking in a crouch. All this takes place to the beat of drums and music of a marching band. As we slowly edged through the door, the music was very low and quiet. As we passed through the door we were ordered upright and the music changed to loud fanfare. The crowd cheered—the Virgin Mary had been presented to the public! Even while struggling underneath, the sensation of it all was a unique high in my life.

We left the church at 8:30 p.m. and returned at 3:30 a. m. We followed a prescribed route to and from the Cathedral. The *capataz*, in front of the float, and two assistants, at each of the back corners, shouted directions to guide the float out of the church and through Seville's narrow streets. The band followed behind and the *penitentes*, about fifteen hundred of them, marched in two lines in their robes and hoods. I received a small break of about a half hour. While carrying the float, beads of sweat rolled down my vibrating arms and soaked head. I distinctly remember thinking "this is not fun." The adjective "work" did not come close to describing the feeling. At the end of the night I had lost eight pounds. When I returned home in New Mexico, I learned that Don Pierce's cancer had inexplicably reversed! It was a small but welcomed break, for eventually he succumbed to the disease.[269]

Effort and miracles aside, I wanted to demonstrate the seriousness with which I accepted the honor of being a *costalero*. I asked José if I could continue to carry *Dulce Nombre* for two more years. I wanted him and his friends to understand that my participation was not a one-time lark done out of curiosity and that at my relatively advanced age for such an activity, I would suffer through two more *salidas*, trips carrying the float of *Dulce Nombre*. In total, I carried a float for three consecutive years. In each of those years four people were there for me—José and Reme, Celia, and Jesús Muñuzuri. Thank goodness, for it is not a task to be done alone, especially for a foreigner.

44
In which the experience is shared

To say that my experience as a *costalero* was an education would be an understatement. The educational process began with the experience that needed to be shared. The first method is obvious. I gave a series of illustrated lectures that were accompanied by music. The second method was a little more convoluted. Still intrigued in cultural connections, the idea of putting together the *hermanos penitentes* from Spain and New Mexico seemed to be an intriguing, if not a natural thing to do. I talked with José and Reme about inviting them to New Mexico where I would set up a schedule of presentations in which they could talk about their experience in Seville. They would give some public as well as private talks. The private talks would be to the *Cofradia de la Conquistadora* in Santa Fe and *Los Hermanos Penitentes* in Taos. After some hesitation, they agreed and proceeded to gather information, images, and prepare notes.

I returned home to sell the idea and organize the schedule. Mr. Pete Tafoya had become a friend of mine through his daughter Guadalupe who worked at the Palace of the Governors for a couple of years. Mr. Tafoya was a very active and influential *penitente* in the Taos Valley. He knew of my experience in Seville and was very agreeable to arranging a reception at his brotherhood's *Morada,* their place of worship in Talpa. The *Cofradia de la Conquistadora* in Santa Fe likewise accepted without hesitation to receive the Spanish guests. I then arranged for two public presentations and informal receptions in Albuquerque and Santa Fe. Albuquerque's South Broadway Cultural Center hosted the talk after which a reception was held at a local hotel. The Palace of the Governors hosted the Santa Fe talk and reception. Funding came from the New Mexico Endowment for the Humanities, Albuquerque businessman and soon to be United States Ambassador to Spain Ed Romero, and the Palace of the Governors.

The whole project worked to perfection. The audiences were large, attentive, and expressed an interest and curiosity that engaged José and Reme. They met Archbishop Robert Sánchez who was very gracious to them. New Mexicans accepted them as their own. This was especially true of the *penitentes* in Talpa who, in an attempt to welcome them in a traditional manner, gave them an unintentional shock.

After an hour plus drive up the Rio Grande Valley from Santa Fe to the Taos Valley we turned off the main highway to a two-lain paved road and then onto a well-worn dirt road that winded around a one-story low-lying, windowless, adobe building that had cemetery next to it. As is common, the building was "L" shaped.[270] We parked among other cars in an open field right at dusk. New Mexican nights, especially at an elevation of seven thousand feet or more can be at once spectacular and very dark.

As we walked toward the building we were met by a man who directed us to wait while he went inside the building. Only when he opened the wood door did we see light and hear a chanting, the last of which was quickly muffled when the door shut. There we stood inside the "L", between the building and cemetery, and in the dark. I found out afterward that my guests had become very worried.

Finally, the door opened and the people inside streamed out in a single-file line all the while chanting a prayer. The line wound behind us and formed a closed circle with us in the middle. By now, José and Reme did not know what to think.

Then the circle unwound and still in single-file ushered us inside the building where we were treated to a wonderful meal of chili, beans, meat, and flour tortillas, after which, José and Reme gave an informal version of their presentation. Happily, translation from Spanish to English was not needed for the *penitentes.* They shared many things, such as prayers and rituals. Their songs and organizational rules contained similarities. But one thing became obviously different and that was secrecy. The question came from one of the New Mexicans.

"What secrets do you have? I mean do you find it necessary to be secretive to maintain your privacy?"

"What do you mean?"

"You know. Do the brothers meet in secret and have rituals that the public cannot attend?"

"Why would we do that?"

The ensuing conversation brought out the differences between the two countries and their respective histories. In Spain, a Catholic country, the brotherhoods are naturally accepted. In New Mexico, which in the 19th century became a part of the primarily Protestant United States, the *penitentes* were seen as cultural and religious degenerates or at the very best as curiosities. Even their own Catholic Church came to despise and condemn them, forcing them to go "underground." While the people and Catholic Church of New Mexico accept the Penitentes today, the memory of that treatment is strong. Out of caution for their self-preservation many of the brotherhoods maintain their independence and distance. The relative perspectives caught everyone by surprise.

José's and Reme's travels in New Mexico fostered a third idea. With the year 1992 approaching, people in the United States began a great deal of planning and complaining about how to commemorate the five hundredth anniversary of Christopher Columbus's first trip to what became America. The legacy born out of that trip was neither Columbus's fault or to his credit. His trip and exploits continue to be a seminal point in American history.

The context as well as reality of U. S. Southwestern history is heavily tinctured by the Columbian, or Spanish, heritage. All the connections between the Iberian Peninsula and the Southwest grew out of this legacy and, after five hundred years, that cultural history had become a large part of the patrimony of the United States whether recognized or not.

The idea of sending the United States' oldest Christian icon, New Mexico's statue of Our Lady, *La Conquistadora*, to be marched in procession during Holy Week in Seville seemed logical enough. My activities as a *costalero* along with José's influence made the whole concept a very real possibility. With the backing of the Church in New Mexico it could become reality.

At the time, Archbishop Robert Sánchez was very popular. He was a New Mexican, very accessible, interested in the area's history, and personally unassuming. Nevertheless, meeting with him on a one-to-one basis was daunting to me. Save for pressing ahead with what I thought was a great idea; the audacity of asking to meet with him would never have come to mind.

Archbishop Sánchez and I met in his Santa Fe office. I gave him an abbreviated account of my history in Seville, which set up the basis for my proposal;

"Your Excellency, can you imagine the message and publicity that marching *La*

Conquistadora in Seville would make? Our cultures are intertwined, especially with our religion. Aside from the Spanish language, there is nothing that could more obviously make the point about our commonality than our religion!"

"Yes. I will need to think about this."

"I can arrange for my *cofradia* in Spain to receive and care for her in their church. They will even create a float and arrange for the *costaleros* to carry her." By now getting carried away, I added; "This could be a spectacular gesture!"

Archbishop Sánchez seemed to like the idea or, at least, the sentiment behind it. Nevertheless, he explained to me that he needed to consult with other people before agreeing to such a proposal. He had to talk with his Senate of Priests, the *Caballeros de Vargas*, and, of course, the *Cofradia de la Conquistadora*. The Caballeros were her official escort for every function and the *Cofradia* cared for her while she was in situ.

Then the Archbishop changed subjects and shared with me a sermon that he was writing. "I am not sure about this part," he said. He then read the part in question in two versions. "Which, if either, do you think is best?"

Somewhat taken aback with an Archbishop asking me to help with a sermon, I replied as only a person in my situation could; "I think that either version will work fine."

A few weeks later I received word that the Senate of Priests had made a decision. In my opinion, to play on an Old Testament biblical analogy, they decided to "cut the baby in half." They liked my idea but they refused to send the original *La Conquistadora* to Seville. The Church had a duplicate statue made by renowned artist Gustave Bauman in 1933.[271] The Senate recommended that the copy be sent to Spain.[272]

I reacted that a duplicate statue would be an insult to the Spanish who marched their own originals, many as old as *La Conquistadora*. Some of these such as the *Virgin de la Macarena* and the *Virgen de la Triana* were much more known and equally as valuable. The people of Seville, in my opinion, would never march a duplicate and besides, if they did, the fact alone would temper all the good publicity that we would get otherwise.

My reasoning fell on deaf ears. New Mexico and the Archdiocese lost a grand opportunity to make some historical and cultural points to bring people closer together. The copy, that I came to call "*La Conquistadora's* little sister," eventually did travel to Seville with Archbishop Sánchez. She was kept in my cofradia's church as arranged by José and Reme. But, she was never carried for Semana Santa.

45
On how formal education became a part of the Spanish connection

The negative reaction to taking *La Conquistadora* to Spain did not dampen the implementation of other programs in Spain. The first Palace of Governors' tour to Spain resulted in subsequent museum sponsored tours that went to Spain, Portugal, Mexico, Guatemala, Peru, and Argentina. I led some of the tours while others like Ambassador Ortiz, Dr. Julio Dávila, Charles Bennett, Donna Pierce, and Celia led or helped lead, "personalized" tours. Ambassador Ortiz led two tours to Guatemala, a place where he had been the United States ambassador. One of the tours coincided with *Semana Santa* in Antigua. Dr. Dávila organized and led a tour to his native Mexico while Charles Bennett and Donna Pierce represented the Palace on other tours to Mexico. Charles led a tour to Peru where the group visited the site of Sipán.

The tours proved to be very beneficial to the Palace and they continue to this day. We priced donations to the Palace's endowment into the tours' total cost. The tours provided us with audiences that had a natural appreciation for history. As a result we made new friends and received support far beyond the priced-in donations. Many of the people became active supporters of the Palace through the Friends and the Foundation. Others continued to financially support the museum. Frank Ortiz collected an extra $8,000 in donations on the first Guatemalan trip. He even auctioned off his well-worn and much ridiculed tennis shoes!

The other museums in the Museum of New Mexico system started organizing tours. The idea spread to museums beyond the Museum of New Mexico system as some of the Palace's staff moved on to other museums and initiated tours based on the model set at the Palace of the Governors. Before long, the tours competed with each other and, at times, the market became saturated.

The Palace's tours were always designed to be educational and to stress the cultural connections to New Mexico. They were organized and priced from expensive first-class tours that we called *"Elegante"* to more affordable tours that we referred to as "budget" tours. In addition, we created a policy of including a staff member along for each trip. Staff's cost was priced in the tour. They stayed on salary and were expected to assist whenever necessary. Eventually, almost every member of the staff went on a foreign tour. Of the two who did not go on a trip, one turned down the offer and the other, Richard Rudisill, who traveled extensively on his own, graciously "stood aside" to permit his colleagues to have the opportunity.

Once again, however, jealousy reared its head. While leading a tour in Spain, my staff informed me that they received a telephone call from a local television station. An assistant to investigative reporter Larry Barker inquired about the tour with staff traveling on state time and receiving what she referred to as a "state stipend," meaning per diem. She wanted to know if they had been granted leave time, were on salary while traveling, and how their trip was being paid. My staff replied that she would need to talk to me and gave her a return date. Somewhat concerned that I might be in trouble, the staff notified me of the potential problem.

We shared the information with the people on the tour and had a few laughs about it. Everyone agreed that the tours involved work for staff as well as an excellent educational opportunity. In fact, the very tour on which we were on was an institute that had mandatory Spanish courses for all the participants, including staff. Without further concern we continued on.

When we returned to Albuquerque, the first person I saw as I left the plane and entered the terminal was Larry Barker studiously looking at the passengers as they passed by him. I fully expected a confrontation right there in public but as I got closer, he continued to look beyond me. Then, another person attracted his attention. I hesitated to satisfy my curiosity and heard him greet his mother as he happily hugged an equally happy elderly woman. This one little episode would be a simile to the whole investigation.

Within days, Barker's assistant telephoned me and asked if she could come in and see the records of all our tours.

I replied with: "What are you looking for."

"I am not sure but I will know if I see it."

"You mean that you don't know what you are looking for? Doesn't that sound illogical to you?"

"Are you going to let me see those records or not?"

"The 'or not' does not apply here. We are a state institution. You can see anything you want. I was just wondering what you are looking for. When do you want to see them?"

"Tomorrow at 8:00 a.m." It was around 4:30 p.m. or the end of the work day. I replied that I had an 8:30 a.m. meeting and that would not give us much time together and very little time to pull the files together. This, of course, was exactly her strategy. She did not need to see me and really wanted to see the records to draw her own conclusions. Realizing this, I quickly replied,

"Fine. Just come in and we will have the files waiting for you. Ask for Karen Gordon, my secretary." I think the woman was a little surprised at the answer. Maybe she was expecting some more resistance.

The next morning the assistant investigative reporter showed up in our offices at the appointed time. I was on my way out but had enough time to answer a couple of questions. After pointing out the stack of files on Karen's desk and showing her to a table and chair that she could use for her investigation, she asked me about the tours.

I gave her a brief history of how they started and why we did them. She asked about staff to which I explained that the tours always had a Palace representative for obvious reasons. But if she was asking about our policy of taking an extra staff member along the answer was that "yes, we do that and I had made that decision because my staff benefits the State of New Mexico way more than what they get paid for and this was my way to provide them with an extra incentive that was at once educational and beneficial."

"Well, who pays for this?"

"The Foundation, which is a private non profit support group and from funds raised through the tour's fees."

"Are they on salary when they travel?"

"Absolutely, they do not make enough as it is. This is part of their work. They are making friends and supporters for the Palace. And, they are expected to work while traveling."

I assured her that I would be available for any questions after my meeting and wished her luck on her research as I left the office. I never saw her again. She looked through the files for about forty-five minutes, thanked Karen, and left.

Soon after, maybe the next day, I received a telephone call from Barker's assistant who told me that they found nothing wrong with the tours and that they would not bother us any more. That communication, I thought, was very decent and very much appreciated. However, we wondered who directed Barker toward us in the first place. We concluded that one of our colleagues in the Museum of New Mexico system had become envious. Beyond that conclusion, we never cared about uncovering the person. We had more important and more positive things to do.

46
Relating to the creation of an institute

The concept of doing something of lasting value with the Palace's sister institution in Spain evolved into a tour variation that became the Palace of the Governor's "Institute of Spanish Culture and Language." We tested people to determine their levels of Spanish language proficiency that ranged from none to advanced level. Then they paid to go to

Spain and be a student in the institute. We scheduled guest scholars to give lectures and have discussions, excursions with specific goals, and met for formal classes in Spanish language at the Museo de la Coria. The institute emphasized historical and cultural connections.

While we were designing the concept of the institute, Dr. Rosalie Otero, a friend who I met while we both served on the Board of Directors for the New Mexico Endowment for the Humanities approached me with a timely proposition. Dr. Otero had become the Chair of the University of New Mexico Honors Program that was conducting summer programs for undergraduate students in Mexico. They called the program "*Conexiones*," Spanish for connections, because the main objective was for students to make historical and cultural connections between Mexico and New Mexico. Now, Dr. Otero wanted to know whether I could establish the "*Conexiones*" program in Spain.

The answer was a quick "yes." Here was a program with the same philosophy as ours that would provide an opportunity to test the institute idea. Trujillo seemed to me to be a perfect place to take students. Also, here was something else I could do in fulfillment of our new sister institutional relationship. I was pleased to organize and lead the University of New Mexico's first summer program to Trujillo.

But, not all went smoothly. The Honors Program had been doing "*Conexiones*" in Mexico in conjunction with the Department of Spanish and Portuguese so that students could get course credits for both Honors and Spanish. Dr. Otero telephoned me with the news that the Spanish Department teachers did not want to go to Trujillo. They preferred Madrid or Barcelona, especially the latter.

"What?" I shot back.

"They want to do the *Conexiones* Program in a larger city."

"Why? Because they prefer it for themselves and are not thinking about the students. Barcelona does not have close to the historical context for New Mexico. Trujillo is the perfect learning environment." And, I rattled off some other points.

"I know, Tom. I am only telling you what they want."

"Fine, then tell them to organize the program themselves because if we are not going to Trujillo, I'm out."

"Now, Tom. It's okay. I will talk to them." She did and in 1995 the first *Conexiones* Program traveled to Trujillo. *Conexiones* has been held every other year since. As of this writing, over 150 students from the University of New Mexico have been placed with families and studied in Trujillo. Each successive trip has improved on the last. One reason for that improvement came when Celia took over directing the program after she was hired to teach in the Honors Program. Dr. Otero correctly concluded that Celia could replace me and I would still help. I was "moved out."

Trujillo turned out to be the perfect place to take students and board them with the local families. The town is small and safe. The community takes care of itself and its guests. The Museo de la Coria has classrooms in a wonderful environment in which to teach, study, and learn. The stories of interaction abound. To date, there has been one marriage between a New Mexican and a *Trujillano.* More than a dozen New Mexican students have returned to Spain to work or study. And, an added benefit has been that the *Conexiones* Program, in its own way, has helped to redefine Trujillo and cause a tourism rebirth.

Trujillo's community is close-knit. It is a place where students not only get to know the locals but become a part of the community. The locals develop a lasting relationship with the students. As part of the program, some students have volunteered, doing everything from working in the Health Center, tending bar, washing dishes in a restaurant, and creating a web-site about Trujillo. The experience has been enriching for everyone.

Two stories involving students are clear examples of Trujillo's close-nit environment. The first example involves a student who unbeknown to the teachers decided to go to a nearby village's fiesta that featured a bull run. This student had enlisted in the military and was finishing his education. In keeping with his career choice he watched his diet, spent an inordinate amount of time on his physical condition, was very competitive, and dependable. He decided to participate in the bull run and by the next day the whole community of Trujillo was talking about it.

"Did you hear about x?"[273]

"No, what?"

"He ran with the bulls! He got out in the street and he took off in a sprint at the first notice of the bull. He only saw the beginning of other people running. I don't think he ever saw the bull."

"*Sí, pero, tiene razón.*" "Yes, but that is logical."

"No. You do not understand. He never saw the bull but he started running when he saw everyone else run. He thought that he was in a race and he kept running to the finish—he came in first!"

"What?"

"Yes! And all the people at the finish saw him sprinting with no one behind him. At first they were confused but then they realized that the runner was an *extranjero,* a foreigner. Then they realized what had happened."

Of such stories legends are made.

During the first *Conexiones* Program, another student had a little trouble showing up on time. As an experienced tour leader I had become a stickler for people being on time. One person can inconvenience many and when this continuously happens, the tour degenerates. In this case, I became convinced that the student was intentionally late as a means to challenge me.

As expected he was late for the departure of our chartered bus on the morning we took an excursion to Guadalupe. This was the last straw and I took his tardiness as a personal challenge. In effect, I became "a snake in the grass." When we arrived at Guadalupe I laid out the schedule and explicitly told the students where and when we would board the bus for our return trip.

Again, as expected, this particular student failed to return to the appointed place on time. All the faculty and students were on the bus but this person was missing again. I sent a student to run back to the plaza to see if he could find the recalcitrant. Ten minutes later the student returned empty handed. By then we had all waited a total of twenty minutes so I made the decision.

Turning to the bus driver I told him; "*Vámonos,*" "Lets go." Without hesitation the driver started up the engine and put it into gear. Before I could turn around and face the students the bus let out a loud "Psssssch" and started moving. I faced the wide-eyed students and said, "Say good-bye to y!" They were stunned.

An hour and fifteen minutes later, the bus let us off in Trujillo's main plaza. Some of the students' surrogate parents were at the plaza, seated at the outside tables that lined the north and east sides of the square.

They already knew that we had left "y" in Guadalupe. They laughed, for his reputation was known.

"Don't worry," they told us in good humor, "he is on his way back in a taxi," a taxi for which he had to pay.

My constantly tardy friend never showed up late again. We had come to an unstated agreement. He would be on time or suffer the consequences.

47
In which the legacy expands

Meanwhile the Palace of the Governors organized two institutes that went to Trujillo. Both of them seemed successful. The second one succeeded despite the unexpected cold and rain. A lack of interest ended the idea of doing more. However, Donna Pierce who took a job at the Denver Museum of Art put together an institute modeled on the Palace and all indications are that it was successful.

As mentioned the University of New Mexico's Conexiones program has continued and, in fact, became the inspiration for a consortium of colleges in South Carolina to organize annual semesters in Trujillo with the Coria as the host institution. Their program is based on UNM's model in that the students are placed with local families, take courses at the Coria, and go on excursions. A rich patron donated a house with a swimming pool to serve as the faculty residence. Like the University of New Mexico, Charleston University, from South Carolina continues to educate students in Trujillo.

New Mexico Highlands University from Las Vegas, New Mexico approached Celia at UNM to ask if she and I could help set up a program in Trujillo. We had a couple of meetings and then met with the students who had signed up for the program. The Highlands program mirrored the UNM program in that they scheduled their trip during the summer, went for a month, decided to go every other year, in the off years from UNM's so they would not compete. After two programs they stopped, although they want to start up again.

Jaime de Salas and I constantly tried to promote our goals for Trujillo. He made trips to New Mexico annually. I arranged for him to meet Dr. Bill Gordon, at the time, the acting President of the University of New Mexico. We also met with Rosalie Otero, the Chair of the Honors Program along with the Chair of the Spanish and Portuguese Department. Eventually, Jaime made numerous trips to Las Vegas to meet with the interested faculty of Highlands University.

During this time President Bill Clinton named Ed Romero the United States Ambassador to Spain. Celia and I met with him in Madrid while he was waiting to be officially received in Spain. The projects in Trujillo took up part of that conversation. It just so happened that another Conexiones program would be in Trujillo during Ambassador Romero's first year in office, so I thought that it would be a neat idea for the United States Ambassador to attend the first night's reception for the students from his home state and city. Of course, Ambassadors have more important work and other priorities. I needed to come up with a plan.

In 1999, Bill Gordon, the recently appointed President of UNM, had not met Ed Romero but he knew of the ambassador. I proposed to Dr. Gordon that he go to Trujillo to personally visit one of his university's foreign programs and meet Ambassador Romero who would be attending the opening festivities. Gordon, like the Ambassador, had priorities and, besides, he said, "I can't start my presidency by spending money and taking trips."

I countered that we had budgeted the previous Conexiones to have an excess of money each year to help with emergencies and occasions such as this. Then, I set the hook;

"Ambassador Romero will be there and this will be an excellent opportunity for you to meet him."

That got his attention. He would think about my proposal. Then I telephoned the embassy in Madrid and asked if the Ambassador had decided to go to Trujillo. "No. No decision has been made," which is to say he probably will not go. "Well, tell him that Bill Gordon, the new President of the University of New Mexico will be there and this will be an excellent opportunity for them to meet."

Then, I waited for a couple of weeks and made a telephone call to each office. Gordon asked if I was sure the Ambassador will be there.

"Yes he will."

"Okay, then. I am going."

Ambassador Romero's assistant asked if President Gordon would be there for sure.

"Yes he will."

"Then the Ambassador will be there, too."

I was not there for the reception for the twenty students, their surrogate parents, and other Trujillanos but I could imagine. Margo Chávez-Charles, who directed the program in 1999 reported the event. Here was the Ambassador of the United States and President of the University of New Mexico in the little town of Trujillo all because that community housed students from New Mexico. Jaime de Salas dutifully arranged for representatives from the University of Extremadura to be there. He also invited the press to witness the speech making and record the event that included an exchange agreement between the two universities. In addition, Salas had the opportunity to meet Ambassador Romero and vice versa as well as solidify his relationship with President Gordon. The whole event embedded a sense of "relevance," as Jaime would say, about the activities of the Museo de la Coria.

Eventually, as Executive Director of the National Hispanic Cultural Center I led a delegation consisting of Ed Lujan, chairman of my Board of Directors, Rod Sánchez, who represented the Intel Corporation, and his wife, Katherine Archuleta, the director of the National Hispanic Cultural Center Foundation, and two staff members. I wanted them to meet Jaime de Salas and see the Museo de la Coria. I had asked them to consider the possibility of installing computers and a telecommunications system in the Coria. This would be the beginning of a distance education system that was one of the NHCC's original goals.

The trip proved very fruitful, for everyone agreed to the idea and Intel donated the equipment worth tens of thousands of dollars. Jaime de Salas and his staff could not believe their good fortune when the boxes full of the necessary equipment began to arrive at the Coria's door. With the help of Jaime's assistant, Miguel, and NHCC staff, the hardware was set up and running in time to telecommunicate from Spain to the NHCC at the very moment the Spanish President, José María Aznar was touring the NHCC in Albuquerque. We had Dr. Chris Garcia, the new Acting President of the University of New Mexico (Dr. Gordon had resigned for another job), Ed Lujan, and the press watching and talking from New Mexico while UNM's Conexiones students, Jaime de Salas, UNM faculty including Celia, and the Mother Superior from the local Catholic High School communicating from Trujillo. Despite some glitches the overall potential appeared obvious. Everyone involved was enthused.[274]

The NHCC subsequently sent staff to Trujillo on two different occasions to initiate a community program on recording personal history. Community volunteers learned how to use the equipment by making a compact disk that recorded their individual histories, using family photographs and background music of their choice. This was an adaptation of a program the NHCC successfully had been using to connect teachers in New Mexico and Mexico. Unfortunately, after I retired from the NHCC, a lack of funds as well as interest doomed the program.

The ripples of cause and effect that began with my first trips to Spain in 1985 and in 1987 will continue to expand throughout time. Jaime de Salas asked me to be on the Board of Directors for the Fundación Xavier de Salas, which oversees the Museo de la Coria. I proudly have held that position for over twenty years.

My colleagues, friends, and family continue to build on that small beginning. For example, a chance dinner in Madrid with Eduardo Garrigues, a former Spanish Consul and ambassador whom, as mentioned, spent time in New Mexico, resulted in three symposiums, four publications, and an exhibition that was installed in the National Portrait Gallery of the Smithsonian Institution.[275]

The meeting with Ed Romero in Madrid mentioned previously resulted in a litany of ideas that we discussed. Per his request I sent him a letter summarizing my ideas. Among those was the suggestion of putting the prestigious Instituto Cervantes in the newly opened National Hispanic Cultural Center in Albuquerque. The Instituto Cervantes is an international Spanish government initiative to promote Spanish language and culture. We knew that a group of influential people in Santa Fe had been advocating that an Instituto Cervantes be opened in Santa Fe. Their idea was to house it in the Paloheimo Mansion in Santa Fe's high-end eastside neighborhood. I suggested to Ambassador Romero that the NHCC had just opened its campus and needed to have programs. Albuquerque would attract more students and attention. Putting the Instituto there was a "perfect marriage." Besides, Ed Romero was one of the founders of the NHCC and wanted to see it succeed. To his credit, the Ambassador latched on to this idea and convinced the Spanish government to place an office of the Instituto in Albuquerque at the NHCC. This was no small accomplishment.

After returning from his service in Spain, Ambassador Romero has continued to work hard in keeping the Instituto Cervantes in Albuquerque. I enjoyed sharing with the public that the Instituto Cervantes has opened operations all over the world and that there are three in the United States. Then, I would list the three locations in alphabetical order; Albuquerque, Chicago, and New York.[276]

48
Relating to another idea thought to be crazy

Late in our careers at the Palace, Charles Bennett and I came up with an idea that most people thought was crazy. We wanted to take a small group of the Native American artisans who sold their wares under the Palace Portal on a short tour of Spain. We had both been to Spain enough to realize that the Spanish would be fascinated with "Indian artisans." Also, by then we had both been involved with the Portal Program for over twenty years. The program is unique in the country. Only Native American vendors are allowed to sell their handmade work under the *portal* of the Palace of the Governors. The *portal*, or porch, lines the north side of Santa Fe's plaza and can be a lucrative place to sell. The artisans, as much as the old Palace itself, have become fixtures in Santa Fe.

After the acrimony of the Columbian Quincentennial in which Native Americans and Spanish speaking people were stigmatized with a stereotypical hatred of one another, the initial reaction from colleagues was a raised eyebrow and "are you crazy?" Well, that was a subject of a different matter. We both knew the artisans and Spain well enough to understand that this would be a fascinating trip that could break down the perceptions that elicited the question. Besides, we were dealing with real people who had moved beyond stereotypes and the dictates of a few.

We made an announcement, solicited applications, and convinced the Museum of New Mexico Foundation to fund the trip. With the help of a committee made up of their peers, nine vendors were selected. They came from various New Mexican tribes and their art work ranged from painting, to pottery and jewelry. Charles and I made the arrangements and escorted the group. We had a couple of pre-trip meetings to explain the nuances like weather, length of travel, necessities, etc. We also shared some history of where we planned to go and why. Again, the theme of connections between there and here took precedence.

Receptions and three shows were arranged in Trujillo and Santa Fe de la Vega, which is located outside of Granada. The second town is the sister city of Santa Fe, New Mexico. In Trujillo, the irrepressible Jaime de Salas arranged for a community reception at the Museo de la Coria. The next day the artisans demonstrated how they created their art. One artist did body painting and was especially popular among the youth. The pottery maker actually brought clay to form pots and had examples of various stages of her craft. The second show in Trujillo was intentionally ironic, for it was held under the *portal* of the Palace de la Conquista on Trujillo's main plaza.

Francisco Pizarro, the famous conqueror of the Inca's in Peru, was born in Trujillo to his father's mistress. He was a vicious man who, in the end, was killed by his own people. As mentioned earlier his Indian lover bore him a mixed-blood daughter who married his half brother Hernando. Hernando built the Palace and, then, was kept in jail for many years. His wife, the daughter of Francisco lived in the Palace. The family wealth easily paid for a multi-storied renaissance palace that still is the defining building on Trujillo's plaza almost five centuries later. Today, the unoccupied, rundown building retains much of its historical magnificence. The building was put to a great use when the American Indians from New Mexico set up underneath its walls and shared their traditions. They talked with primary and secondary school students, gave demonstrations, and even sold some of their work.

As we left Trujillo in our chartered bus, Ken White, one of the participants was seated on the back seat staring at Trujillo as it shrunk in the distance. He cried. This same person, a Navajo or Diné, had collected water at the fountain in Guadalupe.

He knew the story of Guadalupe de Extremadura from our pre-trip lectures. He understood that she was the Virgin of the Americas because of the many people who left Extremadura to go to the Americas. He and the other artisans knew of her importance to historical people like Columbus, Hernán Cortes, Francisco de Orellana, and others like my own direct ancestors. They also knew that the first Indians taken to Europe by Columbus were baptized in the Monastery at Guadalupe and that the baptism font was now a fountain in the village's small main plaza that we all visited. We had discussed the positive and negative aspects of all this history.

Ken White's tribal elders asked that he bring back with him water from that font. With great care and obvious respect, this man, who traveled to Spain as part of our tour, filled two bottles of the special, maybe even, sacred water.

Later on, as we were traveling south to Granada on the train, I ran into him in the lounge car. He was standing at the bar talking to a Spaniard who probably did not understand him. He pointed to an article in Spain's major newspaper *El Pais* that featured our tour with a photograph of him. Apparently he was trying to use his currently achieved star quality to impress this person. I interrupted and asked for the newspaper to see the article.

When I read the caption of the photograph, I was startled to see that he was described as a she! Apparently confused by his long straight hair, the Spanish editors described him as an "Indian woman." He could not read Spanish and did not realize the mistake. One can only imagine what the Spaniard next to him at the bar was thinking.

In Madrid the group insisted on going to a bullfight. I agreed to take them there and Charles agreed to stay with them. This would give me an afternoon off and I was thankful. We all arrived at the bullring very excited. Charles took them to their seats where they witnessed the pageantry and, perhaps, gore of their first bullfight. They were not impressed and wanted to leave to go shopping but Charles told them that the gates had been closed and they would have to stay through all six fights. Nevertheless, outside of Charles's report to me, I never heard a complaint.

Our next stop was Santa Fe de la Vega which is located on the plains or "*vegas*" outside the famous city of Granada. We toured Granada and its environs, were greeted by the mayor of Santa Fe, and treated royally to an outside banquet. The town let out its schools to see and meet the "Indians from America." We met with scheduled groups of primary school youth and let them ask questions. I served as the interpreter.

"Did they speak Spanish?"

"No," or "No, not anymore."

"Do you speak Indian language?"

"Some of us, yes, and some, no."

"How come they were not dressed in Indian clothes?"

"We are wearing Indian clothes. This is how we dress today. The Indian clothes that you are thinking about are only used for special occasions like ceremonies."

Then they asked two of my favorite questions.

"Do you smoke peace pipes?"

"Not any more."

"Do you use smoke signals to communicate?"

And the answer quickly shot back. "No, we use Internet."

49
Concerning an early opportunity to lecture in Spain

Eduardo Garrigues is not overly tall but his mane of white hair, manicured beard, and blue eyes combine with his carriage to create a presence. Foremost he is a novelist, than he is a Spanish diplomat. We first met in the patio of the Palace of the Governors when he and his wife, Pilar Muñoz, moved to New Mexico to live for a year. Their interest in New Mexico became immediately obvious to me.

I was so impressed that I determined to give them an inscribed copy of my recently published biography of Manuel Alvarez. In my haste to impress the couple I inscribed the book to myself. Thus began a relationship that would produce lectures, conferences, special tour stops, and, even, a surprise meeting.

He used his year's leave-of-absence to live in New Mexico and write a novel about his temporary home.[277] Upon returning to Spain he continued his diplomatic career, eventually becoming an ambassador to a couple of countries.

He had become very interested in drawing the people of Spain and the United States closer together. He saw a kindred spirit in me and we began talking. He organized a *Curso de Verano*, a summer course, at the Escorial for the Universidad Completense de Madrid in which the focus was the connections between Spain and the United States. Along with myself, Garrigues invited Orlando Romero and Nasario Garcia, and many others, to give lectures during the week-long class.

The Spanish *Curso de Verano* is a series of summer courses offered to university students as well as interested public. Rather than one teacher, grades, and term papers, a series of invited scholars give lectures and hold discussions over a one or two week period. Any university student is invited to enroll on a space available basis. They receive credit for the attendance and participation. Over the years Celia and I have been invited to participate in a few of these courses. Celia even worked with Jaime de Salas to organize a cooperative course between the Universidad de Extremadura and University of New Mexico. The idea was for each university to host a course every other year. Unfortunately, and even with funding, both universities lost interest leaving the concept to die after two years. Nevertheless, the idea is something that would greatly enhance the educational systems in the United States.

My first *Curso de Verano*, like most initial adventures, is my most memorable. The quality of my colleagues that ranged from ambassadors to university Presidents and well-known intellectuals, interacting with Spanish students was very impressive. The camaraderie of everyone and the location at San Lorenzo de El Escorial, King Felipe II's grand palace and mausoleum that, in part, became the inspiration for France's Versailles Palace, combined to make that week-long class very special.

Of course, my own lecture of a historical overview of Spain in the southwest was notable if not for the substance, but for two tangential events that occurred. The first of these came from my request for a blackboard. Eduardo Garrigues, ever ready to please, set the staff in motion for a blackboard and as the start time for my talk approached, a successful result of the search appeared dubious. Then within minutes before my lecture, a huge blackboard with, at least, three men carrying it, appeared at the classroom's front door. With great effort, much noise, and a lot of finagling, they forced the board through the door and up onto the dais to place it behind the podium.

My blackboard, however, changed the whole dynamic, for it was large enough to block out the official King's portrait up to his nose. He became a characterization of Kilroy. Obviously, given the effort to get the blackboard and the unintended insult to the King, I had an overwhelming need to use the tool. I am sure that Garrigues felt I would make it all worthwhile.

As I began to talk I got caught up in the moment. Here I was speaking to impressive colleagues, Spanish students interested in my field of expertise, and, then, there were the interpreters who attracted my complete attention, for they were seated in a sound proof booth in back of the room facing me while simultaneously translating my English into Spanish. As I spoke, I noticed that they had become more engaged than the audience in my talk. As I progressed through my presentation with a periodic joke or sarcasm I noticed that I had them laughing. As they became more distracted, they scrambled to catch up or explain the translation, which, of course, enticed me to distract them even more. The whole process got to the point where I was talking directly to them, in fact, playing with them. This built up over a ten to fifteen minute period. I could see that their translation had become hopeless, so I acknowledged to everyone that I needed to stop for a few seconds to give the translators a chance to catch up, for which they thanked me with hand signals.

Before finishing the lecture, I used the blackboard to quickly draw an outline of North America and placed New Mexico in it. My original intent of using the board to trace routes and trails, as well as early settlements, had been lost in the moment. The King's denigration, the huge board, and the effort of getting it in the room had all been for naught.

A few days later, as we boarded the plane for our flight home, Eduardo Garrigues reminded me of my unintended gaff by presenting me with a set of felt-tipped colored pens to "prepare for my next lecture."

50
On how history is made with a bull

Eduardo Garrigues and Pilar Muñoz are very gracious hosts. Over the course of years, I have attended receptions in their homes in Madrid and Toledo, took a tour group to Pilar's parent's ranch in Antequera in southern Spain, and benefited from their friendship in many ways. That first *Curso de Verano* was no exception, for the whole faculty was invited to a "fiesta" at a bull ranch that Eduardo's brother ran.

The occasion, we heard, was to test the six month bulls for their fighting ability. Whether true or not, we were greeted with paella, tapas, and sangria, all of which I love to a fault. Dressed in tennis shoes, Levis, and a mountain man shirt, I enjoyed myself as we watched the ranch's designated matador and others tease the bulls.

Eventually, they came to a bull that was especially difficult, for at first, it refused to enter the ring despite their every effort to make to do so. The bull and the staff made all kinds of noise in the bin under the stands while trying to force it into the ring. Extra men with poles rushed to help out. Still it took a while to prod the bull into the ring. Then, when forced into the ring, this bull did not stop to check out his new environment, which is normal. No, this animal charged across the ring and ran over the surprised matador, hitting him square on the chest with his head.

With his ego wounded but otherwise unharmed, the matador got up. The whole episode gave me sublime pleasure, for I at once, liked the bull's stubbornness and was jealous of the matador. The man was slender and good looking to a fault. His outfit, of black, maybe velvet, pantaloons, and a white, open-chest, balloon shirt, had the women among the audience talking. His pink cape only increased their anxiety. Seeing him get his comeuppance pleased me. "Wow!" I reacted. "If this is a real bull, he's dead!"

I was glad that no one in particular heard me because circumstances and my own foolishness would dictate that I eat my words. After making a few passes with the same bull, the matador, as is customary, invited anyone in the audience to "come down" and give it a try. Almost immediately my two friends Nasario Garcia and Orlando Romero, who were also in the faculty of the summer course, started chanting, "Chaa-vez, Chaa-vez," which was picked up by others including their respective wives Jan and Becky.

Plied well with sangria and once again, caught in the moment, I succumbed to the temptation. Within minutes I was in the ring with the bullfighter who already had lost to this bull. He gave me one end of the cape and instructed me to walk next to him toward the bull. When it charges, we were to separate and let the animal run through the cape between us. "Piece of cake," I thought.

Then it happened; the charge, the separation and...the ground shook as a very mad animal rumbled between us. In an instant I sobered up. There was no more fiesta, paella, sangria; just this animal that now was very big. Oh yes, there was the bullfighter who was enjoying the moment at my expense.

We turned around immediately and the bull charged between us again. "This is not fun," I thought. Then my lifeline, the bullfighter, left me alone with the cape and bull. At this point, Orlando who told me later, thought to himself, "Oh my God. We've killed Tom."

As the bull eyed me I asked in Spanish "how much longer?" Someone in the ring asked if I wanted to leave. "Yes!" And, then, I turned away from the bull to walk (or run) out of the ring. "No! no! no! Never turn your back to the bull," came from the exasperated ranch hands. I had no choice but to face the animal. We stared at each other three to five feet apart. I waited for the charge.

Then, all of a sudden the bull had lowered itself on its front knees followed by his back legs. Before I knew it, the bull was laying on the ground–with the hiccups! The ranch hands were incredulous. They could not believe it. As I pompously turned and walked out of the ring they were yelling to the bull, "Out of here," while adding a few not to be repeated adjectives.

I defeated a bull-calf by humiliating it to the point of hiccups. As a historian I can only conclude that this is the only recorded instance of such a victory and, therefore, I made bullfighting history.

As I have told this story through the years, the bull's size has grown. I distinctly remember that it came up to my arm pits but photographic evidence trumps my memory. The bull-calf was maybe mid-chest high or smaller than he seemed to me. Such is memory and imagination.

Part IV

Every Windmill is in the Eye of the Beholder

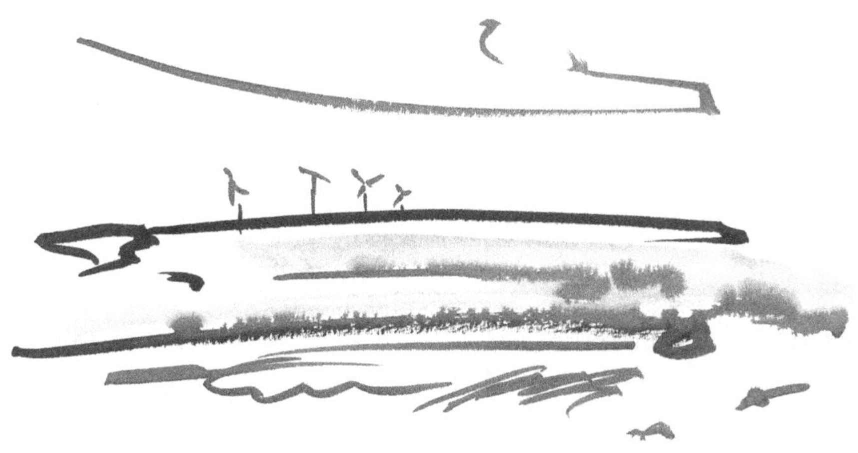

51
About an old man, a fantastic photograph, and a love story

Sometimes in life things turn out differently than they first appeared. At other times the first appearance is correct despite perceptions. Then, there is futility in a wasted or misguided effort. Every person has experienced these sensations.

Don Quixote's most famous adventure was about his encounter with the windmills. The would-be knight and his squire rode up to a series of ten windmills that Don Quixote took to be giants. He had an obligation to slay them and, despite Sancho Panza's protestations otherwise, he charged off lance in hand to nearly kill himself and his horse in the attack.

Upon rushing to help his fallen master, Sancho exclaimed, "Didn't I tell your grace to watch what you were doing, that these were nothing but windmills, and only somebody whose head was full of them wouldn't know that?"

To which, Don Quixote told Sancho to be quiet and proceeded to explain that "matters of war more than any others, are subject to continual change." Therefore he concluded that some magic had been done to turn "these giants into windmills in order to deprive me of the glory of defeating them."[278]

In the end, the two men reversed roles, for on his death bed Don Quixote had come to his senses while the sorrowful Sancho Panza pled with him to become a shepherd. That, too, was a matter of perception that questioned reality if not a plea to keep up the good struggle.

Mariano Chávez was already in his eighties when I met him. I had just started working at the Museum of New Mexico when a smallish, slightly built, balding old man shyly tottered into our shared office. Asking for me, I invited him to sit down. There, we began a relationship that can only be described as enriching.

He wanted to share his life's story and he found a willing audience in me. He was born around the turn of the twentieth century and grew up in the Canadian River Valley north of present-day Roy, New Mexico. His father and grandparents homesteaded there in the 1880s. The family raised sheep and young Mariano grew up a shepherd but not the kind popularly envisioned of a lone man on foot with a crooked staff, and a dog. Mariano, like all the others of his trade in New Mexico, rode a horse and dressed as a cowboy, complete with a rifle attached to his saddle and revolver on his waist.

In the course of our conversations, I introduced him to Diana Ortega De Santis, who helped to put his story on tape.[279] Diana would write an article about Mariano that was published in the Museum's magazine.[280] He joyfully answered all of our questions in Spanish and English. He wove a story full of information about Hispanic life on the eastern plains of New Mexico. At one of our sessions, he showed us some mementos that he had kept. He also showed us some old photographs, which, as he had done with his taped interviews, he agreed to contribute to the Palace of the Governors.

Diana, Mariano, and I were seated around his kitchen table in his modest adobe home in Santa Fe. One photograph caught my attention. Initially, I could not believe what the image depicted. I asked Mariano, "Is that a coyote?" Mariano, anxiously waiting my reaction to that photograph answered, "Yes."

The well-worn and faded photograph is an image of a teenaged Mariano Chávez with his "horse" and a coyote. The coyote has been lassoed with the rope extending around his neck to the pummel of the saddle on Mariano's horse. Young Mariano is standing with his back against the horse facing the growling, teeth-bearing coyote. His revolver is cocked and aimed at the coyote.

Obviously unsaid and unseen in this image is the person who took the photograph. In 1917, when cameras were a little more primitive, the later-day observer is left to ponder at how long Mariano Chávez held that pose before the photograph was shot. Further investigation of the image raises other questions. The terrain looks extremely harsh and broken. How did Mariano get the rope around the coyote's neck? Did he chase the animal down on horse back and, if so, could there be a greater demonstration of dexterity? On the other hand, was the coyote already trapped thus rendering the set up for the photograph relatively safe and if not easy? The elder Mariano Chávez never gave the answers to those questions, for they were never asked.

"Yes," that is a coyote and, then, with an impish smile he told me to turn the photograph over. On the backside, Mariano wrote, "*Mi macho moro y un coyote que cogí*," which translated in New Mexican Spanish with a play on words to, "My brave, spotted mule and a coyote that I caught."

Upon recognizing that Diana and I recognized his play on words, Mariano grinned. Aside from his horse that had to put up with Mariano's prank, the Spanish verb, *cogí*, for "I caught", is a conjunction of the verb *coger*, which also connotes a sexual act in many parts of Spanish America and thus figuratively translated to "...a coyote that I screwed."

Today's animal lovers are hard put to understand such an attitude toward coyotes. After all, they roam through many of our modern western cities and towns where they feed on garbage, small rodents, chickens, and an occasional domestic cat. In Mariano's youth they traveled in packs to attack sheep. In a very real sense, coyotes were a threat to his family's source of income. Thus, in many ways, Mariano Chávez's photograph became a graphic source of information for a period and place in history.

Lest anyone think that Mariano was an inhumane person for their love of the wild, one aspect of his life's story will convince you otherwise. I was soon to learn something about Mariano that could not help but move my feelings, or anyone else's, who heard the story.

Soon after meeting him I realized that I knew both of his sons, Mariano and Epifiano, as well as his grandson, Miguel. We had all met at Chávez family reunions that were very big and active at the time.[281] Miguel is slightly younger than me. He is an artist who specializes in recreating New Mexican Spanish colonial furniture. He also is a community activist who, as of this writing, is a long-time Santa Fe City councilman. His father, Mariano, Jr., and uncle "Epi" have been active in various community organizations for years. Most notably is their association with the Caballeros de Vargas, a group of men dedicated to preserving the memory of Diego de Vargas and Nuestra Señora de la Conquistadora. Given our respective tastes and talents, our paths converged on many an occasion. But it was the family patriarch, Mariano Chávez, the elder, who brought us together.

One day Miguel brought to me his grandfather's invitation to go with them to the old family homestead in the Canadian River Valley. Mariano wanted to show me where he spent his youth so that I could better understand his life's story. I readily agreed to go.

Miguel explained that they had to get permission to traverse private ranch land to get to the site and that we would eventually be driving over some rarely used dirt roads.

While on this trip, I first learned of Mariano's very personal and still emotional story. The first hint came when we stopped at the cemetery in Roy. The graveyard was horribly overgrown with weeds and windblown debris. Mariano got out of the car and asked that Miguel and I stay behind. He wanted to be alone. Miguel answered my inquiring glance with the information that his grandfather's wife was buried there. This began the story, the pieces for which came together from Mariano's family over the next month or so.

On a September's day in 1926 young Antonia "Tonita" Gonzales, Mariano's wife of seven years and a mother of three children, decided to take a ride into town in her brother's new automobile. The car plus the excitement of a Republican convention that had come to town meant that the place would be hopping with activity. Her brother wanted to attend the convention so he invited her along. Along with Tonita's parents and other relatives, she had many friends in town. Also, the place would be full of people. She was anxious to go.

Tonita and her brother met Mariano on the road into town to tell him of their plans. Mariano was too busy tending to the ranch's many chores to join her. Nevertheless, he could not deny her the joy of going. Besides Tonita's happy face conveyed all that he needed to know. In spite of this exuberance, Mariano would maintain for the rest of his life that he had a bad feeling about Tonita's trip into town.

Roy was an agricultural center focused on the Canadian River Valley in New Mexico's eastern plains. The town was much larger than today. Many, if not most, of the people who lived there had moved into the area as homesteaders toward the end of the 19th century. A political convention in Roy was an event worthy of note at the time.

As planned, Tonita met her family and decided to walk with them around the community to take in the excitement. Tonita walked hand-in-hand with her five year old niece while her mother carried Tonita's infant son Mariano, Jr.

At the same time another young woman in town was enjoying the moment. Her husband also had purchased a new automobile and she, like everyone else at the time was fascinated with the new fangled machine. She wanted to try it out and her husband agreed to let her drive. At the time, driver's licenses were not required. The excited woman climbed behind the wheel and proceeded to drive the new car. She quickly lost control of the machine at one of the crowded downtown intersections where none of the people expected to see a careening automobile.

As fate would have it, Tonita and her niece had crossed the street at that very intersection. They were headed toward a store but they never made it there. Tonita saw the out-of-control car coming at them. In a gesture heroic by any standard, she pushed her young niece out of harm's way just before being hit. She saved the little girl's life as her own mother watched in horror from the opposite corner.

Tonita's chest was crushed. She was taken into the store and placed on a cleared counter. One can only imagine the pain of a crushed chest as she lay there beyond help. She suffered for two hours. Her husband, Mariano, was located and brought to her side. He was with her when her pain stopped and she died.

Word of the accident spread through town. Even the convention suspended its activities. Eventually, I was to learn, the story of Tonita's death became somewhat of a local legend. As I told the story to other people who had a connection with Roy, invariably they would interrupt me with the exclamation that they knew about the accident although not the details.

Over fifty years later, Mariano's grandson, the son of Mariano, Jr., who as an infant was held by his horrified grandmother as she witnessed the accident, and I watched Mariano Sr. walk to Tonita's grave. In a scene that I will retain for life, he kneeled among the overgrown vegetation and began to clear the grave site. Then he prayed or, maybe, talked. Never had I seen such an act of love. I would learn later that he never remarried because of his love for Tonita.

Mariano Chávez died in 1981, within a year of our visit to his youthful home. I had gone fishing that Sunday and returned to find a handwritten note stuck to my door.

> "Tom, grandpa passed away today. Please call my father.
> Miguel"[282]

Mariano, Jr. and Epi wanted me to write their father's eulogy. This was unexpected and could hardly be denied. They knew that I had grown close to their father and to say that I was honored by their request does not do justice to my sense of appreciation, responsibility, and, yes, love for the man whose life typified the lives of many people. Everyone has lived an interesting life. Everyone has lived a life strewn with love, humor, and tragedy. We are all touched with those emotions. Mariano was a man who knew and understood that even his humble life had value.

So, I wrote the eulogy that was published as an obituary in the *New Mexican.*[283] My written words became the basis for the eulogy given at Mariano's funeral mass. Like, Don Quixote, Mariano's memory is not lost. He lives through his tapes, his photographs, his family, and his friends. And his beloved Tonita survives through family memory and his photographs. At least two of those photographs capture Tonita's beauty in her wedding dress.[284]

For years after his death the beautiful story of Mariano and Tonita continued to haunt me. I wanted to share it with the greater public. Finally, an opportunity came and I could wait no longer. In 1997, sixteen years after his death, Miguel's daughter Elena, who is as beautiful as her great grandmother Tonita, was chosen to be that year's fiesta queen. The story of her ancestor had to be told and so it was in the local newspaper under the title, "A Long Lost Love Remembered During Fiesta."[285]

52
Concerning the "first Thanksgiving" and sheep

When in April 1598 Juan de Oñate and his colonists traveling north reached the Rio Grande at present-day San Elizaro, Texas south El Paso, Texas and Juaréz, Mexico, they already had undergone hardship, deprivation, and suffering. The succor of the river bottom was a relief that none of them would forget. All of them and their animals hurried to quench their thirst in the water. Indeed, some of the horses drank themselves to death. Game was plentiful at the river bottom and they welcomed a long overdue rest in the shade of the trees. After hunting and fishing, Captain Gaspar Pérez de Villagrá wrote that they,

> "...made A great and excellent campfire,
> And on huge spits and in the coals
> We put a huge supply of meat and fish,
> Placing with liberal hands all that
> Our eager appetites did ask
> To conquer in the most complete sort
> Their great desire for savory food."[286]

The expedition survived the Chihuahuan Desert and arrived at the gateway to what is now New Mexico. They were at a place that they would call El Paso del Norte or El Paso for short. This referred to the riverside pass that would lead them further north into New Mexico, their ultimate goal.

While at the site, Oñate and his people participated in two noteworthy events. First, Oñate did the required *la toma de posesión* or officially taking possession of the land on behalf of the King and God. Next they gave thanks for their survival and success. A mass was held, after which,

> "They did present a great drama
> The noble Captain Farfán had composed"[287]

In early 1980 Sheldon Hall, the Honorary Spanish Consul in El Paso, gathered some friends to plan an April reenactment of Oñate's act of possession. They called their event a commemoration of "the First Thanksgiving" because the historical day of thanks that took place just south of present-day El Paso preceded the inspiration of the official Thanksgiving celebrated in the United States by twenty-three years.[288] Sheldon Hall and his people wanted to make that very point. Their celebration would educate people in their own community as well as the country to a Hispanic heritage in west Texas and the United States that predated the heritage of England.

Sheldon Hall invited New Mexico state senator Tom Benavides and me to participate in the first reenactment. We gladly accepted. They dressed us in period costumes. My outfit included period "balloon pants" and yellow tights. If I did not look like it, I felt like Big Bird, a character in the children's television show, *Sesame Street*. The reenactment script required all of the dressed up participants to move as a colony across a vast parkland open space until we figuratively arrived to the river where the public was invited to watch. We had animals; some dogs, a few horses, a donkey, and a flock of sheep. The grass park in which this was to happen straddles the United States and Mexican border. It is surrounded by freeways and the Rio Grande canal, which is the actual international border between the United States and Mexico.

The procession barely began when it became painfully clear that the sheep would not cooperate, for the flock broke up as individual groups of sheep headed off in different directions. Then it became obvious that no one in the procession had any experience in dealing with sheep. We all ran about waving our arms in a vain attempt to drive the sheep back to a central point. Our efforts exacerbated the situation, for we only spooked the sheep. Within a matter of a few minutes the sheep left the park and got on to the city's streets. Meanwhile, the whole colony was in equal disarray, some of the people were much winded from chasing sheep. We learned that there is more to being a settler than meets the eye.

Fortunately, the people responsible for the sheep came to the rescue. The first thing that they did was to get all of us amateurs out of the way. Sans sheep, we regrouped somewhat disheveled and overheated and continued our procession to a make believe river. We stopped as we approached the audience that no doubt enjoyed the sheep episode. Our Oñate dismounted from his horse while, according to the script, the rest of us kneeled while he gave thanks to God and took possession of the new land.

At that moment one of many photographs were taken and it became an image of an El Paso postcard on which, as clear as day, there I am, kneeling, panting, and internally laughing. Fortunately, my image is small and I was not identified.

El Paso has continued to hold an annual First Thanksgiving celebration. Sheldon Hall took his production to Plymouth where they raised some eyebrows. As Sheldon told it, they had a good time.

On the other hand, some detractors did not like the romance of El Paso's production. They criticized the idea as a historical inaccuracy. After all, Thanksgiving is Thanksgiving and the Pilgrims did it at Plymouth. Nevertheless, Sheldon Hall made his point. He started a conversation and eventually received international press.[289] His foe was not a windmill after all!

53
In which the Smithsonian Institution and Library of Congress learn about "cowboys"

In the summer of that same year, 1980, the Smithsonian Institution's Museum of American History extended an invitation to me to work with Richard Ahlborn. Richard Ahlborn was a curator's curator who had an unlimited curiosity for the collections with which he was charged. Working with him was a great opportunity for me at a time when I was just beginning my museum career. Still a curator with much to learn, my boss Michael Weber enthusiastically agreed to send me east to Washington, DC.

I worked on two projects with Richard Ahlborn. The first and, by far, smallest was reviewing a manuscript about horse saddles that he had written.[290] The second project was an exhibition about cowboy life in Paradise Valley in northwestern Nevada. Teams of anthropologists and folklorists from the Library of Congress and Smithsonian Institution descended upon this valley to record, measure, and collect information and artifacts about cowboy life.

Ahlborn assigned me the task of reviewing thousands of slides and listening to the taped interviews that had been collected. During this process I came upon a panoramic image of Paradise Valley that had as a backdrop the sun setting behind the distant Sierra Nevada Mountains. The sun's rays radiated upward into the sparse clouds. The whole image truly looked like a photograph of paradise. I also had just listened to an interview of an old timer who claimed that he called himself a "buckaroo" and not a "cowboy." "Cowboys," he added, "are those guys over in Wyoming who tuck their pants in their boots."

This statement caught my attention because Ahlborn, with extensive New Mexican connections, had a keen interest in making the relation between modern cowboy life and its Spanish antecedents. Historically, the whole industry was born out of the Spanish experience in America. The Spanish were the first to introduce cattle in the Americas and the cattle-raising industry spread in what is today the United States from Mexico. Historians knew that the term "buckaroo" was a mispronounced derivation of the Spanish term "*vaquero*," which literally means "cowboy." The word comes from *vaca*, or cow and when the *ero* for a male or *era* for a female, is added the translation becomes cowboy or cowgirl.

When I heard the old man call himself *buckaroo*, I latched on to it, connected it to the beautiful image of Paradise Valley and suggested to Ahlborn that we name the exhibition "Buckaroos in Paradise." He immediately agreed. He thought we had a great title. However, when we shared the title with others, some of the staff at the Library of Congress unexpectedly disagreed. They simply refused to accept the title and were pretty adamant about their refusal.

This disagreement caused an impasse, which is a true Washington, DC tradition that led to a meeting in the top floor board room of the National Museum of History. The meeting was called and chaired by Roger Kennedy, the museum's director, who had every intention of settling the disagreement.

The discussion began with representatives from both august institutions present. Arguments went back and forth. Ahlborn pointed out the historical reasons as well as logic behind the title. He noted that the taped conversation backed up his position to use the title. The people from the Library of Congress claimed that the old man was not serious. "He was pulling our legs." Besides, no one could really believe that the term buckaroo was serious.

After about forty minutes of discussion, nothing had been resolved. In fact, the meeting had become interminable. This is when I spoke for the first time.

"Where do you guys get your information? Western movies? I have spent my whole life out west. I was born there. And, I have never heard these people call themselves cowboys or buckaroos. Think! Think for a moment. Do they ride cows? Of course not. They ride horses and what is Spanish for "horse"?

At this point I had everyone's attention and I knew it.

"The Spanish for horse is *caballo,* caa-buy-yo. They call themselves caa-boys. That is cowboys with an accent over the first 'o' and it comes from *caballo.*"

The reaction was immediate. Roger Kennedy, perhaps understanding my ruse spoke first. "We've begun printing the invitations and we need to change them." Upon which he adjourned the meeting.

Ahlborn just stared at me, shook his head, and then laughed. "You just made that up while sitting here didn't you?"

"Yup."

Soon thereafter the exhibition with its catalogue opened with the title "Buckaroos in Paradise: Cowboy Life in Northern Nevada."[291]

54
Regarding a phantom staff member and winning a public contest

In Spain the word for bureaucracy is *burocracia*, which is pronounced, burro-craw-see-ya. Spaniards like to joke that the word's emphasis is on the first syllable "*burro*," the Spanish word for a donkey, which in Spanish or English can be used for an idiot. Government employment, of course, is life in bureaucracy. If the employees refuse to accept the mediocrity that the bureaucracy forces upon them, then the bureaucracy becomes a hindrance.

As an administrator, I believed that my job was to help people do their jobs. Rather than throw up reasons why they could not do something I sought ways to expedite their work. The museum world has a lot of creative people who need to be encouraged rather than hindered. My job was to cut through the "celestial music" so they could create.

Nevertheless, my position was one of many administrative positions in state bureaucracy. I had many an occasion to remind some of the other administrators in the system that they were there to help, not impede. Instead of creating bureaucratic hurdles to impress whoever with their authority, they needed to take pleasure in what they could help accomplish. Dealing with the *burro-cracia* is a constant facet of life in state government work.

Just as was done with the *secretario* of the Archives of the Indies in Seville, we had some opportunities to poke fun as well as make a point. A couple of examples will serve here.

At one point the Palace of the Governors had an opportunity to purchase a sixteenth century "goats-foot lever." This sixteenth century loading mechanism for a crossbow would be a nice acquisition for the collections. The Palace of the Governors had two crossbows.

The staff knew that no one else knew what a goats-foot-lever was, so with some glee, they proceeded to fill out the standard state purchase order. This same form needed to be filled out for pencils, or paper clips, or toilet paper, etc. The fiscal office insisted that all purchases be treated the same, which the staff saw as trying "to fit a square peg in a round hole." The other caveat required that all purchases had to have three bids and their sources cited. Policy allowed for the requester to claim a justified "sole source," which meant that there is one source for the purchase. The fiscal people had trouble believing that anything had a sole source and this is generally true when purchasing pencils, paper clips, toilet paper, etc. Artifacts are a different story.

Nevertheless, the staff dutifully filled out the standard form, filling in the blanks for "price," "quantity, 1," and "Item, Sixteenth century Goats-foot-lever." Sole source was claimed. Sure enough the request was rejected. The terse return note instructed the staff to get three bids. The bureaucracy never bothered to find out what is a goats-foot-lever. All that they knew was that they had a request for purchase and they could reject it because there were no comparative prices for goats-foot-levers.

The staff expected this exact reaction from the bureaucracy and used it to have some fun. They attached pages of published material describing and illustrating a goats-foot-lever to a new purchase request form that once again cited the purchase as a sole source. They added corn seeds and a bottle of wine to the items to be purchased. They justified the last two items by stating that they wanted to grow a historic garden in the Palace's patio and celebrate its harvest with some wine, as was done in times past.

The fiscal people did not appreciate the humor but they had to approve the goats-foot-lever and corn seeds. Alcohol, however, could not be purchased with state money, even for history's sake.

The second opportunity to have some fun at the bureaucracy's expense came a couple of years later and really was aimed at what the staff deemed a ludicrous attitude of one of the Museum of New Mexico's deputy directors. The administration decided to produce an internal newsletter in which the geographically dispersed staff of the Museum of New Mexico's four museums, state monuments, and other departments could share their activities. This, in itself, was a good idea. The nub came when the administration refused to share any information having to do with the staff's participation with community organizations. They only wanted to report on "professional activities." We, at the Palace of the Governors, argued that community involvement is a part of our professional responsibility. Our arguments fell on deaf ears.

I sent the opening salvo when I listed my participation as judge for the New Mexico Junior Miss pageant held in Santa Fe. "Do you have any tattoos?" was one of the questions I put to the young aspirants. I also remember one contestant reciting *Casey at the Bat* as part of the talent competition. Overcome by the pressure, she struck Casey out on four strikes instead of the mandatory three. Of course, my attempt at recognition if not fame, resulted in a telephone call from my supervisor Jean Weber in which she expressed her lack of appreciation for my ploy.

Undaunted, the staff and I decided to have some real fun. We decided to use the newsletter to announce that we had hired a student intern by the name of Jesse Unruh. Now, an observant student of politics at that time would have recognized the real Jesse Unruh as a very influential politician in California. He served in the state legislature for many years and became the state treasurer.

With each issue of the newsletter we shared new information about our bogus Jesse Unruh. He had just moved to New Mexico from California to pursue research in his specialty as a partial requirement for his Masters degree. We sent him to a conference in Quebec where he made a presentation. We gave him a work station with a shared telephone number. We sent him on a tour to all the State monuments to check the care and condition of the Palace's collections on loan to them. Our friend Tom Caperton, the director of state monuments, telephoned to find out about Unruh's inspection schedule, which, of course, we did not know. Outside of the Palace's staff, not even our best friends were in on the scam. Of course, we left Jesse Unruh's schedule open. This allowed us to answer such inquiries with; "when he calls in, we will let you know."

Shortly after we announced the hiring of Jesse Unruh his name appeared on the Office of Cultural Affairs telephone roster. The listed number was shared by the Palace's curators so any calls directed for Unruh were fielded by a staff member. "He's not here right now. Can I take a message?" Or, "hold on. Let me see if I can find him," followed by a muffled shout, "Has anyone seen Jesse?" This, of course, was followed by a distant "no" or "he was just here."

This went on for a period of three or four months. The staff and I anxiously waited for the arrival of the next newsletter to check on the "doings" of Jesse Unruh.

Then, one day, I received a telephone call from the State Personnel Office. They wanted to know whether Jesse Unruh was supposed to be paid because they had not received any paperwork. "Why, yes. He should be paid," I replied. His school is supposed to transfer some money to us and we are waiting for that to happen before filling the paperwork.

Suddenly cooperative, the fiscal people volunteered that if I could send them Jesse Unruh's social security number, they could advance his pay. I thought that this was unbelievable. We could actually get our mythical employee paid! State Personnel volunteered to issue him checks. What a temptation. But, common sense prevailed, for the misuse of state money is the one thing that will result in serious problems. The mere fact that we had pulled off our little ploy to the point where the *burro-cracia* wanted to pay him was enough.

Deciding to end the ongoing ploy, we announced that Jesse Unruh had submitted a letter of resignation and would be returning to California. He had to take his graduate exams and had completed his research while at the museum. The announcement ended with the standard "we will miss him," and, for a while, we did.

Honed by the experience of tweaking our own bureaucracy, we turned our attention to a public entity. As mentioned earlier and as demonstrated throughout this book, the staff and I had determined to raise money for an endowment as well as programs. We also, came to enjoy the weekly seminars held in my office, for they surpassed formal staff meetings in productivity as well as enjoyment. Thus, during one of those seminars, Linda Scheifler, a conservator under contract, pointed out an annual contest run by *The Santa Fe Reporter*. The newspaper posed a series of objective questions about Santa Fe and New Mexico and invited the public to submit their answers. The person(s) with the most correct answers received a check for $500.

The staff decided to enter the contest and use the winnings for some supplies and a staff party. The staff divided the questions and took responsibility for finding the answers. Over the next week staff reported and helped one another until all the questions had been answered. We chose Charles Bennett to be the official contestant and submit the answers. As expected Charles won the contest. Then, he had to go to *The Reporter*'s offices to receive the check where they interviewed and photographed him. When asked how he was able to answer all the questions correctly he replied, in part, that he had at his "disposal resources of...the history library." He added that one of his fellow workers, Jesse Unruh, helped with a question about the opera because he "is an expert on opera." Besides giving us a little publicity, he gave a correct answer, for he and we did use the library as well as the collections, the photographic archives, and each other. Both the interview and the photograph appeared in the next edition of *The Santa Fe Reporter*.[292]

One could argue that such shenanigans are a natural outcome of a group of people who are creative and intelligent. I saw the added benefit of these activities as being a morale builder and I never forgot the words of my predecessor, Mike Weber, who said, "... above all else you need to have a sense of humor" to survive in a government bureaucracy.

Don Quixote constantly convinced others that he was a true knight despite the fact that he was not. Like his creator, Miguel Cervantes, who had an unsuspecting public believing that his novel was history, we latter-day cultural crusaders enjoyed the opportunity to poke a little fun at others, while making a point.

55
Demonstrating how sports can teach heritage

One of those community activities with which I became involved was the booster club at the then College of Santa Fe. The small, private, Catholic, liberal arts school run at that time by the Christian Brothers had a basketball team that competed in the small school level of college basketball. When they hired Lenny Roybal, a local, legendary high school coach to lead the "Fighting Knights," I was convinced to become a booster.

Sports always has been beneficial to my work. Sports permeate the general public's mentality. Familiarity with sports helps relate to the public. I used analogies to sports to make points in lectures as well as teach history.

For example, as a sports fan I had grown up with team names and colors. Beginning with the old baseball Pacific Coast League, I noticed that sports unintentionally taught history. Some of the teams in that league like the San Diego Padres, Los Angeles Angels, and, even, the Hollywood Stars all had nicknames that harkened to their respective city's histories. The Padres referred to the eighteenth century Franciscans who settled California and created the first mission in San Diego. The team even retained the color brown in reference to the modern color of Franciscan habits. Angels is a direct translation of the city's shortened Spanish name Los Angeles, which means the Angels. Other obvious names like the New England Patriots, the University of Mississippi Rebels, the Tennessee Volunteers, and New York Yankees, to name a few, permeate the sports world.

The University of New Mexico's nickname, the Lobos, referenced both New Mexico's Hispanic heritage as well as the Mexican wolf that once roamed the state's foothills and mountains. For a long time Albuquerque's minor league baseball team used the colors of New Mexico's flag and called themselves "The Dukes." Back then the name came from the city's own reference as "the Duke City," which, in turn, referenced the Duke of Alburquerque who was Viceroy of New Spain, today's Mexico, under whom Alburquerque was founded and named in 1706. The new town was named for the viceroy to curry favor. The colors are the same as those of Spain, a country that administered New Mexico for over two and a half centuries.

As fate would have it, I became President of the College of Santa Fe booster club. Charged with generating support and enthusiasm for the basketball program, the club organized dances, membership drives, mailings, ran the concession stand at games, and held team events. Coach Roybal made the job easy because he turned the team into an exciting perennial winner that generated enthusiasm.

After a season when the team made the national playoffs and traveled to Kansas to play in the national tournament, I came up with an idea. The College of Santa Fe did not have a music department and therefore no pepband much less a fight song to play when the team took the court.

I had what I considered a brilliant solution to the problem. Why not hire one of Santa Fe's local Mariachi groups to play "La Negra," which is a very lively, on your feet, fast time song. Like other pep bands they would strike up the music just before each game as the team came on to the court. I knew and still believe that the Santa Fe crowd would go nuts. The violins and trumpets, supplemented by the guitars and *guitarrón*, a base guitar, playing a familiar "party" song would strike the perfect cord for the already enthused home crowd.

What really appealed to me was taking the pep band to Kansas for the national playoffs. I could only imagine what the people in Kansas would think about our unique fight song. With a Hispanic surnamed coach who had recruited more than a few local Hispanic surnamed players for a team that came from Santa Fe, New Mexico, the band fulfilled an image that said something about New Mexico.

I enthusiastically shared my idea with the other club members, coach Roybal, and some school representatives. Everyone liked the idea. I checked all the expenses of hiring the band. The booster club had the money so the question became a matter of priorities.

The last question was never answered, for one afternoon I received a telephone call from the President of the College of Santa Fe, Brother Donald Mouton. He informed me that he and the regents had decided to disband the basketball program and hoped that I understood. I did not understand. Nonetheless I accepted the decision because I was not privy to all the information at Brother Mouton's disposal. That same afternoon, the College of Santa Fe held a news conference in which they announced the end of the basketball program. The pep band idea died with the program.

Years later, the Albuquerque Dukes baseball team moved to Portland, Oregon, leaving the Duke City without a professional baseball team. The city leaders built a new stadium on the location of the old stadium and after a few years absence attracted a new team to Albuquerque.

Unfortunately, an irresistible marketing opportunity took place. *The Simpsons* is a serial cartoon show that features a dysfunctional family whose dufus father, Homer Simpson, works at a nuclear plant. In one episode the father sneaks into the offices of his hometown minor league baseball team to discover the secret plans for the team to move to Albuquerque where they will be called "the Albuquerque Isotopes!" Apparently, the show's writers thought that the name sounded funny.

The real team's owner saw something more. This was a potential marketing bonanza. "Isotopes" hats and jerseys had the name identity for a national market. This proved to be true, for the Albuquerque Isotopes led the nation in the revenue generated from its merchandise among minor league baseball teams.

Nonetheless, I, who was the Executive Director of the National Hispanic Cultural Center at the time, participated in a public protest in favor of retaining the "Dukes" name over a national mockery of becoming the "Isotopes." Martin Chávez, the mayor of Albuquerque came out in favor of retaining the old name. I even received a telephone call at my house from the new team owner who very pleasantly understood my position.

"I could begin a whole lecture on New Mexico history using the Dukes name, logo, and colors." I told him.

"I have no doubt that you could and I would like to attend the lecture," he replied.

I could not fault his logic and, in fact, understood his position, at least, relative to the marketing opportunity. He told me that the legal rights to Dukes name belonged to the old team that had moved to Portland. This was news to me and I subsequently found out that the Pacific Coast League took possession of the rights and, then, turned them over to a private individual from Albuquerque. That person offered to return the rights to the team at no cost if they used the name but, except for throwback games, the offer has not been accepted. Nevertheless, the owner and I hung up on good terms.

Local sports talk show hosts led the campaign in favor of the Isotopes name. Obviously these people considered inconsequential our arguments about historical context and how the old name and colors spoke to the heritage of New Mexico. Taking the opportunity to make one last statement, the National Hispanic Cultural Center held a Dukes tailgate party in its parking lot on opening day of the Isotopes first season. We had fun, a barbeque, live music, and Dukes jerseys. The "Isotopes" name won out and, except for an occasional "throwback" game in which the old uniforms or when a few of the "old-timer" players are brought out, the old name slowly is being forgotten.

As is their want, the local sports pages quickly adopted a shortened form of the name and began referring to the team as the "Topes." Headlines constantly blurted out whether the Topes won or lost. Lost on the writers as well as the talking heads on the radio was when that name is read by the Hispanic community, especially those with connections to Mexico, the name became a local joke. "Topes" means "speed bumps" in Mexico and "bruise" or "bump" in the rest of the Spanish-speaking world. As a result, they read "The Speed Bumps win or loose" and embellished the name with "The Fighting Speed Bumps."

The moral to this story can be assumed. One good joke deserves another.

56
Concerning a mountain man trade fair and buffalo roast

Sam'l Arnold overflowed with ideas. He had spent a successful and colorful life. He was a historian, musician, chef, businessman, and humanitarian. His artist wife, Carrie, who was a member of the Friends of the Palace, always made sure that others did not take one of Sam'l's ideas and draw him into actually doing the work. He had a weakness in helping others as well as seeing one of his ideas come to fruition. Carrie knew that he already had enough to do.

Arnold had been instrumental in the reconstruction of Bent's Fort in La Junta, Colorado. Now a national historical site, Arnold initiated programs at the site, the most popular of which was "winter quarters" where individuals were invited to live in the fort as those who lived there in the 19th century. He became famous for opening a bottle of champagne with a tomahawk, playing the musical saw, and overall playing the role of a nineteenth century fur trader to the hilt. No one could more impressively stand up in full regalia, including his shoulder to floor buffalo coat, lift up his cup of drink and bellow out,

"Here's to the childs whats come afore,
And here's to the Pilgrims whats come after;
May yer trails be free of griz,
Yer packs filled with pews,
and fat buffler in yer pot!
WAUGH!"

With the help of his first wife, Betty, Sam'l Arnold built a replica of Bent's Fort in Morrison, Colorado, overlooking Denver. Arnold's friend and Santa Fe architect Bill Lumpkins helped with the design and techniques. That building became, at once, a residence and The Fort Restaurant. The main dishes reflect Sam'l's lifetime research in frontier recipes. The Arnolds were cultural crusaders who succeeded.

The Arnolds lived in Denver and had a condo in Santa Fe. They had a deep appreciation for the Palace of the Governors. Sam'l constantly came up with ideas for the Palace. We intensely listened because his success lent credence to his thoughts. One of his ideas especially resonated.

He suggested that the Palace of the Governors should host a mountain man trade fair with a buffalo roast dinner. Arnold did not need to convince me about the role of mountain men in New Mexico's history. Many trapped in New Mexico. Others made New Mexico their home. Some intermarried with members of the local population and have left descendents who live in New Mexico today.

As the staff at the Palace discussed the idea we called mountain man re-enactor Jeff Hengesbaugh who, like Sam'l, was another boundless energy, idea person. Hengesbaugh, after all, had traveled on horseback from Tempe, Arizona to Banff, Canada. He and his two companions outfitted themselves as early day mountain men to see if they could survive. They took a camera to document the six-month journey and that was the only modern item they had.

As mentioned, Jeff Hengesbaugh and I had become friends after we met at Bent's Fort. I helped him with a subsequent journey on horseback from Arizona to Santa Fe. I called up the different Pueblo governors' offices to secure permission for Jeff to pass through their reservations. Memories seemed short, for he was constantly stopped and questioned before he was permitted to move on. I drove out of town to meet him coming in and missed him only to find him with his horse on Santa Fe's plaza when I returned to town. Jeff was a natural for our plans.

We came up with a five-day event that we named "The Palace Mountain Man Rendezvous and Buffalo Roast." From Wednesday through Sunday vendors dressed as Mountain Men and women. They set up blankets, lean-tos, and a teepee in the Palace's courtyard. They traded and sold old west antiques and reproductions that ranged from works of art to original flintlock rifles. Period music regaled everyone. A blacksmith worked at his forge in the courtyard adding to the ambience. We arranged for a wild animal park to bring in and demonstrate species native to northern New Mexico. We had artist Kurt Hughey who worked in the Palace Print Shop do the first poster, a silkscreen depiction of a buffalo that has become a collectors' item.

The first "Rendezvous" was held in 1982.[293] For the first few years we held the actual buffalo roast dinner on two evenings; Friday and Saturday nights. Dinner consisted of buffalo roast, rattlesnake, Orlando Romero's *cabrito*, sheep fries and rocky mountain oysters,[294] and a no host bar that featured the Rocky Mountain Hailstorm. The hailstorm was taken out of Sam'l Arnold's recipe book, *Eating Up the Santa Fe Trail.* He found the drink a popular item among traders and trappers at Bent's Fort, which, at the time, had the only ice house in the Rocky Mountain west. During the hot summer months they took the ice, poured in some locally made bourbon, added *yerba buena* or mint leaves, some sugar and a pinch of gun powder. Then they shook the concoction to make a primitive mint julep. This became a favorite item of both staff and museum patron alike.

Along with food and drink we covered the museum's parking lot with straw, pitched a large tent, set out hay bales to sit upon, and let people try their hand at firing muskets, throwing tomahawks, or listen to lectures about the trans-Mississippi west.

Live music and dancing ended the evening. Needless to say we made an impression. The event always paid for itself as well as netted some money for the endowment.[295] Publicity seemed to generate on its own. Many people attended the event dressed in costume. Plus it was really neat to see the Palace of the Governors with its courtyard and parking lot full of people having fun.

Not everything went smoothly. Hengesbaugh gathered up a contingent of mountain men who rode into town on the morning of the first day of the event. They continued to do this each year until they decided to take a longer ride through the mountains from Glorieta. A horse died enroute and was left on the trail. Naturally I received a complaint and called in all the principles for a meeting. With Jeff Hengesbaugh taking the lead we made two decisions. He would have some of the re-enactors go out and bury the carcass and we decided to end the opening parade.

The city initially reacted to the firing of flintlocks by sending the police to us. Obviously, we cannot fire live ammunition in the center of a city even though, as I joked with the officers, "we are aiming at city hall." When the officers found out that we were firing paper wads, everything was okay.

The museum administration worried about throwing tomahawks. As it was conveyed to me they worried that someone might throw the bladed weapon into their own foot. That never happened but we made sure to tell people to let go as they threw.

I did hear a commentator on New Mexico's public radio station read our commercial and then make a sarcastic comment about our "meat feast." Obviously, this guy, who frowned on eating meat, overlooked the salad, corn on the cob, baked beans, or any of the activities being offered.

The greatest problem occurred over alcohol. The vendors all agreed to rules before being accepted into the program. One of these rules was that they could not drink during the day time events. One year they either smuggled liquor into the program or they got drunk at a bar during the hiatus between the end of the daytime market and opening for the roast. Either way a small group of three or four mountain men showed up at the entrance where I always posted myself. They were loaded, foul-mouthed, and obnoxious. I refused to allow them in. This, of course, really made them mad and had it not been for museum security backing me up, I am sure that I would have been in trouble. Fortunately, they left.

The following Monday I was called into Tom Livesay's office where Helmuth Naumer, my old nemesis, waited for me. He wanted to know why his neighbors complained to him about my rudeness. Initially confused over what he was talking about, I gradually came to realize that he was referring to the drunks that I had turned back. Naumer lived out of town in the country and apparently felt a kinship with his neighbors, who were some of the mountain man re-enactors.

Naumer wanted me to write an apology to them. That, I told him, "is out of the question." I then explained what had happened and added that security had filed a report on the incident and, if needed, I could supply a list of witnesses. This ended the discussion and no reprimand was issued.

The Palace Rendezvous and Buffalo Roast has changed over the years. Yet a vestige of it still exists. As mentioned we eliminated the parade. After a couple of years we eliminated the Friday night roast and only did the dinner on Saturday evening. Eventually, the evening festivities were eliminated altogether. The event continues today, however, as the Mountain Man Trade Fair. The Palace Rendezvous and Buffalo Roast was a work intensive event. It was also educational for we used all the senses; sight, smell, taste, hearing, and touching to share a bit of historical information. And, we always made money for the endowment.

That the initial idea lasted over fifteen years and that a part of it is still presented annually every August makes it a successful venture. On the other hand, the fact that all that survives is the trade fair with most of the educational activities eliminated, qualifies the idea as a quixotic adventure.

Sam'l and Carrie Arnold made it a point to travel to Santa Fe every year to attend the Rendezvous and Buffalo Roast. They combined that weekend with annual reservation to the Opera, thus fulfilling two pleasures. Outside of an occasional lecture Sam'l Arnold never had to work on the event that was his idea.

57
On how Christmas came to the Palace

The idea of having Christmas programs at the Palace of the Governors did not receive universal approbation. The idea itself as well as variations of it were criticized from its inception and, probably, continue until now. Most of the criticism was and has been nonsensical. Long before I arrived at the Palace, the staff used various rooms in the Palace for a Victorian Christmas Tree replete with period toys from the collections arrayed underneath.

Immediately after my hiring as the Palace's chief curator, Michael Weber and I put together an exhibition of the collection's Christmas bulbs that led to my introduction of a universal conflict between curators and exhibition designers. We organized the exhibition to demonstrate the evolution of ornaments through time as well as from Europe and into the United States. When installed, we were shocked to see that the designer had organized the ornaments by color, thus obliterating the exhibition's educational value. After complaining, a compromise of sorts resulted in a numbering system that identified each ornament.

Nevertheless, we all understood that Christmas, history, and the Palace of the Governors did have something in common. The idea of Christmas and the Palace were not antithetical. Thus the criticism that the authentic *luminarias* and *farolitos* could cause injury to the public proved false by the very fact that no one was ever injured. A telephone call to a medical doctor at St. Vincent's Hospital confirmed my suspicion to disregard a public complaint that our blinking reindeer would cause an epileptic attack. Then, over thirteen years, we constantly heard the threat that the use of the noun "Christmas," coupled with our presentation of Las Posadas, a traditional Hispanic folk drama of the New Testament's story of Joseph's and Mary's return to Bethlehem and the nativity, put us in violation of our country's separation of church and state laws.

Las Posadas is a traditional community function that has survived decades, if not centuries in New Mexico. "Christmas" only came under attack through political correctness. As a history museum, we dealt with tradition, heritage, and the commonality born out of that past. The fact that the different people who played Santa Claus as well as Joseph and Mary were Jewish, demonstrated an inclusivity that exceeded the goals of political correctness.

With the help of Ruth Holmes who worked for the Bank of Santa Fe that supported our initial efforts, the Palace of the Governors opened its doors to two evenings of simultaneous entertainment, Print Shop activities, apple cider, *biscochitos, farolitos, luminarias,* music, dance, puppets, Christmas trees, and St. Nicholas. Admission was free but, with the suggestion of our secretary Karen Gordon, we asked that everyone donate a canned or boxed food that would be passed on to a local organization to distribute to the less fortunate.

As with the Buffalo Roast, we took every opportunity to educate the public. We included carols in Spanish and passed out song books. Our Santa Clauses received a one-page synopsis of a history of Santa Claus. The name came from Saint Nicolas de Bari, a third century Bishop from Asia Minor who befriended incarcerated children and provided dowries to poor young ladies. He became the patron saint of Greece and all mariners. His remains are buried in Bari, Italy.

Our Santa Claus even sat in an oversized chair that once belonged to New Mexico's own Bishop Lamy, the first Bishop of the Archdiocese of Santa Fe. He wore a distinctive outfit designed and sewed by Christine Tejeda, wife of Museum Deputy Director Skip Pahl. The red and green outfit hinted of a bishop.

We had some unforeseen fun when we worked out a system with Santa's helpers who were children of friends and family of the museum. They talked to the people in line while they waited to see jolly ole St. Nick. In the process, they learned the young aspirant's name and passed it through the ranks to Santa, who greeted each admirer by their first name and sometimes with a personal tidbit. Most of the children accepted this familiarity as par for the course. Some adults could not figure out how he knew the names and information. When asked, we merely replied that he is Santa Claus and, of course, he knew. "You must be an unbeliever," became our standard reply.

From the first night and through the years, Christmas at the Palace attracted between twelve hundred and seventeen hundred visitors each evening. We introduced, indeed welcomed, people to the museum who otherwise might never have gone to the place. I, personally, made sure to station myself at the front door to greet each person and child as they came though the front door. The entertainment was all local, which, in turn, attracted their friends and family. The community saw the museum as opening up to them. We were shedding the time-honored museum elitist label.

Beginning with the Bank of Santa Fe, community support grew. Every year the Palace security force brought to the Palace a life-sized nativity scene that La Fonda Hotel loaned us. Ed Berry, who owned "The Christmas Store" provided ornaments and lights for our many Christmas trees. The downtown businesses opened in the evening for Las Posadas. Even British Airways contributed funds one year. And, of course, we received numerous donations from individuals.

We added Las Posadas in the third year of Christmas at the Palace. The San Antonio Neighborhood Association had been staging the traditional pageant in its neighborhood. Over the years the event had become so popular that the neighborhood became inundated with tourists and buses. What had been a quaint neighborhood activity became a burden and they canceled Las Posadas.

Upon hearing this, from museum supporters, some of whom participated in Las Posadas, we decided to invite the neighborhood association to put on the event in the city's main plaza under Palace sponsorship. We worked out the logistics and agreed to proceed. Instead of going to separate homes on consecutive nights, our Las Posadas would spend one evening to go to different businesses around the plaza and end up entering the Palace's courtyard where all the community would be invited in to see the nativity scene, sing carols, eat more cookies, and have more apple cider.

As portrayed by the San Antonio group, Las Posadas consisted of Joseph leading Mary who was seated on a donkey. They were followed by a choir. At each stop, Joseph knocked on the door and the choir joined him to sing in Spanish asking "the inn keeper" to admit them for the night. They had come to Bethlehem, they sang, for the census, Mary is pregnant, and they need a place to stay. Except for the last stop, the inn keeper refuses them entry because his rooms are full. The San Antonio group added their own nuance, for the inn keepers are portrayed by a singing devil. When they performed on the plaza the devil always appeared from a second floor balcony or porch top. His appearance holding a lantern, all of which was highlighted by flashlights, camera flashes, and hisses from the crowd below, only increased the drama. This setting was even more impressive because we convinced the city to turn off all the street lights and the staff with volunteers passed out two thousand candles.

Las Posadas on the plaza was an instant success. The crowds surprised us. City officials estimated as many as twenty five hundred people joined in the tradition. We hand counted as many as two thousand people crammed into the Palace's courtyard. Within a year we began receiving national publicity and telephone inquiries about Las Posadas.

58
In which reference is made to some complications born out from the subject of the previous chapter

Like anything else, the Christmas programs had some problems. By working two nights of Christmas activities in the Palace, followed by Las Posadas, staff and volunteers were asked to give up a whole weekend the week before Christmas. Every year, the staff organized, set up, and helped produce these programs. Pam Smith and her people in the print shop organized special print related hands-on activities. Orlando Romero and Charles Bennett escorted the "devil" to the appropriate stations; Diana de Santis and James Romero set out the cookies and handled the cider. All the staff worked and helped each other. The logistics for all three nights were complicated and time consuming.

After two years, the San Antonio group did not want to do it any more. They had lost many members from the original group and asked if they could be replaced. We were lucky, for Orlando Romero introduced us to Sister Angie who organized and led Las Posadas in the Parish of Santa Cruz, north of Santa Fe. With Orlando's help we contacted Sister Angie, who instantly agreed to bring her Santa Cruz group to Santa Fe in a school bus to help us maintain a downtown tradition. The people in Santa Cruz even liked the idea of using the San Antonio devils who wanted to continue. Without anyone the wiser Las Posadas continued without skipping a beat.

On occasions, weather interfered. During some years we had to shovel snow to clear a space for Santa's tent in the courtyard. One year we had to cancel Las Posadas. Before the storm hit, the city put up the street barricades that blocked off the plaza. Then it snowed. That night I watched a city police car brake too late and slide sideways into a barrier.

Then there was Pilgrim the donkey. I suppose that whenever a donkey is involved there is potential for a problem and we were no exception. Saul Cohen[296] and his daughter initially played the role of Joseph and Mary. They also volunteered their donkey, Pilgrim, to carry "Mary" through the plaza. Apparently, Pilgrim decided that he did not like the idea, for as we were about to embark on Las Posadas, he bolted. As twenty-five hundred candle-holding, bundled-up people waited on the plaza, we chased Pilgrim through the streets of Santa Fe.

The procession started late without Pilgrim and, to date, a donkey has not been used in Santa Fe's Las Posadas again. As one wag put it that night, we "reduced by one the stable of jackasses working at the museum." We saw it as "early retirement" for Pilgrim.

The devil, like our Santa Claus, unintentionally played on the public's gullibility, for many of the audience could not fathom how the devil got to the second floor of each stop so fast. Almost like magic he would appear. We, of course, had arranged for two devils, to run to alternative stops, usually right through the crowd. As a result, the people saw him telling Joseph and Mary to go away, then among themselves, and within seconds it seemed, appearing on a balcony at the next "*posada.*"

We were constantly questioned about the "magic" of the devil appearing at different locations so fast. We were asked this in spite of the spectacle of both devils joining everyone in the Palace's courtyard at the end of the event! Sometimes questions do not deserve answers.

The weekend of Christmas at the Palace had become so popular that one year I was asked to meet with some City officials. The city had been in contact with the people at Budwiser Beer; whose popular advertising symbol was a large beer wagon pulled by a team of beautifully groomed Clydesdale horses. The company and city wanted to parade the wagon around the plaza as part of our Christmas programs. They thought that the wagon, strewn with Christmas lights, would be a perfect way to entertain the folks before the start of Las Posadas. This, to me, was quite incredible and meant to be a compliment to our efforts. I, like everyone else, thought that the Budweiser wagon was neat. Here I was meeting with company and city officials who wanted to include it for Las Posadas.

They thought that I would jump at the opportunity to include the wagon but I quickly processed the concept and realized that this was not a good idea. For years, now we had separated the first two nights from the more traditional and religious Las Posadas. Now I was faced with the proposition of including a very popular icon that advertised beer with the story of Mary and Joseph and the birth of Christ.

"You want the wagon to parade around the plaza before Las Posadas?"

"Yes." They continued with how neat that would be and what an attraction for the public.

"Do you understand that Las Posadas is a traditional Hispanic rendition based on a passage from the Bible?"

"Yes, but..."

"...And for this very reason we schedule it on Sunday, a day separate from our other more traditional Palace Christmas programs; because some people would see the latter as more commercial than the former?"

This elicited no answers, just stares.

"I'm sorry but we cannot put the two together. That would compromise the significance as well as the context for Las Posadas. The wagon is spectacular but it is a commercial to sell beer."

The city people apparently had expended a lot of effort to get the wagon to Santa Fe. One of them asked if we could reschedule Las Posadas to a different day. I knew that we could not do Las Posadas without city cooperation and permission. It seemed that they were set on bringing the wagon to Santa Fe on the evening of Las Posadas.

I wondered out loud that the wagon would work fine with the Thursday and Friday evening Palace programs and found out, in reply, that Sunday was the only night available for the wagon.

We could not change Las Posadas. Too many arrangements had been made and it was scheduled every year the same way. Then I brought the whole meeting to reality when I concluded, "If you insist on having the wagon on that night, I will cancel Las Posadas. The museum will not be involved with the wagon in conjunction with Las Posadas."

At this a Budweiser representative spoke up and insisted that they, in no way, would be involved in the cancellation of Las Posadas. With this the meeting ended. I offered my apologies, which the Budweiser people refused to accept, for they expressed their understanding.

Las Posadas went on as scheduled and the wagon eventually did come to Santa Fe—at a different time. Las Posadas continues unabated while the overall Christmas at the Palace program has been reduced by a night. Still Christmas at the Palace has become a City of Santa Fe institution.

59
About the benefits of going to lunch

After spending ten months researching in Spain in 1987, I returned to Santa Fe where I was invited to lunch by Judge Harry Bigbee, who, as mentioned, was a long-time friend of two of my uncles. When he was in Santa Fe and not traveling, Judge Bigbee had lunch at the same table, on the same day at the Palace Restaurant. His table sat eight people. Certain people had a standing invitation and others, as happened to me, were invited for that day as a special guest. The invitation came to me through my Uncle Fabián, who was one of Judge Bigbee's best friends and a weekly lunch guest. Fabián, and Judge Bigbee, ran in the same political circles and had known each other for years. Additionally, Judge Bigbee had become fond of Fray Angélico. Upon Fabián's solicitation, Judge Bigbee paid for the publication of a couple of Fray Angélico's books.[297]

So, with more than a little excitement I walked the two blocks from my office to the

Palace Restaurant. I was greeted to a full table that included Fabián and Fray Angélico. Judge Bigbee, who treated for the lunch, ordered for everyone, and clearly was the focal point of any conversation that was to take place. As I learned, he loved to regale his guests with stories and questions that elicited interesting conversation. On this occasion he quickly turned his attention to me and asked about my research in Spain. After I shared a general overview of what I had found, he asked me if I found anything on Franklin.

"Mrs. Bigbee and I are fans of Franklin." He explained to everyone that a person could never get tired learning about Franklin who was a true American genius. When he gave me the knowing nod, I gave him a look of agreement and added that I found a lot of stuff, "even letters that he wrote."

"Like what?"

So with Judge Bigbee intently interested, Fabian looking on proudly, and everyone else politely listening, I launched into an explanation about Franklin's connection to Spanish royalty, diplomats, and intellectuals. Much as I would do with another interested person years later, I summarized Franklin's role with the Conde de Aranda, the Spanish Ambassador to France, and how Franklin had arranged for American corsairs, including John Paul Jones, to take refuge in neutral Spanish ports. I also revealed that Aranda reported that Franklin spoke and understood very little French and, except for their first meeting, they always needed an interpreter present. Finally, I told him about a certificate from the Continental Congress, signed by the Congressional President John Hancock that named Franklin their representative to Spain. Franklin, in an accompanying letter, claimed that he had been named "minister plenipotentiary" to Spain.[298]

Judge Bigbee was impressed. He shared with everyone that he knew nothing of what I had shared. Then he asked what I planned to do with all this new information. I told him that I had decided to digest the overwhelming amount of source material and write a general overview of Spain's involvement in our revolutionary war.

"Have you finished your research?" he asked.

"Oh no, not by a long shot. I have to finish work at the Spanish national archive and then go to two more archives that have more materials."

"Which are these?"

"The National Library of Spain in Madrid, which has documents. The Archive of Simancas in Valladolid has a lot of diplomatic material."

Every person has any number of memorable moments in life and, for me, this was one of them. Judge Bigbee turned to his daughter Elizabeth, who was sitting at the table, and said;

"Elizabeth, I want you to go back to the office and write a check for ten thousand dollars in Dr. Chávez's name. We need to help him finish this interesting research."

I was aghast and my two uncles were completely surprised, for both of their jaws dropped simultaneously. Others, at the table, smiled in approval. Judge Bigbee's smug and pleased look assured me that he meant for me to have the money and finish the research, so all that I could do was thank him.

He asked that when the time came, I should acknowledge Mrs. Bigbee. I fulfilled that request more than once, or so I thought, and am doing so again as I write. When I completed the first six chapters of the manuscript, I sent them to her for comment. She replied with some astute observations. Of course, not all went smoothly. I once wrote a letter to Mrs. Bigbee and spelled her name "Bigby." Elizabeth returned a copy of my letter on which she handwrote the correct spelling with a note,

> "Tom, when you blow it, you really blow it. The name of your donor is spelled BIGBEE. Better luck next time."[299]

I suspect that my apologies to Mrs. Bigbee were accepted because we continued to correspond. However, I am not sure that her daughter was ever really confident in me.

The first opportunity to acknowledge her came when the Daughters of the American Revolution asked me to write a feature article about Spain's role in American independence for their national magazine. I dedicated the article to "Mrs. Allene Penry Bigbee, 1887-1989, a long-time member of the Daughter of the American Revolution...."[300] Unfortunately, here too, I messed up. While Mrs. Bigbee's birth and death dates are correct the name is the mother of Judge Bigbee. Finally, I got it correct when I acknowledged the generosity of Judge and Mrs. Bigbee in the book's forward.[301]

Both Judge and Mrs. Bigbee have passed away. I attended Judge Bigbee's funeral. Their support went along way to helping me complete the research for the book. I also used some of the money to purchase my first computer and to hire translators, including Fray Angélico and Donna Pierce, to help speed up the process. That lunchtime conversation led to the gesture that created the germ of the idea that led to the further research on Franklin, a project that still continues. Some day Franklin's documents in the archives of Spain will be published and made available to all the Franklin fans in the English-speaking world. I only regret that the Bigbees will not be around to enjoy the moment.

60
In which is related a very great honor

Working in a museum and chasing history probably gave rise to the greatest personal honor of my career. One day Fray Angélico walked into my small office and sat down. I watched him as he walked through the reception area and, as always with him, I had an immediate sense of anxiety. I had no idea why he had come to see me. Maybe, I thought, he had a complaint about something missing from the library that he knew was there. Or, perhaps I had irritated him with a quote in the newspaper. But then again, maybe I had done something good, like the time he came into my office to give me his approval for getting the Martínez de Montoya papers. What could it be?

Although he was a small man his presence filled my office. He really did look like the actor and comedian George Burns and the fact that he, like Burns, loved cigars did not dispel the comparison. With Fray Angélico the odor of cigar permeated my office. But, what overwhelmed me were his accomplishments as a writer and humanitarian. And, that he was the eldest brother of ten that included my father was never lost on me.

So there we sat facing each other across a hundred year old desk in an office that measured less than most jail cells; me and this priest, man of letters, idol of my family.

"Father, how are you? What can I do for you?"

"I want you to finish my book."

"What book?"

"The biography of Juan Felipe Ortiz."

I knew that he had written a large manuscript about the Catholic Church in the nineteenth century in which he focused on three priests of the Mexican Period in New Mexico's history; José Antonio Martínez, José Manuel Gallegos, and Juan Felipe Ortiz. He submitted that manuscript to the University of New Mexico Press but they refused to publish it because it was too large. This convinced him to divide it into three books each focusing on the men mentioned above. By the time he came into my office he had published the first two books on Martínez and Gallegos.[302]

The second of these books had been an embarrassment to him because the book's sub-title stated that Gallegos was "New Mexico's First Congressman" and that was incorrect, for he was not New Mexico's first congressmen but the second congressman after Richard N. Weightman. The reviewers did not fail to notice the error. Like an athlete who was at the end of a brilliant career, this intellectual, now in his eighties was not as sharp as he used to be. In fact, he was mentally slowing down and he was self critical enough to realize that what came easily before could not be done now. Yet, he still had not finished the Ortiz book.

"But Father, why do you want me to finish it?"

"Because you are the only other historian in the family and," pointing to his head he continued, "I cannot get what is here to paper."

"Sure you can Father. Just work a little slower." One of the truths of museum work is that you work a lot with elderly people. Retired people make up a majority of museum volunteers and support groups. Indeed, most of the museum's major supporters were, and still are, elderly. As some of the stories in this book relate, we had experience working with people do things late in life.

"No." he replied and then he repeated, "You don't understand. I cannot get what is here," again he pointed to his head, "to here." Where upon he gestured with his hand as if he was writing. "I can't get it on paper."

I still did not understand completely. But I could see that he was serious and making an effort to control his patience with me. So, I acquiesced.

"Okay, Father. What should I do?"

"Go over to the archdiocese offices and ask for my manuscript. I have already spoken with the archbishop[303] to release it to you. I want you to finish it."

So I did as asked. The manuscript was typed with notes on lined notebook paper in Fray Angélico's miniscule handwriting. All the pages had been placed in a blue three-ringed binder.

Not much time passed when what Fray Angélico was trying to tell me became obvious. During one of his afternoon walks he collapsed on a downtown side walk. Taken to the local hospital they quickly diagnosed that he had an advanced tumor on his brain. He passed away within months of coming to my office.[304] What he told me about himself was exactly correct. He did not realize the cause, but he was conscious enough to realize that something prevented him from transferring his thoughts to writing; "from here to there." The tumor prevented it.

In conversations and some exchanged correspondence with the scholar Dr. Nasario García, Fray Angélico acknowledged that he could no longer read or write because "due to the tumor that has been discovered at the top of my brain!" Nasario, who wanted to interview Fray Angélico for a book but was refused, observed that New Mexico's intellectual icon "recognized that for a man in his 80s, both the physical stamina and intellectual acumen—the trademarks of a stellar career as churchman, scholar, and humanist—were no longer inner parts of his persona."[305]

Some years later I finished Fray Angélico's last book. The title itself resulted in both of our contributions and is analogous to our collaboration. His original title of "Wake for A Fat Vicar: A Biography of Vicar Juan Felipe Ortiz" became *Wake for A Fat Vicar: Juan Felipe Ortiz, Bishop Lamy, and the New Mexican Catholic Church in the Middle of the Nineteenth Century*. Fray Angélico and I are listed as co-authors, which is a singular honor for me.

61
Relating to the wonder of a chance meeting

Late in my career Celia and I were invited to a private reception to honor Frederick and Jan Mayer at a private residence in Santa Fe. We arrived slightly late because Celia taught a class that day and had to drive from Albuquerque. I waited at the foot of the dirt driveway for her. She arrived at dusk.

Upon entering the home Donna Pierce greeted us. Pierce held the Mayer Endowed Chair in Spanish Colonial Art at the Denver Art Museum. She knew the Mayers very well.

Without much of an opportunity to orient myself Donna exclaimed, "Mr. Mayer is anxious to meet you. Come with me." She then led me through the crowd.

Pleased with this unexpected news, I dutifully followed her to an elderly, slender man, who was gracefully enjoying the small talk from four or five people vying for his attention. As Donna approached the group, he turned to her and she introduced me. He looked at me with a smile, stuck out his hand to grab mine and said, "I like your book!"

"Which one?" This had become my standard if somewhat flip reply.

"About Spain and the United States."

"Thank you. I think it is my most important work."

"It is very important. I read many books and keep very few but I still have yours."

"Wow! Thank you again."

Then he told me that we needed to talk over dinner later that night. Apparently, arrangements were made to have the two of us seated together at an elegant dinner in Santa Fe's El Farol Restaurant. We talked about my book, the state of Hispanic and Latin American studies in the United States, and that he had made major contributions to, and sat on the boards of the Yale Art Gallery and Denver Art Museum among other institutions. His primary passion was Latin American and Spanish art and history. He had a deep appreciation and curiosity for the contributions of Hispanic and Latin cultures to the United States.

Mr. Mayer asked me what I was working on at the moment. I explained that I had begun a project to transcribe, translate, and annotate all the documents pertinent to Benjamin Franklin that existed in the archives of Spain.

"Did Franklin go to Spain?"

I explained that no, Franklin never went to Spain. However, he corresponded with Spanish officials before, during, and after the Revolutionary War. He also corresponded with the King's son about music and the translation of documents. Also, he was a member of the Spanish Royal Academy of History.

"So, what are you doing?"

"I want to publish all the documents that are known to exist in the Spanish archives. These would be documents that are letters and reports written by him, to him, or are about him."

"Are there many?"

I then gave him the background on how I came across many Franklin documents that I used as source material in my book. Then with the 200th anniversary of Franklin's birth upon us in 2006, a plethora of new biographies of the man had come out. As near as I could tell, all of them had been authored by a prize winning writer but none divulged any new information rather than different interpretations of existing knowledge. None of these writers used the Spanish archives or my book so I felt that a published compilation of this new material would be an appropriate addition to the field. I already had prepared around 150 pages, including an introduction. I would use that as a basis to request funds to finish the project.

Mr. Mayer asked why I needed funds so I explained that a majority of the documents were written in Spanish or French and that, so far, Celia and I had identified six archives with Franklin documents. To date I had photocopied another two hundred or so pages of documents that were in my possession waiting to be processed. If I continued by myself, the project might take up to ten years to complete but if I could hire a team of four to five people, that would include transcribers and translators, the first publication might possibly be ready in three years. There is so much material, I told him, that I foresaw a multi-volume edition.

Obviously surprised and interested in what I was sharing with him, Mr. Mayer asked how much money I needed. I gave him an estimated amount and he inquired; "Does that include your salary?"

"No, I have my retirement. The money is to pay for the team members and some travel."

"But Tom," and he leaned toward me, "you need some money for wine!" By then we knew that we shared an appreciation for red wine. Then he asked, "When will you finalize your budget?"

"Soon."

"When you do, send it to me. I think I can help." He then proceeded to ask if I had thought of various other funding sources with which he had connections. In response to his suggestion for the Henry E. Luce Foundation, I explained that I was familiar with them and that they helped fund the History Library at the Palace of the Governors. "But, they do not support history research projects."

"Yeh, but I know a couple of board members. Maybe I can help there."

"Thanks."

The night ended after a last glass of wine. Mr. Mayer enjoyed himself and was almost the last person to leave. I followed up on our conversation and sent him a letter thanking him for the wonderful time. I also explained that I could not send him a budget proposal for a couple of months.[306] At the time I was working to raise an endowment for the Museum of Spanish Colonial Art and the reason for the occasion during which we met was because the museum had put up an exhibition featuring his and wife's collection of art. I had notified the museum of my resignation at the end of the year so, to avoid a conflict of interest, he would have to wait until then to see a formal request.

As promised, I sent Mr. Mayer a detailed budget that included a cover letter and a rough draft of the first 150 pages of the project. A week later I received a telephone call from a woman who worked at the Denver Art Museum. She informed me that she had received my packet and said, "I am afraid that I have some bad news."

I braced for something to the effect that Mr. Mayer had lost interest in my project or had other priorities.

"Mr. Mayer died last week."

I spent one pleasant evening with this man and, if the effect he had on me is any indication, then I can only imagine the influence that he had on those who really knew him.

62
In which a photograph proves a conversational point

During my lifetime Marc Simmons, PhD, has been one of the better historians of New Mexico. His ability to create wonder about yesterday's people and events permeate his books and articles. He is the state's most popular historian, in part, due to his weekly newspaper articles. While it seemed that at times the field of history was becoming esoteric and incomprehensible, Simmons maintained an equilibrium that not only made history accessible but also attractive.

I had the pleasure of driving Dr. Simmons to his home in Cerrillos one time. Cerrillos is a small village nestled in foothills along the Galisteo Basin about fifteen miles southwest of Santa Fe. The trip took about a half hour mostly on a heavily traveled two lane highway, so we had a chance to talk. Naturally, our subject was history. Simmons started musing about how things we know as history did not happen so long ago. He mentioned Civil War veterans who lived well into the twentieth century, or Wyatt Earp, one of the west's most famous gunmen, who lived into the 1920s. I mentioned a great, great uncle who died in the Civil War battle of Chickamauga in Tennessee.[307] He was my grandfather's uncle and except for my grandfather the family had completely forgotten his story.

My grandfather on my mother's side was from Ohio. On one occasion he told my brother and I, who were both young teenagers at the time, that his uncle was a Civil War hero. He had no details and did not know the story. Not until his son, Allen who is my uncle, decided to delve into family history did we learn that grandpa had reason to be proud. His uncle, Sylvester Sprowl grew up on a farm in Ohio and fought in Union forces that were routed at Chickamauga. In a letter written to his parents by an officer we learn that during the battle the standard bearer was killed. Sylvester picked up the flag and instead of retreating with his comrades, he tried to rally them to hold their ground when he was shot in the chest and left for dead. He died some days later in a Confederate field hospital.[308]

Simmons then told me of an elderly person that he interviewed who, in turn, knew a person whose grandfather had participated in the Revolutionary War. I, taken aback, began to calculate the years but Marc explained that the person fought in the war in his middle teens and lived a long life. He had a son late in life. Yes, this was possible; especially when I considered that my own four grandparents were born in years that ranged from 1879 to 1899. They lived the formative parts of their lives with no automobiles, much less airplanes.

To illustrate the point, my father told me a story of a carpenter who lived for the first three to four decades of his life without indoor plumbing, for it did not exist. He grew up with outhouses that were always placed at a discreet location away from the main dwelling.

When he first heard about the new fangled idea of indoor plumbing he reacted with, "You mean that you put the shitter in the house?" This, to him, was very unsanitary. Yet, today some historians have begun to study outhouses.

This discussion of how history really is not so distant culminated with a photograph in the Palace of the Governors' collection that I published in *An Illustrated History of New Mexico.* The photograph depicts three people, all one hundred years old or older and is titled "The Centenarians." One of the people in that stereograph is identified as Juan Jesús Rivera, age 106. The image was taken around 1880.[309] Computing from the 1880 date means that Mr. Rivera was born before the Declaration of Independence! Here is a photograph of a man who lived in the eighteenth century and, so far as photography goes, the image was taken a full forty years after the invention of photography. Indeed, history really is not distant.

63
Concerning the value of a photograph for retrieving history

I come from a family of veterans. One grandfather fought in World War I. Both my mother and father are World War II veterans. Five uncles and an aunt served in the armed forces. My brother, a sister, and I spent time in the army and one of my daughters was a pilot in the Air Force. My father joined the Marine Corps as a seventeen year old and was sent to the South Pacific where he was off loaded from his ship during the Kamikaze attack on his fleet. He then participated in the invasion of Okinawa and was sent to China. With peace proclaimed he was put in charge of Japanese prisoners of war, primarily to protect them from the Chinese.

Later in life he became a municipal and superior court judge in Los Angeles where he became acquainted with many Japanese-Americans in the legal community. One of these men became the judge who presided over the infamous O. J. Simpson murder trail.

Judge Lance Ito became momentarily famous for the trial's extensive television coverage. He also became a source of a joke among the Spanish speaking community,

"How do you say small judge?"

The answer is, "Judge Ito!"

Another of these men, Hiroshi Fujisaki, presided over Simpson's much less publicized civil trail. Judge Fujisaki once visited me in my office at the Palace of the Governors.

My father was involved in many serious cases that, on occasion, required police security on our house. Most notable of these was when he signed the arrest warrants for members of various militant organizations. He also signed the arrest warrants and then arraigned Charles Manson and his gang. So this is to put into context, how a man who survived World War II, as well as his own career, can influence the decisions of any of his family's members, in this case, me.

My father's friendships with people in the Japanese-American legal community combined with his passion for trout fishing. He was invited to go on the annual weekend fishing trips to Bishop, California and Lake Crowley. The Japanese-American community rented a bus every year to go on this outing. So, one year, I went along. I was a teenager and old enough to retain the many conversations and stories that I heard as we traveled up the Owens Valley along the eastern slopes of the Sierra Nevada Mountains.

At one point some of the people pointed to some roadside ruins of what looked like might have been a small town. The place was Manzanar, a World War II internment camp where the United States government placed Japanese people who had been forcibly removed from the West Coast. Some of the people on the bus where placed there as children and stayed there for the war's duration. I learned that in the war time paranoia, all Japanese on the west coast, whether citizens or not—and for a long time California laws prevented them from becoming citizens or even holding property—were removed from their homes and businesses to inland internment camps.

My father, who had fought Japanese and gone on to a successful legal career, explained to me the injustice, albeit understandable, of the whole Japanese-American "removal." "It was wrong," he told me.

Now, "dear reader," as Cervantes would phrase it, you must be wondering why you had to suffer this short personal diversion. Of such experiences, actions occur. And so, it happened with me.

My memory of fishing with my dad's friends was resurrected while I worked at the Palace of the Governors. The staff in the library received periodic inquiries about "the Japanese internment camp in Santa Fe." Unfortunately, neither the library nor the archives had any information. I remembered that historian Richard Melzer, a colleague who shared an office with me in graduate school, had published an article about the camp in an anthology.[310] As the only source to which we could refer people, I reread his article and searched for other sources. I discovered that, at least, two of the inmates had been buried in the local cemetery but their burial records had been lost. However, an obelisk with Japanese characters still marked their burial sites. The markers can be seen from the nearby road.

The more that I thought about the subject, the lack of information about the camp struck me as odd. I talked to my parents about the situation and they both encouraged me to proceed. My father, I learned, had actually delivered ice to the camp as a teenager with his friend Bill Baca. So, I decided to write about what I called "forgotten history" in my monthly newspaper article. I concluded the article with a potential solution to this overlooked story:

> "So we, in this community, need to look to ourselves for old photographs, letters and records and take them to our museum and History Library. We need to share our history not bury it—no matter how inconvenient. And would it not be nice to acknowledge the fact with a plaque...? Perhaps a monument to all wartime prisoners that list the New Mexican related "detention camps" with the inmates' names that might get people to think in greater depths about our history."[311]

The article resonated, for within a month a committee was formed. I asked my friend Doc Weaver to join me with a number of other community members who had contacted me. As mentioned earlier, Weaver was primarily responsible for the lucrative tile wall project in the library as well as doing the necessary work to get the series of historical novels published. Aside from all his support, he and his wife Alyce had become close, trusted friends. Helping to convince the City of Santa Fe to recognize a piece of its history by putting up a historical marker commemorating the Japanese internment camp would become his shinning, if unheralded, moment with the museum.

Doc, a veteran of Vietnam where he was a pilot and a retired colonel from the United States Air Force, joined the cause without hesitation. He was joined by Joe Ando, a Japanese American who also was a retired colonel from the Air Force. Ando and his parents had been removed from California. He and his mother eventually ended up in a camp in Texas. His father was deemed a community leader and therefore spent the war interred in Santa Fe. Both Doc Weaver and Joe Ando agreed to co-chair the committee.

Santa Fe was a camp of all male, mostly elderly men. These men were doctors, teachers, ministers, agriculturalists, and businessmen. The United States government considered them community leaders and, therefore, dangerous. The government separated them from their families to place them in Santa Fe where the government could keep a closer watch over them.

New Mexico has a special history when it comes to war. The Mexican War was fought, in part, in New Mexico. Over sixty years later General John J. "Blackjack" Pershing set up his base of operation in southern New Mexico to chase Pancho Villa in northern New Mexico. Less than three decades later in the mountains of northern New Mexico, people of the secretive Manhattan Project researched and created the first atom bomb that was first exploded at Trinity Site in central New Mexico. A disproportionate amount of men from New Mexico enlisted to fight in WWII and it was from New Mexico that the 200th and 515th Coast Artillery of the National Guard was called into active service and sent to the Philippines just before the outbreak of that same war.

The 2,000 New Mexicans in those National Guard units were part of the under equipped and under supported American and Philippine force that met and resisted the initial Japanese invasion of the Philippine Islands. General Douglas MacArthur, while fleeing with his wife and pets, ordered the abandoned U. S. forces to surrender, which they did in April 1942 in the single largest surrender of a military force in U. S. history. The captured troops suffered horrendous treatment and deprivation at the hands of their Japanese captors. The underfed prisoners were forced on the famous Bataan Death March. Men were bayoneted, casually shot, had their throats cut, as well as beheaded.[312] Then many of the survivors were packed into the holds of transport ships to be taken to Japan where they were forced to work in mines.

The few that returned home after their liberation justifiably harbored bitter feelings toward their Japanese captors. Quite naturally, then, some of these men, now in their eighties, as well as their families bitterly opposed the idea of commemorating a Japanese internment camp in the capital of their home state.

The committee moved right into the middle of this historical controversy, replete with some extreme emotional and philosophical issues. Opposition to the committee's plans coalesced quickly. Family and friends had to side with the Bataan survivors. To do anything different would dishonor their sacrifice and suffering. One outspoken opponent was a retired lieutenant colonel who never left North America during the war. He was a slender man with a goatee who wore his kaki brown army uniform with a soft hat and a chest full of medals. He did not wear his medals as the customary ribbon in rows over his left pocket. Rather he preferred to hang the medals in a dazzling array on his chest as well as from his cap.[313]

Retired Lieutenant Colonel George Hawthorn personally called me and the members of the committee, "disloyal traitors." He also stated that if a monument or marker went up commemorating the Japanese Camp, he would urinate on it. He refused to believe that any Japanese could have been United States citizens or could have served in the U. S. armed forces.[314]

Here was the nub of the problem, for while Colonel Hawthorn was outspoken in the extreme, those Bataan survivors who openly opposed us, emphasized the hurt that this was causing them. They did not threaten or accuse people of disloyalty. On the other hand, they could not believe that all Japanese were not the same as their captors. The fact that one of our committee, a career veteran, was a son of a camp intern did not initially register with them. Nor did they want to believe that the U. S. Army's 442nd Regimental Combat Team made up of volunteer Japanese Americans was the most decorated U. S. unit in the European theater of war and that many of them had enlisted out of internment camps. This was beyond comprehension.

The committee agreed to be associated with the museum, where we continued to meet. The feelings on both sides of the issue ran deep in the community and the committee needed the city's official approval for a marker because we planned for it to be placed in a city park on a hill overlooking the site of the camp.

Over time the committee agreed on the text for a bronze plaque that would be attached to a large granite boulder. The committee also began the process of going through the city's bureaucracy to win approval. The last procedure is where our effort slowed to a crawl. The task of dealing with the politics fell on Doc Weaver and me.

The process pointed toward the city's leaders making a decision, for the opposition used its many familiar connections to force it into the public forum where the press gave it extensive coverage. Emotional issues are never fun and here was a case where justified emotion existed on both sides. The survivors of the Bataan march came out against the marker and they had long and very deep community ties. The proponents for the marker had very few current residents who had direct ties to the camp. No camp survivors lived in Santa Fe.

While trying to show empathy for both sides, I felt that the real issue was history and how the community chose to treat its history. In sending to Doc Weaver a draft of an "op-ed" that a local newspaper invited me to write, I wrote in a cover note explaining that "I tried to take the high road and not make our position sound like an 'us or them' proposition."[315] I ended the op-ed with the following words,

> "History is not all pleasant, but it is beneficial. To grow and benefit we must learn from our pain, be it physical or emotional; Otherwise the misery wrought by war is for naught."[316]

Upon being confronted with the idea that Japanese loyalty to the United States was fiction, I rather directly, if not brutally, replied in the press that "I'm here to present history and what happened. If people do not want to believe it, I can't control that."[317] This infuriated one of the survivor's relatives, who was a rather large young man. He let it be known that he wanted to see me. My boss, Tom Livesay, thought that I might get "punched out," so, at a subsequent city gathering, he kept watch over me.

That gathering was a city mandated venting session where all sides were invited to confront each other seated in groups of eight or ten people. Gerard Martínez, of the city's office of Intercultural Affairs who helped usher the proposal through the city bureaucracy, came up with the idea and took a risk, for although nobody changed their opinion when it came to "for" or "against," words were connected to human faces and the debate became civil.

The press covered the gathering. Radio people interviewed, television taped, and journalists took notes and snapped photographs. The always observant Doc Weaver saw an opportunity to win some sympathy while seated next to Joe Ando's wife, Millie Ando, who was a camp survivor. She was giving a tearful account of her experience when a newspaper photographer aimed his camera. Doc put his hand on her shoulder as a sign of sympathy. As luck would have it, that photograph was published in the town's main newspaper the next day. The photograph's caption read in part "...Weaver comforts Millie Ando...as she shares her pain...."[318] For the first time, our side had generated some emotion in its favor. The photograph received far more play and had a greater effect than the accompanying article.

As the debate continued everyone began to realize that the matter would have to be decided by the city council. The mayor, who had a vote if the council tied, and the individual city councilors started receiving letters, telephone calls, and actual visits. Some councilors looked at their constituency and said that they could not support the marker because a Bataan survivor and his family lived in that councilor's district. The influence was such that a vote in favor of the marker was a vote against the honor of the survivors' service. That was political suicide. Councilor Patti Bushee expressed support. Carol Robertson López remained in doubt until the night of the vote. We were not sure of her vote until it was cast. Bushee saw that the vote for approval was tenuous so she had it tabled to a subsequent meeting that was set for 27 October 1999.[319]

As the city council meeting and vote neared, Joe Ando shared his collection of memorabilia with the museum. Part of our project was to collect information about the Santa Fe camp and put it in the Palace's library. In the process, we received letters, learned of the existence of a camp newspaper, photocopied drawings of the camp and its inmates, and collected some photographs. We also raised some money that was donated to the library to maintain and preserve the potential collections.

One of Joe Ando's photographs was a rectangular image of all the inmates attending a funeral in the camp. Ando's father was in the image but the overall photograph impressed me, for it hit at the very heart of our message. The inmates were arrayed around a casket behind which stood a young Japanese-American dressed in a uniform of the United States Army. The young soldier had been called from active duty to attend his father's funeral. His father had died of natural causes while an inmate.

Here was photographic evidence of the injustice of the intern camps. The photograph showed Japanese loyalty to, and service in the United States' armed forces. Sensing an opportunity I secured Ando's permission to take the image to *The Santa Fe New Mexican*. The newspaper published the photograph on its front page.[320] A short time later the city council held a meeting in which all sides were invited to express their views. I and others spoke before the council. I listed the historical facts and argued that no community, least of all Santa Fe, should censor history. In the process of my presentation I noted that the nearby National Cemetery contained the final resting places of Confederate soldiers who had died fighting Union troops in the Battle of Glorieta Canyon south of Santa Fe during the Civil War. Surely that example of humanity should dictate to us today to put emotions aside and do what was correct.

All the newspapers endorsed the marker as the evening for the vote approached. *The Santa Fe New Mexican* urged a positive vote as a "modest footnote to a sad chapter."[321] Dick McCord at *The Santa Fe Reporter* wrote that a vote in favor "...would show truth, regret and forgiveness. And, it would give old warriors a last chance to lay down their arms."[322]

At its meeting on 27 October, the council held a role call vote that resulted in a tie. All attention turned to Mayor Larry Delgado who would cast the deciding vote. The mayor was a native of Santa Fe whose ancestors dated centuries back in New Mexico's history. He celebrated his election with a reception in the Palace of the Governors. He was a thoughtful man who had been approached by advocates on all sides of the issue. He had a difficult decision to make and he did so without hesitation. He voted in favor of the motion to create a marker.

The reaction was immediate. Clarence "Porky" Lithgrow, a local politician and son-in-law of a Bataan veteran jumped up from his front row seat and shouted, "You just kicked the Bataan veterans in the teeth in twilight years of their life." People yelled for him to sit down. Then in the middle of the council chambers Lithgrow got into a shouting match with someone in the audience. The Deputy Chief of Police stepped between the two men to end the confrontation.[323] After the council voted to allow the marker *The Albuquerque Journal North* opined that the "vote for the marker deserves praise."[324]

The unveiling of the marker took place on a bluff at the Frank S. Ortiz City Park on 20 April 2002.[325] A fairly large crowd estimated at around three hundred people attended the event. Joe Ando gave the keynote address and Councilor Patti Bushee spoke on behalf of the City. The committee raised enough funds to fly in the only camp survivor that we could locate. When asked about his most lasting memory of his days in the camp, he quipped,

"No women."

More poignant, however, was the marker's text. Doc Weaver wrote an initial draft that was turned into the committee for comment. And comment they did! The text grew way beyond what we could have, so cutting back and editing was turned over to Joe Ando who would worked with me. In the end, we came up with a text that is both tasteful and educational.

> "At this site, due east and below the hill, 4555 men of Japanese ancestry were incarcerated in a Department of Justice Internment Camp from March 1942 to April 1946. Most were excluded by law from becoming United States citizens and were removed primarily from the West Coast and Hawaii.
>
> During World War II, their loyalty to the United States was questioned. Many of the men held here without due process were long time resident religious leaders, businessmen, teachers, fishermen, farmers, and others. No person of Japanese ancestry in the U. S. was ever charged or convicted of espionage throughout the course of the war.
>
> Many of the internees had relatives who served with distinction in the American Armed Forces in Europe and in the Pacific.
>
> This marker is placed here as a reminder that history is a valuable teacher only if we do not forget our past."[326]

Around two hundred people attended the luncheon later that day. Many relatives of those who were interred in Santa Fe attended. Joe Ando led the effort in locating and inviting those key people. As Doc Weaver wrote, "Perhaps one of the most heartwarming aspects of the dedication was to draw together so many with a common bond."[327]

Doc Weaver did not let the moment distract him, for he attended to the necessary detail of sending letters of thanks to the mayor and councilors who voted for the marker.

> "Dear Mayor Delgado;
>
> As I recall, it was almost four years ago when our committee met with you to

discussed [sic] establishing an historic marker to commemorate the memory of the Santa Fe Internment Camp. Never in our wildest dreams did we anticipate it would be such a long journey. From that first meeting until the dedication on April 20, 2002, many events along the way tested not only the committee, but the community as well. Both groups learned a lot about each other and gained immeasurably from the experience. Not only that but we got a history lesson along the way."

He went on to give credit and thanks to the city council and staff "on behalf of Tom Chavez, Joe Ando and the Santa Fe Internment Camp Committee."[328] Weaver also wrote letters to Councilor Bushee, who led the effort with the City Council, and Parks and Recreation Director Ron Shirley along with other important contributors to the project.[329]

Joe Ando continues to collect information about the camp. He moved to Arizona but, as of this writing, continues to correspond and make presentations.

I believe that the photograph of the funeral proved to be the pivotal point in winning approval for the marker. The image vividly depicted a history that needed to be resurrected. The history was not politically correct or joyful but the effort was necessary. History won out and on this occasion we defeated the proverbial windmill.

64
In which is revealed the treasures of an 18th century map

Maps can be just a reveling and intriguing as photographs. Drawing on the influence of Michael Weber, whose specialty is Spanish maps of the Southwest, the Palace's history library has a strong map collection. A map done by Bernardo Miera y Pacheo is the collection's most valued piece.

Miera y Pacheco came to New Mexico from his home in the Valle de Carriedo in the Mountains of Burgos in northern Spain. He came from a family that had distinguished itself in the service of Spain as governors and military men. Miera y Pacheco, however, chose to leave his homeland and travel to New Spain where first in Chihuahua and then in El Paso del Norte he married, began a family, and participated in more than a few military campaigns as a military officer.[330]

By the time he moved to northern New Mexico he had established himself as an intelligent individual. He had become a self-taught cartographer and artist as well as a person of military prowess and a community leader. He became the favorite of the governors of New Mexico, especially governor Francisco Antonio Marín del Valle (1754-1760) who appointed him to various positions. His artwork adorns churches and enhances the collections of museums to this day. Fathers Domínguez and Escalante considered his presence necessary in their famous 1776 journey of exploration. The narratives on his maps and the few remaining letters that he wrote reveal a facet of the man that is even more impressive, for he thought and wrote about a greater vision of the Spanish borderlands. While in New Mexico his letters set up and were the focus of his meeting with Royal officials in Chihuahua. He proposed a coordinated military strategy to create an integrated territory that included California, Nueva Vizcaya, Sonora, Arizona, and New Mexico.[331] He is a figure whose accomplishments and life's work needs more research and a biography.

Early in my career, I remember Mike Weber gloating over a map that the Palace of the Governors under his direction had just purchased. Weber, at the time, was writing his dissertation on Spanish mapping in the Southwest and Northern Mexico.[332] The map was a highly lacquered oil painting of New Mexico that dated to sometime around 1760 and was attributed to Miera y Pacheco. Weber located the map and the museum purchased it for five figures, which was a large expense in those days. The map's acquisition was a major coup for Weber and the museum. Naturally, the map became a center piece to one of Weber's exhibitions in the Palace; *Tierra Incognita: Spanish Mapmaking in the Southwest.*

Miera y Pacheco's map has remained a prize in the collections of the Palace of the Governors. When not included in a subsequent exhibition, *Another Mexico; Spanish Life on the Upper Rio Grande,* it has remained on display in the Fray Angélico Chávez History Library's Robert Olson "map room." And, it has been the source of study almost to the point of assuming a life of its own.

Even though the map was conserved it was not in perfect condition. Some of its cartouche, as well as part of Miera y Pacheco's narrative, is faded or chipped away. The overall tone of the map is dark and lacquered so some of the details are hard to see and nearly impossible to photograph. Yet, the map can grab a person's attention and keep it as time races by. According to Weber, the map had been a presentation copy that Miera y Pacheco painted while in Mexico City. He based it on a map he compiled in 1758.[333]

While in Mexico, Donna Pierce and I accidentally located a copy of the same map hanging in a stairwell of the Museo Nacional del Virreinato in Tepotzatlán, Mexico. Miera y Pacheco apparently made two presentation copies of the same map. Unlike the map at the Palace, the map in Mexico did not have any faded or lost paint. A comparison demonstrated that his words, although written separately, were the same. This meant that the Mexican map could be used to fill in the blanks for the map in New Mexico.

The museum's efforts to borrow the map from the Museo Nacional del Virreinato proved futile. Palace supporter and volunteer, Dr. Julio Davila, a native of Mexico, took on the task himself and convinced the people in Mexico to replicate their map and present it to the Palace.

Dr. Davila had become captivated by the map. After comparing the writing between the two maps, he discovered a notation in the region of the central Rocky Mountains. Miera y Pacheco noted the correct location of the continental divide with a two line sentence, "From this place the rivers flow into the different oceans."

Dr. Davila wrote an article that he presented to the Palace in which he noted Miera y Pacheco's correct location of the continental divide and that he did so a half a century before any English speaker would do the same. Dr. Davila also theorized that Miera y Pacheco might have been the first to identify that feature. On this point, Miera y Pacheco, exactly located what the Francisco Vázquez de Coronado expedition generally noted more than two centuries earlier.[334]

Michael Weber was the first to study and identify the map. Aside from dating it and noting the Miera y Pacheco copied it from his 1758 map, in which Comanche Indians were mentioned for the first time on a map, he noted that the illustrated presentation possibly contained the earliest illustration of a Comanche Indian.[335]

Then while working on a book about Spanish exploration on the Plains, I noticed that Miera y Pacheco had painted a white fortress and buildings with a French flag located at the confluence of two rivers northeast of what is today New Mexico. The barely decipherable writing said that this was French territory. On close inspection the mythical city could only be on the confluence of the Loup and Platte Rivers, the exact location where the 1720 ambush of the Pedro de Villasur expedition took place. The ambush was a New Mexican disaster for which the Spanish blamed the French, which is why one of the Segesser paintings depicts French soldiers.[336] Miera y Pacheco painted that episode into his map some forty years after the infamous battle. Its memory was still strong enough to influence the cartographer.[337] For historians, here was a confluence of a hide painting and oil painted map that documented memory as well as perspective. The incorrect assumption that a French force participated in the Villasur ambush persisted in imagery from 1720 to, at least, 1760.

On another occasion, the map omitted information thus demonstrating a lack of memory or care. As noted earlier, when looking for the lost camp site and route of the 1776 Domínquez and Escalante expedition, maps were consulted in expectation that they might shed some light on the route.[338] In the case of the maps done by Miera y Pacheco, who was on that expedition, cartouches had been placed over the area where we expected to find the camp site. His 1760 map was created before the expedition. If he had some knowledge of the area before the expedition, we will never know, for a cartouche covered the area in question. Even the lack of information said something, for maybe the expedition really was disoriented.

Bernardo Miera y Pacheco's life-story is about to be revealed. His maps, art, exploits, and the few letters so far discovered point to an individual who stood out beyond his times. Students of his work continue to learn, as evidenced from this story of one presentation map.

Thus like Quixote's adventures, Miera y Pacheco's map continues to divulge information to the keen observer; and there are still more lessons to be learned.

65
Revealing the value of the mundane or as artifacts may be perceived

Invariably certain artifacts or works of art surface as favorites of curators who work with museum collections. The reasons are many and they range from the artifact's uniqueness and the story it tells to catching the curator's fancy. Some of these types of artifacts have been described in detail in other parts of this book but there are others; there always will be others.

The Palace of the Governors has a good collection of edged weapons that dates, at least, from the seventeenth century. Most people note the weapons' styles, makes, age, hilts, and so on. Another source is the inscriptions etched into the blades. This interest quickly morphs into a thought process about the people and cultures that used weapons. A common saying on Spanish blades was, "*No me enbaines sin razón*," on one side and, "*No me saques sin honor*," on the reverse side. This translates to "Do not unsheath me without reason" and "Do not sheath me without honor." I came to compare these sayings with a later-day bowie knife that belonged to the Texas Rangers. The knife's blade had, "Hurrah for Hell," one side and "Wakes, Snakes, Bummers beware" on the other side, with "Texas Rangers" on the hilt guard. The mentalities behind the inscriptions are fascinating and telling, for the earlier Spanish inscriptions spoke of honor and caution while the later English inscriptions begged for an excuse to be used. The inscriptions spoke for the people who possessed the weapons and are insights into the respective mentalities of some of yesteryear's people.

The same collection contains a rusted corroded knife blade and a corroded short sword blade that is a couple of centuries old. While neither piece is, or ever was, aesthetically attractive they both fulfilled a desperate function and therein lay their uniqueness.

The knife originated as a file. Some of the original crenelations are still evident. The steel was good so the owner must have felt that a knife would serve him or her better than a file.

The sword blade shares the same type of story, for its original incarnation was as a colonial Spanish plow share. The plow shares looked and were shaped like the bottom of a modern iron. With the pointed end aimed down they were attached to a long piece of wood that was kept steady by the person doing the plowing as it was pulled by oxen. In desperate colonial northern Mexico, iron was a premium commodity that had to be imported overland from central Mexico. Thus, historians and archaeologists have found many examples where iron and metal was reused. In this case, someone reforged the plow share into a sword blade, the reverse of the biblical admonition.

In colonial New Mexico (1598–1821) defense and self-sufficiency were necessities to survival. The plow share and the sword were invaluable commodities to the survival of individuals and the colony. These particular artifacts indicate that, at one point, defense clearly took precedence over crops. The reality of needing a sword even at the cost of a plow share is a stark message. Obviously, for whoever forged the blade, the biblical monstration to "beat your swords into plowshares" had no resonance.

The museum had another artifact that I called a "curious, spurious seal."[339] For a brief moment in time the brass stamp belonged to Manuel Alvarez. It is a thick brass disk roughly the size of a hockey puck. When used to stamp official papers of the United States minor diplomatic office in Santa Fe, Mexico, the image came off as a circular image with the U. S. eagle around which the words "Commercial Agency * U. S. A. * Santa Fe." Alvarez, who was the commercial agent, never used the seal because he received it too late. The seal was shipped to New Mexico in 1846 just as the war between the United States and Mexico broke out. The seal had been packed on one of the caravans scheduled to travel to Santa Fe but held up until the U. S. Army of the West could travel over the Santa Fe Trail and secure New Mexico on its way to the larger goal of California. Thus the seal arrived in Santa Fe after the army had taken over and as agent Alvarez wrote to his Secretary of State James Buchanan, the seal would be of no use "owing to the change of government."[340]

The seal remained in New Mexico to become part of the state history museum's collections. While the seal, in and of itself, does not tell the above story it does make one historical point clear. At one time, the United States recognized New Mexico and its capital as a part of Mexico. The United States also considered the commerce passing through northern New Mexico into and from the United States to be worthy of having a commercial agent in Santa Fe.

As a young curator, I wrote a short article about the seal and concluded with the mistaken reading of its words, "Commercial Agency * Santa Fe * U. S. A." I concluded that someone in the state department had "curious foreknowledge," for they produced a seal before the outbreak of the war yet assumed that Santa Fe would become a part of the United States.[341] After the article's publication I came to realize that, no, what the words meant was that the "U. S. A." pertained to the commercial agency and Santa Fe was that agency's location. This was a moment where I could have used Sancho Panza's advice to avoid being misled and, then, mistaken.

66
Continuing the theme of the previous chapter with a mousetrap, a clock, and some desks.

Then there was a contraption from Chicago that dates to around 1900. At first sight no one could tell what it is supposed to be. Only a label that its maker glued to one of its flat surfaces revealed its true identity. The manufacturer proudly proclaimed in print that the contraption is "The Best Mousetrap in the World."

The instructions then laid out the convoluted way in which the trap would bring the unfortunate rodent to its end. Start with a discrete trail of kernels of corn or some other mouse temptation that will attract the furry pest through a series of trapdoors that open to different wire mesh tunnels from ground level up to a platform that has one opening over a jar of water. As the mouse follows the food trail through each door it can not turn back because each door only opens one way. So the mouse must continue to its evitable death by drowning in the glass jar.

I was never sure what to make of the "best mousetrap in the world." I do know that as I shared it with visitors they were as fascinated as I that someone had spent the time and effort to create such a complicated gizmo to kill a mouse. Even more astounding was that the company actually marketed the trap! We never figured out what it all meant. Then again we have never seen a mouse trap ever remotely similar to that one. Even the mundane can be fascinating if for nothing else the secrets that it has yet to reveal.

Unlike mousetraps, clocks have held people's fascination since their inception. They are fascinating contraptions, works of precision, and art all at once. Their construction, along with the science and math behind their development all conspire to make clocks, watches, or time pieces, in general, prime items for collectors and museums alike.

Charles Bennett was able to acquire a clock for the Palace of the Governors that fit all of these attractions and more. He convinced a family to contribute an heirloom railroad clock that came from the turn-of-the-century train depot in Columbus, New Mexico. The depot still exists but the tracks and trains no longer pass by. Columbus is a small indescete village that sits on the Mexican border in southern New Mexico and for a short time became a part of international news.

On 9 March 1916 Pancho Villa's men sneaked across the border, surprised a small U. S. Army contingent, and raided the town. Within hours the Villistas looted and burned most of the town, killed ten civilians and eight soldiers while suffering a disproportionate 170 deaths themselves. They lost over a fourth of their force. The national press's headlines screamed that the United States had been invaded. The Federal government reacted to the outcry by sending General John J. "Blackjack" Pershing and a military force that included airplanes, tanks, automobiles, and machine guns to locate and defeat Villa, which they never did.

Reasons for the raid vary from Villa's irritation with the Untied States for allowing his opponent's troops to be transported on trains over U. S. territory, to his reaction to the United States' foreign policy relative to Germany's role in the Mexican revolution; and, the most likely reason, that he became upset over some weapons deals gone bad with the Ravel Brothers, whose store was in Columbus. The store was one a many buildings burnt to the ground.

When the shooting started, station master Louis Jagers was working behind the counter. He immediately ducked to the floor as bullets flew around him, shattering windows and splintering wood. When it was over he noticed that one of the random bullets had hit the wall clock, shattering its glass face, severing the pendulum, and stopping the time at 4:11 am.

Upon his retirement years later, he was presented with the clock as a memento of his life-threatening experience. With the hands still frozen in time and the bullet hole very much evident, the clock became a family heirloom that Jagers' descendents appreciated. They had a special form fitting case made to store the clock. A few years, after Jagers' death his granddaughter decided that the clock needed to be in a museum. She contacted Charles Bennett and he quickly convinced her that the Palace of the Governors was the perfect place for her grandfather's clock.

The clock is unique. Aside from its age and intrinsic value as a railroad clock, it is a historical artifact that documents a time and place. In fact it documents the exact time of day when Pancho Villa's men raided Columbus, New Mexico as well as "invading" the United States. The bullet hole with an entry in front and exit in back is testimony to the firepower of some of the invaders' weapons.

Charles made sure that the gift would receive the credit that it was due. He arranged for the press to attend a formal ceremony in the courtyard of the Palace of the Governors. Jagers' family made a public presentation of their gift. As the speeches were made one could only wonder at this artifact that was witness to what its owner at the station must have felt during the raid. It was, as we could see, a moment when time stood still.

Tomas Jaehn, the Palace's current head librarian took an interest in the clock and, for a few years, took the time piece back to Columbus for the town's annual celebration. Tomas did make one improvement. After being asked how the bullet got through the clock's glass cover without breaking it, Tomas had the cover removed. Obviously, the new glass cover was added after the fact, something lost on many people.

Some desks are legendary. The desk in the oval office of the White House is a prime example. Desks where kings of various countries sat and desks of writers and scientists are numerous. For example, my desk at the Palace of the Governors belonged to Territorial Governor L. Bradford Prince and dates to 1891.

The Prince desk gave rise to a minor episode when a Presidential candidate scheduled a campaign stop in Santa Fe's plaza. The candidate was Walter Mondale who was Vice President of the United States at the time. Because of his position, he needed direct access to the White House at all times in case of an emergency. As a result, Charles Bennett's office, right off my own office, was designated the emergency command post. The secret service came into our offices to make sure that they were safe and then hooked up a special telephone with direct access to the White House.

Two secret service agents showed up unannounced at my office to explain that I needed to step aside while they combed the cubicle. These two young men brought in a dog that sniffed at everything. The men kept straight faces behind sun glasses that they continued to wear indoors. Conversation was out of the question. They looked under my desk and behind the bookcases and behind the books in the cases. They checked the curtains and under the cushions in my office couch as well as the light fixture above my desk. It was all very impressive.

When they finished and were about to leave I could not help but to tell them about a secret liquor cabinet in my hundred year old desk. The cabinet was hidden behind one of the desk's side panels, which opened when pushed on a certain location. Upon opening the panel and revealing the space that contained some bottles of spirits I commented in good humor that, "Someone could have hidden enough plastic explosive in there to blow up downtown Santa Fe." There was no reply. The cold stares that I received from both men were enough to tell me that they did not think I was funny.

Another Territorial Governor had a desk, if you want to call it that. His desk was a writing board the fit across the arms of a Morris-style lounge chair. Both the board and chair belong to the museum. What make these artifacts interesting is that they belonged to Lew Wallace, who after serving as a general in the Civil War was appointed governor of the Territory. Of course, Wallace is known to the vast majority of the fans of literature as the author of *Ben Hur*.[342] He finished his epic book while serving in New Mexico and living in the Palace of the Governors. Legend has it that he sat at that very chair and wrote the finishing touches of his novel on that writing board. The truth of the legend is more likely than not and only needs corroborating evidence to be confirmed.

My two favorite desks dated a few decades earlier. The first of these was a very large "quartermaster's desk" from Santa Fe's Fort Marcy. As mentioned earlier, this desk belonged to Bruce Ellis who bequeathed it to the museum. The desk is huge and is moved in four parts that fit together. When compiled the desk stands around seven feet high. The U. S. Army transported the desk down the Santa Fe Trail sometime toward the end of the Mexican War.

Fort Marcy was established in August 1846 with the construction of a star shaped defensive work on top of a hill 650 yards northeast of the plaza. The garrison and its administrative offices were housed in the town. The garrison lasted in Santa Fe until 1894.

The quartermaster was the person who ordered and then kept track of supplies. Initially, this was especially important at Fort Marcy, for until the July 1851 establishment of Fort Union outside of Las Vegas fifty miles to the east, Fort Marcy was the supply depot for all military operations in New Mexico. Of necessity, then, the quartermaster had to keep good records. His desk fitted his purpose, for it had over eighty cubby-holes in which to file information. With a large desk-top and every drawer and cubby-hole within three feet of the person seated at the desk, the quartermaster could work his mastery without moving from his work station.

Comparing the desk to a mainframe computer seemed to be the best way to explain it to the general public. You had the main work station with the table top, and then you had various functions with the drawers, and up right file holders. The cubby-holes became "the files."

Another desk belonged to U. S. Brigadier General Stephen Watts Kearny, the commanding officer of the U. S. Army of the West that occupied New Mexico in 1846 and, then, moved on to secure California during the Mexican War. Kearny spent most of his time in the field and ensconced in his field tent. He did his writing on a very fine "field desk" that traveled with him.

When closed, Kearny's field desk looked like an oversized wooden brief case or an artists supply case. It opened to a felt writing area, a couple of cubby-holes, an ink well, and file folders. The desk even had a secret compartment that no doubt reflected the high security of Kearny's work. Whereas the Fort Marcy quarter master desk was a "main frame," Kearny's field desk was a "lap top."

The field desk was another of Charles Bennett's acquisitions. He collaborated with some of Kearny's descendents and did as he had done with the Columbus clock, convinced them that the unique desk should be preserved for posterity at the Palace of the Governors. After all, Kearny and, no doubt, his field desk had occupied the building for a brief period of time.

Desks, clocks, and even mousetraps might appear to be mundane at first thought but their place in history makes them unique. Whether they were packed down the Santa Fe Trail, or people made history on or around them, they are priceless treasures; survivors of yesteryear with stories to share.

67
Relating to the roles of two 16th century artifacts that helped to secure millions of dollars

While in route to Washington, DC., Frank Ortiz warned me that if his wife found out he would be in big trouble and I had better not tell. He was referring to his wife's bright, cherry red hat box that contained the Palace's 16th century *morrión*. His embarrassment being seen with the box added to the scene he presented. We joked about it, for we were in a light-hearted mood. We had been invited to Washington, DC to appear before the Senate Finance Committee chaired by New Mexico's senior senator Republican Pete Domenici and co-chaired by our junior senator Democrat Jeff Bingaman. So we had leadership in both parties on our side and we knew it.

The preparations had been done long before our trip. We were after millions of dollars in appropriations to help fund the construction of the new state history museum. Thanks in great part to Frank Ortiz who took advantage of his many trips to Washington, DC to pester every member of New Mexico's delegation as well as the Hispanic caucus,[343] many of the Congressmen were aware of the Palace's request. In addition, both senators had toured the Palace of the Governors and its collections. Senator Bingaman and his wife had an authentic interest in history. They had started their own collection of my books.

Senator Domenici, as a member of the majority party in both houses of Congress, had accumulated enough time in office to become a very influential person. So when he agreed to visit the Palace of the Governors to spend a couple of hours touring the facilities and reviewing our preliminary architectural plans, we made sure to present him with our best, most direct, and clear sales pitch. His familiarity with Ambassador Ortiz and my family connection to Ernie Vigil, the director of his Santa Fe office, did not hurt. Both Ortiz and Vigil accompanied us on the tour.

All went well that day. The senator expressed his interest in the project. He reacted to different points, seemed disappointed at our unsuccessful attempts at getting appropriations through the House of Representatives. After years of trying to attract Representative Bill Richardson's support, he finally introduced a bill for us as his last act before he left Congress to be United States Ambassador to the United Nations. The bill was reintroduced by his successor Bill Redmond who was not re-elected. Neither bill had a chance. Senator Domenici opinioned that we should have started with him. "Oh, oh," we thought.

Then we went to the rare book room in the recently renovated and opened Fray Angélico Chávez Library. I had a few of my favorite old books pulled and waiting in their specially made slip cases. They were presented on top of the room's hand made table and the senator seemed interested. I presented *La Cronica del Rey Don Rodrigo*, a 1549 book about Rodrigo, the last Visigoth king of Spain.[344] I explained the story about Rodrico and noted that the book was printed with wooden type. I shared with him a couple other rare books and, then I opened a slip case and pulled out an original edition of the second volume of Giovanni Batista Ramusio's *Navigationi et Viaggi*. As I opened it I explained that this book was published in Venice in 1556 and what was especially interesting to me because it contained the first published account of the Francisco Vásquez de Coronado expedition into New Mexico just fifteen years after the fact.[345]

I then laid the book open to the page where that account began with the heading in Italian,

RELATIONE CHE MANDO FRANCESCO
Vazquez di Coronado, Capitano Generale della gente che su mandata...

that continued for another four lines. Senator Domenici, visibly moved, asked if he could sit down and touch the book. I handed him some white cotton gloves to put on and invited him to spend all the time that he wanted with the book. As everyone there knew, Senator Domenici was very proud of his Italian heritage and here in front of him was a four-and-one-half century old connection between Italy and his native state New Mexico.

He handled the book with awe and began to read some of the text. He looked up and commented on his appreciation of the moment and received the nodding approval of everyone. From that moment on there was never any doubt that Senator Domenici would help get the new museum built.[346]

In Washington, Frank Ortiz and I made the rounds. We visited the offices and talked with each member of New Mexico's delegation. We shared the contents of the red hat box; Pedro Ortega y Rivera's *morrión* that dated from the sixteenth century. It impressed everyone who saw it. With its engravings of the Virgin of Remedies on one side with an image of a man in period clothing kneeling before a cross on the other side, the *morrión* was an impressive piece to represent the Palace's collections in support of our prepared statements before the committee. In fact, it elicited more questions about the collections, which gave us an opportunity to stress that they were in danger in their current storage. Our meetings included a review of what the members of the Senate finance committee would ask us.

I was surprised that we had to read prepared statements. I always thought that people could appear before our Congressional committees and make their cases. Not true. Both of us had to write out our statements and submit them in advance. We were instructed to keep with our scripts and to stay seated at our assigned places because we would be televised on C-Span, the cable system that televises Congressional activities.

We both read our statements but keeping me in my seat proved to be impossible because the *morrión* became an attraction. I had to take it before various members of the committee for an up close look. After we completed our presentations we were surprised when a representative of the National Park Service spoke out against our funding request. First, he argued that the Park Service did not have the budget to support the Palace of the Governors, which, after all is a state institution and not a part of the Federaly funded Park Service. Moreover, he reminded the committee that the Park Service had more than enough of its own buildings that needed repair.

The Park Service's opposition caught Ambassador Ortiz and I by surprise. We were unaware that the money for our request would come out of the Park Service's budget and we knew that Federal money had been used for state and local projects in the past. The Park Service's argument did not make sense to us.

Senators Domenici and Bingaman, whether surprised or not, took matters in hand. Domenici started with a rhetorical question that posed whether Park Service's representative or his organization realized that the Park Service would be used to pass money through it rather than from it? And, if he did, did he realize that there would be no fiscal impact on his organization? The all-of-sudden nervous and visibly sweating witness knew that he was in trouble. His weak answer that he did not understand the funding process was only the beginning. Senator Domenici yielded to Senator Bingaman who referred to different sections of the proposed legislation to make comments and ask questions directed to the poor guy. No, he really was not familiar with the bill, he had been sent to testify by his superiors.

"Well then, was the Park Service equally unaware of the proposed legislation?" No answer.

Senator Bingaman yielded back to Senator Domenici, who asked the man if he had ever been to the Palace of the Governors and was he aware of the Palace's collections? Followed by, was he prepared to argue that the building and its collections are not part "of our national patrimony?"

When New Mexico's two senators finished with the Park Service's representative, they left him figuratively lying prostrate on the witness table with blooding running out of the side of his mouth. Clearly the committee would act favorably and the Park Service had made a tactical error. Eventually the full senate, the house of Representatives, and Presidents Clinton and Bush (II) approved our measure that provided a total of fifteen million dollars towards the construction of a new history museum and a Museum of New Mexico administration building that was required to free up space for the history museum.

The Federal appropriation was not near enough. We knew this and expected to get the balance from the State. After all, as the Park Service argued, we are a state institution. The Federal appropriation helped in two ways. Obviously, Federal support at that amount attracted the attention of our state legislators as well as the governor in a positive way. Secondly, we asked that the Federal legislation make the money available on a matching basis with a ten year time limit. Now we could argue before the state legislature that we had ten years to come up with a match or lose the money. This at once pressured the legislature to act while allowing them time to provide the match over time, which relieved pressure.

Before I left the Palace, the state had acted and a total of twenty-six million dollars had been raised. Subsequent state appropriations would complete the funding for the buildings. Ambassador Ortiz and I had no doubt that a book and a helmet from the Palace's collections helped secure the funding that led the way to the new museum.

68
In which the museum attempted to reach alternative youth

Charles Bennett was always quick to remind me of the salient fact that a museum without collections is not a museum. Conversely, collections are the basis of a museum. An apt analogy would be a library without books is not a library.

So we focused on collections with the realization that the Historical Society of New Mexico had created the heart of the collections at the Palace of the Governors and, indeed, the Museum of New Mexico. Here was an organization that had been collecting since the 1859.[347] Thanks to the HSNM the Palace of the Governors had a head start on an invaluable collection.[348] Then, as shown in this book, the staff proceeded to significantly add to the collection's quality.

We knew that everything a museum does emanates from its collections. Like books in a library, the collections are a source of knowledge that the museum staff is obligated to disseminate to the public. Obviously, this meant exhibitions, demonstrations, publications, tours, etc. It meant taking artifacts as well as reproductions to schools and retirement centers, as well as authenticating period costumes for movies or Santa Fe's fiestas.

All of this and more became a part of our life as cultural crusaders. With the help of Alex Traub and his organization called Culture Net, we joined up with SER, a public school initiative to "save" young adults who had dropped out of high school but still wanted to pursue their education.

Alex Traub is a photographer by profession and had become deeply involved in computer technology. Sometimes his unbelievable enthusiasm for his work put people off. That was not the case with us.

He and Charles Bennett put together a program where the students were taught photography, history and the humanities, museum work, and computer science. They assigned the students to work on a project that resulted in an internet site that focused on the Civil War in New Mexico. To get to that end they introduced the students to the different parts of the Palace's collections; artifacts, the Print Shop, photographic archives, and the research library with its rare books and manuscript collections. The curators in each section worked with the students in small groups to teach them how things were identified, catalogued, and conserved.

Charles took on the task of teaching them historical context that eventually would focus on the Civil War in New Mexico. Alex Traub taught photography where, in a specially set up studio in the Palace, the students photographed artifacts. The SER school had a classroom with computers where Alex, Charles, and the regular faculty along with the Santa Fe Community College who provided technical instruction and support and taught the students how to create a site on the computer.

They took all of this information to write a narrative, select and photograph appropriate artifacts and documents, reproduce historical photographs, and, then, enter them into a computer where they formatted and designed the final site. The project required individual initiative as well as team work, for in the end they had to consolidate all their information and skills to form one site.[349]

The program lasted two semesters and I really enjoyed seeing the students react so favorably. The staff, especially, took pleasure in having appreciative students working with them. Unfortunately, not every good thing lasts. Sometimes, like a shooting star, good things must be enjoyed for the moment.

Issues over funding and disbursement of the funds ended the program. This was one occasion where we could not find our way through the *burro-cracia.* I joked about the students as being "stressed students" but we found out that they were not stressed at all. They had a hunger for education, especially if they thought that they were being taught something that is relevant. While our quest to help lasted a short time, I am sure that it was not for naught. Some quests are short lived but nonetheless successful.

69
Concerning some chases that turned out well and not-so-well

The staff continued its aggressive pursuit of collections. We inherited a collection that had a special quality about it, so we did not collect solely to add to the collections. Because of the Historical Society's record keeping, their donation provided a basis of a collection that could be summed up with the time-honored, elitist sounding, museum word; "provenance." Pronounced pro-vaa-naance, it sounds as if you would say the word patio with the long "a." So while the word can be a turn off in common company it is an exciting term when positively applied to a piece in collections. What it means is that the piece has a history from its inception to the present. We know where it is from, who made it or owned it, and how it came down through history to its current owner.

The Segesser Paintings had a good provenance. The vara stick from the Mesilla Valley and the two military desks are excellent examples of having good provenance. We could even document whose library originally had what books with some of our rare books. A .58 calibre Hawkins Plains rifle that has been on exhibit at the Palace for years was owned by mountain man Auguste LeCome, who traded with the Zuní and Navajo tribes. Then there is D. H. Lawrence's satchel and the pieces of Franciscan clothing, all of which derive their authenticity and value from their provenance.

Naturally, then, when staff came across something that should be in our collections and it had impeccable provenance as well, then the chase was really on.

So it was, to give an example, when Diana De Santis received information from a person who had possession of a tin chandelier that once hung in the Palace of the Governors. She went after it. Her research verified the claim. Here was an artifact that definitely needed to be returned to the Palace, so with no misgivings whatsoever Diana and I checked out a car from the state motor pool and headed south on a four hour drive to Deming, New Mexico. Diana had little trouble securing the chandelier from a charmed and gracious donor.

Charles Bennett learned of the existence of an interesting silver place set that belonged to Major General Mariano Arista, who was in the Mexican army and Zachery Talyor's adversary in an 1846 battle near Brownsville, Texas during the Mexican War.[350] Apparently, the morning attack caught General Arista by surprise just as he was sitting down to breakfast in his tent outside of Matamoros. His abandoned sterling silver tableware was found by a U. S. soldier who collected it for himself as a spoil of war.

The soldier and his descendents dutifully kept records of the tableware as it was handed down through generations. They even had all the owners names etched into the plate in chronological order. At the time, the last descendent to own the place setting, who lived in Colorado, decided let out the word that it was available. Charles contacted them and through written correspondence and telephone conversations in his understated and unassuming way he successfully, almost too easily, received the donation of General Mariano Arista's silver tableware. For the rest of our careers at the Palace of the Governors we heard the occasional mussing; "How did that place setting end up there?" We loved the reaction.

On another occasion Diana curated an exhibition about New Mexican filigree jewelry. She named the exhibition *Golden Lace.* As she always did, she created a first class exhibition perfectly fitted for the Palace of the Governors. While researching the exhibition she learned that my own family had some pieces of filigree that had to be included.

My great grandmother divided a large filigree necklace among three of her daughters. Two of the three smaller necklaces had been handed down mother to daughter through three generations and still existed. The pieces now resided with two great, great granddaughters.

Diana contacted my cousins and was able to borrow the necklaces for the exhibition. Both Consuelo Chávez and Victoria Sosaya Murphy were pleased to share a bit of their family's heritage. Diana interviewed them, collected photographs of the original sisters; Aurelia, Nicolasa, and Victoria Roybal.[351] A photograph of Nicolasa actually showed her wearing the necklace that Diana put on exhibit.

Naturally both Diana and I thought that the necklaces were prime museum pieces, so we asked to have them donated to the museum. Here is where such a request requires a tough decision, for the museum's motives run up against everything that a family heirloom means to the owners. The necklaces had been passed down through four generations if you count the originator. Each woman treasured the jewelry for what it meant. Now as current recipients of the necklaces they had been asked to cut off the family tradition and give their prized heirlooms to public trust in a museum.

With understandable trepidation both Victoria and Consuelo considered the request. Victoria decided to keep her necklace and Consuelo reluctantly and hesitantly donated hers. Both understood that their respective necklaces were treasures, works of art that were once part of the same necklace that had become family heirlooms.

Unfortunately, the unthinkable happened. Barring a miracle, Victoria's necklace may never be in a museum or handed down, for within a couple of years after it was on exhibition someone robbed Victoria's house and, among other things, stole the necklace. Diana was able to provide good documentary photographs of the piece. On the other hand, the one surviving piece sits in the museum as lone evidence of a once incredibly beautiful work of art that was lovingly divided between three sisters.

This story is not the only story to end badly. Indeed, it is one of many. Charles suffered a similar fate when his combined interests of material culture and military history led him in pursuit of a Civil War era rifle.

While preparing for an exhibition on Jewish pioneers in New Mexico, we included information on Louis Felsenthal, who had become the subject of a well-documented biography[352] that featured a current photograph of Felsenthal's Maynard Carbine rifle along with a close-up of an engraved plaque attached to the stock that had the owner's name. Felsenthal used this rifle during his military service that included the Civil War in New Mexico.

The photographer was identified under the photographs so Charles got to work and quickly found out that the rifle belonged to some Felsenthal descendents. He located them and asked if they would consider giving up the carbine for the "Jewish Pioneers" exhibition. They answered "no." Charles did not get the sense that they were adamant so he patiently pursued the matter. However, his patience did not pay off, for the owner died and the carbine was lost when the estate was dispersed. And so was a piece of Louis Felsenthal's history.

Like Sancho Panza's donkey, which he lost in the end, the discontinued SER project, the lost necklace, and the lost carbine did enjoy some time in the limelight. Maybe all of them, the donkey included, will be found again or resurrected in some form.

Figuratively speaking one donkey did not get away, for a few years after Charles retired he received the news that the Palace of the Governors had come to an agreement for the purchase of a rare book. The book was printed by Padre Antonio José Martínez, who was responsible for establishing the first printing press in New Mexico and who printed books mostly on religious matters. Those books, printed in the 1840s, have become lost over time. The surviving copies are very, very rare. The Fray Angélico Chávez Library had none.

Charles learned that an existing copy of one of these books belonged to his elderly landlady and fellow member of the Raton, New Mexico Museum Board. The book is *Instrucciones de derecho real de Castilla y de Indias* and was written by José María Álvarez. It is only one of five copies known to exist and is worth thousands of dollars. After the landlady passed away, Charles tried to convince her brother that the book should be donated to the Palace of the Governors' library but he had other ideas and kept the book.

After Charles retired, he told both Tomas Jaehn, in the library and Tom Leech, who took Pam Smith's place in the Palace Print Shop, about the book. Upon Charles's advice they continued to pursue the book. In March of 2009, the brother, Tom Burch, agreed to sell the book to the Palace at a discount. With the generous support of Robin McKinney Martin, who owns *The Santa Fe New Mexican*, the seed planted by Charles many years before, bore fruit. As of this printing, the acquisition of Padre Martínez's book is the latest manifestation of a Palace of the Governors' aggressive policy to pursue collections begun almost over a quarter-of-a-century before.

Part V

The Joust is For Real

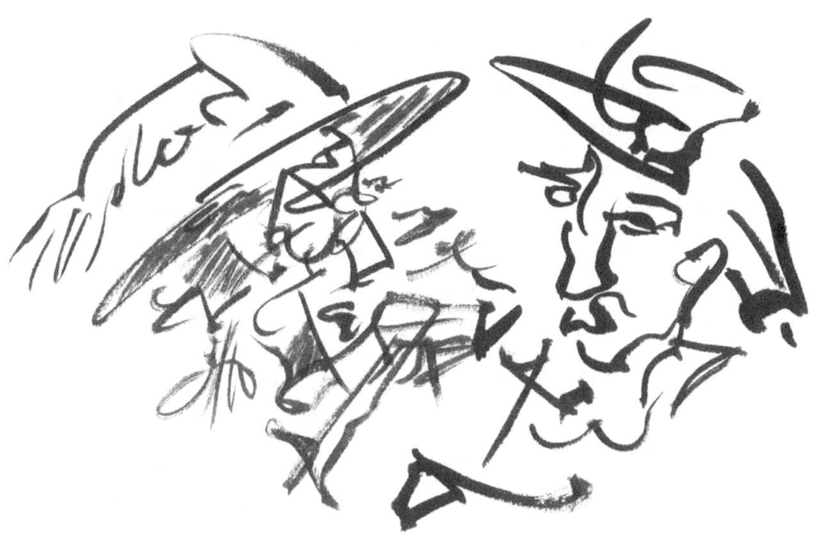

70
On the meaning of ta-ta-Ta-Ta-TA-TA-TA

Barely heard, the sound started in the distance. ta-ta-Ta-Ta-TA-TA-TA. We could hear it getting louder as it came closer. First out of sight and, then, the helicopter came into view. At first, we thought nothing of it. We had been inside attending a Museum of New Mexico board of regents meeting when a welcomed recess had been called. Some of us took advantage of the opportunity to step outside into the fresh air. We stood around and chatted under the portal that frames the entrance to the welcome center and exhibition hall of the Coronado State Monument. The view to the south, across the Rio Grande's cottonwood river bottom to the Sandia Mountains is gorgeous. And, it was the enjoyment of this view that the approaching helicopter interrupted.

We soon realized that the black helicopter was coming to us and when it landed in a whirl of dust and rocks in the nearby unpaved parking lot. Toney Anaya, the governor of New Mexico, jumped out and quick-stepped toward us.

At the governor's request, the regents met in executive session, which is to say that they would deal with personnel matters and the public as well as staff could not attend.

"What's going on?" "What's happening?" People asked to no one in particular. I answered, "Say goodbye to Jean Weber." And, indeed, that was the case. Weber, the director of the Museum of New Mexico resigned her position. Welcome to the reality of politics and culture in New Mexico.

The episode at Coronado Monument was the culmination of a series of events over time. It was a vivid reminder that politics, art, and the humanities are not exclusive of one another. The governor had his own reasons for his actions. The staff, which knew that Weber was in trouble, was divided over the quality of her leadership. The staff at the Museum of International Folk Art openly supported her by creating and wearing lapel pins of support. Significantly, no other part of the Museum of New Mexico system followed suit.

Don Quixote was tricked into giving up his knight errant pursuits when he lost a fake joust. Only, Quixote, did not know the true nature of the competition and he was knocked off his horse and nearly killed. He never knew the truth of the matter. For him the joust was very real.

As partially documented earlier in this book, Jean Weber and I had some differences. I became the acting director of the Palace of the Governors soon after Weber was hired. After two years in the acting position I walked into her office and handed her a letter that, at once, offered my resignation as acting director of the Palace and, then, informed her that I remained a candidate to be named the permanent director. The letter continued to spell out that my qualifications, including two years on-the-job experience and a PhD that, in my opinion, made me more qualified for the job than anyone. I did this in full knowledge that the governor had embarked on a program of giving priority to New Mexicans for state jobs and that Weber, who was creating new administrative positions as she reorganized the Museum of New Mexico, had yet to find a qualified New Mexican to hire. Indeed, rumor was rampant that Weber had a favorite for the position whom she had hired on a research grant. This person, who came to the museum from Texas, had neither the experience nor education to match mine.

The concept that native-born New Mexicans, especially Hispanics were not qualified, incapable, or incompetent for being professional museum personnel was obvious in the Museum of New Mexico's own hiring practices. I, for example, would become the first native born New Mexican of any ethnicity to be hired in the Museum's administration. One museum director stated to a joint staff meeting of my staff and her's that she would love to hire a Hispanic New Mexican but that she could not find any qualified for the job. I and my staff looked at each other in amazement over the overt ignorance of that statement, for there was our head librarian Orlando Romero, his assistant Hazel Romero, our curator of collections Diana Ortega DeSantis, Arthur Olivas who worked as our curator of photographs, and our registrar James Romero. Never mind that I who was this person's equal on the organizational chart, was there as well.

My letter of resignation to Jean Weber concluded that if she hired anyone but me for the position of director of the Palace of the Governors, I would file a suit against the Museum and her. When she first opened the letter, she stated, "So you do not want to continue?"

"No, keep reading. I am resigning my position as acting director but I am still a candidate for the permanent position and there is no one more qualified than me on the face of this earth."

She read the complete letter. I did not need to comment on the threat to take legal action. When finished she looked up at me from behind her desk and said, "I didn't know that you wanted the job."

I could only reply, "Well, I do."

Without another word and without hesitation, she picked up her telephone and called the personnel office to have me hired on the spot.

71
Concerning the paradox of politics and culture

Now, after a bumptious journey, Weber had resigned. Politics should not have been a surprise. Everyone in State government depended on legislative funding for salaries, operating costs, collections acquisitions, etc. A year did not pass by but when we were not asking the legislature and, consequently, the governor for something.

During the almost three decades that I worked for the state, from 1979 until 2005, the Office of Cultural Affairs was organized, initially as a sub cabinet level post and, finally, with full cabinet status. Two of the people appointed to the cabinet secretary position were wives of politicians.[353] Whether qualified or not, all the secretaries were political appointees. Indeed, the members of the Boards of Regents for all the State cultural institutions were appointed by the governor. Obviously, politics in New Mexico's cultural institutions is a way of life.

Fortunately, for those of us who considered ourselves professionals on a quest, New Mexico has been good to arts and humanities as well as natural history and the environment. While not documented, I always sensed and believed that New Mexico spends more on culture through museums, preservation, etc. on a per capita basis than any other state in the Union. As can be seen from some of the stories in this book, I always found the legislature to be helpful.

Nevertheless, Tom Livesay, who replaced Jean Weber, eventually irritated Governor Gary Johnson or his advisors enough to be forced to resign as well. Livesay did not have to suffer a helicopter visit rather than a walk in downtown Santa Fe where the Secretary of Cultural Affairs, Edson Way, delivered the message.[354]

Ironically, both Livesay and Way respectively were the best directors of the Museum of New Mexico and Secretary for Cultural Affairs for whom I worked. Both, in my opinion, are decent individuals who were professionals in the world of cultural institutions. While, on occasion, I had differences with both of them, I respected them, their positions, knowledge, and talent. Edson Way spent a good deal of his early life working ranches, became an anthropologist, and eventually directed, at least, four museums in the state. He lost his job when Bill Richardson became governor. He, too, was a political casualty.

Former first lady Clara Apodaca[355] was an obvious political appointee. Her popularity with the state legislature helped the museum system. In addition, she helped me personally. When others would not, she personally took me before the state personnel board to secure a raise in my salary. I was impressed with the fact that her mere presence and prestige seemed to be enough to garner the board's complete acquiescence that I receive a raise in pay. Thus, while I, as a career professional with all the required degrees, might complain about political appointments, I learned that there could be a silver lining to the political cloud.

72
In which is related the story of how dog meat got the governor's attention

Sometimes advocacy is not needed to make a point. Sometimes merely doing your job or standing up to controversy can make a point or become a problem. So it was that Helmuth Naumer, at the time the Secretary for Cultural Affairs appointed by Governor Gary Carruthers and carried over into Bruce King's third term, used what he saw as another opportunity to try to rein me in. In the process, he made a bad judgment that resulted in a meeting in the office of James B. Lewis, Governor King's Chief of Staff. And the whole controversy began over the issue of dog meat!

Among other things, Sam'l Arnold was student of cooking in the old west. He wrote a book of old recipes from the Rocky Mountain West in the nineteenth century. As mentioned a recipe for the "Rocky Mountain Hailstorm" that was used at Bent's Fort on the Arkansas River in the 1830s and 1840s, became a drink that the Palace of the Governors served every year at its Mountain Man Buffalo Roast.[356] The casual observer would think that serving up a primitive mint julep that called for a pinch of gun powder would have caused some trouble for the museum; and I can speak from personal experience about the drink's potency. Outside of a couple of personal headaches the Hailstorm never caused a problem.

However, another seemingly innocuous recipe in the book did cause a problem. Arnold included a recipe that the Cheyenne Indians used to make dog meat stew. The warm concoction was popular among the tribe as well as its many non Indian visitors. Some of the latter thought enough of the meal to mention it in their journals or share it with third parties. Hence, Arnold, in his research found the recipe and included it in his book.[357]

Naturally enough, the Palace's history library received and catalogued a copy of Arnold's book.[358] That should have been the end of the story but it wasn't, for political correctness in the extreme combined with community activism to result in a confrontation.

Before we moved into the Fray Angélico Chávez Library, the photographic archives, manuscripts, and book collections were housed in the very cramped quarters of the old armory's ground floor. The same building behind the Palace of the Governors also housed the administrative offices upstairs and collections storage in part of the ground floor and the whole basement. The floors were wood and a wooden stairway connected the upstairs offices, including my own, to the library and photographic archives, which had a direct entrance from the street.[359]

One day I heard some arguing that soon turned into shouting. Then it stopped. A little time passed and it started again but, it seemed, louder and more heated. I rushed downstairs from my office. I recognized Dick Rudisill's voice but not the others. I found Dr. Rudisill, an unassuming intellectual man in his fifties, backed against a wall in what we called the map room. A woman, who turned out to be Jerilou Hammett was yelling at him. Orlando Romero was trying to appease her while her husband looked on from a few feet away.

I quickly found out that she and her husband were upset because the museum had accepted Arnold's book with the dog meat recipe. In their minds, the recipe was degrading to Indians and they were determined that the book be removed from the library. Unfortunately, rather than take their complaint and demand to Orlando Romero, the head librarian, or to me, they latched on to the first employee that they saw and that was Dr. Rudisill, who had nothing to do with the book.

At first, he did not know what Hammett was talking about. Apparently, because she did not receive instant gratification, Hammett became verbally abusive with Rudisill. Eventually, security was called and the couple were escorted off the premises, which, of course, infuriated them. The matter was not over, for the Hammetts were well-known and tenacious community activists.

After quizzing both Rudisill and Romero I was able to piece together the story that Jerilou Hammett had caught Rudisill unannounced and apparently became infuriated with his lack of understanding. At one point, she pushed or grabbed him to get his attention. Rudisill, in his manner, told her in an elevated voice to, "unhand me, madam!" At this point, Romero, who was back in the stacks, came rushing out and interceded. The Hammetts considered him a friend and fellow activist, so he succeeded in bringing some calmness into the matter and convinced them to leave.

Some minutes later, however, the Hammetts returned to the library where they found Rudisill still searching in the reference books. Once again they, mainly Jerilou, started yelling at Rudisill, who by now became upset over the undeserved treatment that he was receiving. This was the point where I showed up and with the arrival of museum security, the Hammetts left.

Within days I received a telephone message from Helmuth Naumer. The Hammetts had met with him and claimed that they had been mistreated by state employees. In particular, they singled out Dick Rudisill. Naumer told me that I had problems with my staff. My employees, he claimed, had a bad attitude toward the public and he intended to change that right now.

Helmuth Naumer grew up a son of a Santa Fe artist and lived a privileged life. Most of his advanced education and formal career had taken place in Texas. He had a resonant baritone voice and was very much aware that he could use it as well as his presence to intimidate people. As related earlier in this book, Naumer and I did not care for each other. In fact, just a month before this episode Naumer and I had the aforementioned conflict over the drunks who tried to crash the Buffalo Roast. So, given our earlier conflict with the Segesser Paintings and this recent flap, he apparently thought that now he had a real opportunity to get me.

He ordered me to take disciplinary action against Dr. Rudisill. I replied that I knew about the incident and did not believe that any such action was warranted. He then made the outrageous statement that if I did not take action against Rudisill, he would "fire him himself." I was in disbelief, for even Naumer had to realize that state personnel codes prohibited such quick punitive action. So, now irritated, I told the secretary for the Office of Cultural Affairs that he did not have the authority to take such an action and if he tried, I would join Dr. Rudisill in his defense before the State Personnel Board.

Naumer quickly countered with the charge that I was "insubordinate" and that he would take action against me. I refused to change my position so we hung up without the usual salutations. If Naumer was predictable in anything, I knew that he meant what he said.

Within the hour I received a telephone call from James Lewis. Lewis, a politician from Albuquerque who had a short career in boxing, had earned a reputation as a man who got things done. Everyone agreed that Governor King made a great decision when he chose Lewis to be his Chief of Staff. I had never met him but only heard about him so when he announced himself, I knew I was in trouble—except for one thing. James Lewis is a decent man.

He was following up Naumer's complaint that I was insubordinate. He wanted me to understand that the governor did not appreciate such an attitude. I replied that I understood, even appreciated the governor's position and, then, asked him if Naumer had told him how I had been insubordinate. Yes, he replied, I had refused to take disciplinary action against an employee for abusing a member of the public.

I quickly retorted that I had been told to "discipline" the employee and if I did not act Naumer would fire him and that I felt that neither action was justified. Lewis listened, paused, and then asked for more information. We finished with a suggestion that he do what Naumer refused to do; investigate the matter before demanding action. "Actually, Mr. Lewis, I challenge you to come down here unannounced and question the people involved. If you conclude that a personnel action should be taken, then I will follow up."

Lewis, who has gone onto a well deserved career in New Mexico,[360] actually heeded our conversation, for he took the time to interview the involved parties. At the time I did not know what, if anything, he was doing. I waited to hear what action he would take against me.

Then came the summons to Tom Livesay, Dick Rudisill, and myself to meet in Lewis's office on the fourth floor in the state capitol building. When we arrived, we learned that the Hammetts and Naumer also had been invited. It appeared, the conflict would come to a head at this meeting. Livesay had the passive look of a noninvolved person. Rudisill appeared visibly worried, for neither the place nor the company were his environment. Naumer and the Hammetts talked with each other and looked confident. I did not know what to expect. While I had been in the executive offices on the fourth floor of the state capital building, I had never been asked to attend a meeting like this.

Lewis entered the room and sat down at the head of a long table. He thanked all of us for being there. He assured us that this would not be a long meeting and then proceeded to explain that he had received a complaint of insubordination against "Dr. Chávez" from Helmuth Naumer and that he had looked into the matter. He called us together to share his conclusion. Then he stated that he found that there was no basis for disciplinary action to be taken against either Dr. Rudisill or myself. He turned to Naumer and requested that he write a letter stating why "Dr. Chávez is an exemplary state employee" and place it in "his personnel file." He concluded that nothing more needed to be said, thanked all of us again, and left the room. With the meeting adjourned, we all had a quiet ride down the elevator. Dr. Rudisill and I had a rather pleasant walk back to the Palace and I acquired a great respect for James Lewis.

73
In which politics resulted in a failed attempt and disappointment

Late in my career at the Palace of the Governors, I suffered the first real consequence of adverse politics. With Tom Livesay's departure, I decided to apply for the job. I felt that after two decades as director of the Palace of the Governors, a promotion to the director of the Museum of New Mexico would be a logical step. I believed that many of the people who had worked with me through my career would support me. Some of these people had become regents of the system and they were the ones who would make the final decision. One impediment to my candidacy would have been Helmuth Naumer but for health reasons he had resigned his position and had been replaced by Edson Way. I felt comfortable in my qualifications as well as with the search committee that was compiled by regents of the Museum of New Mexico and board members of the MNM Foundation.

"Hindsight," Sancho Panza noted, "is worth its value in gold," for after the fact I realized that my candidacy had, at least, two problems. The first should have been obvious, for some of my colleagues in the system opposed me. Given the anonymous letter incident during the FBI affair and the press's inquiry into the Palace's foreign tours, I could not be surprised. Then again, at the time, I had the longest tenure of anyone in the Museum of New Mexico administration, so, I suppose, that there was opposition because I was too familiar with the system.

The real disappointment came from some of the very people that I counted upon. The first clue came at a reception in Frank Ortiz's house. Ortiz had been appointed to the Board of Regents and when I took him aside to proudly inform him that I had decided to apply for the director's position, he instantly replied, "You won't be successful."

"Why not?" I asked. But no reply came. He merely turned a way from me and walked away. What a strange and, to me, unexpected reaction.

Later, Ambassador Ortiz came to the Palace of the Governors to make a lame attempt to convince me to withdraw my application. I asked him to give me a reason and he gave the same answer as before.

"That's not good enough."

"Tom, you are more valuable here [as director of the Palace of the Governors] than as director of the Museum of New Mexico."

"But that is illogical and unfair! Besides, Frank, we could get more achieved for the Palace with me as director of the whole system"

"I'm just telling you..."

"Thanks Frank."

At the time, Tom Wilson had been hired as the interim director of the Museum of New Mexico to replace the recently departed Tom Livesay. He had worked in other museum administrations and had some vague early connections with New Mexico. Edson Way hired him the same day he fired Livesay. In fact, Wilson moved into the director's office the same day. Wilson also applied for the permanent job.

So here I was discouraged by an ally and regent, competing against someone who seemed to have support from the governor's office. Meanwhile other applications came in and the search committee began its work. I heard from one committee member that another criticized me for my lack of administrative ability. Then Jim Leopold, another friend who was a regent and search committee member came to my office. Leopold was a local banker and served with me on the board of the Santa Fe Chamber of Commerce. He was always a very affable man.

Aside from Frank Ortiz, who took a personal interest in the museum, regents rarely visited with me in my office. Leopold came through my door unannounced. He had been sent by the search committee with a request and "please don't kill the messenger."

He then proceeded to ask me to withdrawal my candidacy for director. I replied as I had with Ortiz. "Give me a reason to do that." Leopold said that hiring me the director of the Museum of New Mexico "was not in the cards." As to why, there was no answer except that I should consider withdrawing.

"No, Jim, I need a reason."

A few days later another regent and member of the search committee came into my office. Mike Arnold was a large, balding, and very imposing man. His message was direct.

"Tom, you need to withdraw."

"Why?"

"Because you won't be selected."

"How do you know that? The process is not finished. I haven't even been interviewed."

"Tom, I am telling you that you will not be selected. The decision has been made."

"So I won't even be interviewed. Why should I withdrawal if the decision has been made? My withdrawal would be a moot point."

Visibly frustrated, he rose and left my office.

The search narrowed down to two men. Not surprisingly, Tom Wilson was one. He was pitted against a person who was working in a prestigious western institution in Oklahoma. We, in the Palace of the Governors, met and interviewed both candidates. Ortiz acted as if everything was normal and sought my advice about the two finalists, which was unenthusiastically given.

One day in a telephone call Frank Ortiz told me that I needed to get over my "snit," to which I replied with "Gee, thanks for your support, friend. You did not do a thing on my behalf and never gave me a reason why." Then, he repeated, his rationale; "Tom, you are more valuable to us at the Palace of the Governors."

"What?" I shot back incredulously, "You are penalizing me for a good job performance? Why couldn't you even grant me an interview? You know, Frank, you are supposed to be Mr. Hispanic around here. When is the next time you will have the opportunity to hire a Hispanic New Mexican director of the Museum?" And I answered my own question. "Not in your lifetime buddy."

Clearly, all career advancement opportunities in the Museum of New Mexico had been closed to me. Supporters assumed that I would be content with the situation. I wasn't. With twenty-five years of service behind me, the decision to retire from the Palace of the Governors came easy. Besides, I rationalized to myself, leaders of countries much less a museum director, do not nor should not last that long.

The announcement came out in June 2001. I would retire at the end of March 2002, which meant that I would stay around long enough to help secure the passage of a major legislative appropriation for the new history museum. "That'll make for a happy retirement...," I said. "The state needs the building. It was never about me...."[361]

74
Regarding the tale of Guadalupe and her mythical bikini

Before I left the Palace, another ugly bout with politics surfaced as a result of an exhibition held at the Museum of International Folk Art. A Hispanic curator, along with the consultation of a committee made up of three Hispanic women, installed an exhibition of Hispanic artists who used modern mediums for religious themes.

California artist Alma López did a photographic collage of Guadalupe that was used on the exhibition's invitation to the opening. She compiled an image of a defiant Guadalupe wearing a short skirt of roses, standing over a photograph of a topless female "angel" who was, in reality, a friend of the artist. The image would cause problems on a number of levels, some of which had nothing to do with the image itself.

Because the depiction of a Catholic-Mexican icon who is Our Lady of Guadalupe, the mother of God, was scantly clad and the angel under her was a photograph of a topless woman, some objections became obvious. The ensuing public protest pitted some community activists against the museum. Rather than talk and calmly express their concern to allow the museum to react and possibly even agree to some solutions, the activists called in the press, riled up some of the community's more pious people, and forced confrontations all the while demanding that the museum take the exhibition down. Either the museum acquiesce to their demands or else.

So the museum was forced into a defensive position. Frank Ortiz, still a regent, personally demanded that Tom Wilson cancel the exhibition. Wilson held an emergency administrative staff meeting in which the Museum of New Mexico's options were discussed. He asked each person in attendance for their opinion.

I gave a history of Guadalupe and wondered why other parts of the exhibition such as an interactive altar had not been singled out. Then I addressed what I considered the two main issues. The first had to do with Frank Ortiz's demand and the role of the regents. I felt that Ortiz had acted out of line with his individual demand and if he wanted the exhibition cancelled he had a legal process to follow. He could secure a regents vote at a public meeting. Then, Wilson, with his job on the line would have to decide to obey that mandate or not. As it stood at the moment, one regent did not have the authority to demand anything of the director.

Secondly, I understood and appreciated the concerns of the community but found the motives of their leaders doubtful. They seemed more concerned about getting publicity than results, for if they cared about the latter, they would have been less confrontational. Because of their actions, the Museum of New Mexico as a public, cultural institution was left with no option but to ignore the activists. The Museum could not acquiesce to confrontational demands. This meant that any decision would and should be made on the museum's terms. While open to public discussion and change, no cultural institution should be forced to make policy under such reactionary conditions.

Thus, I continued, the museum staff as represented by the administration should wait to see what direction, if any, the regents would take and, then, draw its own conclusions. The leadership at the Folk Art Museum and Tom Wilson decided not to wait for the regents to meet. They moved up the end date of the exhibition in what became a failed attempt to placate the public.

In the meantime, while the activists made demands and were allowed to review internal museum memorandums, correspondence, and minutes, a very hot e-mail debate raged over the sexual orientation and religiosity of the artist. Then, regents decided to hold their anticipated meeting out-of-town in Las Cruces in the state's far south, where they took no action whatsoever.

75
In which Swastikas and Guadalupe create a dilemma

Meanwhile, back in Santa Fe some very sick people spray painted swastika signs on the doors of the Guadalupe church and on an image of Guadalupe that is located outdoors by the Santa Fe River. Could the crazed activists have done this to embarrass the Museum by accusing it or its employees of being the culprit? The hatred involved in such an act equated, in my mind, to the same crazed mentality that led to the lack of logic and inhumanity of flying passenger jets into buildings; which had happened only weeks before in New York and Washington, DC.

Ta-ta-ta-Ta-Ta-TA-TA, here it came. In my mind's eye I could see an ominous immediate future for the Museum of New Mexico, including all its branches. Within days we had another administrative staff meeting that was held in the old meeting room of the Palace of the Governors. Before we began, I asked Joyce Ice, the Director of the Museum of International Folk Art for a quick word away from our colleagues. Dr. Ice is an intelligent, silent woman, who has her say when needed. Nor is she a vindictive or jealous person. She also has a sense of humor and likes baseball, which is enough for me. So, I had no doubts about confronting her with any type of idea.

With the swastika incidents, the exhibition in her museum, no action taken by the regents, and important legislation for the museum coming up in the next legislative session, I suggested to Dr. Ice that she consider the possibility of moving up the closing date of the exhibition once again. The exhibition should be closed as soon as possible to prevent the activists from linking the Museum of New Mexico to the people who painted the swastikas. They will imply that we are one and the same; Guadalupe haters with no appreciation for the Hispanic/Catholic community. Not only will this create a public relations problem but it will hurt us with our legislative funding requests. The other side of the argument, I knew, was that the Museum had nothing to do with the swastika graffiti and that I was suggesting to Dr. Ice the appearance that the Museum "cave in" as a result of something that may have been done intentionally to put us in that position.

I felt that once the regents refused to take any action, the Museum staff was free to make its own decisions in the matter without any pressure. Moreover, we opened the exhibition, withstood the initial storm of protest, did not give in to the pressure, and, in a sense, forced the regents to back off. We, the Museum of New Mexico staff, had made our point. Now was the time to take the moral high road. I did not express these last thoughts to Joyce Ice clearly enough and I probably should have taken a little more time to explain my position.

She replied, "That's an interesting idea. I will think about it."

And, with that, we went into the meeting. I was anxious to hear Tom Wilson's summary of the recent regents meeting in Las Cruces. We knew from the newspapers that the regents did not take any formal action but I wanted to hear about their discussion and, maybe, informal thoughts.

Wilson continued to conduct the administrative meeting as if the regents' meeting never happened. He made no mention of Guadalupe or the regents; nothing. Nor did anyone else. I hoped that maybe Joyce Ice would ask about the regents and broach the idea of my suggestion at which point I would support her. Nonetheless, the meeting droned on as each administrator made reports with no apparent concern about the controversy surrounding Guadalupe.

I felt like don Quixote when he was tricked into a joust. He was the only person who did not understand that the joust was an elaborate hoax to force him away from his quests. The only problem was that the joust actually happened. Quixote faced an adversary, they charged each other with lances aimed and Quixote was hit and knocked off his horse. The joust was for real. Yet, here I sat in an administrative staff meeting listening to my colleagues who seemed oblivious to the reality of our own joust. I wasn't a half-crazed Don Quixote, or his philosophic servant, both of whom would dare to venture where others would not. So I raised my hand to attract Wilson's attention and asked, "What happened at the regents meeting?"

"Nothing."

"That's it? They did nothing? I can get that from the newspapers. Did they say anything?"

Nothing worth talking about."

Then I laid out my thoughts about closing the exhibit, the realities of dealing with the legislature, and thus taking the moral high ground before our detractors condemned us to the opposite.

Wilson quickly replied with a firm "no."

I repeated a listing of the potential problems that the Museum would have and emphasized public perception and legislative relations.

"No," he answered again.

"Why not?"

"Because the artist will sue us."

"How do you know that? She didn't sue us when we moved the closing date up. This would amount to another month's advance. How could she sue us over our decision anyway?"

Wilson was steadfast. "No, it is not legally possible."

"How about I personally hire an attorney to give us some real legal advice?" The rest of the people seated at the meeting had become conspicuously quiet. Apparently, they were not used to their director and boss being confronted like this. Apparently, too, they had no desire to have a serious conversation about the matter. A lot had changed since the previous meeting when Wilson actively sought their advice.

By now the beet red Wilson had had enough of my questioning and ended the conversation. The Museum kept the exhibition up, was indeed grouped with whoever painted the swastikas, and was scolded before every legislative committee that considered museum support, including the annual budget. The controversy would linger through time and, in fact, is vividly remembered today in various academic symposiums and the newspapers, and in the legislature. Not long after Bill Richardson replaced Gary Johnson as governor. The new governor "resigned" both Edson Way and Tom Wilson. No one doubted that the Guadalupe scandal was a part of the reason for Wilson's departure.

Frank Ortiz was never aware of what I had tried. Instead, he sent me an insulting note in which he called me "stupid" and an "unbeliever." While the former cannot be debated, for that is a subjective judgment, the latter certainly can be questioned. Ambassador Ortiz, a member of the Catholic organization, Opus Dei, had no business or any basis to make a comment about my faith.

The activists were bolstered by some serious people. Henry Casso, educator, ex-priest, intelligent, caring, forthright, and religious man, traveled from Albuquerque to condemn the Museum of New Mexico before the state legislature. His strong feelings about the depiction of Guadalupe made him a natural ally to Frank Ortiz and they became fast friends. Ortiz drew Casso into helping the Palace of the Governors with its legislation as we tried to separate the Palace from the Guadalupe fiasco. Casso also became a member of the Board of Directors of the National Hispanic Cultural Center soon after I was appointed its Executive Director. During Ortiz's last years, Henry Casso did yeoman's work to publicly acknowledge his new friend's many life's achievements.

76
About the passions of a Virgin

Born out of the influence of the Catholic Church in the area's history, New Mexican art understandably is permeated with Church iconography. Depictions of the Virgin Mary in her various manifestations make up a large percentage of that art. Devotion to Mary has been an obvious feature of Spanish Catholics, probably dating to a number of miracles attributed to her in Spain and then in the Americas. The most obvious is the appearance of Mary to Saint James the Apostle while the latter traveled in Spain. She appeared over a pillar and instructed the apostle to build a church on the spot. Our Lady of the Pilar, located in the City of Saragossa, became the most popular Virgin Mary of Spain, for not only did she appear on Spanish soil but, if true, she did so before her actual mortal death, which is an act unique in the lore of Mary.

When Spain was occupied by the Muslims out of North Africa, the Christians commonly hid their statues and over time lost track of the hiding places. Thus, as the Christians slowly retook their lost territory, expanding from the north to the south over the next seven centuries, a common miracle story repeated itself. Religious icons, especially statues of Mary were discovered in caves, buried in the ground, etc.

The legend of Guadalupe, for example, dates to 1324 when a man rounding up his cows saw an apparition of the Virgin Mary who told him to look for her in a nearby cave. There, he found a statue of Mary. Because the cave was near the Guadalupe River, the statue was given the name of Guadalupe, which means "hidden river" or "hidden water." Historians can date the cult of Guadalupe to as early as 1327–1328. The statue itself dates to around the end of the 12th century.[362]

Over the years many miracles have been attributed to Our Lady of Guadalupe and she became the patroness of Extremadura, that region of Spain where she was found and where many of the first Spanish explorers, conquerors, and settlers originated. For example, Hernando Cortes, Francisco Pizarro, and Francisco Arellano came from Extremadura. Christopher Columbus had his first audience with King Fernando and Queen Isabel at the Monastery of Guadalupe, did a pilgrimage of thanks to the holy place after his first voyage in 1693, and during his second voyage in 1694 named a Caribbean Island after Guadalupe. Then, upon returning from his second voyage he took two Native American Indians to Guadalupe where they became the first American Indians to be baptized in Europe. The Extremadurans obviously transposed the *morena* or dark complexioned Virgin of Guadalupe of Extremadura to America, especially Mexico where with the miracle of Tepeyac in 1521[363] she eventually became the patroness of Mexico.

Of course, the Virgin of Guadalupe was not the only manifestation of Mary to come to the Americas. Depending on which part of the Americas, different manifestations became popular. The Virgin of Lujan is the patroness of Argentina, for example, and, initially, Our Lady of the Remedies was the most popular Virgin in Mexico, at least, among the Spanish. She is displayed as an upright triangular image. The Native people never warmed up to her because of her popularity with the conquering Spanish soldiers. Instead, a non-Marion image attracted their attention. This was St. Joseph, San José, the kindly father of Christ who acquired imagery with hollyhock flowers, which, in Mexico, are referred to as St. Joseph's cane.

Devotion to Guadalupe in Mexico slowly surpassed St. Joseph and for that matter all other images and saints. The first church built on the site of the miracle, which also was the location of an Aztec holy place dedicated to "our mother' Tonantzin, is mentioned in 1565. The first written description of the miracle of Tepeyac, the hill where the Virgin of Guadalupe appeared, dates to 1597.[364] Eventually, Guadalupe became the patroness of Mexico and appeared on banners during the independence movement.

This evolution of iconography and faith is evident in New Mexico and the southwest. The Virgin of Remedies (*Remedios*), popular with the Spanish, was carried on banners of the first settlers in 1598 and was brought back during the reconquest of Diego de Vargas in 1692–1693. The *morrión* found in New Mexico and that traveled to Washington, DC also depicted the Virgin of Remedies.

Then the Virgin of Rosario, or of the Rosary, became popular in New Mexico. A statue brought to New Mexico by Fray Alonso Benavides, was changed from Our Lady of the Annunciation to Our Lady of the Rosary in the 1620s. She became popularly known as Our Lady of the Conquest (*Conquistadora*), which, as mentioned, became mistranslated in the nineteenth and twentieth centuries. Nuestra Señora de la Conquistadora became the patroness of New Mexico.

By the end of the eighteenth century, Guadalupe of Mexico came to New Mexico when the mission at the Zuñí Pueblos received her name. The church dedicated to Guadalupe at Peña Blanca opened in December 1869 and Santa Fe's parish church of Guadalupe was built in at the end of the nineteenth century. Located at the west end of town on the road heading south to Mexico, the latter church is still used today, with a new and very impressive statue of Guadalupe standing next to the building. After centuries of migration north out of Mexico, Guadalupe has become the most popular Virgin in New Mexico as well as throughout the southwest.

While San José remains very popular throughout the Hispanic world and Nuestra Señora de la Conquistadora remains popular with her own confraternity in historical chapels in Santa Fe's Cathedral/Basilica and at the cemetery in Santa Fe, it was the very popular Guadalupe of Mexico that became the focal point for a controversy touched off by art that quickly spread into a debate of sexuality and politics.

77
In which success is snatched from failure

As I worked during the last months of my tenure at the Palace of the Governors, I was both anxious and whimsical. The end of a wonderful even awe-inspiring time was approaching. With staff help we compiled two reports or roadmaps of what had been done and needed to be done.[365] *The Santa Fe New Mexican* ran an article in which they pointedly asked if I harbored any bitterness over the way that I had been treated over my application for the director's position. I replied that I was "disappointed that I was not named and insulted that I was not interviewed" for I felt that "they at least owed me that [an interview] after 22 years."[366]

The Santa Fe New Mexican featured me in its prestigious Friday insert, *Pasatiempo.* Starting with a "hero" photograph of me on its cover with the oversized words "Adiós y gracias," and followed up with a well-intended but overstated synopsis that begins with,

> "Knowing that Santa Fe's outspoken historian Tom Chávez is at his post as the director of the Palace of the Governors is a lot like knowing that God is in Heaven."

The newspaper's inspiration for that exaggerated comment may have come from a quote that I gave them in the main article. After asking me to comment on the accomplishments during my tenure, including raising the money for the new history museum which "took the effort of a lot of people," they asked how I felt leaving before the new museum was built. I replied, "I've spent four years in the desert getting them to the chosen land and they can take it from here. I'm happy with that."[367]

Just before announcing my retirement, something quite unexpected happened. While in Spain, I received a message at a hotel desk that Edson Way was trying to reach me. I tried to telephone him but could only leave a message that I had returned his call and would return from Spain in a week. I left it there and did not even consider what he wanted even though I probably could have ventured an opinion based on previous history, for almost two years before Edson Way telephoned me in my office to ask if I would be willing to step in as acting director of the National Hispanic Cultural Center. Without going into details he explained that he was having problems with the current director and might have to fire him from the position.

I explained that I would be willing to help but would only do so part-time because I had enough to do at the Palace of the Governors. Also, I told him that because of my work at the Palace, I was not interested in a permanent transfer to the NHCC even though such a transfer meant a promotion within the state bureaucracy. Edson thanked me and said that he might be calling soon.

A short time after that conversation the Executive Director of the National Hispanic Cultural Center was given one afternoon to clear out of his office. The newspapers and now ex director reported the episode as non controversial. Dr. Adrian Bustamate, a very qualified and experienced man who, at one time, served on the Museum of New Mexico Board of Regents and, later, as Cultural Affairs officer, accepted the position of interim director until a search committee could select a new permanent director. This was supposed to happen within six months.

Thirteen months later my resignation from the Palace of the Governors became a matter of public record. Edward Lujan, the chairman of the NHCC Board of Directors, knew me for many years. He, Adrian Bustamante, and I served together on the Board of the Hispanic Culture Foundation that created the dream, plan, and reality of the NHCC. Lujan later said,

> "I've known Tom and his family for more than twenty years, and quite frankly I wanted him before this, but you don't steal people out of a sister agency. When he said that he was going to retire, all bets were off."[368]

Upon my return from Spain, Edson Way asked to meet in my office. Maybe, I figured, he wanted to talk about my connections in Spain. Within fifteen minutes of his telephone call, he was in my office and closed the door. He wanted me to take over the National Hispanic Cultural Center. He said that, "I was perfect for the job." Dr. Bustamante wanted out because he had been extended way beyond the original six months. Given how I had been treated by my own people, I was astounded and privately very pleased at what I was hearing. Here was the secretary for Cultural Affairs offering me a job for which I had not applied. Nor did they want to interview me. I told Edson that I would seriously consider his offer.

Later that same day Adrian Bustamante telephoned me. He knew that Edson had offered me the job and wanted me to know that he thought I was a great choice and "please take it." He wanted to return to full retirement.

Ed Lujan came to my office the next day. Ed is as decent a man as any that have lived. The NHCC was his dream and had become "his baby." He would not take "no" for an answer and even threatened to sit in my office until I said "yes."

Actually, I was very flattered by him, Adrian, and Edson. I could hardly have said "no." Also, Celia already worked in Albuquerque at the University of New Mexico and a quick calculation meant that the promotion being offered would mean a large increase in my retirement. Financially, taking the job was a no brainer. More importantly, the challenge intrigued me immensely. I was ready for a change so I told Ed Lujan that I would accept the offer.

Although I had announced my intentions to leave the Palace of the Governors to my staff and in the press,[369] I had not submitted an official letter of resignation. I already decided that I would continue at the Palace of the Governors through the next legislative session that would end in March 2002. We had a very large amount of money for the construction of the new museum on the line. Getting that legislation passed would be a pleasing and important milestone for me. So I told Ed Lujan, Edson Way, and Adrian

Bustamante that I could not start at the NHCC until April 1, a day that rang true for me. They laughed at the date but accepted my proposal. With this I sat down and penned my official letter of resignation that also noted the offer and my acceptance for the new position.[370]

Before leaving the Palace I gave the last of my fundraising lectures. Rather than give a serious of lectures over five weeks, one five hour lecture would do. Held at La Fonda Hotel the lecture, billed as "The Mother of All Lectures" and advertised with certain guest appearances, including "life-long nemesis Herr Professor von Ludwig Duck," attracted a large crowd and netted over $11,000![371]

Then the legislature came through with the last of our bills to help meet the Federal match for the new museum. Representatives Lucky Varela and Kiki Saavedra, sponsored a bill for $11 million and Ben Lujan, the new Speaker of the House put his new authority on the line to get the bill passed. Unfortunately, Governor Johnson told me at a reception in the Governor's Mansion that he had other priorities and would be vetoing the bill. In his direct and honest way he said, "Tom, you can't have your desert before the main course." Somewhat taken aback, I could only reply that the money for the new museum could hardly be mistaken for desert and that nonetheless, "When I was little I did eat desert first to make sure I had room for it." Nonetheless, I was chagrined as I left the mansion. A few days later, I heard or read the news that Governor Johnson signed the bill. He gave us our main course![372]

The Santa Fe New Mexican ran a front page headline that read "Governor OKs funds for New Mexico's 'Crown Jewel'"[373] and followed with an editorial the following day:

> "It might not be All's Well That Ends Well—but from the budgetary wars emerged a promising survivor: the Palace the Governors."[374]

We now had a total of $26 million dollars in place for the new museum and administrative building that would be needed. While we knew that we would need more, we had enough to know that the museum would become reality.

So, I left the Palace satisfied and began a new challenge with a new staff in a different city. Governor Johnson approved my new appointment. He later told me that he "always thought that I was perfect for the job." I agreed to work at the NHCC for two-and-a-half years at which point we would complete its most pressing project, which was to finish the fundraising and construction of the new Roy E. Disney Center for Performing Arts.

I quickly learned that I inherited a great and gratifying opportunity along with another tremendous staff that was waiting to show what it could do. Apparently the Board of Regents and search committee at the Museum of New Mexico unwittingly did me a great favor.

78
Wherein is given a brief description of a new adventure

By the time that I arrived at the National Hispanic Cultural Center, Ed Lujan had thoroughly briefed me on what I was getting into. I also met with the Board of Directors as well as the Foundation board. Set on fifty-five acres next to the Rio Grande in south Albuquerque, the NHCC campus had three buildings completed and another under construction. The institution had been open for three years and had a staff that had started working a couple of years before the opening. I would become the NHCC's fifth director over that span of time.

The completed buildings consisted of a very large modern structure that hinted of Meso-American pyramids that lined the back end of the campus and defined one side of the campus's main brick-lined plaza. The second floor housed the administrative offices of both the Center and its foundation. My office, notably, was located about where human sacrifices would take place if the pyramid were real. The building also housed the Center's art museum with three large galleries, ample storage, curatorial offices, and a gift shop. Another modernistic *torreon* or tower that harkened back to the prolific *torreones* throughout the Hispanic world greeted visitors at the Center's front gate. Santa Fe artist Frederico Vigil had been hired to apply a gigantic fresco on the *torreon*'s interior walls. The "*maestro*" as I called him, had applied the first necessary stucco coat on the walls and was drawing up conceptual drawings for what already was indicated to be a major work of art.

The third building was a restored and renovated adobe, pueblo-style elementary school building. Shaped like a giant squared off "U" wrapped around a patio with an incomplete fountain, the building housed the NHCC's library, a banquet hall, and a restaurant.

A new $22 million performing arts center was under construction. This would become my major challenge, for we still had to raise six million dollars to complete the cost of construction as well as additional money to plan and pay for the first year's programs. In the mean time we had to maintain the continuing programs in education, literary arts, and exhibitions.

Along with this we needed to plan two additional buildings that respectively would house the Center's educational programs and the Instituto Cervantes. Staff for both groups currently worked out of the main building. To help with this, Ed Lujan pledged to work with me in the legislature.

The Foundation started in the early 1980s when a group of Albuquerque Hispanic civic leaders met. They conceived the idea, really a dream, of creating the National Hispanic Cultural Center. As mentioned, many of the people who have crossed the pages of this book were active members of this foundation; Ed Lujan, Ed Romero, Frank Ortiz, Adrian Bustamante, Tish Frank, Concha Ortiz y Pino de Kleven, and many others including myself. Arturo Ortega, an Albuquerque attorney was a primary catalyst for the whole movement that resulted in the NHCC. I remember attending meetings in the board room of his downtown law office. His elegance and demeanor is a legacy that many people connected to the Center maintain to this day. I inherited a Foundation that had a sense of mission but, with the recent success with the City of Albuquerque's contribution of land, the construction of the completed buildings, and the successful handoff to the State; had become lost in the shuffle. As desired and planned, the NHCC had become a state institution with a governor appointed Board of Directors to set policy. When I came to the NHCC, the foundation had been without a hired director for over a year. Some board members openly wondered whether the Center's director should double as the Foundation's director. My answer was an emphatic, "no."

Ed Lujan wanted a career professional to lead the Center. The dream was becoming reality but its first years were turbulent to say the least. Both the Center and its Foundation had gone through a number of directors, some of which had been forced out.

In the two years and nine months that I worked there, we hired a foundation director, renamed the foundation to "National Hispanic Cultural Center Foundation," completed and opened the Roy E. Disney Center for Performing Arts, progressed on the *Torreon*'s fresco, had preliminary architectural plans for the new education and international buildings completed, raised the first few million dollars for the education building, purchased additional land and a warehouse across the street, completed the library's water fountain, improved the landscaping, expanded staff, and produced excellent programs and exhibitions. Most importantly, we had begun to create a positive reputation for the NHCC both nationally and locally.

Many factors went into that success. Legislative support, Federal support, a tremendously supportive and creative staff, and a renewed Foundation all conspired to create rapid and exciting progress. The dream was becoming reality.

79
Relating to an unknown story of a lost church bell in Albuquerque and an "I" beam from the Twin Towers in New York

The epoch defining moment of September 11, 2001 had occurred by the time I began my new job at the NHCC on April fools day of 2002. The smoldering and imagined smell of the collapsed Twin Towers and destroyed side of the Pentagon permeated the souls of everyone. Yet the narrative that would be our history marched on.

I was informed that the NHCC had a large brass church bell. As told to me by my new deputy director, Gene Henley, the bell was one of a matching pair that hung in the steeple of the neighborhood church on south 4th Street just a few blocks from the NHCC. Sagrada Corazon, or Sacred Heart, is the parish church for the Barelas neighborhood. Barelas is a poor neighborhood with mostly second and third generation Mexican-Americans living there. Some young upwardly mobile people had started to move in and downtown Albuquerque is slowly encroaching on the area. The construction of the NHCC on a fifty-five acre campus on Barelas's southern edge redefined the neighborhood as well as the Albuquerque skyline.

The NHCC's family understood that while it wanted to live up to its name, it also had to have support of its own neighborhood to say nothing of the city and the state. Here I was, in the first days of my new job, and the always meticulous Gene Henley told me the full story of the bell. The church suffered a fire in which the steeple was destroyed. Both bells disappeared. The NHCC staff located one of the bells in a south Albuquerque scrap yard and finagled a price to acquire it for the NHCC's collections.

As a result the NHCC had a bell that rightfully belonged to Sacred Heart Church. "No," I was reminded, "we saved the bell that belonged to the church but now it is State property."

Gene Henley was a master at working with the state bureaucracy. I, of course, felt that I had a little experience myself. He knew and played by the rules. I fudged on occasion. So we had a discussion, the gist of which was how to get the bell, which is now state property, back to its original owner. Henley initially confronted me with "it can't be done" and "no way." I looked for openings. "Has it been accessioned into the collections? If so, it can be deaccesioned. If not, how 'bout we declare it surplus like we do with worn out furniture?" "Maybe we can work a permanent loan to the church?"

"No," "no," "no."

Then an opportunity came that we could not overlook. The parishioners somehow had received permission to take an "I" beam from ground zero of the Twin Towers in New York. A trucking firm and union agreed to transport the beam from New York to Albuquerque for free. The parish priest, the Archbishop, and other parish representatives flew to New York to receive this very special gift.

The church planned to use the "I" beam in the construction of its new steeple. They came to the NHCC to ask if they could store it on our campus until the construction began. We had a better idea. We set the beam up outside in a very tasteful way and invited the public to come and see it. We completely realized that the beam would be an emotional attraction. People prayed and meditated before it, left flowers, touched it, and just stared at it.

The NHCC had both the beam and the bell. Both belonged to the church. We concluded that if the "I" beam was going into the church's new tower then the bell should hang in the tower as well so we just decided to return the bell.

News of this excited the parish. They held a special celebration for the bell's return. Then they had a larger celebration with the beam and the bell that featured the New Mexico Symphony Orchestra with a special concert inside the church. All the town's dignitaries attended.

Today, Sacred Heart Church on south 4th street has its new bell tower. If a passerby looks carefully a glint of the bell can be seen. The beam is buried inside the tower. A plaque inside the church tells the tale of the tower's hidden treasure. The Barelas neighborhood and its parish church share a history with the NHCC that will surface periodically for generations to come.

80
About the visit of the Prince and the dedication of his building

Thanks to Ambassador Ed Romero, the Royal family of Spain had become familiar with the National Hispanic Cultural Center. Prince Felipe, normally called *el Principe*, the heir apparent to the Spanish throne, had been to New Mexico. Since I met him in 1988 at the Palace of the Governors, he had returned to New Mexico to participate in the announcement of an endowed chair at the University of New Mexico. Iberdrola, a corporation from Spain, endowed and established The Prince of Asturias[375] Endowed Chair in Information Science and Technology. Ed Romero arranged it all.

Now the former ambassador turned his attention to the NHCC international building that would house the Instituto Cervantes. At his suggestion, we agreed to name the planned building the Felipe de Asturias International building. Hopefully, this would help give us an international presence and help with the raising the funds necessary to build the edifice.

The Prince agreed to fly to Albuquerque for a dedication ceremony. This got us all excited. Our excitement increased with the additional news that he would be traveling with his new wife Letizia, whom, they recently announced, was pregnant with their first child, a son. After cutting back on grandiose plans for a fundraising banquet, musical concert, and so on, we settled on a tour of the campus and a simple ceremony on the grounds where the new building will go. After speeches, His Highness would take a shovel and symbolically turn over the first dirt.

Then we got down to "nuts and bolts." The prince's front people proceeded to tell us what we could and could not do right down to how much time we had. We walked through the agreed upon itinerary and shared our proposed program for the groundbreaking ceremony. This resulted in a curt announcement that, "The Prince does not give speeches."

"But," I replied; "he did before." He gave a speech on the plaza in Santa Fe and in a special indoor ceremony at UNM. He also spoke at the Houston banquet that I attended.

"No, he does not give speeches."

"Okay." I looked at Ed Lujan who seemed as puzzled as I. We revised the itinerary in which we had a few dignitaries give welcoming words. I would read prepared words putting the whole event in context and then invite the Prince to step in front of the low stage to turn over some dirt.

We set up bleachers, a canopied stage, bought special shovels, ran up more than one Spanish flag, and waited for the royal couple to arrive at the designated place. When their caravan arrived and they alighted from the limousine we introduced ourselves and the dignitaries who would share the stage; Ed Lujan, Ed Romero, Albuquerque Mayor Martin Chávez, Foundation President Katherine Archuleta, and Ed López, chairman of the Foundation Board.

On an overcast and drizzly day the crowd applauded and cheered. The program began on schedule and continued without a hitch. I read my speech and the others said their words of welcome. I led the Prince off the stage and handed him a shovel. We both bent over and took up a shovel full of dirt and paused. His Highness quietly asked me, "Where do I put it?"

I quipped in reply, "On me for all I care." He laughed as he followed my instructions to return the dirt back to its original location.

Then we went back on stage where he retook his place and I went before the microphone to thank him and close the ceremonies. As I was in mid-sentence I heard behind me a "pssst, pssssst." I turned around to confront the Prince, all six foot six of him leaning toward me.

"Can I say something?" he asked almost humbly.

"Como me manda," "as you command me" I replied in Spanish. He laughed again, pulled a sheaf of notes out of his interior coat pocket and proceeded to give an elegant and very thoughtful speech.

When he finished, I closed the ceremony. As we walked to a private reception the member of his entourage who insisted that the Prince did not give speeches came up to me and apologized. The Spanish, like most Europeans, may insist on something but when they are mistaken they own up to it. This was a small case in point.

To date, construction on the building has not started. The building was a part of the original plan and dream for the NHCC. The plans still exist. Eventually, it will become reality. The idea remains and the Instituto Cervantes is waiting. On that day Felipe, the Prince of Asturias, who knows, he may be the King of Spain, will return and give a speech because he does.

81
Concerning a Maestro, his fresco, and the culture police

Frederico Vigil was a middle-aged, medium height, lanky genius of an artist. He looks like an artist. He usually dresses in clothes with paint blotches all over them. He wears his full head of black turning to grey hair over his ears and combed to one side. He sports a goatee. But he does not come off as a mad artist for his facial lines hint of his disposition that is given away by his brown eyes. My grandfather would call them "smiling eyes." I cannot help but smile when I see him and his smile is quicker in return. He likes to laugh, complain in good humor, and share a glass of wine, preferably from Spain. He has been a friend for years.

We never really spent a lot of time together, for we both were too busy for that. We became friends in the early 1980s when he asked me to write an essay in a handout booklet about his work for a traveling exhibition of his paintings.[376] I spoke at the exhibition's openings in Santa Fe, Farmington, and Albuquerque. From then on we maintained a friendship that supported each other's endeavors. When word leaked out about the treatment of my unsuccessful application for director of the Museum of New Mexico, Frederico was one of the few who wrote a letter to the editor on my behalf. In short, we have a mutual admiration for each other. For my part, he truly deserves to be called "Maestro."

Born and raised in Santa Fe where he graduated with a degree in biology from the College of Santa Fe, he grew up infused with the rich history of his New Mexican heritage. That pride has become the trademark of his art. His emphasis on history with its ironies as well as lessons is an integral aspect of his work. His art is his quest.

Frederico Vigil paints history. He has used *dichos*, words strung together to create time-honored sayings with messages. He has used words from historical documents. He incorporates the words into his art both literally and figuratively. The words convey images or images convey words. The images come out of history and his vibrant colors wash the viewer with richness, indeed, wonder of that past.

He is one of a few artists in the United States to paint in the medium of *buon fresco*, which means like Michelangelo did, he applies his colors to fresh or just applied wet stucco so that the colors permeate the wall and lasts for centuries. Frederico was the perfect choice to paint the interior of the *Torreón* or stylized watch-tower that stands at the main entrance to the NHCC campus.

That Frederico had begun work on a *buon fresco* that would fill up the inside walls of the NHCC's *torreón* pleased me. I would be a part of that endeavor and Frederico and I could spend some time together. Now we would see each other on a regular basis.

But, like all worthy projects, there were problems. The budget was not realistic and Frederico had not been paid much for his work to date. We quickly had a series of meetings and settled on a budget of $300,000 that we adjusted up to $380,000. The money paid for supplies, assistants, workshops taught by Frederico, and his salary. Still, the price was cheap by any standard.

Now, except for some initial expenses already paid, we needed to raise the money. With this, Michael and Marianne O'Shaughnessy, long-time admirers of Frederico Vigil, stepped forward with a $100,000 lead gift from the I. A. O'Shaughnessy Foundation that needed to be matched.[377] The NHCC Foundation met the match when they committed to another $115,000 and we succeeded in raising the rest.

Still, the finances were not settled. Frederico needed funds on which to survive so we agreed to put him under contract so he could get a regular bi-weekly salary. This, too, raised issues. The O'Shaughnessy's did not like the idea of contracting for art and Frederico became very suspicious of the whole process. He hired an attorney.

The irony of this situation was not lost on me, for Frederico and I now became adversaries. In addition, I had alienated Michael and Marianne O'Shaughnessy who also were friends. I sent an email to Michael explaining my position and what I felt needed to be done. I thought that I was helping Frederico and concluded with my feelings in the matter:

> "I am in the precarious position of caring for a friend/sensitive artist and representing the state and, now, because of the first friend, I am running the risk of offending you, another friend."[378]

The next day I met with Frederico's attorney and expressed the same sentiment. I asked him to review the contract to resolve the dispute.[379] During all of this Frederico kept working, money was being raised, and he was paid on a bi-weekly basis. The issue was not resolved until after I retired at the end of 2004.

At the same time another problem surfaced. Word filtered to me that the New Mexico Hispanic Culture Preservation League had objections about Frederico and his fresco. At first, I could not imagine a problem. Frederico is a Hispanic New Mexican, descendent from a prominent New Mexican family. The fresco' subject matter would showcase the history of the Hispanic world with a focus on New Mexico. To assure accuracy as well as balance, we formed a committee of historians to periodically meet with Frederico to exchange ideas and, in some cases, make suggestions about the design and emphasis of figures.

The concept was to begin the narrative in Spain, Mexico, and New Mexico before Columbus embarked on his epic journey. From there the visual narrative would spiral up the walls as it passed through time and place to New Mexico and end with an offering of hope for the future.

Frederico created scale renderings of the fresco as the ideas developed. He even created a scale model cylinder the inside of which he placed his scaled renderings to get a hint at how they would look. He put a charcoal grid on the Torreón's wall and transposed the scaled drawing to the wall. I could see from early on that he was creating something very, very special.

Still, complaints from the Preservation League periodically filtered in. They were an Albuquerque based organization that formed to promote New Mexico's Hispanic heritage. Their formation was a direct reaction to a recent spat of pan-Indian attacks in opposition to the placement of a statue of New Mexico's first governor Juan de Oñate in Albuquerque. The League held annual banquets during which they presented awards to selected individuals who supported Hispanic culture. They also worked for, and promoted, the teaching of New Mexico history in the State's pubic schools.

I knew some of the League's key members and was pleased to find out that their current president, Robert Rodríquez, a native of Cuba but a staunch New Mexican, was a docent for the NHCC. One of my first acts at the NHCC was to invite the Preservation League to hold its board of directors meetings in the NHCC board room. They held, at least, a couple of meetings. The NHCC, under Ed Lujan's direction and with his contribution always purchased a table at the Preservation League's annual banquet. So, I gladly befriended the organization and my good intention was returned by their promotion of my book, *Spain and the Independence of the United States.*

Rubén Sálaz Márquez, an active member of the Preservation League had been appointed to the NHCC Board of Directors. While I did not realize it at the time, Sálaz and I had a short history. A little more than two years before, in March of 2001, Sálaz used his influence with someone in the State legislature to have his book on the history of New Mexico nominated to be New Mexico's "official chronology of New Mexico's past." By that time the book had been badly received by many professionals and organizations. The book originated as a project of the NHCC whose advisory committee rejected the manuscript. Nevertheless, the House of Representatives passed a measure to make it the official state's history on a 38-21 vote. The bill (HB 653) was sent to the senate for final consideration when the press contacted me.

I was not aware of the issue nor had I read the book. When told, I reacted with a definitive answer. "What is a state doing promoting an official history? Totalitarian states create official histories not free democratic states." I then added that history is always a work-in-progress, and it should not be frozen in time. "To try to create an official history, that is an insult to our history." The bill died and soon thereafter Sálaz stormed into the Palace of the Governor's gift shop and demanded that all his books be removed from the shelves.[380] As a staunch member of the Preservation League, Sálaz received an appointment from Governor Richardson to the NHCC Board of Directors.

I was surprised to realize the depth of the Preservation League's opposition to the fresco, for their coolness to Frederico Vigil and his work became acrimonious. I took the position that anyone could voice an opinion and we should listen. After Frederico and the committee of historians finally agreed on the themes, Frederico drew up a scaled depiction of what he wanted to put on the wall. I scheduled a special Board of Director's meeting to present the drawings for final approval. The Preservation League was notified and invited to the open meeting.

Bob Rodríquez then sent a written complaint to Sálaz who passed it on to Board Chairman Ed Lujan.[381] Ed asked me to write a reply.

My one page letter explained the process, the committee of historians, and that the board of directors had to approve the drawings before the artist proceeded. Regarding his complaint that the history of New Mexico was under represented, I assured him that he was mistaken. However, I reminded him that "art can be a matter of taste despite the subject" even among like-minded people. Nonetheless, the NHCC was a "national" center and the fresco would reflect that as well.[382]

We then invited the Preservation League's Board of Directors for a private tour and explanation of the Torreón and the work in process. We explained the process, showed the guests the scaled drawings that would be presented to the NHCC Board of Directors for approval, and tried to answer questions. "Tried" is the operative term, for the Preservation League's Board of Directors spoke of a conspiracy to circumvent public input into the project, which was ridiculous on the face of it for here were the critics making their point at a transparent meeting. I reiterated the NHCC's intent for an open and transparent process but they were not convinced. I began to realize that the Preservation League's opposition to the fresco had more to do with the artist than the work.

Robert Rodríquez responded to the tour with a letter to me and copied to the NHCC Board of Directors. He stated that the Preservation League is:

> "...now quite certain that the drawings proposed have a definite emphasis on Mexican/Central American Indian groups and a neglect of Spain, New Mexico, the Southwest and the United States...."

He continued with:

> "It appears as though the basic purpose of the mural in the torreón it [sic] to promote the '*mestizo*' theme of racial mixing while ignoring the history and culture of Hispanics..."

He then presented a twenty-one point list of suggested available subjects to be included on the wall. He also expressed the Preservation League's concern that the Board of Directors would "be circumvented on this matter," recommended that all work on the project be temporarily suspended, and offered the Preservation League's assistance.[383]

Here was a classic, if confusing, "stick and carrot" technique. On one hand they claim to be my friends and wish to help and on the other hand they accused me of duplicity. The list and commentary about "racial mixing" really muddied the conversation, for he included suggestions for themes that already had been included and had been shown to him and his colleagues. He was completely off base from an historical perspective, for Spain, New Mexico, the Southwest, and United States took up the majority of the proposed fresco's space.

The meeting and subsequent letter clarified the perplexing bitter-sweet relationship that I would have with the Preservation League. It became clear to me that short of canceling the project, the Preservation League or, at least, Rodríquez and Sálaz, who now voiced the same line, would not be satisfied.

That letter, coupled by the unfortunate comment directed at Frederico Vigil put me and the staff on notice. Two of the Preservation League's major representatives, one a NHCC Board member and the other a NHCC docent, had become very confrontational with the NHCC.

I replied to Rodríquez with a short letter in which he was thanked for his concern. I defended the qualifications of the people working on the project and that many of his suggestions "already are being incorporated in the work." I also reminded him that the drawings would be completed in anticipation to a special board meeting scheduled for 20 June 2003. I invited him and his board to attend and voice their concerns.[384]

On 13 June 2003, the NHCC sent out a public announcement with an agenda for the special board meeting. Blazed across the sheet in upper case bold letters was the announcement that "THIS MEETING IS OPEN TO THE PUBLIC AND PUBLIC COMMENTS ARE WELCOME." In response, the Preservation League made sure to invite all its members to be there.[385]

82
Which continues with an account of an unfortunate disagreement along with other dire matters

I asked Frederico Vigil not to attend the meeting. It is his job, I told him, to be creative and do the art and it is my job to deal with the politics. I meant what I said. I also knew that the issue had become personal. Some members of the Preservation League were now complaining about his previous artwork as well as about him. That kind of opposition was acrimonious and I did not want him to face it or get involved in an unnecessary confrontation.

Besides, the finished sketches bespoke of a spectacular finished product. I shared my confidence with Frederico. We had considered Rodríquez's letter, many of his suggestions had been incorporated in the work, and I had a good idea of their position. Let me deal with the meeting. Frederico agreed.

As Chairman of the Board, Ed Lujan ran a tight meeting. He set up the agenda, laid out the ground rules, and proceded. Stuart Ashman, the State's Secretary for Cultural Affiars attended. I led off by unveiling the proposed artwork and argued on its behalf. Then members of the consulting committee of historians were invited to speak after which the members of the Board of Directors made comments. All the questions were directed to me and all of them were pertinent. They ranged from observations of what was missing to questions about the project's procedure. When the Board finished, Ed Lujan invited public comment. John Lucero and his wife, Conchita, both founding members of the Preservation League, made comments and asked some questions. They praised me but felt that the NHCC, especially the fresco, had gone astray. To them, the fresco seemed to be too much about Mexico and Indians. They argued that the fresco should emphasize more of Spain and New Mexico.

The Lucero's concerns were heart-felt and sincere. I felt that they had misread what they had seen and tried to point out that actually the proposed sketches had more of Spain then they realized. I noted that the *Dama del Elche,* Columbus, the Hapsburg Eagle, and Spain's role in United States' independence all appeared in the drawings. Actually, I disliked correcting Mr. Lucero in public but went ahead, hoping that he and Conchita would understand. Their questions and comments seemed reasonable and I tried to respond in kind.

Other public members spoke in praise of the project and the artist. Representatives from the Barelas neighborhood offered comments and the neighborhood association endorsed the proposed drawings. One neighborhood association representative said that "we need to look beyond" our own backyard. He added that space had limitations and the artist cannot put everything in the fresco so we need to have faith in the experts.

Robert Rodríquez stood up and pretty much repeated what he had written in his letter. He felt that the whole proposed depiction added up to an anti-Spanish view and an endorsement of the Black Legend. He incorrectly noted that "only the Mexican flag is represented," and added that, we need "to tell the truth." In his opinion, the fresco was a Mexican point-of-view, not a world view.[386]

I took notes of all the comments, for we wanted to consider everything as we progressed to a final product. In response to the Mexican flag comment, I observed that the Hapsburg Eagle, which represented Spain, was larger than the flag and New Mexico's flag would be included as well.

The meeting concluded with a Board vote. A motion was made and seconded for approval of the fresco's concept. An amendment was included that instructed the artist, the committee of historians, and me to take into consideration the public's comments.[387] Rubén Sálaz was the only Board member to speak in opposition to the project. During the motion's discussion he went off on a tangent arguing that the Board did not have legal authority to take action because "the law states that Board members have a strong knowledge of New Mexico's Hispanic History." The lawmakers, he expounded, "want us to be Hispano rather than Chicano."

After the Board was assured that the committee and artist would seriously consider the public comments as well as others that might be conveyed to us, the motion was called to question and the Board voted in favor of the fresco project. Rubén Sálaz cast the only "no" vote.

A few days later I received a very polite and reasoned letter from Conchita Lucero. She reiterated the concern that both she and her husband had expressed. She offered some specific observations. "Benito Juarez [the Mexican President who defeated Maximilian] is quite large in comparison to Queen Isabel and King Ferdinand, who did more in the Golden Age than any other leader," "could we utilize the *nichos* to greater advantage," or add to Spain's role in support "of the thirteen colonies in their struggle for independence." She added a couple of criticisms about the conduct of some people at the meeting and, then, thanked me for the opportunity to express her concerns before the board of "Torreón advisors."[388]

Overall, I felt good about the proceedings. I also wanted to review the drawings in light of the comments, which Frederico and the history committee did. Some adjustments were made. For example, the whole order of subject matter was moved so that the first thing a visitor would see upon entering the building would be Santiago, the patron saint of Spain. Now Frederico could begin drawing up his images on tracing paper in anticipation of tracing them on the wall. Once this was done, we would see how the models transposed onto the actual walls. Then we could make more modifications.

83
On how the matter of the previous chapter continues to surface

Despite all that had passed and had been done, some members of the Preservation League continued to agitate. On 22 September 2003 Robert Rodríquez wrote a letter to the State Attorney General that was copied to Ed Lujan and me. Rodríquez requested that

Attorney General Patricia Madrid "immediately" investigate the NHCC's violation of the State Public Meetings Act for its next schedualed board meeting. Rodríquez claimed that the meeting room could not accommodate the Preservation League's many members who planned to attend.[389]

Although the Attorney General's office did not react and the board meeting was held without incident, I realized somewhat ambivalently that some people, like Rodríquez, would not quit in their effort to stop the fresco from being completed. Both Rodríquez and Sálaz, who continued to argue against the project on the Board, approached me as if we were old friends. Nevertheless, their letters and comments had become tiresome. Their approach sharply contrasted to the reasoned position of the Luceros and others.

In another effort to placate the Preservation League, Foundation director Katherine Archuleta arranged a private tour of the fresco then in process. She asked that Frederico be there to answer questions. The tour quickly turned into a confrontation with John Lucero verbally attacking the artist. Frederico would later say that he believed that Lucero was trying to entice him into a fight.[390]

Confrontations aside, Frederico had the Board's approval to proceed. He began work and the fresco started to take shape. The cartoons filled the walls and he began to apply the colors for the four Virgins; Guadalupe from Mexico, La Conquistadora from New Mexico, Remedios out of history, and Guadalupe from Spain. The brilliant colors and cartoons hinted at the ultimate reality that Frederico's work would be a master piece.

Meanwhile, the NHCC had begun attracting national as well as local interest. A number of favorable articles came out in newspapers and magazines. Under headlines like "National Influence: Hispanic Cultural Center, Once seen as a Bust Has Become the Model for Cities Across the Country,"[391] "The National Hispanic Cultural Center's Slippery Slide Toward Success,"[392] "National Hispanic Cultural Center finding way to open performance building despite budget Cuts,"[393] and the "Hispanic Cultural Center is envy of other Cities."[394] Representatives in a group visiting from Los Angeles called the Center a model "that represents the greatest and largest vision for a Hispanic cultural center in the United States."[395] A *Los Angeles Times* article openly wondered how a distant place like Albuquerque and not Los Angeles could have such an institution.[396] A newspaper in Dallas called the NHCC a "Southwest surprise" and added the bi-line, "'City at the end of the World' becomes a Mecca of Hispanic Culture."[397] All these articles described and praised various aspects of the NHCC, including the fresco. More than a few of the articles featured photographs of Frederico Vigil working on his masterpiece, which continues to attract attention.[398]

The NHCC had become a unique success story. It was far in advance of other larger communities who wanted to create something similar. The fresco was one of the attention getters. The local public had become interested in this "sleeping giant."

All of a sudden, it seemed, the fresco became very popular. Poor Frederico seemed to spend more time talking to visitors than working on his art. Finally, we tried to set a schedule to keep people and reporters away so he could work uninterrupted.

Under the title "Towering Task," *The Albuquerque Journal* published an article in its Sunday "Arts and Culture" section. The article featured Frederico's now famous fresco but brought up some of the Preservation League's complaints. The article conveyed my position that the League had been under the misconception that the fresco was solely about New Mexico rather than a larger Pan Hispanic history that focused on New Mexico. Frederico who finally had an opportunity to speak out in reaction to months of personal as well as artistic criticism took advantage of the opportunity:

> "I don't mind people having an opinion...as long as its an educated opinion, and I feel that some of them are uneducated as to what they were talking about, true facts in history."[399]

Robert Rodríquez reacted with a letter to Governor Bill Richardson that he copied to the Board of Directors, the legislative leadership, Stuart Ashman, and me. He accused the NHCC of racism for promoting "*mestizaje,* the mixing of European and Amerindian races." Rodríquez repeated Salas's early criticism about the historical expertise of the NHCC Board members and concluded with a request that the NHCC be investigated before the "*fresco* painting actually begins."[400]

The Governor, who never demonstrated an interest in the NHCC, had Secretary Stuart Ashman reply. He wrote a recap of all the research done by various historians and the Board meeting that Ashman attended. He observed that Rodríquez "offered support for the consensus," and that "input from many constituencies, including the League, was incorporated into the design at various stages of its development.[401]

Ashman put his finger on the precise problem in replying to the Preservation League's president. They came off as bitter, ever virulent, and cooperative, depending on who represented them, whether they were face to face or writing letters. One thing was clear, despite my well-intentioned efforts to include them in the process; they would not let up in their opposition. They did not like Frederico Vigil at all.

By this time the staff, including myself, had become completely exasperated with the Preservation League. We started referring to them as the "culture Nazis." Mentally, we began to think of them as being a fringe organization. We rallied behind Frederico and his fresco. In fact, the vast majority of the public increasingly supported the project.

In April of 2004, Rubén Sálaz wrote another letter attacking Vigil. This time he complained to Ed Lujan about an NHCC mailing that featured a Frederico Vigil painting of Sor Juana Inés de la Cruz that the NHCC used for a poster.

Sor Juana Inés de la Cruz is a seventeenth century nun who lived in Mexico City. She is considered one of the Americas greatest poets. She was a playwright and a theologian who the Church forced to renounce her work. She did this in spectacular fashion by signing a confession in which she renounced her writings, in her own blood.

Sálaz saw in Frederico's painting the bloody hand and some of his other imagery pertinent to her life as "scatological." He asked Lujan who was "promoting this scatological direction at the Center?"[402]

Ed Lujan left the reply to me. Sálaz, it seemed, knew very little about Sor Juana's life. In answer, I defined the painting for him image by image. In each case I pointed out that nothing in the work was even close to the standard definition of scatological. I even quoted the definition from the dictionary. I questioned his motive and invited him to openly state "what it is that concerns you."[403] That never happened, at least, to me.

A few years later, Frederico reminisced with me about the Preservation League and their effort to derail the fresco. He reminded me that the same people protested an earlier work that he completed in Española and that "a nut" had defaced another of his frescos at St. Johns College in Santa Fe.

I shared with him the story of Don Quixote who chased off the guards and released some prisoners condemned to the galleys. He mistakenly believed that they were unjustly being mistreated. The old knight thought that he was doing good but the newly released criminals turned on him and beat the heck out of him all the while thanking him for their undeserved freedom before they ran off.[404] Beat to a pulp and left on the ground, don Quixote was left "grief-stricken at seeing himself so injured by the very people for whom he had done so much good."[405]

"You see, Frederico, we crusaders mean good but sometimes, many times, the beneficiaries do not appreciate what we do. Does Quixote's episode with the prisoners ring a bell with you?"

Frederico laughed. He always liked a good humorous story with a point.[406]

In truth and seriously, the thirteenth century Italian Catholic philosopher and theologian, St. Thomas Aquinas, summed it up best when he wrote:

> "The same spirit that hovered over the waters at the beginning of creation hovers over the mind of the artist at work."[407]

Now complete, the fresco has become an attraction by itself. This was intended, for the staff and supporters wanted to create a campus that included buildings, art, plazas, waterworks, lighting schemes, workspaces, as well as programs that each alone would be an attraction.

The daunting task is Frederico's *Magnus opus*. The Torreón's interior walls are forty feet high. The surface on which he applied his fresco begins twelve feet above the ground floor and extends up cylindrical walls to the ceiling, which is also included as part of his composition. In short, Frederico's work covers an estimated total of 4,000 square feet.

84
In which private support came to the rescue

One individual and his wife, however, keyed the final push for the Performing Arts Center. Roy E. Disney and Patti Disney already had agreed to a million dollar contribution, $500,000 of which had been paid, toward the construction of the Performing Arts Center.

They came to the NHCC through Frank Zuniga, a long-time Disney employee who retired to Albuquerque. Frank is a native of New Mexico, born in Gallup. He introduced the Disneys to the NHCC and to Ed Lujan. The Disney's liked Ed Lujan and developed an obvious interest in the Center's plans. They agreed with Frank Zuniga to premier the Disney movie, *The Wonderful Ice Cream Suit,* in Albuquerque to raise funds for the NHCC.

Of course, the State had to be a major partner in the funding formula. While, the majority of the funding for construction of the fine arts center came from Federal and private sources, we included the State in our funding strategy. In anticipation of a June opening, the NHCC went through the Office of Cultural Affairs with a major funding package that included staff, some operating costs, equipment, and furniture.

The Office of Cultural Affairs gave the NHCC every indication of its support but a number of things conspired to derail the effort. The Office of Cultural Affairs already had cut the NHCC operating budget by over 14% to divert funds to the Museum of New Mexico. A series of meetings with Edson Way elicited promises that the funds would be restored but no action followed.

However, Bill Richardson, the newly elected governor, quickly replaced Edson Way with Ruben Smith. After about a year, Richardson fired Smith and replaced him with

Stuart Ashman. The new administration did not back our legislative efforts to fund the performing arts center. We continued to lobby for our legislative initiative without knowing that we had no support from the Office of Cultural Affairs. When we found out that no bill had been introduced, Ed Lujan and I scrambled to get one introduced but it was too late and died without action.

Now the NHCC had a real problem. Some hard decisions needed to be made. I met with staff, Foundation leadership, NHCC supporters, and Ed Lujan to devise a plan. In April 2003, roughly a month after the dire fiscal information had become official, I met with the NHCC Board of Directors. Simply put, I had to inform the Board about the status of the budget, how I planned to use the budget, and the status of the required revenues to open the performing arts center.

I told them that the decreased budget meant that the NHCC would cut programs and the failure to get any money from the legislature for the Performing Arts Center meant that we would have to make an emergency request from the State's Board of Finance that is chaired by the Governor. If that failed we would need to find some minor funds "to moth ball" the Performing Arts Center until funding became available. This all came out in the newspaper the next day[408] and Governor Richardson reacted badly. According to an anonymous aid, he stormed out of office wanting to know "who the f... is Tom Chávez?"

The Albuquerque Journal ran an article the following day in which the Governor said that I wanted "to pressure" him "into funding the Hispanic Cultural Center...." The same edition ran an editorial that endorsed the NHCC, adding that, "...it's unfortunate the project finds itself begging for money" and the State, meaning the Governor, should support the effort. "Doing so will ensure a return on the millions of dollars already invested in the project."[409]

Now the Governor was really mad. He dispatched Ed Romero to tell me that he "did not play that way" and did not appreciate my use of the press. With Ed Lujan seated at my side, I asked Ambassador Romero what the Governor would prefer; that I lie to his appointed Board of Directors or violate the State's open meetings act and meet with them in secret? Ed Lujan agreed, stating that I only did what was required of me. Ed Romero asked that I stay calm and, then, read the article that upset the governor. He later telephoned to say that there was nothing in the article that should have irritated the Governor and that he would talk to him.

This was not our first encounter with the governor, for shortly after he took office, I received a telephone call from Ruben Smith, his first Secretary of Cultural Affairs, and Ben Lujan, Jr., the departments head fiscal officer.[410] Smith wanted me to cancel five NHCC contracts and proceeded to list them. He said that the governor needed the money.

Somewhat taken aback, I observed that the contracts had been let, people were working, and that the contracts had been legally processed through the State's procurement process and approved by his office. Canceling them now would violate the contract.

Ben Lujan chimed in to point out that the small print covered me.

Still not convinced I replied that this was not right. These people were working in good faith and how was I to expect them ever to work for the NHCC or state again if we arbitrarily cut them off?

My concerns were of no matter. Smith's and Lujan's only concern was that the governor wanted the money.

To this I replied that if that was the case, either one of them had the authority to cut off the contracts and to go ahead because I would not do it. They offered me the evening to think about it and get back to them the next day.

The next morning I wrote a long e-mail to Ruben Smith in which I laid out value of the work being done under the targeted contracts and that every one of them had been partially fulfilled. That justification, alone, argued against ending them. Then I repeated that I thought ending them without reason would be illegal and added that, legalities aside, I found the idea "ethically repugnant." I concluded that I would not cancel the contracts.

My inaction did not win any friends in Santa Fe. On the other hand, neither Smith nor Lujan used their authority to cancel the contracts. It seems that they needed someone further from the Governor to do the dirty work. My subsequent actions, regarding the NHCC budget must have reminded the Governor of my lack of cooperation.

Nevertheless, we did something right, for the Governor's administration started restoring some budget and the Governor and the Board of Finance approved the NHCC request for $200,000. With this small success, we reviewed schedules and decided that we could set a goal for a soft April opening of the Performing Arts Center. Shortly thereafter, the opening was moved to June and changed to a "hard" opening. This was still contingent on private support. Nevertheless, we were optimistic. Any success with the State would help with private support.

I expressed that as a historian I felt that it did not matter when we opened. "What matters to me is that one hundred years from now somebody will look back and say, 'Those people really did a neat thing for us...'" We knew that we would get the money, "It's just a matter of when."[411]

At the time, the politics delayed construction as well as fundraising. The money would be coming in later rather than sooner, which put us in a cash flow bind. As a result, Gene Henley, who met with the architects and construction supervisors on a weekly basis, informed me that the building could not be turned over to us in time to meet the

June date on which we had been planning our major opening. The building would not be complete. Some of the fixtures and cosmetics would be missing. On top of that, the deficit in the state budget meant that we would not have the necessary staff to train and operate the highly technical building in time for the opening.

Gene Henley met with the architect and construction people to receive a solid completion date. The funding would be my problem. The answer came back that it would be, at least, another two months. I made an executive decision. We will delay opening the Performing Arts Center for another three months.

The foundation and the Center planned to invest almost a quarter of a million dollars in a three day opening celebration in June. We even tried to get Placido Domingo to headline the event. Initial publicity had gone out. No one at the foundation or on my board of directors liked my position to delay the opening again. The staff ducked the debate but made sure that I knew that they could use the time.[412] I argued before both boards of directors that we had invested so much in the new building that it would be a shame to open it partially completed. It would be a mistake to open it before its time. We should open when the building was complete so that people, from the start, would see it in all its glory. After all, this would be a seminal moment for the future of the National Hispanic Cultural Center. I argued that we could not "short-change ourselves."

Ed Lujan was visibly upset to hear this position but agreed with me. In fact, he stood by me when I took the news to the board of directors. The foundation proved to be a little more difficult. They had been raising money and planning the festivities for the opening. My news initially left them speechless out of frustration.

In her office Katherine Archuleta blurted out to me, "Fine, but you tell the Disneys." She felt that the Disneys would be real upset. To make her point, she dialed Roy Disney's office and handed me the telephone. Roy Disney had an assistant who was, at once, very blunt, outspoken, and protective of him. She apparently did not share her boss's favorable view of New Mexico.

Upon hearing about my decision and rationale, she reacted with a sarcastic tirade about "you people." Obviously, rude and possibly racist, she threatened that Roy Disney would not appreciate any additional delay. My only reply was that "I made the decision and I will take the blame." I told her that if either Roy or Patti have a question, "please have them call me."

As I thought about the condescending conversation, I decided that I had better not leave it to Roy's assistant to convey the message. Instead, I penned a letter explaining my position and using that as a basis to request that Roy and Pattie consider a second million dollar gift. I also added my observations of his assistant's attitude and unfortunate words and requested that I not have to deal with her again.

A few weeks later, in November, Clifford Miller who was Roy Disney's colleague, accountant, and advisor telephoned me at home. Miller had joined the Disneys more than once on their trips to New Mexico so we knew each other. He told me that Roy had received my letter while traveling in Europe and asked him to deal with it. He asked that I overlook the acrimonious conversation with Roy's assistant and implied that she would not be involved with us any more. In return, I backed off any outlandish accusations and openly surmised that maybe I got her at a bad time. Nonetheless, we agreed that we should move on.

Then he surprised me. Roy found my letter very interesting. Could I fill in some detail about the funding problems? I did. Roy agreed to my request and more, for he and Clifford Miller understood from my letter that we needed the money sooner rather than later. "That," I confirmed, "is correct." We need to pay the contractor so he can pay his workers. Roy agreed to move up his payments on the balance of the first million dollars and then agreed to pay a second million dollars in two parts; the first half before New Years and the second half immediately after. To help us with raising other monies we agreed that half of the second gift had to be matched in $100,000 increments.[413]

In one of the great understated questions of my life, Miller asked if that arrangement was alright with me.

"Are you kidding? Yes! That would be great!"

Within a month Katherine Archuleta was able to write Clifford Miller and the Disneys that the NHCC would be receiving a total of $425,000 from the Bank of America, the Journal Publishing Company, and the McCune Foundation. In addition the Bank of America would contribute an additional $125,000 over the next couple of years and the total Journal gift would be $500,000![414] Now, with funding in place, we could open the Performing Arts Center with all the bells and whistles.

85
Dalí, Disney, and an opportunity partially fulfilled

Before the story of the previous chapter occurred, I had met Roy and Patti, who insisted on being called by their first names. I had faith in their appreciation for my position. They like Ed Lujan would understand the rationale behind delaying the opening.

Both of them always seemed to me to be very friendly, observant, curious, and engaging. At least in my case, they had a knack of making me comfortable around them. I always felt that they were good honest people who asked for the same in return.

At one time Roy told me a story about Salvador Dalí, the famous Spanish surrealist artist. In the late 1940s Dalí had been hired to work at the Disney studios in California. Roy met him while Dalí did the art for an animated film. "Wow," I thought, "What an idea!"

"What happened?"

Well, Dalí worked on it for a while and left. For one reason or another, the project was dropped and the Dalí illustrations were filed away and forgotten. But they recently had been rediscovered. Roy, who grew up in the Disney animation studios decided to finish the project. He put together a "Dalí short" that was nominated for an Oscar. When he first told me the story, the nomination had been made while Oscar night was still in the future.

My reaction to Roy's story was like a shot-gun blast with pellets flying in every direction. "What was Dalí like?"

"Very creative. He liked to say that 'other people are crazy but don't know it. I know when I am crazed and I can withdraw from it.' But, he was a genius and knew it."

"Where are the illustrations?"

"The company has them."

"Are they available? Can we host an exhibition of them here at the Center?"

"That is an interesting thought."

Two days later, as the Disney's were departing, Roy turned to me to say, "I will remember our discussion about your idea for an exhibit."

"How about the movie? Is it done?"

"Well, it is not a movie but a short about fifteen minutes long."

"Can we show it at the Center?" The new building had three auditoriums, two of which were equipped to show movies.

"Yes, that could be arranged."

"Better yet! Why don't you come out to present the movie in person as part of the grand opening?"

"That's a good thought. Let me think about it."

Roy and Patti did attend the three day opening. And Roy did present the Dalí film, called *Destinos*, which in my biased opinion deserved the Oscar it did not win. "It should have won." Patti whispered to me.

During that weekend I learned that Patti loved Zarzuelas, so I asked them about helping the NHCC become a national center for Zarzuelas. Zarzuelas are Spanish short, light operas or operettas. I felt that New Mexico would be a natural place for them. NHCC staffer Javier Lorenzo, a specialist in conducting Zarzuelas, informed me that the University of New Mexico had a collection of unpublished and never performed Zarzuela scores.[415] New Mexico already had some operatic fame for its Santa Fe Opera. The NHCC could build on that audience and existing resources to become a national center for Zarzuelas.

My staff already had informed me that the NHCC would need an additional $90,000 for each Zarzuela that we produced. We had enough in our budget to do one each year. One Zarzuela hardly makes a series so I asked Roy if he and Patti could fund a second Zarzuela for each of the next five years, to give the NHCC a chance to develop an audience. I added that we would name the series the Patti Disney Zarzuela Series. Pattie squealed with delight when Roy and I broached the idea to her.

I also learned that the Dalí illustrations belonged to the Disney Company and because Roy had been on the losing end of a company takeover, he could not get them for an exhibition. At least for the moment, for he and his allies were fighting back.

Since then Roy regained influence and some control of the company that bears his family name. Maybe our not-too-forgotten conversation will surface again. I particularly enjoyed Dalí's reference to baseball and, of course, Don Quixote in the short. Both Roy and Patti continued to support the National Hispanic Cultural Center. Unfortunately, for the NHCC and the Disney Company both Roy and Patti passed away within seven years of the opening. Maybe an exhibition of Dalí cartoons was not so quixotic, even if it did not happen.

In September 2004 we opened the Roy E. Disney Center for Performing Arts with a full week of activities that culminated on a three day weekend. We called the opening *Maravilla!* Disney's film was one of the weekend events. The culminating evening featured a variety show ranging from dance to song. We had modern dance, flamenco, the New Mexico Symphony Orchestra, arias, and jazz. The performers came from coast to coast and the local talent shined. They all performed before a packed house in the Center's Journal Auditorium.[416]

During intermission Roy and Patti Disney caught my attention and called me to their seats. I squatted down to hear them and Patti said, "Tom, we wanted to tell you that you were right about delaying the opening. This is wonderful." They put their words to print when they subsequently sent a letter exclaiming the "enormous success of the whole weekend. What a place! What an evening! What an honor to be a part of it all!"[417]

86
Concerning another less substantial story of Salvador Dalí

A family tradition holds that Fray Angélico Chávez met Salvador Dalí while both men were in New York. Although there is no solid proof of this meeting, both men were in New York in the 1950s so the meeting is conceivable.

Nevertheless, the point becomes interesting if not moot in the context of Fray Angélico's poetry, for he based a long, ingenious poem on a 1950 Dalí painting called *The Virgin of Port Llegat* in which Fray Angélico wrote about the artist's "spirituality and the atomic system."[418] He described three images depicted in one painting; the visual one; an intellectual metaphoric "Sphinx of Christendom;" and a visual intellectual picture "painted for us by astronomy and astrophysics." Considered by many, but not all to have been Fray Angélico's most ambitious and best poem, twice Pulitzer Prize winner Paul Horgan wrote:

> "As literature, as philosophy, as prayer, [the poem] is a most significant production; and, in its invocation of harmony between Christian Truth, ancient myth and the evolution of scientific thought in Western civilization, it may be a work of prophecy as well."[419]

When Fray Angélico sent his poem to be published in an anthology being edited by the famous intellectual T. S. Elliott, the latter thought so much of the work that he refused publication. Instead, Elliott wrote to the author that the poem should be published on its own, which is what happened.[420] It was published as a limited edition book with its own slip-case. After publication of the poem, a historian and curator of Dalí's life and works wrote in a now lost pamphlet accompanying an exhibition of Dalí art, that Fray Angélico truly understood Dalí's fascination with the atomic cosmos. A. Reynolds Morse, who may have been the same person who wrote the lost pamphlet, wrote the poem "was the first serious recognition that a message could be found in Dalí's religious art."[421] All this came to me as I became more familiar with Fray Angélico's work and life.

I met a man in Santa Fe, whose name I have long since forgotten. He was a former ambassador from a South American country like Columbia or Bolivia. Before that he worked for newspapers, at one time in Spain.

At a gathering in his house he shared with me his collection of Meso-American pre-Columbian art, I guess, because of my connection with the Art of Ancient America exhibition. While not a large collection, it was impressive.

Our conversation turned to his life and some of his exploits as a young newsman. He interviewed Salvador Dalí. He went to Dali's home at Port Lligat, north of Barcelona were Dalí escorted him through the house even pointing out where he and his lover and wife, Gala, "make love." When the reporter asked Dalí "who besides yourself, is your favorite artist?" Dalí replied, "Velázquez."[422] Dalí went on to explain that of all the painters through history only Velázquez shared with him an understanding of the many dimensions of the atomic cosmos.

"Indeed," I thought, for Dalí even groomed himself as a reincarnate Velázquez. The famous Dalí moustache was not a whimsical touch to outrage or attract attention, although it did both. Rather it was a paean to Velázquez who sported a similar moustache.

A few years after that conversation I finally made it to the Teatre-Museu Dalí, commonly referred to as the Dalí Museum, in Figueres, Spain. Everything about that museum is multi-dimensional. Of course, Dalí designed it himself. I was astounded by his drawings using mirrors to create three dimensional images or with my favorite Dalí painting, a large portrait of Abraham Lincoln that when viewed with the naked eye is Lincoln but when seen through the wrong end of binoculars becomes a standing nude of Gala. But I was overwhelmed to see a work of art that he did in memory of his friend Frederico García Lorca, who was brutally executed by Nationalist soldiers during the Spanish Civil War.

The work is a sculpted head of Velázquez that, except for the hint of seventeenth century clothing, could be Dalí himself. Dalí painted an intricate miniature rendition of Velázquez's most famous work, *Las Mininas*, on the forehead. Here is a work that took us through time and more, for *Las Mininas*, itself is famous for using three dimensions by drawing the viewing audience into the scene.

Just like Dalí's painting, *The Virgin of Port Lligat*, where dimension, indeed gravity, exist but are suspended, Fray Angélico, the South American journalist, Velázquez, and, even, Roy Disney had been drawn into the cosmos that only a few had ventured to understand. Now even the NHCC had been touched.

And so the pendulum keeps docking over time
and space
The spin of worlds in welkin hive and warbler's nest,
While in the middle she,
Both magnified and magnifying in her portaled breast
The central Infant, watches how His playing brings
More births in bread through lovelier alchemy
To fill the hungry with good things.[423]

87
On how Sancho Panza's wish to rule an island relates to reality; or the meaning of "Anybody but Chávez"

When Ed Lujan first asked me to take the job at the National Hispanic Cultural Center, I asked for a little time then I told Ed Lujan and the Board of Directors that I would take the job for two-and-a-half years. Those extra years would give me the maximum years required for retirement and I had no desire to work for the State beyond that point.

True to my word I announced my intended retirement date but Ed Lujan refused to accept my plan.[424] He invited Celia and me to spend the weekend with him and his wonderful diminutive wife, Virginia, at their summer mountain home in Pendaries north of Las Vegas. Once again, he worked his persuasive magic.

By then the NHCC was becoming very successful. The Performing Arts Center was funded with a definite scheduled opening. A number of very good exhibitions had opened in the museum to rave reviews. Intel had donated a technical system in Trujillo, Spain so we were positioned to initiate distance education. We purchased the land and a warehouse across the street from our main campus and we had begun funding and planning for a new education building. Ed Lujan ran through these achievements. I had to admit that working with him, the staff, and the foundation had been a very gratifying experience.

Ed Lujan made a simple request, "stay on to help set up the first year's programming in the Performing Arts Center." I could not say no but I warned that this would be the last time because Celia would be taking a sabbatical in 2005 and I wanted to travel with her. Ed acknowledged my sentiment but, then again, he is a delightfully devious man. We agreed that I could retire at the end of 2004 but volunteer to help with the transition until Celia and I left on her sabbatical.

Work continued at a breakneck pace. The opening season was set and the three-day opening of the Performing Arts Center proved to be spectacular if not the fundraiser that we expected. Nevertheless, we set the tone.

Then two problems surfaced that fall. The first involved the foundation, for, suddenly, it could not raise the funds to support the opening season. In part, due to the large expenditures made for the opening, the foundation did not have the expected funds.

This resulted in some meetings between Gene Henley, Katherine Archuleta, Demesia Padilla and I in October of 2004. Padilla served as chair of the foundation board of directors and because she was a professional accountant, her private company kept the foundation's books. I was not surprised at the foundation's finances so much as Padilla's lack of comprehension about the different operations of the foundation and the NHCC. We had to adjust the first year's program to cut costs. Henley and I wrote up a counter proposal for the rest of the season.[425]

We wrote that "the message is acceptable and understandable but the delivery was not complete...We all accept and understand that the...Foundation does not have funds...." However, the memorandum continued that I "became concerned about the finances and financial relationship between our two organizations" and proceeded to correct a series of misconceptions as stated in the meetings. Despite the necessity of correcting their errors, the larger and more important message was understood, for the memorandum included a detailed plan of how the NHCC would cope with the situation.[426] Archuleta and Padilla replied with a reiteration of their position and a reiteration of their misconceptions.

I did not realize it then but would find out later, that Archuleta and Padilla did not appreciate being corrected, for after I retired, they left the foundation deeply in debt. Nevertheless, while we worked on the revised schedule and financial problems, politics raised its ugly head.

The second problem arose when Governor Bill Richardson broke a promise to Ed Lujan and removed him from the NHCC Board of Directors. The Governor replaced Lujan as the Chair of the Board with Las Vegas politician Matt Martínez. We thought that Martínez supported Lujan but found out after the fact that he secretly campaigned for the position.

Ed Lujan will never admit publicly that he was hurt or that the governor's deceitful action had something to do with Lujan's subsequent health problems, including a heart attack.

Ed Lujan is the ultimate cultural crusader and from its inception the NHCC has been his dream. Ed Lujan, his family, and his business had contributed hundreds of thousands of dollars to the NHCC. He and Ed Romero were the reason for all the state and federal support that came to the institution. Now, unexpectedly and without reason, Governor Richardson "fired" him.

Naturally, reaction to Lujan's removal got back to the governor who quickly tried to "spin" out of his act by announcing that he had named Lujan an "emeritus" board member. Notwithstanding that the NHCC's by laws did not accommodate such a position, Ed Lujan and those around him saw that for what is was—nothing.

Nevertheless, Ed Lujan kept attending Board meetings. As we moved closer to my retirement date, Ed Lujan and members of the Board started talking to me about extending again. This time they could not counter my reasons for leaving. Celia and I planned to go to Argentina and nothing would change our minds.

However, Ed Lujan latched on to my offer to help with the transition. He figured out that I would be available from New Year through the end of February and, then, be in Argentina for three months. Ever clever, he made two requests; if he and Virginia met Celia and me in Argentina would I take them to see their namesake, the Virgin of Lujan, who is the patroness of Argentina? Then he asked whether I would agree to be reappointed the NHCC's Executive Director when I returned from Argentina. After some more discussions, especially with Celia, I agreed but only after I addressed the Board.

At the subsequent Board meeting I repeated that I agreed to Ed Lujan's proposal but qualified that by telling the Board that its priority needed to be the NHCC and not me. If they thought that my absence would be a problem, had a better candidate, or felt that change was necessary then they should do what they considered best for the NHCC. The Board listened, asked me to leave the room, and took a vote. They unanimously voted to re-hire me.

I retired, continued to keep office hours, and worked with Gene Henley who became the acting director. Celia and I left for Argentina in March of 2005. During the last week of our stay in Argentina Ed and Virginia Lujan joined us in Buenos Aires. We all booked rooms in the Hotel Dorá, a well-located place that caters to business people. As it turned out, Ed and I had some business to do.

While in Argentina I corresponded with both Stuart Ashman and Gene Henley. I heard enough to know that the Governor's heavy hand as applied by Ashman and Board chairman Martínez had begun to force people from their positions at the NHCC. Ashman also candidly wrote me that the Board had reconsidered its vote to hire me because it wanted to do a search. Eventually, he added that they did not want to interview me. In addition, one of the governor's new surrogates, now working at the NHCC announced that I had withdrawn my candidacy for the position. I responded with a missive sent to everyone involved, in which I denied that statement.

Obviously reminded of my experience at the Museum of New Mexico, I was anxious to hear from my friend and colleague Ed Lujan. We met at our hotel in Buenos Aires where he asked if we could sit at a table at the far end of the lobby. His demeanor singled the importance of the moment and I moved to the designated table without hesitation.

Ed Lujan told me about the Board meeting where Stuart Ashman attended and convinced the Board to reconsider its vote to rehire me. Ashman represented Governor Richardson who, he said, wanted an open search for the position. The Board asked why: they already had who they wanted. The discussion continued until Ed Lujan interrupted by asking Ashman what did the governor really want. Ashman replied that Bill Richardson's message is "anybody but Chávez." Thus, the Board, which is appointed by the governor, followed orders to open the search but not include me.

I listened to Ed tell me this story somewhat expecting its conclusion, for in light of Ashman's correspondence to me it made sense. Finally, I was retired and it was time to move on.

I said something to Ed about how both of us had been "chumped by Richardson so we are in good company." I was reminded of Sancho Panza's statement when he resigned from his dream position as a ruler of an island.

> "I'd rather lie down in the shade of an oak tree in summer and
> wrap myself in an old bald sheepskin in winter, in freedom, than
> lie between linen sheets and wear sables, subject to a governorship."[427]

In the case of Bill Richardson, Sancho Panza may have been understated.

But, Ed Lujan had not finished, for he handed me a multi-page memorandum that Katherine Archuleta and Demesia Padilla wrote and sent to Stuart Ashman. Apparently, they harbored some resentment over our exchanges in October. The Foundation, they wrote, was broke. Verbosely, if misguided and in false detail, they blamed the NHCC as the culprit.[428] Ashman shared the missive with Ed Lujan who became incensed. With a copy in hand he confronted Archuleta and repeated to her what he told Ashman. This memorandum was a diatribe and nothing more than an attempt to "CYOA, cover your own ass."

Now, I was incensed. Unlike Ed Lujan who has the capacity to ignore such attacks, I had to do something. The memorandum did not mention me but named Gene Henley. Still, it was all about my leadership and reflected on my integrity.

With Ed's encouragement I drafted a multi-page, point-by-point, no holds barred reply. I went through five drafts and sent it to Ashman, Martínez, the NHCC Board of Directors, NHCC staff, and selected members of the Foundation's Board.[429] Whether or not my corrective answer had any effect on subsequent actions is beside the point, for within weeks Padilla had been removed from the Chair of the Foundation Board eventually to be elected New Mexico's State Treasurer and Katherine Archuleta left the state for another job, to work in politics in Denver.

They inexplicably left the Foundation in deep debt.[430] Then we learned that an employee in the Foundation's offices, who worked the budget, was, in fact, an employee of Padilla's accounting firm. Archuleta hired Padilla's firm to do the Foundation's required audits. Small wonder there were no answers.

On the other hand, I had retired and could parody Sancho Panza, for I came into the position of Executive Director "without a *blanca*, and I'm leaving without one," which, he added, "is very different from how" others leave.[431]

Perhaps that is the point. There is a difference between crusaders and soldiers; warriors and followers. Crusaders and warriors pursue a belief or a goal for the improvement of something besides themselves. A soldier takes orders and does what is told. Belief in anything is not necessary for the soldier, which is how we get mercenaries.[432] In this sense, a soldier may become a warrior but a warrior could never become a soldier.

Just as Don Quixote and Sancho Panza suffered many disappointments during their adventures, so too do later-day crusaders, for like the indomitable duo, the purpose as well as the ideal will not die.

88
In which dreams of Queen Isabel's art collection and the treasures of Guadalupe remain illusive

Nothing started ever ends. Cause and effect are triumphant. My travels to Spain and Europe gave rise to ideas for three blockbuster exhibitions, two of which I actively pursued. I never had time to try to sell the idea of an exhibition that I called "Encounter," the concept of which was about Cortés and Montezuma, Spain and the Mexicas (Aztecs), the encounter and defeat of Tenochtitlan. While the concept is not new, for many books have been written on the subject, the reality of creating an exhibition is daunting. Such an exhibition would be complicated because all the artifacts and art would have to be collected through secured loans from many institutions which are dispersed on two continents and many countries. All of the artifacts would be very rare and valuable. The logistics of securing permission for them to be on loan to one place at the same time would take a minor miracle and tremendous expense.

The other two exhibitions, however, are possible, for their logistics are relatively easier. The Monastery of Guadalupe in Extremadura and the Royal Chapel of the Cathedral of Granada in Granada have holdings that would make spectacular exhibitions. As mentioned earlier, the former is a magnificent *mudejar* building with deep historical connections to Mexico and the Southwest of the United States. It houses a treasure trove of items dedicated or gifted to the Virgin of Guadalupe that has been collected over eight centuries.

The Royal Chapel in Granada is the final resting place of King Ferdinand and Queen Isabel along with their daughter Juana la Loca and her husband Felipe the Handsome.

In a commentary of the time, their remains repose under a detailed sculpture of all four royals lying in state. Unlike the other images, the Handsome's head does not indent his pillow, which is to say, as legend would have it, that the artist and his commissioners did not think well of the consort's intellect. A room located next to the royal tomb houses the sixteenth century art collection of Queen Isabel, including her jewelry box.

"The Treasures of Guadalupe," as I called the proposed exhibtion, has a simple concept of selecting forty to fifty artifacts from the Monastery's collections. They would be exhibited with the history of Guadalupe de Extremadura, in a contextual setting that would include her image; architectural features copied from the Monastery, and recorded Marian music. The only possible additions beyond the Monastery collections might be the supposed gold scorpion pendent sent by Cortés that is in private possession along with some latter-day depictions of Guadalupe.

My Spanish friends in Spain had positive reactions to this idea. What a great concept. What a great way to show a special connection between Spain and the United States and specifically to demonstrate another historical and cultural connection from Extremadura. "Great idea, Tom."

Then the unanimous pessimism came. The Monastery will never loan any of its collections. It never has loaned anything and never will. Furthermore, the Spanish government has no authority to facilitate such a loan. The collection belongs to the Catholic Church.

Jaime de Salas was among those who expressed the above to me. However, he was willing to help so far as he could. He noted that the Franciscans, who had charge of the Monastery, had recently opened up enough to allow some much needed preservation work on their building. Maybe with this example in their experience they, at least, would consider my idea. Jaime advised that the cultural affairs office of the government of Extremadura should be solicited for its support before approaching the father prior at Guadalupe.

The Franciscan community needed to work with someone they could trust and this needed to be a regional authority. Jaime met with and identified Francisco Pérez Guedan, the Director General del Patrimonio for the region of Extremadura. Jaime found him "very open to the issue" and said that he would help organize and partially fund an exhibition on Guadalupe. Jaime briefed him on the NHCC. Jaime had done a good job[433] but he was not finished, for he wanted me to meet Pérez Guedan and, then, meet with the Prior of Guadalupe, Fray Guillermo Cerrato, O.F.M.[434]

I agreed with Jaime's suggestion but noted that I could not afford to travel back and forth from New Mexico for separate meetings. Could the necessary meetings be arranged within a one week period and, more significantly, would it be proper?

"Yes." Jaime de Salas proceeded to make a date with the cultural affairs office. I was left with the task to present the idea to my own people and supporters, for if this worked out we would be looking at an estimated two million dollar price tag. I needed to know whether the Foundation and some of its key financial backers felt that this was an idea worth pursuing. To this I received nothing but enthusiasm in reply. It appeared that this time, I would be joined by a chorus of backers and so charged off on another quixotic foray.

Jaime also gave me the name and mailing address of Father Cerrato. Salas told me that I should arrange that meeting. On 12 April 2004 I sent an introductory letter. I described the NHCC and described my "dream of doing an exhibition about Guadalupe and the monastery." I wrote that I would be in Trujillo, which is about an hour from Guadalupe, and would love to meet with him about my "idea" and "its possibilities."[435]

Father Cerrato agreed and a meeting was scheduled in May on the day after my meeting with the government official in Cáceres. On the appointed day I rented a taxi in Trujillo and with Danny López, the NHCC's young public information officer, in tow, headed up to the Monastery of Guadalupe.

All the routes to Guadalupe are scenic, winding, two lane roads. The Monastery and its surrounding village sit below a mountain gap. As planned, we arrived early enough to take an organized public tour. I wanted Danny to see the collections and realize the possibility of what I was after. I had taken that tour as many as a dozen times by then and have taken it many more times since. The priest vestments dating to the fourteenth century with semi-precious as well as precious stones and pearls sewn into them, many times with gold or silver thread; the collection of choral song books, many oversized so the choir can read them from a distance; centuries-old books with their illuminated miniature illustrations; the art collection of many old masters; and, most amazing of all, the Virgin of Guadalupe's "treasure room" where the statue's vestments, crowns, orbs, and jewelry behind glass, startle and overwhelm the visitor. One crown is reputed to have four thousand diamonds.[436]

Just to have one or two items from that room in the exhibition would be worthy of note. And the formal tours through the Monastery do not visit the library and archive that has, among other items, the letters about Cortés's golden scorpion.[437]

We met the Prior after completing the tour. He escorted us through the Monastery and its main courtyard, into a second interior courtyard that now houses the Monastery's hotel, restaurant, and a coffee bar. Father Cerrato treated us to coffee and we sat down to discuss a possible exhibition.

Physically, the Prior was an older mirror image of Danny; above medium height, slender, clean shaven and good looking. He was pensive and proved to be generous with his time. He also was patient with my presentation and request. Occasionally he nodded ever so slightly. Clearly appearing to be in agreement, he never agreed. Neither did he say, "No." He asked a couple of questions about New Mexico and my intentions with the collections.

The Monastery holds the largest and greatest collection of Francisco de Zubarán paintings that were done in 1638 and 1639. The most important of these masterpieces hang on walls for which they originally were intended. They have not been moved since the seventeenth century. These particular paintings are very large, measuring 2.90 meters high by 2.22 meters wide.[438] With their ornate frames they must be enormously heavy.

Father Cerrato wanted me to understand that those paintings could not be loaned under any circumstance. We agreed. In closing, he escorted Danny and I to the Monastery's gift shop at the entrance. He stated that he would think about what we had discussed. I was ecstatic.

The good Prior seemed to be a reasonable man. He warned me that his position in charge of the Monastery was not permanent and that his Order of Franciscans rotated their members into that position. He told us that he would be attending a general meeting "within the month" and that while he expected to be retained, anything could happen. We exchanged e-mail addresses and agreed to keep up a correspondence.

Upon my return to Albuquerque I sent an elaborate e-mail to Father Cerrato in which I gave more details of the envisioned exhibition. I excitedly waited for his reaction but it never came. I understood his silence to mean that either he did not want to proceed or that he had been rotated out of the Prior position. Jaime de Salas advised that I let the matter drop for the time being. It appeared, I had chased an illusion.

The matter of the Queen Isabel's art collection followed a different route but with the same conclusion. I was very heartened with the idea of traveling twenty to twenty-five pieces of her collection. While on the trip to Washington, DC on which Frank Ortiz and I testified on behalf of the proposed new history museum, we made an appointment to introduce ourselves to the Spanish Ambassador. We met in the ambassador's large but not so elaborate office. Frank Ortiz, himself a retired ambassador, knew our host so he began the conversation. The two of them talked about old times and Ortiz steered the subject matter to the new history museum that we planned to open in the future. At this point, I joined in the conversation. We talked about the museum and the shared histories of Spain and the Southwest. Almost casually I stated that I wanted to open the new museum with a "blockbuster exhibition" of Queen Isabel's art collection currently at the Royal Chapel in Granada. Frank Ortiz almost came out of his chair and the Spanish ambassador stared at me opened mouthed and dumbfounded. I smiled, probably like an idiot in their minds.

From behind his desk the Spanish Ambassador sat up and spoke first. "That is an interesting idea."

I explained that the collection is the Church's patrimony so this could be a difficult proposition. He replied that it could be done.

I suggested that perhaps with the help of the Spanish government, the Church would agree to a loan. Moreover, I not only wanted to open the new museum with this exhibition but I wanted to travel it to Washington, DC or New York. The ambassador was speechless. Then he spoke, "Yes, yes. That is an interesting idea."

Afterwards Frank Ortiz remained overwhelmed. He kept asking me where I came up with that idea. How could I conjure up the nerve to present it to the ambassador? How come he had not heard about it before now?

I explained that I had seen the collection and was fascinated with the story that during Isabel's reign from 1474 until her death in 1504, she and her husband Ferdinand never had a capital city. Instead the Catholic Monarchs traveled with their court and art collection from city to city. So now her traveling collection had found a permanent home. "It needed to travel again." I noted factiously.

Later on in Santa Fe my friends David Margolis and Jean Moss were driving with me back to town after my first visit at John Bourne's house. Seeing for the first time the magnitude of Bourne's collection overtook me and got me to start talking about Isabel's art collection. David Margolis is a descendent of a rabbi. At the time I did not know what Jean's religion, if any, was. So I was taken aback when in mid-thought about Isabel, Jean Moss spoke up from the back seat,

"Why would you bring that Jew hater's art to New Mexico? I wouldn't have anything to do with her!"

This time I was dumbfounded and speechless. Of course, I knew the history. By virtue of Isabel's marriage to Ferdinand of Aragón, the Kingdoms of Castile and Aragón were joined to form Spain. To solidify their new political entity they had to fight against interlopers, create alliances, and defeat the last Muslim enclave at Granada. In the process they sent Columbus sailing west where he encountered the Americas, married their daughter to a Hapsburg and declared Catholicism the state religion. This last act resulted in a declaration that all Muslims and Jews had to convert to the state religion or leave the country. To make sure that the conversions were authentic, the Monarchs resurrected the Spanish Inquisition. This is what earned them the moniker of Catholic Kings and, in the late 20th century, a movement to have them beautified by the Church. Nevertheless, the work of the Inquisition is not a positive page in Spanish history.

Jean Moss is a slight, liberal woman born out of the sixties. She is intelligent and not hesitant to speak her mind. She also has a sense of humor that sometimes can be very ironic, even biting. So, she saw her opportunity and took advantage. My silence, even unease, to her comment was obvious. David, who was sitting in the front with me, merely stared forward and said nothing. Jean broke the silence with loud laughter.

"Hah! I got you! You're speechless!" And, she laughed some more. She has been quick to remind me of that moment ever since. Many years later Jean and David joined Celia and I and Charles Bennett and his wife Marcia de Chadenedes on a personalized tour of Spain. We had a great time although we never made it to Granada. We meant to go there and see Isabel's collection, but did not.

The idea of the exhibition has gone down the same road as the Guadalupe exhibition. It has not happened but the possibility still exists. However, this was a quest that never really began.

89
Regarding the loss of creativity: Distance Education, "Hey Mozart," and "María de Buenos Aires"

Unlike my departure, my tenure at the NHCC began with a lot of fanfare. I inherited a staff that was poised to perform. They were like a tethered stallion that needed to run free. And run they did! They ran the gamut from cutting edge to tending to the miniscule, the staff worked beyond any expectation to position the NHCC on the national stage. Attendance jumped, revenues increased, and the publicity followed suit.

We hired additional staff to operate the new performing arts center and they, too, unleashed a creative approach that would do justice to any performing arts center in the country.

The staff tried many things and most worked. I felt that they had proven themselves. I warned them to "circle wagons," for success breeds jealousy and I feared that politics might be their undoing if they did not stand together.

As demonstrated in the previous chapters, I was correct. Even if the staff stood united, which it didn't, it probably could not have withstood the onslaught of blatant political interference that followed. Within the first six months after my departure, over a dozen people were forced out, left in disgust, or were terminated. These people ranged from Gene Henley, the Deputy Director, to Program Directors Dr. Helen Lucero and David Sánchez. Curator Andrew Conners, exhibition designer Andrew John Cecil and others created staff voids that will be difficult to fill.

Programs as well, fell to the political knife. Simply put, Governor Richardson and his people fulfilled their desire to drastically cut the program budget and staff, not to save money but to redirect it in fulfillment of the Governor's appetite for political patronage. His administration rampaged through a well-respected, first class working team to create positions for his political groupies. And, in the process, he and his henchmen came close to ruining some lives.

One of the programs ruined by Richardson's politics was the NHCC's beginning effort at creating an educational connection with Trujillo, Spain. With the generosity of Intel, the NHCC opened its first high tech partner on foreign soil at the Coria Museum. The effort started with great promise. NHCC staff helped install the equipment and even began programming. Dr. Shelle Luaces (who through marriage is now Varetten de Sánchez) went to Trujillo twice to train teachers and community volunteers on the new equipment.

Jaime de Salas, of course, was elated with all this attention. He insisted that we talk with the Mother Superior at the local Catholic School and have her invite her faculty to see the new installation and a demonstration of how they could use it. Shelle and I made the appointment and went to meet the Mother Superior. After being escorted into the office, which, as might be expected was sparse, very quiet, and had a crucifix on the wall, we were asked to wait.

Shelle seemed a little nervous. Why not? This was a new experience for her. So, to break the ice, I leaned over to her and said, "Don't screw this up." And, then, laughed.

The meeting went off without a hitch. The Mother Superior, herself, went to the Coria to see the demonstration. She even tried her hand at working on the equipment.

The program started up and we had the beginning of community involvement. The NHCC wanted to include the teachers of Trujillo in a program in which it was training teachers of northern New Mexico and in Chihuahua, Mexico to individually create and record story lines on a disk. The stories, usually biographies or something about the community in which they lived, included images and background music. They had to develop a study plan for classroom application as part of their project. Then the teachers from both countries shared their disks and supplemental material. This showed great potential for international cooperation among teachers and the exchange of information promised enriched classroom experiences for their students. Now, the NHCC could include teachers from Spain with those from New Mexico and Mexico.

The promise was never filled, for the Governor's machinations resulted in a lack of funds and staff that killed off any chance of moving forward. Intel's generosity was wasted but not just in Trujillo.

David Sánchez originally had been hired to design, install, and maintain the NHCC's technical systems. As the money became available he purchased equipment under my authority. The equipment included all the NHCC's computers, the computer laboratory, and everything necessary for a new Media Arts Center that was designed into the new Performing Arts Center.

Sánchez oversaw the selection and installation of the equipment sent to Trujillo. As the Media Arts Center received its equipment, I named him the NHCC's director of media arts. Under his expertise, the NHCC had field as well as studio production capabilities plus high-end editing and duplication facilities that would be the envy of any other studio.

Along with Shelle, I counted on David to implement the NHCC's distance education program beginning at the Museo de la Coria in Spain. However, neither distant education nor the Media Arts Program came to fruition, for both became casualties to Governor Richardson's budget priorities that, combined with Sánchez's lateral transfer out of the directorship of Media Arts, killed any chance of what had begun as two promising programs.

When I heard that he had been removed from Media Arts, I wrote to Gene Henley, "...so guess what, David is looking for another job."[439] David Sánchez resigned from the NHCC soon thereafter. In disgust he wrote a letter to my successor and the NHCC's Board of Directors. Upon first reaction one might assume that such letters to a group of the Governor's appointees are futile, for they surely will take no action—and they did not. Nevertheless, his thoughts, the belief of a warrior, are a matter of record for future historians. The crusader idealist lives beyond the moment in time. The blatant non-believer cares about now, consequences be dammed, especially in this age of spin.

Sánchez succinctly summed up the situation when he wrote that,

> "...many former and current employees...all have expended a considerable amount of effort and passion in the Center and its mission. To see our accomplishments put aside is extremely painful, personally as well as professionally...."[440]

To date, neither distant education, contact with Trujillo, nor Media Arts has been resurrected.

Two other ingenious ideas all but killed because of politics are given here as examples. More importantly two sterling staff members were forced out of the NHCC to be replaced by patronage people. Javier Lorenzo is from Argentina. He and his wife moved to New Mexico to attend the University of New Mexico. He received a Masters of Arts degree in Music and she received a Masters of Education degree. Javier has an extensive background in music as well. He is a musician, a conductor, and scholar. The NHCC secured a work permit to hire him.

At the same time the NHCC hired Tomás Lozano, a native of Spain, who by virtue of marriage, lived in New Mexico. He, too, is a scholar of music who has reproduced historical musical instruments, played them in various groups and concerts, is recorded, and has done extensive documentary research in music history.

Both of these very creative men were hired to help bring in innovative programs for the Performing Arts Center. Their connections and thought processes quickly became evident. Along with existing staff led by Dr. Reeve Love and Joseph Wasson, they formed schedules of entertainment for the first two years that was nothing short of eye-popping. As has been mentioned, problems with funding required that the NHCC cut back on the programs halfway through the first year.

Javier Larenzo wanted to do a full-scale production of Astor Piazzola's "*operita*" *María de Buenos Aires* that, so far as we knew, had never been done in the United States. The operetta was always sung with an orchestra in a concert format. Lorenzo proposed a major production with sets, dancers, actors, lighting schemes, and so on. Together we planned and created a budget. We decided to put on six shows at a cost of $230,000. We felt that we could cover the expense through sponsorships, ticket revenues, state funds, and foundation support.

As it turned out, the production was spectacular. The expense reflected the immensity and grandeur of it all. Many of the technicians and performers were brought to New Mexico from Buenos Aires. The dancers and most of the orchestra were auditioned and recruited locally. At that time in New Mexico, only the Santa Fe Opera could have produced such a show in-house.

Ticket sales started off slow but word got out. Buses were chartered to bring in patrons from Santa Fe. Attendance increased for each of the shows until the last two performances sold out. Still the revenues did not overcome the expenses. The cost to the Foundation and State together ran into six figures.

I felt that the cost was worth the effort for a few reasons. The show enhanced the NHCC's reputation as an innovator and very capable institution. I always felt that this international production made a point to our constituency. Organized and directed by Javier Lorenzo, the NHCC put on a first class in-house production. The technical staff was challenged and the exercise allowed us to test our own capabilities in the new auditorium. So, beyond the expense, *María de Buenos Aires* benefited the NHCC.

The NHCC's production of *María de Buenos Aires* was an act of genius. Although the actual shows took place two months after I retired, I considered it one of my proudest moments at the NHCC. That production was a quest completed. It should have set the table for future such successes but the governor interfered.

Always thinking creatively, Tom Lozano and Javier Lorenzo sought permission to take a concept done in New York and apply it in New Mexico. They proceeded to tell me about "Hey Mozart," a musical program that went to elementary schools to identify and encourage future musical composers.

Lozano and Lorenzo wanted to establish a similar program in New Mexico. They volunteered to contact schools to solicit and select seven to twelve year old students to share original ditties. Then they would have the ditties orchestrated, recorded and performed. The whole idea seemed grandiose and impossible but I could not say no. The two men went out to organize and begin "Hey Mozart" in New Mexico. Almost as quickly they suffered two distractions. I retired and both Lozano and Lorenzo were laid off by the new regime. They were told that there was no money to pay their salaries while at the same time Governor Richardson-appointed employees started working at the NHCC at much higher salaries.

Tragically, Javier Lorenzo, without a job and a work permit, received quick notice from the U. S. Immigration Service telling him that he had one month to take his family and leave the United States. Tom Lozano took a job tending tables at a local restaurant. A few months later he and his wife moved out-of-state.

The two of them spent what was left of their limited funds and time to pursue "Hey Mozart" on their own. With Brooks McIntyre, an interested and active volunteer helping them, they convinced the NHCC and New Mexico Symphony Orchestra to participate in the idea. They also went to New York to convince the music faculty and graduate students at Hartwick College to orchestrate the ditties and then, with a philharmonic orchestra, they recorded the music at a New York studio. They created a disk of fifteen children's melodies and called it *Hey, Mozart!New Mexico.*

On the night of the concert each of the selected students were invited on stage to perform their respective melodies. The master of ceremonies asked them a few questions and then invited them to listen to the full orchestra play the orchestrated version. It was a magical evening.

The dust cover to the disk had the following words:

> "The CD in your hands is the result of intense labor of love for the arts. Bursting forth to our astonished ears is this fine demonstration of the talent in young New Mexico children. We hope it serves as inspiration to all child composers."[441]

The NHCC has not produced an in-house show of the caliber of *María de Buenos Aires* or started a program like *Hey, Mozart!* since that time. The latter has continued but not as an NHCC or State effort. Brooks McIntrye has kept it afloat. Both Tom Lozano and Javier Lorenzo are cultural crusaders. Those words and their efforts fell on the deaf ears of politics. Now they are benefiting societies elsewhere. But New Mexico has not lost them, for *Hey, Mozart!* has continued, Tom Lozano subsequently published a genius of a book on the history of New Mexican music titled *Cantemos al Alba: Origins of Songs, Sounds, and Liturgical Drama of Hispanic New Mexico*, and Javier Lorenzo has started teaching music through distant education. Quite naturally, he has co-taught courses in the University of New Mexico's General Honors Program and some of the readings come from Lozano's book.[442] Politicians and politics can set back the crusaders but never will stop them.

So, it was not without reason that I wrote an op-ed piece for *The Santa Fe New Mexican* with the headline "Redirect funding from politicians to creative artists." I wrote a description of Lozano's and Lorenzo's genius and how rudely they were laid-off. I concluded:

> These are the kinds of people being sacrificed on the governor's altar to fulfill his appetite for patronage. We...should redirect our monetary support from politicians to...creative geniuses like Tom Lozano and Javier Lorenzo.[443]

The Governor would never understand but Cervantes would agree.[444] The problem, however, is not local but universal. The constant questions, criticisms, and calls to cut the budgets, for example, of the National Endowment of Arts or Humanities are indicators of the same problem. The problem is a universal challenge and is the environment in which cultural crusaders must exist. It is reality.

90
The quest continues; new institutions and new generations

Don Quixote's end came as a result of the cure his friends and family endeavored to put on him. They burned his books, tricked him through a joust to return home and, then, convinced him of his madness. What they really did was to strip him of all hope and desire, of any reason to live. He retired to bed were he slowly lapsed into death.

While in bed, Sancho Panza, who also helped betray the old knight, was the first to realize what was happening. With tears streaming down his face Sancho pleaded with his beloved companion to rise up. Sancho Panza now understood Quixote's reality and belatedly plead that Dulcinea does indeed exist and that the two of them had yet to fulfill their stated desire to be shepherds. In short, Sancho Panza knew that the quest was Quixote's salvation. But, his recognition of this different reality was too late, for Don Quixote, the protagonist of a long novel died.

His creator, Miguel Cervantes, wrote of a man whose spirit would live beyond death or a novel's end. Quixote's spirit has never died. Even within and beyond the book, the vision is in the eye of the beholder–and the quest continues. Perhaps Cervantes' message is that when hope is taken away, humankind will die.

On Labor Day weekend in May 2009, the new State History Museum opened to forever change the landscape for history and its preservation in the State of New Mexico. Just two weeks before, in reaction to my application for the vacant position of Executive Director of the NHCC, Stuart Ashman, on behalf of the governor, sent me a letter in which he stated that "...there were candidates that more closely fit the selection criteria."[445] In fact, most of the six finalists did not fit the published criteria at all.

No single person is indispensable to the potential of the National Hispanic Cultural Center. Like all institutions, the NHCC will survive many setbacks as well as achievements. The investments of good people, effort, and actual money have set it on its way. Someday it will fulfill its potential.

While the Palace of the Governors, like the NHCC, will suffer from the politics of moment and eventually survive, it is the dreams and determination of a staff in a particular time as well as the support of many people who came forward from the community that are the reason that New Mexico has a history museum representative of the state's rich history.

The quest continues. Inspiring or not, accomplishments are real and beneficial. Both institutions will continue to attract cultural crusaders who will battle all the contrarians to do amazing and wonderful things. Such people always exist. They will always push to bring their ideas and ideals to fruition; and humankind will continue to benefit. They will brush off compensation and political hardball. They will deal with reality but move under different influences and motives. The adventure continues for us all. As Sancho Panza said, "...it is better to earn a living with the crowd than a reputation with the elite."[446]

Because of these mostly unheralded people, cultural institutions and organizations will continue to upgrade society's quality of life, educate, and improve social discussions. New crusaders, warriors that they are, will mount their figurative Rociantes and sally forth to create new dialogues and forums, yes, even new institutions for the benefit of anyone who wishes to partake.

Every person has a bit of Don Quixote in them. Every person has or has had a spark of idealism about themselves, their friends or families, or their society. Teachers, scientists, musicians, lawyers, laborers, every profession has crusaders. And, anyone who has tried to maintain their focus or pursue the goal of their crusade while trying to keep dignity of their idealism intact knows that it is a task fraught with obstacles. They will prevail "no matter how Envy attempts to hide them or Malice to obscure them."[447]

Crusaders are mortal but the cause is infinite. When Don Quixote finally died at the end of his book, Miguel Cervantes wrote:

> "Here lies the mighty Gentleman who rose to such heights of valor that death itself did not triumph over his life with his death. ...for it was his great good fortune to live a madman, and die sane.[448]

But, he also wrote:

> "Let's have more quixoticies: let Don Quixote go charging and Sancho Panza keep talking, and whatever else happens, that will make us happy."[449]

Epilogue

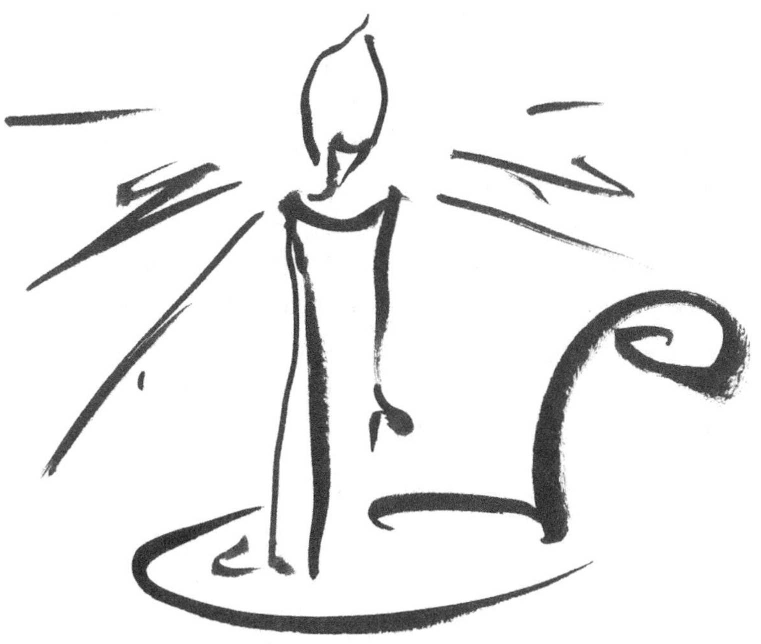

I write these closing lines in Guanajuato, Mexico as I sit at an outdoor restaurant and bar in front of the Hotel Luna that faces the Jardines de Union, a plaza as pretty as any. Underneath the well manicured trees that completely shade the plaza, life bustles in every direction. The plaza is full and so are the city's streets for Celia and I have come to enjoy the Festival Internacional Cervantino, an international celebration of Miguel Cervantes.

I think about the sense of symmetry that Cervantes would appreciate, for here I am attending a festival celebrating him. And the festival's location is in America, a place to which he wanted to travel but was refused permission to do so. Centuries after his death, I am finishing a tome that is in many ways inspired by his own classic work.

Hopefully, to paraphrase Don Quixote, my words have not plummeted from the peaks of my simplicity into the depths of my ignorance.[450] Rather, they will continue and boost the lifelong quest of myself and many others both in these pages and beyond.

I remember speaking about Fray Angélico Chávez who at one time called himself a "true cousin" of Don Quixote.[451] I said that years from now people will remember him but they will have no idea who the governors were during his life. People remember Cervantes and not who his king was. Indeed, Cervantes' protagonists Don Quixote and Sancho Panza are more famous than most kings throughout history. The general public can tell you who Shakespeare is but do not concern themselves much about who ruled the government under which he lived. But, then, there are warrior leaders. Carlos the III of Spain created the Prado Museum. Teddy Roosevelt, President of the United States, created national parks. Maybe there is immortality for some crusaders.

So surrounded by music, art, drama, literature, and history that cannot be escaped in Guanajuato, I scribble the last lines of this self-indulgent effort; the latest of thrusts at the windmills of our time. "*Vale.*"[452]

NOTES

Part I

1. Frank Springer, "Address Delivered by Hon. Frank Springer at the Dedication of New Museum Building, Santa Fe, New Mexico, November 25, 1917," Papers of the School of American Research, 42 (1917), 2; quoted in David L. Caffey, *Frank Springer of New Mexico: From the Colfax County War to the Emergence of Modern Santa Fe,* (College Station: Texas A & M University Press, 2006), 147.
2. Miguel de Cervantes, *The Adventures ofDon Quixote,* translated by Edith Grossman, (New York: HarperCollins Publishers, Inc., 2003), 3. This edition of *Don Quixote* is the only edition used for citations in this book. *Rocinante* is the name of Don Quixote's horse.
3. Cervantes, Part I, chapter ix, p.68.
4. Harry S. Truman, quoted in Merle Miller, *Plain Speaking: An Oral Biography of Harry S. Truman,* (New York: G. P. Putnam's Sons, 1973), 25.
5. Thomas E. Chávez, *New Mexico: Past and Future,* (Albuquerque: University of New Mexico Press, 2006).
6. For clarity's sake, the Palace of the Governors is used here in an organizational sense, for, at the time, the Education Program was physically housed in the Palace of the Governors.
7. See Richard Polese, "An Introduction," *El Palacio: Quarterly Journal of the Museum of New Mexico,* (Vol. 82, no. 4, Winter, 1976), 2. The whole edition was dedicated to the Malaspina expedition with articles by Donald Cutter, Mike Weber, and others.
8. Marc Simmons and Frank Turley, *Southwestern Colonial Ironwork: The Spanish Blacksmithing Tradition from Texas to California,* (Santa Fe: Museum of New Mexico Press, 1980).
9. Dr. Yvonne Lange, the legendary director of the Museum of International Folk Art first called me that name.
10. In fact, the Palace requested money from the International Folk Art Foundation on one occasion and were quickly turned down. See Thomas E. Chávez to Tish Frank, President, International Folk Art Foundation, 29 November 1984, Box 2, folder 7; and Box 1, folder 24b; Tish Frank to T. Chávez, Box 1, folder 29a, Segesser Hide Paintings Documentation Collection (Hereafter Segesser Collection), FAC/POG.
11. The accounts of these gifts can be found in the records of the Museum of New Mexico Foundation.
12. A plaque in the library gives the exact date as 9 July 1892. A copy of the deed is on file at the Palace of the Governors/State History Museum.
13. Quoted in Frank V. Ortiz, *Ambassador Ortiz: Lessons from a Life of Service,* (Albuquerque: University of New Mexico Press, 205), 191.
14. John O. West, "The Artistic Journey of José Cisneros," in José Cisneros, *Riders Across the Centuries: Horsemen of the Spanish Borderlands,* (El Paso: The University of Texas at El Paso, 1084), xiv.

15. Gaspar de Villagrá, *Historia de la Nueva México*, (Alcalá de Henares, Luis Martínez Grande, 1610). At the time, we were led to believe that eighteen copies of the book were known to exist.
16. Ortiz, *Lessons*, 193.
17. In New Mexico, the cities of Santa Fe and Albuquerque celebrated anniversaries of their respective "foundings" and this gave rise to a historical discussion about the definition of "founding." For example, when trying to establish who were the "founding" people versus those who "settled" in the area before the "founding." Then, in the case of Santa Fe, the argument extends to "founding" being an official act and in this scenario Martínez de Montoya is not the founder even though he clearly established a village a few years before the 1610 date the modern city uses. Ironically, there is no document whatsoever that establishes an official, therefore, legal founding date for Santa Fe. See Part II, chapter 12 herein.
18. Hotz, *Indian Skin Paintings...*, (Norman, Oklahoma: University of Oklahoma Press, 1960).
19. Eric Ferraris to T. Chávez, 17 May 1984, Box 1, folder 11, Segesser Hide Paintings Collection., (Hereafter, Segesser Collection) FAC/POG.
20. T. Chávez to Andre von Segesser, 18 May 1984, Ibid.
21. Andre von Segesser to T. Chávez, 30 June 1984, Box 1, folder 16, Segesser Collection.
22. T. Chávez to Eric Ferraris, 5 August 1984, Box, 1, folder 17, Ibid.
23. Editors of Time-Life Books, *The Spanish West*, (Alexandria, Virginia: Time-Life Books, 1976), 72-73.
24. Hotz, *Indian Skin Paintings*, plate 8.
25. Ibid., plate 3.
26. A shorter version of this story is shared in Thomas E. Chávez, "History Comes Home: America's Oldest Historical Paintings of Settlers and Indians Return after Two Centuries in Switzerland," *Art & Antiques*, (November 1986), 75-77, 114. Also see, T. Chávez to Andre von Segesser, 6 June 1984, Box 1, folder 14; Andre von Segesser to T. Chávez, 22 December 1984, Box 1, folder 27; and Telex, Renate Wenke-Lukas to T. Chávez, 17 January 1985, Box 1, folder 29; all in Segesser Collection.
27. Renate Wenke-Lukas to T. Chávez, 24 April 1985, Box 1, folder 30; and Deutsches Ledermuseum [Gunter Gall] to T. Chávez, 9 July 1985, "Report on the Segesser Paintings," Box 3, folder 17, Segesser Collection.
28. Skip Pahl, Acting Director, MNM to T. Chávez, 22 October 1984, Box 2, folder 3, Ibid.
29. T. Chávez to Pahl, 22 October 1984, Box 2, folder 4, Ibid. Pahl hand wrote the "Do you believe this crap?" note across this memorandum. The memorandum with the note has not been been located. The memorandum cited here is a copy of the one sent to Pahl.
30. See T. Chávez, "The Segesser Paintings," *The Denver Westerners Roundup*, November-December 1991, 10.
31. A 105 page transcription of the public forum is in "Public Forum, " 8 August 1986, Box 6, folder 28, Segesser Collection.
32. Boyd's definitive work is *Popular Arts of Spanish New Mexico*, (Santa Fe: Museum of New Mexico Press, 1974).
33. Boyd to Gottfried Hotz, 6 November 1959, Box 1, folder 1, (copy) Segesser Collection; and "Palace of the Governors, Report of the Segesser Paintings," Segesser Collection. The letter refers to letters that Hotz wrote to both Bertha Dutton and Oliver LaFarge seeking information.
34. Boyd to Savoie Lottinville, 15 March 1961, Box 5, folder 5, p; and 17 March 1961, Box 5, folder 5, q, Segesser Collection.

35. See Alvin M. Josephy to T. Chávez, 29 March 1988, Box 4, folder 11, Segesser Collection in which Josephy related his dealings with Hotz and attached copies of correspondence between him and Hotz. Josephy establishes that Hotz researched throughout the Southwest and into Mexico.
36. Dust cover, Hotz, *Indian Skin Paintings.*
37. *New Mexico Historical Review* to Boyd, 10 December 1970; 9 February 1971; and 20 April 1971, v, all in Box 5, folder 5, Segesser Collection. The last letter refers to "Hotz's horror."
38. Oliver LaFarge to Alfred Steinmann, 1 June 1960, (copy to Boyd), Box 5, folder 5, m, Ibid.
39. E. Boyd, book review of Hotz, *Indian Skin Paintings*, in *New Mexico Historical Review,* Vol. XLVI, no. 3, (July 1971), 271-76. Most reviews generally ran up to one page. Body admitted that "finally" Hotz came to New Mexico and parts of Texas. She continued to error in saying that he did not go to Chihuahua or Arizona.
40. Oliver LaFarge to Gottfried Hotz, 20 November 1959, Box 5, folder 5, I; Segesser Collection.
41. Jane Ivanovich to Boyd, 3 November 1959, Box 5, folder 5, g, Ibid.
42. E. Boyd, book review, 275.
43. Boyd to Hotz, 1960, as quoted Hotz, *Skin Paintings,* 227-228; and Boyd to Dr. Savoie Lottinville, 15 March 1961, copy in Box 5, folder 5, p, Segesser Collection.
44. An interesting observation is that by the time I was in graduate school at the University of New Mexico from 1976-1980, Hotz's book was required reading. So within six years Hotz had been vindicated.
45. Phillip von Segesser von Brunegg to Thomás Apodaca, 20 February 1758, Consulados, Archivo General de Indias, Seville, Spain; a copy is in the Segesser Collection.
46. Segesser Paintings conservation report, Palace of the Governors.
47. Fray Angélico Chávez, "The Unique Tomb of Fathers Zarate and de la Llana in Santa Fe," *NMHR*, Vol. XL, no. 2, (April 1965), 101, 104-05.
48. T. Chávez, "Santa Fe's Own: A History of Fiesta," *El Palacio*, Vol. 91, no. 1 (Spring 1985) and in *Vivan Las Fiestas!*, Donna Pierce, editor, (Santa Fe: Museum of New Mexico Press, 1985), 5 & 17.
49. Fray Alonso de Benavides, *Memorial of 1630*, Cyprian Lynch, O. F. M., translator, (Washington, DC: American Academy of Franciscan History, 1954), xv, 33 and 55. La Conquistadora has had many names. She was originally Our Lady of the Assumption, and then became Our Lady of the Rosary. "Conquistadora" is a nickname and, recently, "de la Paz," or "of the Peace" has been added.
50. T. Chávez, "Santa Fe's Own," 14.
51. Register of Nuestra Señora del Rosario, 1760; and Duplicado del Navio nombrado Nuestra Señora del Rosario, 1760; and Sr. Con.dor Princ.pal de la Real Casa de Contratación, folio 40, 30 March 1761, Contratación, legajo 2564, Archivo General de Indias (hereafter AGI). This information was published for the first time in T. Chávez, "The Villasur Expedition and the Segesser Hide Paintings," *Spain and the Plains: Myths and Realities of Spanish Exploration and Settlement on the Great Plains*, Ralph H. Vigil, Frances W. Kaye, and John R. Wunder, editors, (Niwot, Colorado: University Press of Colorado, 1994), 90-113, see specifically p. 109.
52. Ibid.
53. Charles Bennett to Richard Alhborn, 23 June 1987; Lonn Taylor to Thomas Livesay, 21 August 1987; "Amendment to Agreement for lease with purchase of the Segesser I and Segesser II

Hide Paintings," 16 June 1988, Box 2, folder 3; Taylor to Livesay, 10 July 1987, and 21 August 1987; Livesay to Taylor, 14 September 1987; "Agreement for Purchase...," undated and unsigned; Livesay to David Phillips and Bennett, 8 October 1987, Box 3, folder 4, Segesser Collection.

54. Ibid.; and for the negotiations between the Smithsonian Institution and Museum of New Mexico (Foundation) see the correspondence between Lonn Taylor (SI), Helmuth Naumer (MNMFdn), and Tom Livesay (MNM), from 12 June to 14 September 1987, Box 3, folders 41, 48, 53, and 61, Segesser Collection.
55. Donna Pierce to T. Chávez, 21 June 2009, Author's collection. Frank and Barbara are the parents of Congresswoman Gabrielle Giffords who survived a shot to her head in an assassination attempt in Tucson, Arizona.
56. Keith Easthouse, "New Mexico, Smithsonian to Share Hides?" *The Santa Fe Reporter*, 25 November 1987, p. 5.
57. Ibid., 3 & 5.
58. Memorandum, T. Chávez to Livesay, 8 January 1988, Box 3, folder 83, Segesser Collection.
59. "The Report to the New Mexico State Legislature in January 1988," Box 5, folders 3 & 4, Ibid.
60. T. Chávez, "History Comes Home: America's Oldest Historical Paintings of Settlers and Indians Return After Two Centuries in Switzerland," *El Palacio*, Vol. 95, no. 1, (Fall/Winter 1989), 49.
61. The actual legislation is Section 6, Appropriations Act, HB 2, second session, 38th Legislature, January and February 1988. The legislation was for $395,000. Herr Segesser made up the balance of $5,000 by crediting us for a fee we paid to extend the loan. See In-loan agreement, No. 1986.057.2, 11 May 1987, Box 11, folder 3, Segesser Collection.
62. The story of the "lost" first check and subsequent issuance of the second check is documented in Box 4, folders 28, 33, 37, 39, 40, 43, 47, 48, and 56, Ibid.
63. T. Chávez, *Roundup*, 11 & 13.
64. The award is dated 23 April 1988.
65. As of this writing the manuscript has been published by the Rio Grande Press. The title is *A Moment in Time: The Odyssey of New Mexico's Segesser Hide Paintings.*
66. Chávez, *Roundup*, 6 as well as the book review of the revised edition in the same journal, p. 15, mistakenly notes that the University of New Mexico Press issued the revised edition. Gottfried Hotz, *The Segesser Hide Paintings: Masterpieces Depicting Spanish Colonial New Mexico*, (Santa Fe: Museum of New Mexico Press, 1991).
67. This was stated by Fran Levine, the current Director of the Palace of the Governors and New Mexico History Museum in a meeting in the offices of the Museum of New Mexico Foundation.

Part II

68. Cervantes, 2nd Part, Chapter X, 519.
69. Martínez de Montoya Documents, Fray Angélico Chávez History Library, Palace of the Governors; and France V. Scholes, "Juan Martínez de Montoya; Settler and Conquistador of New Mexico," *NMHR*, (October, 1944, Vol. XIX, no. 4), 337-342. Scholes gives most of the information related here.
70. Juan de Oñate to Viceroy Luis de Velasco, 24 August 1607, cited in Scholes, "Martínez de Montoya," 340.
71. For Oñate's resignation see Oñate to Viceroy Don Luis de Velasco, San Gabriel, 24 August 1607,

1042-1045; For the acceptance of Oñate's resignation see Royal Order Addressed to Oñate, 27 February 1608, 1048-1049; and for Martínez de Montoya's appointment as interim governor, see Appointment of Juan Martínez de Montoya as interim Governor, 16 February 1608, 1051-1053, all in George P. Hammond and Agapito Rey, *Don Juan de Oñate: Colonizer of New Mexico,* Part II, (Albuquerque: University of New Mexico Press, 1953) The originals are in the Archivo General de Indias, Audiencia de Mexico, legajo 27.

72. Scholes, "Martínez de Montoya," *NMHR*, 341.
73. "Instructions of Peralta," Lansing B. Bloom, transcriber, and Irene Chavez, translator, *NMHR*, (April, 1929, Vol. IV, no. 2), 178 & 179.
74. Exclusive of the Martínez de Montoya documents, historians have identified a few people who may have lived in the area called Santa Fe before 1607 although there is no hint that a town or plaza had been established. For example, see A. Chávez, *Origins of New Mexico Famiiles*, 41 for a Juan Griego who declared that he was born in Santa Fe. The combination of his age and year of his declaration puts the year of his birth at 1605.
75. France V. Scholes, "Juan Martínez de Montoya, Settler and Conquistador of New Mexico," *NMHR,* (October, 1944, Vol. XIX, no. 4), 337-342.
76. Ibid., 341.
77. Interview with David Snow, 2 April 2007, Santa Fe, New Mexico.
78. Scholes, "Martínez de Montoya," 338, note 2. The full title is, *D. Juan Saez Maurigade, vecino de esta Corte, sobre que se incluya en la descendencia directa del Capitán D. Juan Martínez de Montoya, descubridor, conquistador y poblador que fue en las Americas y Governador del Nuevo México.*
79. *Nuevas Leyes de Las Minas de España: 1625 Edición de Juan de Oñate,* Homer E. Milford, Richard Flint, Shirley Cushing Flint and Geraldine Vigil, translators and editors, (Santa Fe: Sunstone Press, 1998).
80. I believe he went to London for the wedding of one of his sons. Ambassador Ortiz does not mention his involvement with the Martínez de Montoya documents in his autobiography. Ortiz, *Lessons.*
81. For example, historians David Snow, Dedie Snow, and José Esquibel have all pointed out birth dates of individuals who claim to have been born in Santa Fe before 1610. See Fray Angélico Chávez, *Origins of New Mexico Families: A Genealogy of the Spanish Colonial Period,* (Santa Fe: Museum of New Mexico Press, 1992), 41.
82. Hazel Romero, "State Archives an Unlikely Treasure," *La Herencia,*(Winter 2002, Vol. 36); and Chávez, *New Mexico: Past and Future.*
83. Donna Pierce and Charles Carrillo both figured out that Miera y Pacheco created the altar screen. I first heard about this discovery from Pierce.
84. To see what it may have looked like with its original colors see, Eleanor Adams and Fray Angélico Chávez, translators and annotators, *The Missions of New Mexico, 1776: A Description by Fray Francisco Atanasio Dominguez with other Contemporary Documents,* (Albuquerque: University of New Mexico Press, 1956), front piece.
85. Ibid., 34. The official title of the painting is *La Madre Santísima de la Luz*. The work is attributed to Miguel Cabrera, a famous eighteenth century artist in Mexico.
86. For a good brief summary of La Castrense see John L. Kessell, *The Missions of New Mexico Since 1776,* (Albuquerque: University of New Mexico Press, 1980), 44-48.
87. Ibid., xi.

88. Ibid.
89. The loan records are on file at the Palace of the Governors. The Sisters of Loretto loaned the painting to the Palace of the Governors from 20 September 1994 to 20 December 1994.
90. The history of the statue is based on Fray Angélico Chávez, "Nuestra Señora de la Macana," *New Mexico Historical Review,* (Vol. XXXIV, no. 2, April, 1959), 80-97. The article was reproduced with the republication of his novel about the statue. See Chávez, *The Lady From Toledo: An Historical Novel in Santa Fe,* (Santa Fe: Friends of the Palace Press, 1993), 169-192. For the Robeldos and Romero see footnote 12, pp. 185-86 in the book.
91. This story is first related in Agustín de Ventancurt, *Teatro Mexicano,* (México City, 1697), 276-85.
92. Ibid., as quoted in A. Chávez, *Lady From Toledo,* 184-85.
93. Diego de Vargas to the Conde de Galve, Santa Fe, 16 January 1694 in John L. Kessell, Rick Hendricks and Meredith Dodge, editors, *Blood on the Boulders: The Journals of Don Diego de Vargas, New Mexico, 1694-1697,* Book I, (Albuquerque: University of New Mexico Press, 1998), 51 & 449.
94. Alfred B. Thomas, *Forgotten Frontiers: A Study of the Spanish Indian Policy of Juan Bautista de Anza, 1777-1787,* (Norman: University of Oklahoma Press, 1969 [1932]), 134.
95. Juan Bautista de Anza to Teodoro de Croix, 1 November 1779, Ibid., 142.
96. Gaspar Pérez de Villagrá, *Historia de la Nueva México,* (Alcalá de Henares, 1610). The most recent and complete edition is Miguel Encinias, Alfred Rodríguez and Joseph P. Sánchez, translators and editors, *Historia de la Nueva México, 1610,* Albuquerque: University of New Mexico Press, 1992). This last publication is used and cited for this book.
97. Marc Simmons, *The Last Conquistador: Juan de Oñate and the Settling of the Far Southwest,* (Norman: University of Oklahoma Press, 1991), 119-123 & 128-129.
98. Ibid., 130; Villagrá, Canto XIX, stanzas 157-165, p.178.
99. Villagrá, Canto, XIX, stanzas 195-197, p. 179.
100. Ibid., stanzas 198-200, p. 179.
101. Ibid., stanzas 221-244, p. 180.
102. Hernán Cortés to Carlos V, 13 October 1520 in Anthony Pagden, translator and editor, *Hernán Cortés: Letters from Mexico,* (Hew Haven and London: Yale University Press, 1986), 141 & 145, n. 105. Cortés was hit with rocks and he spent twenty days recovering. He was hit on the head a second time while in Honduras.
103. Codex cited in Sebastión García Rodríguez, O.F.M., editor, *Guadalupe: Siete Siglos de Fe y de Cultura,* (Guadalupe: Ediciones Guadalupe, 1993), 513. Cited as codex 83, folio 27, Archivo Monasterio Guadalupe (AMG). The codex is also cited in same author, *Guadalupe de Extremadura en America,* (Guadalupe: Comunidad Francicana de Guadalupe, 1997), 77-79.
104. Ibid., cited as codex 85, folio 69; and codex 90, folio 20.
105. Fray Cosme de Barcelona in Ibid., cited as codex 83, folio 27.
106. See Mary L. Davis and Greta Pack, *Mexican Jewelry,* (Austin: University of Texas Press, 1963, 1982), 48-50.
107. Federico Gómez de Orozco, "?El Exvoto de don Hernando Cortes?," *Anales del Instituto de Investigaciones Estéticas,* (no. 8, 1942), 51-54.
108. Roger Atwood incorrectly wrote that Bourne's father was the collector. Roger Atwood, *Stealing History; Tomb Raiders, Smugglers, and the Looting of the Ancient World,* (New York: St. Martin's Press, 2004), 191.

109. For John Bourne's own account see John Bourne, "Recollections of My Early Travels in Chiapas: The Discovery of Bonampak," *El Palacio*, Vol. 108, no. 1, (February 2003), 10-15.
110. On the Malaspina exhibition see, "The Malaspina Expedition: 'In the Pursuit of Knowledge'," *El Palacio*, (Vol. 82, no. 4, Winter 1976).
111. As a historian I have always had trouble with and rejected the commonly used "pre-history" term as semantical nonsense.
112. Dr. Furst also was Professor Emeritus of Anthropology and Latin American Studies at State University of New York at Albany.
113. Peter T. Furst, "Art of Ancient America," *Art of Ancient America: 1500 B. C. Through 1500 A. D.*, (Santa Fe: Museum of New Mexico, n. d.), 20.
114. Ibid., 24.
115. Ibid., 14.
116. The painting belonged to Anne Samuel Arnold who supported the museum. Upon her death, her daughter, Armanda S. Croy, gave the work of art to the Palace of the Governors under the state's newly created "New Mexico Acceptance Act." See, "In the Collections," *El Palacio*, Vol. 107, no. 4 (November 2002), 35.
117. Pierce to T. Chávez, 7 September 2009, Author's Collection.
118. "Priceless Spanish Colonial Artwork Donated to the Palace of the Governos," Press release on *Museum of New Mexico.org.*
119. Quoted in Atwood, *Stealing History*, 188.
120. This is corroborated in a headline article of the local newspaper in which the FBI agents said that museum officials and the donor are, "cooperating with the agency." *The Santa Fe New Mexican*, 2 October 1998.
121. For example, see Walter Alva, "Discovering the New World's Richest Unlooted Moche Tomb," Vol. 174, no. 4, (October 1988); and "New Moche Tomb: Royal Splendor in Peru," Vol. 177, no. 6 (June 2000), both in *National Geographic Magazine*. Also, see Christopher B. Donnan, "Unraveling the Mystery of the Warrior-Priest," Vol. 174, no. 4, (October 1988), *National Geographic Magazine.*
122. *The Santa Fe New Mexican*, 1 October 1998 & 2 October 1998.
123. *The Santa Fe New Mexican*, 2 October 1998.
124. Roger Atwood, *Stealing History*; and Sidney D. Kirkpatrick, *Lords of Sipán: A True Story of Pre-Inca Tombs, Archaeology, and Crime*, (New York: William Morrow and Company, Inc., 1992) both treat Alva favorably but have to mention that he had his detractors and why.
125. Roger Atwood, *Stealing History*, 52-53; and Sidney D. Kirkpatrick, *Lords of Sipan*, 69-71, 104-05, 130.
126. Atwood, *Stealing History*, 197.
127. *The Santa Fe New Mexican*, 25 October 1998.
128. Atwood, *Stealing History*, 203-04.
129. *The Santa Fe New Mexican*, 2 October 1998.
130. *The Santa Fe New Mexican*, Ibid., and 1 October 1998.
131. *The Santa Fe New Mexican*, 20 October 1998. The original letter is dated 2 October 1998. A copy is in the author's personal file as well as at the Palace of the Governors. Atwood, *Stealing History*, 305, n. 15, cites the same letter as unpublished. He apparently never realized that it was published in the newspaper and used a copy in the Palace of the Governor's files.

132. Cervantes, 2nd Part, Chapter X, 520.
133. Ibid., 2nd Part, Chapter XI, 521.
134. Walter Alva and Christopher B. Donnan, *Tumbas Reales de Sipán*, (Los Angeles: University of California, 1993).
135. Atwood, *Stealing History*, 201.
136. Atwood, *Stealing History*, 190.
137. Frank V. Ortiz, *Ambassador Ortiz: Letters From A Life of Service*, (Albuquerque: University of New Mexico Press, 2005), 190.
138. Roger Atwood, "A Public Desservice?", *ARTnews*, Vol. 102, no. 2 (February 2003).
139. Atwood, *Stealing History*, 197. Contrary to Atwood's narrative, Alva never offered a long-term loan and public talk.
140. Ibid., 203.
141. Ibid., 197.
142. Atwood, *Stealing History*, 195. Atwood used the journalistic technique of stating that early in the 1980s the "New Mexico officials learned of the paintings and approached the Segesser family to negotiate their return." He does not explain how I became involved. In fact, those museum officials were Charles Bennett and I. See Part I, chapters 5-10 herein for a more detailed description regarding the Segesser Paintings.
143. Findings and Decision of the Government Council of the Canton of Lucerne, Switzerland, 8 June 1988, Box 4, folder 21, Segesser Collection, POG/FAC.
144. Chávez to Ludwig von Segesser, 2 February 1889, Box 4, folder 64; and Ludwig von Segesser to Chávez, 16 March 1989, Box 4, folder 65, Ibid.
145. Quoted in Atwood, *Stealing History*, 204.
146. *The Santa Fe New Mexican*, 31 May 2008, C-1, C-3.
147. Atwood's and the FBI's point-of-view continues to resonate with *The Santa Fe New Mexican* and, apparently, with the current staff of the Palace of the Governors. See Ibid. for an article in which the sub headline reads, "In 1998, archaeologist suggested Bourne collection contained looted pieces."
148. Quote in Ibid., 204-05.
149. John Bourne, "Travels in Chiapas," *El Palacio*,10-15.
150. "On Exhibit," Ibid., 16-17.
151. *Journal North*, 8 December 2011.
152. Simon Barrett, "Interview with George C. Baldwin; Author of *The Science Was Fun*," *Blogcritics Magazine*, (an online magazine), 27 January 2007.
153. George Baldwin subsequently published an important book for the general public. George C. Baldwin, *The Science Was Fun: Selected Recollections of a Life in Science*, (Bloomington, Indiana: Authorhouse, 2006).
154. The article was written by Charles Kelly who took a trip through Glenn Canyon to visit and record historical sites and inscriptions before they became submerged by the rising waters of Lake Powell. Charles Kelly, "At 80 He Is Still an Explorer," *The Saturday Evening Post*, 6 May 1939; and George C. Baldwin, "The Vanishing Inscription," *Journal of the Southwest*, Vol. 41, no. 2, (Summer 1999), 120, 124, & 144.
155. Herbert E. Bolton, *Pageant in the Wilderness: The Story of the Escalante Expedition to the Interior Basin, 1776*, (Salt Lake City: Utah State Historical Society, 1951).

156. See Ted J. Warner, editor, and Fray Angélico Chávez, trans., *The Domínguez-Escalante Journal: Their Expedition Through Colorado, Utah, and New Mexico in 1776*, (Provo, Utah: Brigham Young University Press, 1976), 99-100.
157. Fray Francisco Garces, *A Record of Travels in Arizona and California, 1775 & 1776*, John Gavin, trans. and edit., (San Francisco: John Howell Books, 1967), 72. The Domínguez-Escalante Expedition left Santa Fe on 29 July 1776. They arrived at Oraibi, one of the Hopi Pueblos, on 16 November 1776. See, Chávez and Warner, *The Domínguez-Escalante Journal*, 109. Garces arrived at Oraibi on 2 July and left two days later. Garces, 69-77.
158. John Francis Bannon, *Herbert Eugene Bolton: The Historian and the Man, 1870-1953*, (Tucson: University of Arizona Press, 1978), 212.
159. Jesse Nusbaum, as quoted in Ibid., 213.
160. Baldwin, "Vanishing Inscription," 123.
161. See Part IV, chapter 64.
162. Jim Knipmeyer, *Butch Cassidy Was Here: Historic Inscriptions of the Colorado Plateau*, (Salt Lake City: University of Utah Press, 2002), 12-13 and a color photograph in the front of the book with the caption, "177—near Kabito, Arizona."
163. George C. Baldwin, "The Vanishing Inscription," 119-176.
164. All the above information and more can be gleaned from James Smithsonian's mausoleum room at the Smithsonian Institution. Also see, Heather Ewings, *The Lost World of James Smtihson: Science, Revolution, and the Birth of the Smithsonian*, (London: Bloombury USA, 2007).
165. Now called The School of Advanced Research.
166. Charles H. Lange and Carroll L. Riley, *Bandelier: The Life and Adventures of Adolph Bandelier*, (Salt Lake City: University of Utah Press, 1996), 210, 225 & 237.
167. Ibid., 237. One contemporary of the time remembers actually sitting on the chest unaware of what was inside of it until one of the staff members gleefully told him. Luther Wilson to the author, September, 2007.
168. Ibid. Some popular lore states that the ashes were spread at the Shrine of the Stone Lions, an ancient place of worship. I believe Lange and Riley. After all, Lange was there.
169. Marc Simmons, *The Last Conquistador: Juan de Oñate and the Settling of the Far Southwest*, Norman: University of Oklahoma Press, 1991, 193-194. Eric Beerman, "The Death of an Old Conquistador: New Light on Juan de Oñate," *NMHR*, Vol. 54, no. 4 (October 1979), 25; Beerman states that he died in "his home" in Guadalcanal.
170. For Diego de Vargas's Will, dated 7 April 1704, see John L. Kessell, editor, *Remote Beyond Compare: Letters of don Diego de Vargas to His Family from New Spain and New Mexico, 1675-1706*, (Albuquerque: University of New Mexico Press, 1089), 84.
171. T. Chávez, *Spain and Independence*, 214.
172. Two good studies of Anza are the classic Alfred Barnaby Thomas, translator and editor, *Forgotten Frontiers: A Study of the Spanish Indian Policy of Don Juan Bautista de Anza Governor of New Mexico, 1777–1787*, (Norman: University of Oklahoma Press, 1969 [originally 191932]); and Donald T. Garate, *Juan Bautista de Anza: Basque Explorer in the New World*, (Reno: University of Nevada Press, 2003).
173. A brief history and report on the Anza portrait may be located on-line and was prepared by the Center for Advanced Technology in Education, University of Oregon, copywrite 1998-2000; also see Palace of the Governors accession records.

174. For Oñate's years in Spain see Eric Beerman, *NMHR,* 305-319.
175. Homer Milford, Richard Flint, Shirley Cushing Flint, and Geraldine Vigil, editors and translators, *Nuevas Leyes de las Minas de España: 1625 edición de Juan de Oñate,* (Santa Fe: Sunstone Press, 1988).
176. Beerman, *HSNM,* 310-313. Oñate's Will is dated 4 October 1625.
177. John L. Kessell, *Remote Beyond Compare,* 3 & 5.
178. Luis Soler Pudrol, *La Real, Muy Ilustre y Primitiva Congregación de San Isidro Labrador de Naturales de Madrid,* (Madrid: Talleres Gricos Escelicer, S. A., 1966), 34-35.
179. Ibid., 38.
180. Charles Penny to T. Chávez, 26 February 1999; and Pedro Vela Vázquez to T. Chávez, 14 July 1998, Author's Collection.
181. Soler Puchol, 93.
182. Beerman, *HSNM,* 314.
183. Nancy Brown to Chávez, n.d., author's collection.
184. The Royal Austrians were the Hapsburgs who ruled Spain at the time. King Carlos V's oldest daughter married Maximillian II who became the Holy Roman Emperor. She became the Empress María of Austria. When her husband died in 1576, she returned to Spain where in Madrid she entered the Convent of the Descalzes Reales. Because of her fondness for the Jusuits, she became a major benefactor for the school.
185. Encinías, Rodríguez, and Sánchez, editors and translators, *Historia de la Nueva México,* XI.
186. Justo Corbacho, *Una Pequeña Gran Historia: Guíabreve del Instituto San Isidro,* (Madrid: Publications San Isidro, 2004, original in 1995).
187. Penny to T. Chávez, 26 February 1999, Author's Collection.
188. Beerman also found Oñate's Last Will and Testament in those records. Beerman, *HSNM,* 1979.
189. For example, see Marc Simmons, *The last Conquistador* and Eric Beerman, "The Death of an Old Conquistador...", *NMHR.*
190. This much earlier military chapel should not be confused with the church, *Nuestra Señora de la Luz,* constructed in 1760 and 1761, that became popularly known *la capilla castrense,* or simply, *La Castrense,* the military chapel. This church lasted until 1859, when Bishop Lamy sold the building. See, John L. Kessell, *The Missions of New Mexico Since 1776,* (Albuquerque: University of New Mexico Press, 1980), 44-45.
191. Two reports repeat the same good narrative survey of all the archaeological excavations of the Palace of the Governors and its environs. See Stephen S. Post, "A Data Recovery Plan for Excavation of the New Mexico Museum of History Site—700 Years of Human Occupation Near the Palace of the Governors in Santa Fe, New Mexico," Draft, Office of Archaeological Studies, Santa Fe, 2002, (Archaeological Notes 311), 3-6; and Stephen S. Post and Yvonne R. Oaks, "A Twenty-first century Archaeological Study of the Palace of the Governors: A Data Recovery Plan for Excavation of the Museum of New Mexico Administrative Parking Lot at 113 Lincoln Avenue in Downtown Santa Fe, Office of Archaeological Studies, 2002 (Archaeological Notes 311), 3-6.
192. Archaeologist Steve Post, interview, 3 February 2009. Post was the lead archaeologist in charge of the excavations conducted in back of the Palace of the Governors in anticipation of the construction of the new history museum.
193. Diego de Vargas to Viceroy Conde de Galve, El Paso, 2 January 1693, translated and quoted in J. Manuel Espinosa, *Crusaders of the Rio Grande,* (Chicago: Institute of Jesuit History, 1942), 116.

194. John Kessell, *Remote Beyond Compare: Letters of don Diego de Vargas to His Family from New Spain and New Mexico, 1675-1706*, (Albuquerque: University of New Mexico Press, 1989), 89-90.
195. Draft anonymous manuscript, n.d., Burial Suit files, A.87.75.1, Museum of International Folk Art, Santa Fe. This well-written manuscript is based on interviews with some documentary backup.
196. Burial Suit files. The depth of the grave is given as "about two feet, eight inches" in an Anonymously written manuscript, and approximately 78.7 cm in Terri Schindel, "Conservation of Grave Garments From Spanish Colonial Santa Fe, 1690-1710, TCC no. 1059-A, May 1988, p. 11, Burial Suit files, (Hereafter, Conservation Report).
197. Whether the Archdiocese gave or loaned the suit to the museum became a bone (pardon the play on words) of contention that was resolved with a loan in perpetuity to the museum. See, "Memorandum of Understanding Between the Museum of New Mexico and the Catholic Archdiocese of Santa Fe Regarding the Care and Conservation in Perpetuity of the Colonial Suit, 19 June 1992," Burial Files, MOIFA.
198. Vargas file, MOIFA.
199. Ellis, *Lamy's Santa Fe Cathedral*, 172.
200. Kessell, *Remote Beyond Compare*, 84.
201. Ibid.
202. Burial Suit Files.
203. The date of the visit is given as 4 September 1986 in Jim Wilke, "Report" and 1985 in Donna Pierce to Joyce Ice, 11 March 1991; both in Burial Suit files.
204. Nora Fisher to Yvonne Lange, 25 February 1974, Ibid.
205. Pierce to Ice, 11 March 1991; Sarah E. Alley to Charlene Cerny, 13 January 1992, Ibid.; and Pierce to T. Chávez, 21 June, 2009, Author's Collection. Pierce remembers that the suit had a small wooden cross about two inches high with round glass insets.
206. *Albuquerque Journal*, 26 July 1992.
207. Even Terri Schindel, as she worked through the daunting task of conserving the suit gave it the name of Diego. Vargas appeared to her in dreams to advise her and, as she related, he even tried the suit on. He advised that the waist coat was "too small." Of course, she never listened, for she realized these were dreams and conservators and scholars cannot base conclusions on a hunch, even if originating from a dream. Unedited draft, Conservation Burial Suit Folder, notebook A.87.75-1 "Colonial Suit," MoIFA.
208. Charlene Cerny to Claire Munzenrider, 14 August 1990, Burial Suit files.
209. Landis Smith, another conservator at the Museum of New Mexico.
210. Munzenrider to Cerny, 27 August 1990. Cerny wrote a note to Farwell Gavin to implement the solution on this memorandum.
211. See, for example, *The Albuquerque Journal*, 26 July 1992, in which mentions that Vargas was buried in the *parroquia*.
212. Anonymous draft, Burial Suit files, MOIFA.
213. Schindel, "Conservation Report," Burial Suit files, MOIFA; Pierce to T. Chávez, 7 September 2009, Author's collection.
214. Anonymous Draft, Ibid. The anonymous writer has recently been revealed as Dr. Donna Pierce. Pierce to T. Chávez, 21 June, 2009, Author's Collection.
215. Ibid.

Part III

216. Cervantes, Part 2, Chapter lxxi, 923.
217. Pamela Smith with Richard Polese, *Passions in Print: Private Press Artistry in New Mexico, 1834-Present,* (Santa Fe: Museum of New Mexico Press, 2006), 158-160.
218. Ibid., 161, 163, and 167.
219. Mauro Montoya Collection (AC 152), Fray Angélico Chávez History Library, FAC.
220. Diana Ortega DeSantis, *The Journal of José Salaices, 1789-1818,* (Santa Fe: Press of the Palace of the Governors, 1998).
221. Catherine Ferguson was born in Mexico City. Her parents were U. S. citizens. She graduated from the University of Arizona with a major in art and moved to New Mexico in 1974 where she became an artist of Catholic religious icons.
222. "Introductory Cover," *New World Saints.*
223. Smith, *Passions,* 167.
224. *New World Saints,* (Santa Fe: Press of the Palace of the Governors, 1995), Introduction, right side.
225. Smith, *Passions,* 10.
226. Kevin Ryan, "Foreword," in William F. Clark, *Remembering Santa Fe,* (Salt Lake City: Gibbs Smith, Publisher, 2004), n.p. Kevin Ryan is Clark's grandson who helped finish the original limited edition of this, Clark's last book, that was published under the title *Recuerdos de Santa Fe* in 1990.
227. Lawrence Clark Powell, *My New Mexico Literary Friends,* (Santa Fe: Press of the Palace of the Governors, 1986).
228. Marc Simmons, "Foreword," *Ibid.,* 1.
229. Smith, *Passions,* 167.
230. Bruce Ellis bequeathed the desk to the Palace of the Governors, where it now resides.
231. Bruce T. Ellis, *Bishop Lamy's Cathedral with the Records of the Old Spanish Church (Parroquia) and Convent Formerly on the Site,* (Albuquerque: HSNM/University of New Mexico Press, 1982).
232. Ibid., viii-ix.
233. Les Savage, Jr., *The Royal City,* (Santa Fe: Friends of the Palace Press, 1988).
234. Walter O"Meara, "Author's Note," *The Spanish Bride,* (Santa Fe: Friends of the Palae Press, 1990), n.p.
235. "Author's Note," O'Mera, *The Spanish Bride.*
236. Fray Angélico Chávez, *Origins of New Mexico Families: A Genealogy of the Spanish Colonial Period,* (Santa Fe: Museum of New Mexico Press, 1992). The book has an interesting publishing history, for counting the Museum of New Mexico's publication it was issued on four different occasions by four different publishing houses. The book was originally published as *Origins of New Mexico Families in the Spanish Colonial Period,* (Santa Fe: Historical Society of New Mexico, 1954), it came out with the same title in 1973, (Albuquerque: University of Albuquerque with Calvin Horn Publisher), and in 1975, (Santa Fe: William Gannon). Another nuance is the slight change to the dedication from the first edition to the last. Any biographer of Chávez might want to check that.
237. *El Palacio Magazine* (1956-1957).

238. Thomas J. Steele, S. J., Foreword in Fray Angélico Chávez, *My Penitente Land: Reflections on Spanish New Mexico,* (Santa Fe: Museum of New Mexico Press, 1993 [1974]), v.
239. The lecture was given as a fundraiser for the Museum of Spanish Colonial Arts at La Fonda Hotel on 24 February 2007.
240. Thomas E. Chávez, *Quest for Quivera: Spanish Explores on the Great Plains, 1540-1821,* (Tucson: Southwest Parks and Monuments Association, 1992), 50.
241. T. Chávez, *Manuel Alvarez: A Southwestern Biography, 1794 to 1856,* (Niwot: University Press of Colorado, 1989), 61.
242. T. Chávez, *Spain and the Independence of the United States: An Intrinsic Gift,* (Albuquerque: University of New Mexico Press, 2002), plates 1 and 3. See Fernández y Fernández to Louise Stiver, (copied to Governor Bill Richardson), 20 December 2004; and Stiver to Fernández y Fernández, 11 January 2005, both letters in the Author's Collection.
243. Presidential debate, Univisión, 9 September 2007. In fairness, none of the other candidates gave good answers to the question either.
244. Bill Richardson with Michael Ruby, *Between Worlds: The Making of an American Life,* (New York: G. P. Putnam's Sons, 2005), 29-30. The most glaring error was his claim to having been drafted to play professional baseball.
245. The Memorial may be located in Dispatches from United States Consuls in Santa Fe, Mexico, Manuel Alvarez, 1839-1840, Microfilm 199, Record Group 59, National Archives of the United States of America, Washington, DC. The Fray Angélico Chávez Library, Palace of the Governors, has a microfilm copy. There is some initial disarray in the arrangement of the attached letters. Some are missing and others are out of order.
246. Thomas E. Chávez, editor, *Conflict and Acculturation: Manuel Alvarez's 1842 Memorial,* (Santa Fe: Museum of New Mexico Press, 1989).
247. Thomas E. Chávez, *An Illustrated History of New Mexico,* (Niwot: University Press of Colorado, 1992), ix-x.
248. David V. Holtby to T. Chávez, Albuquerque, 17 February 1986, Author's collection.
249. Thomas E. Chávez, *España y la Independencia de Estados Unidos,* Translation by Teresa Carretero y Amado Diéguez, (Madrid: Taurus Historia, 2006).
250. "Spain and the American Revolution," *Discover American History, Cobblestone,* Vol. 21, no. 8, (November, 2000).
251. Reyes Calderón Cuadrado, *Empresarios españoles en el proceso de independencia norteamericana: La Casa Gardoqui e hijos de Bilbao,* (Madrid: Unión Editiorial, S. A., 2004). The portrait is of Diego María de Gardoqui who was Spain's first ambassador to the United States.
252. Román Álvarez, *Abelgas: Paisajes, Evacaiones y Remembranzas,* (Salamanca: Ediciones Almar, 2003), 104-05. The erroneous title of my biography of Alvarez is *Manuel Alvarez, 1794-1856: A Southwestern Biography.*
253. Cervantes, *Don Quixote,* part one, chapter ix, 68. "...since historians must and ought to be exact, truthful, and absolutely free of passions, for neither interest, fear, rancor, nor affection should make them deviate from the path of truth, whose mother is history, the rival of time, repository of great deeds, witness to the past, example and adviser to the present, and forewarning to the future."
254. Mary J. Straw Cook, *Loretto: The Sisters and Their Santa Fe Chapel,* (Santa Fe: Museum of New Mexico Press, 2002).

255. Mary Jean Cook, "?Porqué (sic) Monterrey?: The Death and Mysterious Burial of Merchant Manuel Alvarez, Part I," *Wagon Tracks,* Vol. 19, no. 3, (May, 2005), 6-9. Inexplicably (to me) the article has the *imprintur* of a one paragraph introduction written by Marc Simmons.
256. Mary J. Straw Cook, *Doña Tules: Santa Fe's Courtesan and Gambler,* (Albuquerque: University of New Mexico Press, 2007), 92.
257. Ibid., 148, n. 97.
258. Ibid., 92.
259. Cervantes, *Don Quixote,* Prologue, Second part, 458.
260. "Letterbook of Brigadier General Edward Hand," 13 April-25 August 1778, vol. 1, no. 156, Record Group 93, National Archives of the United States of America. The full account of Willing's exploits is given in T. Chávez, *Spain and the Independence of the United States,* 104.
261. Richard B. Morris, *The Peacemakers: The Great Powers and American Independence,* (New York: Harper Torchbooks, 1965). Snodgrass's film was *The Work of Peace,* (1984) that he did for the Smithsonian Institution.
262. Roger Snodgrass to T. Chávez, 29 January 1986, Author's collection.
263. María Jesús Pablos to T. Chávez, 13 June 1986, Western Union Mailgram, Ibid. The short message was, "US Spanish Joint Committee grant awarded stop letter follows."
264. "Tom Chavez's Banner Years," in the "Journal North" of *The Albuquerque Journal,* 25 January 1987.
265. See Aline Griffith, *The Earth Rests Lightly,* (New York: Holt, Rhinehart & Winston, 1963). Griffth was an American spy in Spain during WWII and married into nobility to become as she was known in Spain as María Aline Griffth y Dexter, the Condesa de Quintanilla. This book is a first person account of the exploits of her and her friends in Trujillo, including the search for Sansón's remains.
266. Not all people who sing *saetas* are gypsies.
267. I received two invitations. The second resulted from another friend in Seville, César Correa. Both were unsolicited and I accepted the first one received. For the quote; El Hermano Mayor de la...Hermandad de Nuestro Padre Jesús...y María Stma. Del Dulce Nombre to T. Chávez, 19 December 1987, Author's Collection. For the second invitation; Hipolito de Oya Jiménez-Placer to César Correa García, 29 February 1988; and César Correa to T. Chávez, 10 February 1988, Author's Collection. The second invitation came from the Confraternity of Nuestra Señora del Valle.
268. In southern Spain Spanish is spoken in a type of slang called Andalucian or "Andalu" in which words and letters are dropped. "Tos" is "Todos" meaning in this case "Everyone."
269. I gave Mr. Pierce a lapel pin from my *cofradia.* Although not Catholic and very particular about what he wore on his ever present baseball cap, he wore that pin religiously. I received a letter from his wife, Pat, who explained this to me to the point of when he lost the backing, he insisted on searching until he found it. He would not accept a replacement. Pat Pierce to T. Chávez, 6 June 1989, Author's Collection.
270. The buildings in which the Hermanos Penitentes meet and pray are called *Moradas.*
271. A. Chávez, "Our Lady of the Conquest," *Vivan Las Fiestas/ El Palacio Magazine,* Donna Pierce, edit., (Santa Fe: Museum of New Mexico Press, 1985), 20.
272. Archbishop Robert F. Sánchez to T. Chávez, 17 December 1989, Box 1, folder 7, Chávez Collection, FAC.

273. For the students' privacy I will not use their names.
274. "N.M. Clicks With Spain," *The Albuquerque Journal*, 10 July 2003.
275. The exhibition opened on 27 September 2007 and was titled, "Legacy: Spain and the United States in the Age of Independence, 1763-1848." The three symposiums were: "La Ilustración española en la independencia de los Estados Unidos: Benjamin Franklin," "Norteamérica a finales del Siglo XVIII: España y los Estados Unidos (en el aniversario del namcimiento de Benjamín Franklin)" both held in Madrid 17-19 May 2006, and "The Spanish Contribution to the Independence of the United States: Between Reform and Revolution," Washington, DC, 27-29 September 2007. Two of the four publications have come to fruition; Gonzalo Anes and Eduardo Garrigues, editors, *La Ilustración Española en la Independencia de los Estados Unidos: Benjamín Franklin*, (Madrid: Real Academia de la Historia, 2000) and no author/editor, *Legacy: Spain and the United States in the Age of Independence, 1763-1848*, (Washington, DC: Smithsonian Institution, 2000). The two forthcoming anthologies are compiled from the papers presented in the 2006 conference in Madrid and the 2007 conference in Washington, DC. The author has an article in *La Ilustración*, which is "Los Padres Fundadores y España: Un Examen del Conocimiento Americano de la Ayuda de España en el Nacimiento de Estados Unidos," 199-209.
276. As of this writing, talk continues about opening an Instituto Cervantes in Los Angeles.
277. Eduardo Garrigues, *West of Babylon*, (Albuquerque: University of New Mexico Press, 2002). Garrigues hired New Mexican writer Nasario Garcia, who with the help of his wife Jan, translated the book into English for publication at UNM Press.

Part IV

278. Cervantes, Chapter VIII, 59.
279. Those tapes, never transcribed, were left in the collections of the Palace of the Governors.
280. Diana de Santis, "The Hispanic Shepherd of New Mexico's Eastern Plains," *El Palacio Magazine*, Spring, 1982, (Vol. 88, no. 1), 12-13. The article notes that three interviews were held on 19 and 20 November 1980 and 28 January 1981.
281. Regretfully, the reunions have not taken place in years.
282. Maraino Chávez died on Sunday, 12 July 1981.
283. *The Santa Fe New Mexican*, 13 July 1981, A2.
284. As mentioned the tapes are in the collections of the Palace of the Governors. His photographs, likewise, reside in the photographic collections of the Fray Angélico Chávez Library, Palace of the Governors. The photograph of the "macho moro" and the "coyote que cogi" has been published twice. See T. Chávez, *Illustrated History*, 193; and *New Mexico: Past and Future*, 178.
285. T. Chávez, "A Long Lost Love Remembered During Fiesta," The "Outlook" section, *The Santa Fe New Mexican*, 7 September 1997, F-1, F-6.
286. Villagrá, *Historia de la Nueva México, 1610*, canto XIV, lines 164-170, p. 127. The autor changed the word "completest" to "most complete" in a nod to clearer English.
287. Ibid., lines 318-19, p. 131.
288. The year of the Oñate "Thanksgiving" is 1598 and the year of the Pilgrims' "Thanksgiving" is 1621.
289. *El Pais*, Madrid, Spain, 1996. *El Pais* is the largest circulating newspaper in Spain.

290. Richard E. Ahlborn, editor, *Man Made Mobile: Early Saddles of Western North America*, (Washington, DC: Smithsonian Institution Press, 1980).
291. Howard W. Marshall and Richard E. Ahlborn, *Buckaroos in Paradise: Cowboy Life in Northern Nevada*, (Washington, DC: Library of Congress, 1980)
292. *The Santa Fe Reporter*, 29 May 1985, p. 4. The *Reporter* named the contest "The Great Santa Fe Quiz." Charles won the first one.
293. In 2009 the Palace of the Governors had a twenty-five year anniversary of the event. This celebration was off by two years. For the anniversary event see "Invitation to the celebrate the 25th anniversary;" and for the 1982 event see "The Weekly Calendar and TV Section," *The Santa Fe Reporter*, August 22, 1982; Benita Bubt, "Bite a Buffalo: Sample Mountain Man Grub at the Rendezvous Roast," *The Santa Fe New Mexican*, Section C, August 25, 1982; *Pasatiempo, The Santa Fe New Mexican*, August 27, 1982 (This last citation includes a cover image of Kurt Hughey's poster image); all in Palace Rendezvous and Buffalo Roast Vertical File, FAC. Also see Palace of the Governors Annual Report, Fiscal Years 70 and 71, Vertical Files, FAC.
294. These two delicacies featured the testicles of sheep and bulls respectively.
295. The first year Palace Rendezvous and Buffalo Roast was financed by a loan from the Museum of New Mexico Foundation. The event grossed enough to cover the loan and net $3,500. Palace of the Governors, Annual Report, Fiscal Year 71, 1.
296. Saul Cohen is a prominent Santa Fe attorney, noted bibliophile, and a longtime Museum of New Mexico Foundation trustee.
297. Fray Angélico dedicated his book *Tres Macho, He Said* to Judge Bigbee's wife, Betty Roe Bigbee, "Fair Lady Chesterfield of Santa Fe." For Fabián Chávez see David Roybal, *Taking on Giants: Fabián Chávez Jr. and New Mexico Politics*, (Albuquerque: University of New Mexico Press, 2008).
298. All this information with the proper citations was subsequently published in my book. See Chávez, *Spain and the Independence*, (Albuquerque: University of New Mexico Press, 2002).
299. T. Chávez to Mrs. Bigby (Bigbee), 13 March 1988, with return note from Elizabeth, Chávez files. Elizabeth Bigbee signed the note with "EBK" and the uppercase is in the original.
300. T. Chávez, "Spain and the Independence of the United States," *Daughters of the American Revolution Magazine*, February 1992 (Vol. 126, no. 2). The dedication came in bold print at the end of the article on page 190.
301. Chávez, *Spain and the Independence*, xi.
302. *But Time and Chance: The Story of Padre Martínez of Taos, 1793–1867*, (Santa Fe: Sunstone Press, 1981) and *Trés Macho He Said: Padre Gallegos of Albuquerque; New Mexico's First Congressman*, (Santa Fe, 1985).
303. Archbishop Sánchez, who convinced Fray Angélico to move from a rented apartment and live with his Franciscan brethren at the Cathedral.
304. Fray Angélico Chávez passed away on 18 March 1996, a month short of his eighty-sixth birthday.
305. Nasario García, *Cantares: Canticles and Poems of Youth, 1925-1932*, (Houston: Arte Público Press, 2000), xvii-xviii.
306. T. Chávez to Frederick Mayer, February 2007.
307. The battle of Chickamauga took place on 19-20 September 1863. The Confederate forces routed the Union troops in this pivotal battle. Soon thereafter, Ulysses Grant took command of the Union's western forces and was victorious at nearby Chattanooga. As a result President Abraham Lincoln appointed him to the newly created post of General of the Armies and the rest is history.

308. Captain S. J. Firestone, Co. A, 19th Regiment, to Benedict Sprowl and family, 10 October 1863, copy in possession of the author, original in the National Archives.
309. T. Chávez, *Illustrated History,* 114. Photograph by George C. Bennett, MNM 15348.
310. Richard Melzer, "Casualties of Caution and Fear: Life in Santa Fe's Japanese Internment Camp, 1942-46," *Essays in Twentieth-Century New Mexico History*, Judith Boyce DeMark, edit., (Albuquerque: University of New Mexico Press, 1994),213-240.
311. T. Chávez, "The Forgotten History of Internment Camps," Opinion, *The Santa Fe New Mexican,* F-1, F-3.
312. Lt. General Masaharu Homma, who was in charge of the prisoners, was later tried and convicted of war crimes. He was executed outside of Manila.
313. See a photograph of George Hawthorn in *The Albuquerque Journal*, 28 October 1993, p. 1.
314. Regarding "urinate" see *The Santa Fe New Mexican,* 28 August 1999. Regarding "traitors" Hawthorn added in a letter to the editor, "...you are guilty of giving aid or comfort to our enemies and stirring up discontent...and you can be charged with *sedition* [italicized in the original] if your acts were deliberate." This letter is clipped from a newspaper and undated in Box 1, folder 4, Santa Fe Japanese Internment Camp Records, (AC 369), FAC.
315. T. Chávez to Doc Weaver, 27 August 1999, Box 1, folder 2, Internment Camp Records.
316. *The Journal North,* 29 August 1999; also in Box 1, folder, 4, Ibid.
317. *The Journal North,* 15 August 1999.
318. *The Santa Fe New Mexican,* 24 August 1999.
319. *The Albuquerque Journal*, 28 October 1999.
320. *The Santa Fe New Mexican,* Sunday, 22 August 1999, A-9. The image appeared twice in print. The second appeared with an "Op. Ed." that *The Journal North* invited me to write. *The Journal North,* 29 August 1999.
321. Ibid., 11 August 1999.
322. *The Santa Fe Reporter*, 25-31 August 1999.
323. *The Albuquerque Journal*, 27 October 1999.
324. *The Journal North,* 31 October 1999.
325. "Santa Fe Internment Camp Historical Marker Dedication" itinerary, Author's files. The park was named for the father of Ambassador Frank Ortiz.
326. Sometime later an elementary school did a play based on the internment camp. For one of the props the children created a replica of the marker and boulder to which it is attached. For a while that replica resided in the main reading room to the Fray Angélico Chávez History Library, Palace of the Governors.
327. R. C. Doc Weaver to Honorable Larry Delgado, Mayor, 9 May 2002, Author's files.
328. Ibid.
329. All the letters are dated 9 May 2002. The supporters who received letters are Miles Chaffe of Milestone, Bill Coppola of Coppola Concrete Supply, Inc., and Charlie Smith of C. Smith Construction, all in Ibid.
330. A. Chávez, *New Mexico Families, 229-230.*
331. The story of Miera y Pacheco's vision and his attempt to convince Spanish officialdom of his grand plan was presented by Paul Kraemer, "Miera y Pacheco and the Gila Apaches," at the 2008 Annual Conference of the Historical Society of New Mexico, Deming, New Mexico, 25 April 2008; and published under the same title in *La Crónica de Nueva México*, no. 76 (July 2008), 1 & 2.

332. Michael Frederick Weber, "Tierra Incognita: The Spanish Cartography of the American Southwest, 1540-1808", Dissertation, University of New Mexico, 1986.
333. Ibid., 170.
334. The various narratives of the Vázquez de Coronado expedition indicate that they were in the middle of a large continent and that somewhere between the east and west "cordilleras" or mountain ranges, the rivers flowed into the North (Atlantic Ocean) or South (Pacific Ocean) Seas. A hand drawn map makes no reference to a continental divide. Richard Flint and Shirley Cushing Flint are the only historians to give the Vázquez de Coronado expedition credit for noting the continental divide. See Richard Flint, *No Settlement, No Conquest: A History of the Coronado Entrada*, (Albuquerque: University of New Mexico Press, 2008).
335. Weber, "Tierra Incognita," 165.
336. Segesser II.
337. See T. Chávez, *Quest for Quivira*, 42-43, for a blow up of the French city on the Miera y Pacheco map.
338. See Part II, Chapter 24 herein.
339. T. Chávez, "A Curious, Spurious Seal," *El Palacio*, Summer 1980, (Vol. 86, no. 2), 40-41.
340. Manuel Alvarez to James Buchanan, 4 September 1846, United States Consular Dispatches, Santa Fe, Manuel Alvarez, Vol. 1, Record Group no. 199, National Archives, Washington, DC.
341. Chávez, "Curious, Spurious Seal," 41.
342. Among other items that belonged to Lew Wallace the Palace of the Governors' Fray Angélico Chávez Library has the largest collection in the world of first editions of his book, *Ben Hur*, in foreign languages.
343. Ortiz, *Ambassador Ortiz*, 194-95.
344. Pedro de Corral, *La Cronica del Rey Don Rodrigo*, (Toledo: Juan Ferrer, 1549).
345. Giovanni Batista Ramusio, *Delle Navigationi et viaggi...*, Vol. II, (Venice, 1556). Ramusio's three volumes dealt with travels. His first volume (1550) dealt with Africa and his third volume (1559) was about Asia, including Marco Polo's journey.
346. Ortiz, *Ambassador Ortiz*, 194-95.
347. For an early view of the Historical Society se James T. Stensvaag, "Clio on the Frontier: The Intellectual Evolution of the Historical Society of New Mexico, 1859-1925," *HSNM*, Vol. 55, no. 4 (October 1980), 293-308.
348. History Unit Staff, "Historical Society of New Mexico Donation to the Museum of New Mexico: The Vast Riches of the Historical Society's Gift Touches Each Collection with the Museum," *El Palacio*, Vol. 90, no. 3 (Fall-Winter, 1984), 6-13.
349. That site can still be seen at New Mexico Culture Net—The Civil War in New Mexico, 1861-1862.
350. Arista later briefly became the President of Mexico. An entry in the Presidential Palace in Mexico City still bears his name.
351. Chávez, *Origins of New Mexico Families*, 334-35. Chávez names the daughters and their other siblings as well as the parents, Romauldo Roybal and María Monica González. There was a fourth sister, Eva, who did not figure in this story of the necklace.
352. Jacqueline Dorgan Meketa, *Louis Felsenthal: Citizen-Soldier of Territorial New Mexico*, (Albuquerque: University of New Mexico Press, 1982).

Part V

353. Jill Cooper, wife of Tom Udall who was himself hired as a State's attorney for Energy and Minerals before he won election as the Attorney General, then became a multi-term United States Congressman, and finally in 2008 was elected to the U. S. Senate; and Clara Apodaca, former first lady with Governor Jerry Apodaca, subsequently received an appointment to Secretary for Cultural Affairs.
354. As told to the author by Edson Way.
355. Wife of Governor Jerry Apodaca who was governor from 1975 to 1978.
356. Sam'l Arnold, *Eating Up the Santa Fe Trail: Recipes and Lore from the Old West,* (Golden, Colorado: Fulcrum Publications, 2001). Another of his popular books was *Frying Pans West,* (Denver: The Fur Press, 1969). Arnold hosted a nationally syndicated televised cooking show of the same name.
357. Arnold, *Eating Up the Santa Fe Trail,* 45-48.
358. The Palace had other reasons for possessing the book. Sam'l Arnold's wife, Carrie, a member of the Friends of the Palace, illustrated the book. Her water color graces the cover and features David Margolis, a long-time member of the Friends.
359. Washington Street.
360. He was elected to two terms as the State Treasurer.
361. *The Albuquerque Journal,* "Journal North," 30 June 2001, D1 & D3; and *The Santa Fe New Mexican,* 30 June 2001, A11.
362. For a good overview of the story of Guadalupe and her monastery in Spain see Sebatián García Rodríguez, O. F. M., *Guadalupe: Siete Siglos de Fe y de Cultura,* (Guadalupe, Extremadursa, Spain; Ediciones Guadalupe, 1993). Specifically for the name, place and time see pp. 11-12.
363. Also spelled "Tepeac."
364. Still one of the best overviews of the story of Guadalupe and Mexico is Jacques Lafaye, *Quetzalcóatl and Guadalupe: The Formation of Mexican National Consciousness, 1531-1813,* (Chicago: The University of Chicago Press, 1974).
365. "The Palace of the Governors Millennium Plan: Technology & Increased Collections Access," "Palace of the Governors History Annex: A Program of the Museum of New Mexico," and "Palace of the Governors Exit Reports," FAC.
366. *The Albuquerque Journal,* 7 September 2000, D3; Also see *The Santa Fe New Mexican,* 8 September 2000, B3; editorial in *The Albuquerque Journal,* 10 September 2000.
367. "Adiós y Gracias," *Pasatiempo,* March 22-28, 2002.
368. Ed Lujan as quoted in Ibid., 40.
369. *The Albuquerque Journal,* "Journal North," 28 June 2001.
370. Chávez to Thomas Wilson, 11 December 2001, Author's Collection.
371. *The Santa Fe New Mexican, "Pasatiempo,"* 36; *The Albuquerque Journal,* "Metro & New Mexico," B8.
372. *The Santa Fe New Mexican,* "Pasatiempo," 36. For the long campaign leading up to the bill's successful passage see "Lujan faces test in Palace appropriation," editorial, *The Santa Fe New Mexican,* 28 February 2001; "Museum Fund Quest," *The Albuquerque Journal North,* 5 February 2001; and an article written by the author, "For the Palace and the People," "Insight & Opinion, c-1 & c-2, *The Albuquerque Tribune,* 27 February 2001.

373. *The Santa Fe New Mexican,* 7 March 2002, A1 & A4.
374. Ibid., 8 March 2002, A9.
375. The Prince of Asturias is the official title of the heir to the throne of Spain, in this case, Felipe.
376. T. Chávez, "Funciones: Traditions for the Future," *Funciones: Communal Ceremonies of Hispanic Life*, (July 1983).
377. T. Chávez to Michael O'Shaughnessy, 8 May 2002; Michael O'Shaughnessy to T. Chávez, 21 June 2002, Author's collection.
378. T. Chávez to Michael O'Shaughnessy, 23 August 2004, Author's Collection.
379. Alberto A. León to T. Chávez, 24 August 2004, Ibid.
380. "Museum official blasts state history bill," *The Santa Fe New Mexican,* 3 March 2001, A1 & A2.
381. Bob Rodríquez to Ruben Sálaz Márquez, 9 March 2003, Author's collection.
382. T. Chávez to Rodríquez, 25 March 2003, Ibid.
383. Rodríquez to T. Chávez, 27 May 2003, Author's collection.
384. T. Chávez to Rodrígúez, 9 June 2003, Ibid.
385. Conchita Lucero to membership, 15 June 2003, Ibid. This was an e-mail.
386. Minutes, both on tape and in hard copy, on file at the NHCC; and T. Chávez, notes from the 20 June 2003 Special NHCC Board of Directors' Meeting.
387. Ibid.
388. Conchita Lucero to T. Chávez, (copied to the NHCC Board of Directors and History Committee), n. d., Author's collection.
389. Rodríquez to Patricia Madrid, Attorney General, 22 September 2003, Ibid.
390. Frederico Vigil, interviewed on 24 September 2008.
391. *The Albuquerque Journal,* no date, Author's collection.
392. *The Grossmonts Weekly*, September 11-18, 2003.
393. *The Albuquerque Journal,* 29 September 2003.
394. *The Santa Fe New Mexican*, 15 May 2005.
395. *The Albuquerque Journal,* 24 August 2002.
396. *The Los Angeles Times*, 21 September 2004. The headline reads, "New Mexico's Vision: L.A.'s Dream."
397. *The Dallas Fort Worth Star-Telegram*, April 2005.
398. For example, see "Gallery: History Al Fresco," in *Delta Sky*, (August, 2008), 113.
399. "Arts and Culture Section," *The Albuquerque Journal*, 4 January 2004.
400. Rodríquez to Governor Bill Richardson, 21 January 2004, Author's collection.
401. Stuart A. Ashman to Rodríquez, 3 February 2004, Ibid.
402. Sálaz to Ed Lujan, 17 April 2004, Ibid.
403. T. Chávez to Sálaz, 22 April 2004, Ibid.
404. Cervantes, Part III, Chapter XXII, 163-172.
405. Cervantes, Part III, Chapter XXII, 172.
406. Vigil interview, 24 September 2008.
407. St. Thomas Aquinas as quoted in Fox, *The Hidden Spirituality*, 92.
408. *Albuquerque Journal*, 11 April 2003, A1 & A7.
409. Ibid., 12 April 2003.
410. Ben Lujan's farther is Ben Lujan, Sr. who was the Speaker of the State House of Representatives. With the help of his father and Governor Richardson, Junior was elected to the State Public

Regulations Commission and then to the United States Congress from New Mexico's first district.

411. *Albuquerque Journal*, 29 September 2003, A1 & A2.
412. For example, Joseph Wasson to T. Chávez, 29 December 2003; and 2 June 2004, (emails), Author's collection.
413. Roy E. Disney to Archuleta, 6 November 2003, Author's collection.
414. Archuleta to Clifford Miller, 10 December 2003 with the following attachments; Andrew Plepher (Bank of America) to Archuleta, 25 November 2003; T. H. Lang (*Journal*) to Archuleta, 13 November 2003; and Hank Beukema (McCune Foundation) to Archuleta, 8 December 2003, Author's collection. Also see R. Disney to Archuleta and T. Chávez, 13 January 2004, Author's collection.
415. Manuel Areu Collection of Nineteenth Century Zarzuelas, 1849-1992, Center for Southwestern Research, Zimmerman Library, University of New Mexico.
416. For example, from Fort Worth, see *The Sunday Star-Telegram*, "Travel Section," H1, H3 & H4.
417. Roy and Patti Disney to T. Chávez and Archuleta, 21 September 2004, Author's collection.
418. For a more in depth look into Chávez's interpretation of Dali's painting see Ellen McCracken, *The Life and Writing of Fray Angélico Chávez: A New Mexico Renaissance Man*, (Albuquerque: University of New Mexico Press, 2009), 279-284.
419. Dust cover jacket, Fray Angélico Chávez, *The Virgin of Port Llegat*, Fresno, California: Academy Library Guild, 1959).
420. T. S. Elliott to Fray Angélico Chávez, 7 August 1958, AC 40, Box 4, Folder 14, FAC Library.
421. As quoted in McCracken, *Chavez*, fnt 27, p. 439.
422. Diego Rodríquez de Silva Velázquez (1599-1660).
423. A. Chávez, *Virgin of Port Lligat*, 35.
424. T. Chávez to Stuart Ashman and Edward Lujan, 4 December 2003, Author's collections. I mis-typed my intended retirement date for 1 April 2004, which already had passed.
425. Memorandum, T. Chávez to Katherine Archuleta, n.d. (October 2004), Author's collection. The first sentence of this memorandum is "This is a reaction paper to our meeting held on 13 October 2004."
426. Ibid.
427. Cervantes, 2nd Part, Chapter LIII, 808.
428. Memorandum, Demesia Padilla and Katherine Archuleta, 9 March 2005, Author's collection.
429. T. Chávez to Ashman and Matt Martínez, 8 May 2005, Author's collection. The letter was copied to Archuleta, Padilla, Gene Henley, Ed Lujan, and Shelle Luaces.
430. Fortunately, Archuleta's successor, Clara Apodaca, has been able to correct the economic situation and has the foundation, at least, out of the red.
431. Cervantes, 2nd Part, Chapter LIII, 808. This edition does not give a translation for "*blanca*," while other translations translate the word to "farthing." See, for example, the translation of *The Adventures of Don Quixote* by J. M. Cohen, (Baltimore: Penguin Books, 1970), 814.
432. For an in depth discussion of the difference between warriors and soldiers see Matthew Fox, "The Hidden Spirituality of Men" *Ode*, (October 2008), 60-64; Matthew Fox, *The Hidden Spirituality of Men: Ten Metaphors to Awaken the Sacred Masculine*, (New World Library, 2008).
433. Jaime de Salas to T. Chávez, 4 November 2003 (email), Author's collection.

434. Salas to T. Chávez, 5 January 2004; 18 February 2004; 17 February 2004; 19 February 2004; and 24 February 2004; T. Chávez to Salas, 17 February 2004 (all emails), Author's collection.
435. T. Chávez to Reverando Padre Guillermo Cerrato, O.F.M., 12 April 2004, Author's collection.
436. For a great overview of both the Monastery and its collections see, Sebastián García Rodríquez, *Guadalupe: Siete Siglos.*
437. Ibid., 513-14.
438. Ibid., 332; and footnote 20, 352.
439. T. Chávez to Gene Henley, 11 October 2005, Author's collection.
440. David Sánchez to the Board of Directors and Executive Director, 29 January 2006.
441. *Hey, Mozart! New Mexico,* compact disk, (Hey, Mozart! Hartwick College Child Composer Project—Crisol Bufons Corporation, 2006).
442. Lozano's book was published by the University of New Mexico Press in 2007 and the class that Lorenzo co-taught was called "Drums and Dreams of Liberation: Latin American Music as Text."
443. *The Santa Fe New Mexican,* 30 April 2006.
444. In his subsequent run for President of the United States, Bill Richardson reportedly raised $22 million. He never garnered more than 5% of the vote in any primary and quit the campaign early with a campaign debt that he was trying to pay back as late as December of 2008. Richardson was selected by Barack Obama to be part of his economic team as Secretary of Commerce. See *The Albuquerque Journal,* 10 December 2008; and *The Santa Fe New Mexican,* 12 December 2008, A1 & A7. Richardson subsequently withdrew his name for consideration because of a Federal grand jury investigation touching on his administration and his fundraising.
445. Stuart Ashman to T. Chávez, 24 April 2009, Author's Collection. That application was made at the request of NHCC Foundation leadership and some staff. Clara Apodaca, Ambassador Ed Romero, and Ed Lujan wrote letters of recommendation. Apodaca to Ashman, 16 December 2008; Lujan to Ana Canales, NHCC Exec. Director Search Committee, 9 December 2008; and Romero to Ashman, 19 December 2008, all in Author's Collection.
446. Cervantes, first part, chapter xlviii, 415.
447. Ibid., chapter xlvii, 410.
448. Ibid., 2nd part, Chapter LXXIV, 939.
449. Ibid., 2nd part, Chapter IV, 482.
450. Cervantes, 2nd part, Chapter LXXIV, 939.
451. Ibid., 2nd part, Chapter IV, 482.
452. Cervantes, 2nd Part, Chapter XII, 528.
453. A. Chávez , 21 June 1992, Box 4, folder 19, Angélico Chávez collection, FAC Library. See also, A. Chávez, *Chávez: A Distnctive American Clan of New Mexico,* (New Edition, Santa Fe: Sunstone Press, 2009), 146.
454. From the last line of *Don Quixote.*

www.ingramcontent.com/pod-product-compliance
Lightning Source LLC
LaVergne TN
LVHW081257100826
845148LV00005B/898
* 9 7 8 0 8 6 5 3 4 8 9 8 1 *